This is the tumultuous inside story of our most amazing war, and a vivid account of the only invasion of the United States. Few periods in our history are less familiar to the average American. Most people remember the Battle of New Orleans, the burning of Washington and the writing of the Star Spangled Banner. But not many realize how unnecessary this war was, how inadequate were our preparations. Written in a straightforward manner, with a touch of acid humor, *The War of 1812* throws new light on this little-known period.

Beginning with the crucial years of Madison's first administration, the author shows how the young War Hawks led by Henry Clay plunged this country into conflict at a time when the American Navy consisted of only a few ships and the American Army of a few scattered posts of regulars. These irresponsible young firebrands believed that Canada could be conquered by Kentucky militia men alone. They listened with unconcealed contempt to the brilliant though unpopular warnings of Randolph of Roanoke.

The War of 1812 covers every phase of fighting on land and at sea. The Navy, though small in size, was officered by younger men who had had battle experience against the Barbary pirates. On the Great Lakes American ships under the leader-

ship of such officers as Perry and MacDonough fought the British to a standstill and wrested from them the control of the internal waterways, isolating the British garrisons in Canada.

On land the Army was officered by older men who had not seen action since the Revolutionary days. The results were disastrous and a blow to American pride. The turn came only in 1814 with the Battle of Plattsburg, the Battle of Horseshoe Bend and the repulse of the British attack at Baltimore when the younger officers like Andrew Jackson, Izard, Totten and Macomb came to the fore. But by that time peace negotiations were well under way and the greatest American victory at New Orleans came, ironically, one week after the peace terms had been arranged at Ghent.

The author has the gift of making history entertaining and exciting reading. His book is a clear and detailed story of one of the strangest wars, perhaps, in history, and one of lasting importance to the United States.

THE WAR OF 1812

THE
WAR OF 1812

By

FRANCIS F. BEIRNE

MAPS BY
DOROTHY DE FONTAINE

NEW YORK

E. P. DUTTON & CO., INC.

1949

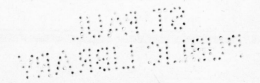

To
R. R. B.

CONTENTS

Preface 11

CHAPTER
I. "Free Trade and Sailors' Rights" 15
II. "Great Bunglers, Indeed" 24
III. American Blood Is Spilled 31
IV. A Noble Experiment Fails 41
V. President Madison Inherits Trouble 47
VI. Tecumseh and Tippecanoe 56
VII. The War Hawks Swoop Down 64
VIII. Two Clever Rogues and Other Intrigues 77
IX. As Britain Yields, We Declare War 87
X. General Hull's Martyrdom 96
XI. Disaster on the Niagara Front 109
XII. Our Frigates Make History 124
XIII. Harrison Has His Problems 138
XIV. We, Too, Burn a Capital 154
XV. Marauders on the Chesapeake 168
XVI. "Don't Give Up the Ship" 183
XVII. Perry on Lake Erie 200
XVIII. A Victory in Canada at Last! 213
XIX. Wilkinson in Quest of Laurels 221
XX. Jackson Justifies a Nickname 232
XXI. Glory, But Nothing More 250
XXII. Washington Burned, the Government in Flight . . 264
XXIII. Plattsburg Stands Fast 289
XXIV. "The Flag Was Still There" 304
XXV. The Die-hards Play Their Hand 322
XXVI. The Final Chapter at Sea 335
XXVII. Old Hickory Avenges His Scar 353
XXVIII. Ghent, City of Peace 374
Conclusion 387
Bibliography 393
Index 399

LIST OF MAPS

Map   I.   Northwest Front 97
Map   II. Niagara Front 110
Map   III. Northern Front 156
Map   IV. Battle of Craney Island 175
Map   V.   Creek Campaign 233
Map   VI. Washington Campaign 267
Map   VII. Battle of Plattsburg (Land) 294
Map   VIII. Battle of Plattsburg (Sea) 295
Map   IX. Battle of Baltimore 310
Map   X.   New Orleans Campaign 348
Map   XI. New Orleans, January 8 360

PREFACE

THE WAR OF 1812 receives mention, of course, in all general histories of the United States. In recent years individual incidents or special phases have served as subjects for historical or fictional treatment. But, so far as the writer has been able to discover, not since Benson J. Lossing published his *Field Book* in 1868 has anyone presented a volume devoted exclusively to the war as a whole.

The present work was, therefore, undertaken with the purpose of filling the gap and bringing up to date events which happened long ago but which have an important bearing on the happenings of today. It is the belief of the writer that those who persevere until the end of the story will discover many things that they have forgotten, or never knew, and many that will surprise them. It is his hope that they will feel their effort has been worth while.

I am indebted to Mr. Philip M. Wagner, editor of the Baltimore *Sun* for first suggesting a book. He proposed a humorous approach. But as the work progressed it soon became apparent that, while the war frequently assumed the nature of *opéra bouffe,* there were heroic episodes and serious overtones that did not lend themselves to frivolous handling. In the end the plan adopted was to let the story tell itself.

In preparing the volume I have depended principally upon Lossing's *Field Book* and Henry Adams' *History of the Administrations of Thomas Jefferson and James Madison.* Lossing cannot be classified as a scholar in the narrow sense of the term. But he was an enthusiast whose work gives evidence throughout of complete familiarity with the best authorities of his day. He visited all the important scenes of action, talked with many eyewitnesses and made delightful sketches to illustrate his book. Though his style is a trifle florid and his partisanship sometimes seems to influence his judgment he stands up well when checked against other writers. Only the captious would scorn his important contribution to the subject.

Henry Adams is the perfect antidote to Lossing's vergings toward the sentimental. No consideration of national patriotism or provincial pride discouraged him from describing individuals and events

11

exactly as he saw them. His reputation as a historian needs no elaboration.

Other sources of material will be found in the bibliography. I should, however, like to express especial indebtedness to the late Mr. Edward M. Barrows for, among other things, the general description of sea battles and the account of the engagement between the *President* and the *Little Belt*, which appear in his life of Matthew Calbraith Perry; to Mr. Julius W. Pratt for the light thrown on the intrigues over the Floridas in his *Expansionists of 1812;* to Mr. Samuel Eliot Morison for the judicial evaluation of the Hartford Convention in his life of Harrison Gray Otis; to Mr. Marquis James for his scholarly handling of Andrew Jackson's operations in the Creek War and in the defense of New Orleans; and to Mr. Gerald W. Johnson for his vivid sketches of Jackson, John Randolph and Henry Clay in the titles under his name in the bibliography. Mr. Neil Swanson's *The Perilous Fight* represents by far the most thorough research on the battles of Bladensburg and Baltimore and is of inestimable value to anyone interested in those engagements.

I have used Henry Adams' version of the controversial episode of the Henry letters. In an article in the *American Magazine* in 1895, several years after the appearance of his history, Adams stated that he had re-examined the evidence and found his account correct with the exception of one unimportant detail.

My profound gratitude is due Edith Rossiter Bevan for reading the manuscript and making a number of first-rate suggestions, and to my wife, Rosamond Randall Beirne, for her assistance in collecting material, making the first drafts of the maps, and for innumerable personal sacrifices while work on the book was in progress.

Acknowledgment also is due Mrs. Gaylord Lee Clark for permission to use the letter from her collection of McHenry correspondence which appears at the end of Chapter XXIV, and to the staffs of the Enoch Pratt Free Library and the Maryland Historical Society for their courteous response to many requests and inquiries. Last but not least I wish to thank Mr. Frank Henry and Mr. Frank Jay Markey, of New York, for exceptional favors which cannot be specified here but whose nature they know well.

FRANCIS F. BEIRNE

Ruxton, Maryland, May, 1948

THE WAR OF 1812

CHAPTER ONE

"Free Trade and Sailors' Rights"

ON MARCH 4, 1805, Thomas Jefferson delivered his second inaugural address and embarked upon another four years as President of the United States. Looking back over his first term in office he had more than a little reason to be gratified with his achievements.

The country had, on the whole, enjoyed a period of comparative peace and prosperity. After a truce of a year, Great Britain and France were again at each other's throats and Europe was in turmoil; but Jefferson might pride himself upon the fact that, thanks to the policy of no entangling alliances with foreign powers proclaimed in his first inaugural, the United States thus far had kept out of the conflict. The Barbary pirates had given trouble. They had, however, been severely dealt with by the infant United States Navy and temporarily subdued. Though Jefferson shared his fellow Republicans' prejudice against the Navy he would have been less than human had he not experienced a feeling of profound admiration for the boldness and courage of Commodore Preble's officers and men. A young nation had stepped in, and won, where the ancient powers of Europe feared to tread.

Far more important than this were the successful diplomatic negotiations which culminated in the purchase of Louisiana. Lesser men might quibble over both the constitutional right and the practical wisdom of laying out $15,000,000 on a wilderness. Was there not already more than enough land east of the Appalachians for a modest population of 7,000,000 souls; and was not $15,000,000 a lot of money to risk on a single speculation? Jefferson reflected less upon the past than he planned for the future. If he had had any doubt about his course he was reassured by the reports brought back by his explorers of the vast expanses of territory, the natural resources,

15

and the infinite variety of the flora and fauna included in his recent purchase. Meriwether Lewis and William Clark, who crossed the continent from St. Louis to the mouth of the Columbia River; Zebulon M. Pike, who discovered the peak that bears his name, and others drew aside the curtain that hitherto had concealed the true immensity and the potential wealth of the new dominions.

Where others looked toward the West and saw only endless forests and barren prairies Jefferson, with prophetic vision, saw prosperous towns and cities, rich farmlands planted to wheat and corn and other crops, the whole connected by good roads and peopled by men and women dwelling in peace and plenty and, through the aid of public education, striving after higher standards of living and culture.

When he bought Louisiana Jefferson sacrificed much of his theory of the limited powers and duties of government to political expediency. Having strayed that far might he not, without too great violence to his conscience, take another forward step to develop the nation which promised to be the outcome of his first transgression? His second inaugural revealed his decision when it spoke of an amendment to the Constitution to permit the setting aside of an annual fund to be spent on "rivers, canals, roads, arts, manufactures, education and other great objects within each state."

More to the point, these were not the idle dreams of a philosopher. The funds for such improvements were within sight. In spite of the cost of the war with Tripoli and of the Louisiana purchase, Jefferson's astute Secretary of the Treasury, Albert Gallatin, could assure him that revenues were running well ahead of expenditures; and that, if the nation continued to prosper, the whole of the public debt would be resolved by the year 1817. Better still, Gallatin, whose calculations were generally reliable, estimated that by 1809 the principal of the debt would be so reduced that $3,000,000 could be safely allocated every year to the noble program of internal improvements already taking definite shape in the President's mind.

With these great achievements to his credit and such brilliant prospects ahead Mr. Jefferson need pay little heed to the New England orator who declaimed from the rostrum that "We have a country governed by blockheads and knaves," or the slanders of the Federalist press or the sneering comments on his literary style. He could well forget Alexander Hamilton's denunciation of him as "a hypocrite." To the taunts of his enemies whose stronghold was New England he had but to reply *"Res ipsa loquitur."* To all appearances his philosophic theories, so scornfully treated in some quarters, were paying off handsomely.

As impatient as Jefferson was to keep his gaze fixed on the West and its brilliant future, other forces beyond his control demanded his attention in the opposite direction where lay the old and degenerate past. There was, for example, the matter of the Floridas which were then in the possession of Spain. Jefferson perceived that his new empire was not entirely secure so long as a foreign power was entrenched on its flank. Spain herself was too weak to be greatly feared, yet her very weakness denied the assurance that her property would not pass into the hands of a more dangerous owner. However, Jefferson's diplomatic agents were at work at the court of His Catholic Majesty; and, though the negotiations were being subjected to all the tedious delays that Spanish cunning could devise, something positive might yet come out of them.

There was still another annoying matter that demanded immediate attention. Though the nation's treasury was full to overflowing, this happy circumstance was not due to the application of Mr. Jefferson's philosophic theories. A more direct and practical reason rested in the carrying trade of the Atlantic and the world events which had suddenly converted it into a gold mine for the vigorous young American republic. Since 1795 Great Britain had been pretty well occupied with her wars against revolutionary France, with the result that the Stars and Stripes had begun to replace the Union Jack to an alarming extent on the high seas. In the course of eleven years Britain had seen American foreign trade almost treble, jumping from $26,000,000 in 1795 to $60,000,000 in 1806, and the end was not yet in sight. American trade was continuing to increase at the rate of 700,000 tons a year. American merchants and shipowners were growing fabulously wealthy and British seamen, who should be fighting their country's battles, were deserting to benefit by the better living conditions and higher pay prevailing in the American merchant marine.

Furthermore, to add insult to injury, this state of affairs was due in large part to Britain's own Admiralty. There was a law known as the "Rule of 1756," accepted by all nations, which held that no ship could, during time of war, engage in trade forbidden to it in time of peace. Now in time of peace France reserved to herself the exclusive right of trading with her colonies. But, with the outbreak of hostilities, France fround it convenient to grant this right to American ships in direct violation of the Rule of 1756, and the British Admiralty acquiesced. In the test case of the *Polly* the Admiralty ruled that an American vessel which sailed from the French colonies and stopped at an American port, unloaded her cargo and reloaded it before proceeding to a European port, was not actually engaged in direct trade, and hence did not violate the Rule.

So the British traders stormed the Admiralty with their protests and with such good effect that the learned Sir William Scott, who had rendered the decision in the case of the *Polly*, looked into his law books again and, with all the solemnity peculiar to courts of justice, reversed the Admiralty's position. In the test case of the *Essex* in 1805 he handed down the opinion that the broken voyage no longer met the requirements of the Rule, and that an American vessel engaged in trade between the French colonies and the mother country would hereafter be subject to seizure and confiscation, just as though she had been an enemy vessel.

It was now the turn of the American merchants to grow alarmed. They appealed to Congress; and Congress, after giving the matter due study and consideration, determined upon a commission to settle all points of dispute existing between the two countries. Pursuant to the wishes of Congress and the merchants the President appointed the Honorable William Pinkney, an eminent Maryland lawyer, as High Commissioner to assist the American Minister, James Monroe, in the negotiations with the British Government. Mr. Pinkney set sail in May, 1806.

Pinkney's departure caused concern in several quarters. Friends of Mr. Pinkney were concerned because Mr. Pinkney was a Federalist and, in the eyes of his fellow Federalists, he was committing an unforgivable sin in accepting an appointment from the high priest of the despised Republican party. Friends of Monroe were concerned because they saw in the dispatch of Mr. Pinkney to serve as joint commissioner with Monroe the sordid hand of politics. Though three years more remained of Mr. Jefferson's second term, as is the

American way, thoughts already were turning to his successor. Little James Madison, Secretary of State, was nearest the throne and a prime favorite of the President. His most dangerous competitor was Monroe. Now if, by hook or crook, the innumerable difficulties between Great Britain and the United States were settled and Mr. Monroe were to return home with a treaty in his pocket which he alone had negotiated, even the power and prestige of Jefferson might prove too little to offset Monroe's appeal to the electorate. Thus Mr. Madison might lose the succession in what jealous New England Federalists were already dubbing "The Virginia Dynasty." On the other hand, if Mr. Pinkney were to share the laurels, Mr. Monroe would to that extent be reduced in the public estimation. If the treaty were to fail, then of course little was to be feared from Mr. Monroe. That is what Monroe's friends thought.

As for Pinkney, his conscience was at rest. For how could he, a loyal citizen, refuse his talents to his country, even though they were sought by a Republican? Had he not proved his worth already as commissioner in the negotiation of Jay's treaty? Had he not within the year returned to Maryland from London after having extracted no less than $500,000 in claims for his native state from the haughty government of England? Pinkney was at home in London. An orator of no mean ability who, his enemies charged, practiced daily before his mirror, he could not have failed to jump at the opportunity of going daily to Westminster to see and hear the world's greatest exponents of the art. These same enemies gossiped that Pinkney wore corsets and blacked beneath the eyes to enhance the tragic effect of his presence. They added that the words he spoke were, unfortunatly, hardly equal to the manner in which he spoke them. But then among these enemies were rival lawyers at the Maryland bar and competition for practice was keen. Some political commentators of the day went so far as to insinuate that Jefferson intended the mission to fail so that, having offered American friendship to Great Britain, and being refused, he might proceed with a French alliance which was closer to his heart.

There was, however, another question at issue, important or unimportant according to one's political views and condition of life. That was the matter of impressment. Great Britain, in endeavoring to round up deserters from her navy, had long been making a practice of searching American merchant vessels and hauling off what sailors suited her. It did no good for sailors so seized to protest that they were native-born Americans or had become naturalized. They were impressed into the British service just the same. As for those who claimed to be American-born, Great Britain held that the burden of proof rested with them. When others claimed naturalization, Great Britain maintained there was no such thing. Once a Briton always a Briton. Of course if a foreigner wanted to become a naturalized Briton that was quite another matter. The British courts had so ruled. Little James Madison with admirable logic had pointed out to the British the inconsistency of their position. But the British refused to be persuaded. It was conceivable to them that others might want to become Britons. It was altogether inconceivable that a Briton would voluntarily want to be anything else, or could be if he wanted to.

In the confusion that resulted from this difference of opinion, the sailors themselves were not helpful. It was suggested that each American sailor carry on his person a "protection," issued by the mayor of a town, a consul or other official, giving the sailor's description and the place of his birth. This was done, but not infrequently sailors lost their protections. Furthermore, they paid some official a dollar for a protection; but then, when they came up with a British deserter who answered the description on the protection, they sold it to him for from ten to twenty dollars, thus earning a neat profit and doing a good turn to a fellow tar into the bargain. And who could stop officials from making money on the side by issuing protections to sailors who did not qualify for them? Obviously every protection was under suspicion, a useless piece of paper to display to a press gang.

American shipowners cultivated a tolerant attitude toward impressment. Seizure of American vessels and goods was an outrage which must be corrected; but the taking of a few American sailors, while it might be regretted, was nothing about which to lose one's head. After all, they maintained, it merely put the sailors to a temporary inconvenience. The United States Government retained an officer in London and another in the West Indies to receive complaints from Americans who alleged they had been impressed. The vast majority found their way home. As the wealthy New Englander and Federalist leader, Timothy Pickering, saw it, the whole matter of impressment was grossly exaggerated. True enough another New Englander, John Quincy Adams, asserted that there had been several thousand cases and every one of them "was on a par with murder." But then, all the Adamses were peculiar. And what could you expect of John Quincy who had only recently given proof positive of his mental instability by deserting the Federalist for the Republican party? Why bring up this annoying question of impressment when trade was so good?

Nonetheless, petitions asking for redress of the evil began to flow to Congress from the seaport towns. They could not be ignored. So Congress asked the Secretary of State to furnish it with a report on impressments. Mr. Madison complied, reporting that since the resumption of hostilities between Great Britain and France in 1803 there had been no less than 2,273 cases of American sailors being impressed. Public reaction to the announcement was immediate and unfavorable. Republican papers, such as the Philadelphia *Aurora*, the Boston *Patriot* and the Baltimore *Whig*, demanded action, while Federalist papers contended that the impressment issue was merely a Republican method of arousing antagonism against Great Britain in order to play the game of France.

These protests were too numerous to be ignored, even had Jefferson cared to disregard them. Furthermore, they came from persons loyal to the Republican cause; while, on the other hand, it was chiefly the wealthy Federalists who preferred to gloss over the injustice done. As a mission was about to engage in the settlement of difficulties existing between Great Britain and the United States it was only natural that Jefferson should include the delicate subject of impressment in the agenda. He went even further than that. He demanded that Great Britain relinquish her claim to impressment if any treaty was to be made at all.

To demand that Great Britain give up impressment was an order of considerable proportions. Here she was in a struggle of life and death with Napoleon and not only were the Yankee upstarts growing rich and impudent on her trade, but they were demanding that she abandon a time-honored practice that would make it virtually impossible to recapture deserters. Why, it was rumored, as many as twenty thousand deserters were already in the American merchant

21

marine! As a man of discernment and one who had had considerable experience with England, Mr. Pinkney must have realized the immensity of the task that lay before him. Possibly he put a few extra hours into practicing eloquence before his mirror.

Jefferson, it must be admitted in justice to him, was peculiarly oblivious to the obstacle he had placed in the way of his commissioners. He wrote optimistically to Monroe in London: "No two countries upon earth have so many points of common interest and friendship; and their rulers must be great bunglers, indeed, if with such dispositions they break asunder." Gracefully overlooking the fear and contempt the Republicans felt for a navy, which had led them to lay down not a single capital ship and to put their trust in less than two hundred gunboats too top-heavy to go to sea, he proceeded to deliver a threat: "We have the seamen and materials for fifty ships of the line and half that number of frigates; and were France to give us the money and England the dispositions to equip them; they would give to England serious proofs of the stock from which they are sprung and the school in which they have been taught. Were, on the other hand, England to give the money and France the dispositions to place us on the sea in all our force, the whole world out of the continent of Europe, might be our joint monopoly." As though the British Navy were nonexistent, as though her frigates were not now lying off our coasts, intercepting and searching our merchantmen, and as though he had at his command squadrons of ships of the line and frigates to drive them off he concluded: "We begin to broach the idea that we consider the whole Gulf Stream as of our waters, in which hostilities and cruising are to be frowned on for the present, and prohibited as soon as either consent or force will permit us."

Let England accept the terms dictated, or else the United States would ask France for money to build 75 warships; and, having received the money and built the ships, the United States would proceed to punish England for her arrogance. That, in substance, was what Jefferson said to Monroe. It was so easy, if Great Britain could only be made to understand.

Jefferson's confidence was not the only ammunition with which the commissioners were supplied. Congress had debated the issue involved in the *Essex* case at length and had considered several plans of action. The United States might go to war with Great Britain. But war was not a Republican weapon. An embargo might be declared. But some argued that an embargo was too drastic; that, in fact, it was the equivalent of war. Then there was negotiation. The time was favorable. For Pitt, who in his later years had proved none too kindly toward American traders, was dead. His ministry had been succeeded by Lord Grenville's so-called "Ministry of all the Talents." And of all the talents ninety per cent rested in the person of Charles James Fox who assumed the portfolio of Foreign Secretary. The liberal Fox had always shown himself a sympathetic friend of the United States. No better man could be found for negotiation. And upon negotiation Congress had decided. But this was not enough to satisfy the more hot-blooded members. There must be a threat, and one which Great Britain could understand. So Congress proposed a non-importation act declaring, in effect, that unless Great Britain gave satisfaction in the negotiations to be conducted, in the following November she would be forbidden to import into the United States certain of her products. The bill was passed while the acid John Randolph of Roanoke jeered: "What is it? A milk and water bill. A dose of chicken broth, to be taken six months hence."

Still, William Pinkney might view the situation with satisfaction. As much as he loved his native Maryland, he was about to make another entrance upon a greater stage. Here would be a test of his abilities more worthy of them than the petty legal squabbles of his neighbors. And, above all, there was a sense of fulfilling a duty to his country. He had been successful before in bringing home $500,-000. Might he not follow up that success by bringing home this time a treaty? For an ambitious man the situation was interesting, to say the least.

CHAPTER TWO

"Great Bunglers, Indeed"

MONROE, having spent nine months in Spain endeavoring without
success to effect the purchase of the East Florida, returned to London in January, 1806. During his previous sojourn in England,
when the Tories were in power, he had not been altogether happy
in his position. He was known as a friend of France. He also was
a friend of Jefferson, and Jefferson, whether by thoughtlessness
or design, had greatly offended England's Minister to the United
States. Anthony Merry was a punctilious person, very conscious of
his own importance and of the respect due an emissary of King
George III. He and Mrs. Merry had resented bitterly the President's
introduction of the system of pell-mell at White House functions,
according to which guests pushed forward into the President's
drawing room with no regard for precedence. As the rules of precedence would have put them at the top of the list, he and Mrs. Merry
had protested the slight, but without success. Nor did Minister
Merry consider it proper that, on less formal occasions, Mr. Jefferson
should receive His Majesty's servant, wearing a dressing gown and
bedroom slippers, and providing a door for Merry's exit so situated
that he virtually had to bow himself out.

Jefferson had decidedly got the better of Merry, but Merry had
returned home with a full report on his treatment. In retaliation,
Merry's friends gratified their spite on the unoffending Monroe. The
American Minister, serious of mind and slow to comprehend sub-
tlety, was no match for the English wits of the dinner table who
knew how to insult his country while maintaining an appearance
of amiability and politeness. His only defense was silence.

From Fox, however, he could count at least upon unfailing courtesy and consideration. And with Fox now in the Foreign Office it

was not impossible that he might obtain concessions for his country that Pitt had refused to yield. Yet there was a vast difference between what Fox would have liked to do, and what he was capable of doing. At the very moment when Great Britain needed all of her energies to combat Napoleon, her domestic situation was in a state of chaos. George III, the old king, passed successively from sanity to insanity; and unfortunately, nobody could tell when he would return to sanity again. Meanwhile his son, George, having scandalized the country by divorcing his unprepossessing German wife, Caroline, amused himself with his mistresses, wrangled with his father and intrigued with the politicians. Ministers were at a loss to know whose favors to curry; which of the royal personages to follow. Those who were in power today might, through a turn in the King's condition, be out on the streets tomorrow. The Grenville ministry held office by a slender thread and no one was more conscious of it than its members.

With the best intentions in the world toward the United States, Fox hesitated to make a move for fear of bringing down upon his head the wrath of the mercantile interests and the country Tories. To make matters worse, news was reaching England of the acrimonious debates in Congress on the non-importation act. The bill was obviously intended as a threat, but it was a threat that was not backed by force. A nation whose fleet had acquired unchallenged mastery of the sea through the victory at Trafalgar was not to be browbeaten by a nation brandishing a few top-heavy gunboats. English manufacturers, who did a prosperous business with the United States, might have been counted upon to show concern; but they, too, were silent. When news of the passage of the bill reached England it did not frighten, it merely irritated. Fox complained bitterly to Monroe that it made negotiations considerably more difficult.

However, Fox had aroused Monroe's hopes that something would be done and he was as good as his word. But how make concessions to American shippers without playing into the hands of the opposition and risking the fall of the ministry. An ingenious fellow, Fox at last hit upon what seemed at the time an excellent plan that would be satisfactory to all parties. At his instigation an order in council was issued declaring the coast of France blockaded from

25

Brest to the River Elbe, adding that a strict blockade would be maintained only between the River Seine and Ostend. The virtue of the order lay in the fact that while it gave the appearance of further restricting neutral commerce, which satisfied the British mercantile interests, actually it allowed greater freedom to American ships. Its weakness was that it established a paper blockade, a principle to which the United States had never before been willing to agree. At the time, though the proposal was a subterfuge, it seemed innocent enough. Fox never dreamed that harm would come of it, and when he explained it to Monroe, the latter was completely satisfied. Monroe immediately wrote home to his government pointing out the advantage American trade was to derive.

The order in council was issued on May 6, 1806. About the same time Monroe learned of Mr. Pinkney's appointment and that the negotiations were to pass from his individual hands to that of a commission. He at once comprehended that he had ceased to enjoy Jefferson's full confidence. It was a blow to his pride that he could not fully conceal. On June 24 Commissioner Pinkney landed in England, and his reception by Monroe was distinctly cold. But both were intelligent men, and it was not long before Monroe had recovered from his pique and was working on cordial terms with his fellow commissioner. Simultaneously Fox was taken seriously ill and the physicians announced that his condition was hopeless. Further delay ensued while the British Government looked about for new negotiators. Eventually Lord Holland, Fox's nephew, and Lord Auckland were selected.

The new British commissioners, both of them Whigs, treated Monroe and Pinkney with the greatest courtesy and consideration, a treatment in marked contrast to that accorded by the Tory friends of Anthony Merry. But, like Fox, they were restrained by their fear of the Tory opposition. It was late summer when the negotiations were started. Jefferson had directed his representatives to make three demands. Great Britain must abandon the right to search American merchant ships, she must return to the United States the right to trade with the French and Spanish colonies upon the terms enjoyed prior to the *Essex* decision. She must pay indemnity for goods seized as a result of that decision. These demands must be yielded before a treaty was even to be considered.

26

No sooner had the commissioners met than the matter of impressment at once became a stumbling block. The British commissioners offered for consideration a situation that might arise if Great Britain were formally to abandon her right of search. Suppose, said they, a British man-of-war and an American merchant ship were lying in the same harbor. Suppose sailors from the British man-of-war were to desert to the American ship. Was the commander of the man-of-war to stand idly by and allow the American ship to sail out of the harbor with the deserters aboard? Yet such an instance might occur if the right of search were surrendered. Obviously His Majesty's Government would not hear of such a thing.

On the other hand, the British commissioners acknowledged that there were times when mistakes were made and Americans, erroneously taken for deserters, were impressed into the British service. Nobody more than His Majesty's commissioners realized the injustice thus done to Americans, and nobody regretted it more. Surely this was a matter that could be settled without the formality of a treaty. This seemed fair enough to Monroe and Pinkney and so, in violation of the strict orders of Jefferson, they agreed to accept a note, to be attached to the treaty in lieu of a formal surrender of the right of search, which read:

"That His Majesty's Government, animated by an earnest desire to remove every cause of dissatisfaction, has directed His Majesty's Commissioners to give to Mr. Monroe and to Mr. Pinkney the most positive assurance that instructions have been given, and shall be repeated and enforced, for the observance of the greatest caution in the impressing of British seamen, and that the strictest care shall be taken to preserve the citizens of the United States from any molestation or injury and that immediate and prompt redress shall be offered upon any representation of injury sustained by them."

Fox breathed his last on September 13 and was succeeded in the Foreign Office by Lord Howick. Holland and Auckland were not affected by the change. With impressment out of the way, the negotiations proceeded to what Monroe and Pinkney imagined to be a favorable conclusion. As Monroe later pointed out to Jefferson, no less than eleven of the articles in the treaty of 1794 were included in the new treaty. It would perhaps have been better had Monroe and Pinkney been dealing with the most unsympathetic and reactionary Tories, for then they might have been on their guard. As it was they were charmed by the kindliness of Lords Holland and Auckland. Fully conscious of the difficulties under which the latter were working the American commissioners seemed to go out of their way to be accommodating. Desirous of obtaining the treaty for which they had been commissioned, they overlooked the fact that the treaty to which they agreed contained none of the three principal stipulations Jefferson had made a *sine qua non*. Right of search was not abandoned. No promise was made to pay damages arising out of the *Essex* decision. The theory of the broken voyage as defined in the case of the *Polly* was not resumed. Instead, American trade between French and Spanish colonies and their mother countries was to be permitted only when American vessels so engaged paid to the United States Customs a tax of not less than two per cent ad valorem. In other words, Great Britain was undertaking to dictate to the United States what duties she should demand of her own vessels, a purely domestic matter. An astounding proposal, yet Monroe and Pinkney accepted it.

Furthermore, the treaty did not mention trade with the British West Indies, with Canada, Nova Scotia or New Brunswick. It permitted trade with the East Indies only by ships going directly to and fro, and which did not put into a European port on the way. Critics declared it worse than the treaty negotiated by John Jay. Monroe and Pinkney defended it as the best that could be obtained under existing circumstances, when Great Britain was still exulting in her triumphs on the seas and everybody knew that the United States had neither the power nor the will to fight.

The last and most telling blow was yet to fall. In the autumn of 1806, while the British and American negotiators were at work in London, events of great moment were taking place on the continent. On October 14 the battles of Jena and Auerstädt were fought, crushing the last opposition to the French invasion of Prussia. On October 27 Napoleon entered Berlin in triumph. In the whole of Europe Russia and Great Britain alone remained to be conquered. Almost exactly a year before the Emperor's army had camped on the sands facing Dover, ready at a moment's notice to cross the Channel. Only in the nick of time had Nelson returned from his wild goose chase across the Atlantic to destroy the French fleet at Trafalgar and thus deny to Napoleon the few hours' mastery of the sea he needed to land his army on the English shore. If the conquest of Britain by arms was denied him there was another means by which Napoleon could accomplish the same end, a means peculiarly fitting for a "nation of shopkeepers." He would strike at her trade. Fox, now lying cold in his grave, unwittingly had given Napoleon a model to follow.

On November 21 Napoleon issued his Berlin Decree. Fox's order in council of May had laid down a paper blockade of the French coast. The Berlin Decree laid down a paper blockade of the whole of Great Britain. It prohibited all commerce and correspondence with the British Isles, adding that no vessel coming directly from England or from the English colonies should be received in any French port, and that any vessel contravening the order should be seized. Here was a paper blockade, indeed; a blockade that violated the generally accepted laws of the nations. For justification Napoleon had only to point to Fox's order in council of the previous May.

When news of the Berlin Decree reached England, the commissioners were putting the finishing touches on the treaty. The Berlin Decree furnished the last touch. For the British commissioners announced then and there that, unless the United States refused to recognize the decree, Great Britain would not ratify the treaty. So determined were Monroe and Pinkney to complete their task that they accepted even this provision. The treaty was signed by the commissioners on December 31.

On January 3 Monroe wrote to Jefferson announcing the signing of the treaty. His letter crossed one from the Secretary of State in which Madison advised him that Jefferson was of the opinion that, if impressment were not included, it would be better to sign no treaty at all. Early in March Jefferson received a copy of the treaty. Having read it he did not even take the trouble to submit it to the Senate. He simply filed it away. Nine months of negotiation had gone for naught. The differences between the United States and Great Britain were as far from solution as ever, and Monroe farther from the Presidency. Diplomacy involving such great names as those of Charles James Fox, Jefferson, Madison and Monroe had ignominiously failed.

"No two countries upon earth have so many points of common interest," Jefferson had written, "and their rulers must be great bunglers, indeed, if with such dispositions they break asunder." Who were the bunglers? It may be assumed that Jefferson did not include himself among them.

CHAPTER THREE

American Blood Is Spilled

IF FORTUNE did not smile on George Canning at his birth, she made amends by endowing him with a splendid intellect and a consuming ambition. The son of a disinherited father and a penniless mother, the boy was sent through Eton and Christ Church College, Oxford, with funds supplied by his wealthy uncle, Stratford Canning, a London banker.

George made good use of his time both at public school and at the University. Sir Spencer Walpole described him as the most distinguished boy ever known at Eton. At Oxford he maintained his reputation for brilliance by winning the Chancellor's prize for Latin verse. After her husband's death, when George was a year old, his mother went on the stage, and some of those who saw Canning perform in Parliament remarked wryly that he inherited from her a gift for acting. An actress mother was, in those days, scarcely advantageous to social preferment; but, during his time at Christ Church, George had learned to cultivate the right people. If, at the start, his position was precarious, he strengthened it by making an alliance with a lady and an heiress who brought him a fortune of £100,000. Fresh from the University Canning entered Parliament, and at the age of 26 was an undersecretary and one of Pitt's ablest lieutenants. He has gone down in history as being probably England's greatest foreign secretary in the nineteenth century, but this estimate refers no doubt to his maturer years. In his youth he was so impatient to get on with his career that not infrequently he exhibited a bland indifference to the amenities. It was said of him by his contemporaries that he was incapable of delivering a speech without making a new enemy. "It is Canning's misfortune," declared one critic, "that nobody will believe that he can take his tea without a stratagem";

while another observed that "by an unhappy perversion of mind he always would rather have obtained his end by a crooked path than a straight one." Said a third, "Canning can never be a gentleman for more than three hours at a time." Added to these shortcomings was an irritability of temper and an astonishing lack of tact.

When, on March 18, 1807, the Grenville ministry fell and was succeeded in office by the Tory government of Lord Portland, Canning found himself elevated to the important position of Foreign Secretary. It was with Canning that the American commissioners now had to deal, and the radical change from the cordiality of Holland and Auckland to the frigidity of Canning must have been painful in the extreme. To a man of Canning's temperament, pitted as he was against the most powerful and astute politician of Europe in the person of the Emperor Napoleon, it must have been equally irritating to have to give occasional ear to the persistent complaints of representatives of a small and insignificant country three thousand miles away.

Since the first of the year world conditions, instead of growing better, had become worse. Coincident with the transmission of the treaty by the commissioners to their home government in Washington, Great Britain had issued another order in council on January 7, in reply to the Berlin Decree. This order forbade all vessels to engage in the coastwise trade of France and her allies or of any ports to which British vessels were denied. It was a severe blow to American commerce in the Mediterranean where vessels were accustomed to sail from port to port, seeking the best market. Immediately upon the publication of the Berlin Decree, John Armstrong, American Minister to France, had hastened to inquire its effect on American ships. He had been assured by Decrès, French Minister of Marine, that the decree was not intended to be applied to them. But anyone who had had dealings with Napoleon knew how valueless such assurance was likely to be.

As the months wore on and spring gave way to early summer Monroe and Pinkney approached Canning with a suggestion for the resumption of negotiations. Canning replied that it was impossible to resume negotiations upon a treaty which had been agreed upon, signed and then had been rejected by one of the contracting parties. And so it appeared that the two Americans would have plenty of leisure time to enjoy the beauties of England in the rare days of June. Canning was left to watch with penetrating eye the measures Napoleon was taking to ensnare his fellow emperor, Alexander of Russia.

That eye stood him in good stead when, in July, the two Emperors, meeting on a raft constructed over the River Niemen so that they might be insured absolute secrecy, agreed upon the measures that were to be embodied in the Treaty of Tilsit. One of the secret stipulations was that the Danish fleet, then lying in the harbor of Copenhagen, should be handed over to Napoleon. But before Napoleon had time to act, a British fleet entered the harbor, demanded the Danish fleet for safekeeping, and, when the demand was denied, seized it. How Canning, in faraway London, discovered what was taking place on the raft in the River Niemen remains today one of the great mysteries of history. But discover it he did, and thereby accomplished the greatest coup of his career.

In the very moment of this gigantic triumph Canning had to pause to give attention to an annoying incident that had occurred a few weeks before off the Virginia Capes. In the month of June, 1807, several British men-of-war lay in the American waters of Lynnhaven Bay, Virginia. Among them were the *Leopard* and the *Melampus*. Several sailors were reported to have deserted from the *Melampus*, rowed to Norfolk and there enlisted in the United States Navy. According to the advices which reached Vice-Admiral George Berkeley, in command of the British naval station at Halifax, the offending sailors had paraded the streets of Norfolk under the American flag and before the very eyes of their former commanders. Yet the American authorities had ignored demands for their return.

When Vice-Admiral Berkeley heard the story every fiber in his august body contracted. He sat down at once with quill pen and paper and dashed off an order to the British squadron in Lynnhaven Bay to the effect that if any British man-of-war encountered on the high seas any American ship bearing the deserters, the commander of the British man-of-war must immediately board the American ship and seize the deserters.

On June 19, fresh from the navy yard at Washington, the United States frigate *Chesapeake* put into Norfolk. She was under the command of Captain Gordon, and also bore the flag of Commodore James Barron. She was bound for the Mediterranean and, owing to the inefficiency of the navy yard, was already late for her rendezvous. She had halted briefly at Norfolk to fill up her crew. Having accomplished this task she put to sea on June 21. Her guns had not been mounted; her crew had been mustered only three times. It was the intention of Commodore Barron to put her into shape when she got to sea and thereby save valuable time. He did not dream that any immediate danger awaited her.

However, as the *Chesapeake* sailed out, the *Leopard* hoisted anchor and followed. Just outside the three-mile limit the *Leopard* drew near and hailed. The *Chesapeake* luffed and waited while a boat was lowered from the *Leopard* and came alongside. It contained an officer who presented the compliments of Captain Humphries of the *Leopard* to Commodore Barron and requested the Commodore to permit the officer to muster the crew and search for the four British deserters believed to be aboard. Commodore Barron replied that he had mustered the crew himself, that he had taken particular pains to see that no deserters were aboard and was satisfied that there were none. He added that it was against the regulations of the United States Navy to permit the officer of a foreign vessel to muster an American crew and, consequently, he must refuse the request.

The British officer returned to the *Leopard* which was now lying within pistol-shot distance of the *Chesapeake*. From the *Leopard* came a voice through a trumpet, "The Vice-Admiral's orders must be obeyed." Barron made no response. A moment later a shot from the *Leopard* crossed the *Chesapeake's* bow, followed almost immediately by a broadside that riddled her hull, tore through her rigging, killed three of her crew and wounded 18 more, including Commodore Barron. The bombardment continued 15 minutes. The *Chesapeake* was incapable of reply. Barron was desirous of having at least one shot fired and this was accomplished, an officer carrying a hot coal from the galley stove to the cannon. The Commodore then ordered the colors to be struck.

In a few minutes Captain Humphries came aboard and Barron offered to surrender his ship. Humphries declined the surrender, apologized for the damage he had done, but insisted upon searching the *Chesapeake* for the deserters. The four men sought were soon found in the hold and brought on deck. They admitted that they had deserted from the *Melampus*, but three of them claimed that they were Americans who had previously been impressed into the British service. According to some accounts all three were Negroes. The fourth was unquestionably a Briton, Ratford by name, who had escaped Barron's notice by enlisting under the name of Wilson.

Captain Humphries took his prisoners and departed for Halifax. Ratford later was hanged. One prisoner died in captivity and the other two several years later were returned to the deck of the *Chesapeake* from which they had been taken. The *Chesapeake* limped back to Norfolk to tell the distressing tale and to stir the country to wrath from end to end. For once Federalists and Republicans forgot party animosities. From north, south and west a universal cry for revenge went up. Senator Pickering and a few friends alone refused to join the tumult, instead asserting that Britain had acted within her rights. "At that moment," Jefferson later declared, "I had the issue of peace or war in my hand."

At last Jefferson, who little more than a year before had boasted of making the Gulf Stream the national boundary, who had threatened to teach England a lesson, realized the nation's utter unpreparedness for war. He let the issue slip from his grasp, if it had ever been there, and clung to the hope that the action of the *Leopard* had been a tragic error for which the British Government would make prompt and proper amends. Yet something must be done to appease the anger of the people. On July 2 the President issued a proclamation reciting the details of the outrage and forbidding British men-of-war to enter the ports of the United States. Then, a painful reminder of the country's impotence, he added that, since there was no force to compel them to stay out, should British men-of-war enter the ports in disregard of the proclamation, loyal citizens would deny them all aid and comfort. The proclamation did something to allay the storm, but the country still needed a scapegoat. Commodore Barron was the most suitable person to fill the role. He was charged with failure to prepare his ship for action, court-martialed, found guilty and retired from the service for five years without pay.

The incompetence of the Navy Department, which was in large part to blame for delaying the departure of the *Chesapeake,* was thus neatly concealed.

No sooner did Canning learn of the encounter between the *Chesapeake* and the *Leopard* than he realized the blunder that Berkeley and Humphries had made. His Majesty's Government might be arrogant, but never in its bluffest moments had it claimed the right to board and search an alien man-of-war. A merchantman might be treated indifferently, but an insult to a man-of-war was an insult to a nation that thoroughly justified a resort to arms. British statesmen had been assured by their observers in America that the United States would never fight over impressment and the orders in council. But that she would not fight over an insult to the flag Canning could not be too sure. And, to be frank, Great Britain did not want war with the United States. She had her hands full enough in Europe. For all his pride Canning was ready to offer apology and punish the offenders. There seemed no other way out. On the other hand he had to consider the anti-American group in England, and also that Berkeley was the brother of a lord.

It was the irony of fate that the excuse Canning so much needed was presented to him by Monroe and Jefferson. Upon receiving the news Monroe seized upon it as a practical means of settling the whole issue of impressment, something for which he had waited so long that he had almost ceased hoping. On July 29 Monroe addressed a formal note to Canning in which he called attention to the aggression. He could not resist adding, "I might state other examples of great indignity and outrage."

Canning was prompt to divine Monroe's course. Replying on August 3, he assured Monroe that if the circumstances of the encounter between the *Leopard* and the *Chesapeake* were as Monroe had described them, His Majesty would have no difficulty in disowning the act and manifesting his displeasure with the conduct of his officers. He concluded somewhat tartly, "With respect to the other causes of complaint (whatever they may be) which are hinted at in your note, I perfectly agree with you, in the sentiment which you express, as to the propriety of not involving them in a question which is of itself of sufficient importance to claim a separate and most serious consideration."

Monroe hardly expected to be taken so literally in the matter of confining the conversations to the one issue. But Canning made it clear that he had no intention of allowing the *Chesapeake* affair to be used as an entering wedge for a renewal of the impressment controversy. Thus having defended himself against attack, Canning was waiting and ready to take the offensive. The opportunity came as soon as he received word of the President's proclamation. Up to this point he had been apologetic and conciliatory, but immediately his attitude stiffened.

Having received an unofficial copy of the proclamation from the British Minister to the United States, Canning sat down and penned a note to Monroe asking for verification. The following day Monroe replied that he had not yet heard from his government. For a month Canning was silent on the subject. So, on September 7, Monroe sent him a reminder. Canning permitted a fortnight to pass and then wrote a blistering letter. "Before I proceed to observe upon that part of it which relates more immediately to the question now at issue between our two governments," he began, "I am commanded, in the first instance, to express the surprise which is felt at the total omission of a subject upon which I had already been commanded to apply to you for information, the proclamation purported to have been issued by the President of the United States." In language which could not have been meant to be other than insulting, suggesting as it did that Monroe had not told him the truth, he continued, "Of this paper, when I last addressed you upon it, you professed not to have any knowledge beyond what the ordinary channels of public information afforded, nor any authority to declare it to be authentic." Canning then proceeded to demand from Monroe official acknowledgment of the proclamation. He pointed out that the whole matter now had resolved itself into one of reparation, but that the Government of the United States had taken reparation into its own hands by declaring its ports closed to British men-of-war; that it had resorted to these measures of retaliation previous to any direct application for redress to the British Government or to the British Minister in America. He concluded with the categorical demand: "I am further to inquire whether you are authorized to withdraw the proclamation on the knowledge of His Majesty's disavowal of the act which occasioned its publication?"

Without doubt, by failing to demand redress before issuing his proclamation Jefferson had given Canning an excuse. But, having gone thus far, the President was unwilling to acknowledge the original error. Worse still, Monroe received from him in September instructions to demand a disavowal of the principle of impressment along with a disavowal of Berkeley's order. This was a stipulation that Jefferson ought to have known was incapable of fulfillment. No doubt he was goaded into action by the public outcry that followed the attack on the *Chesapeake*. He did not realize that Canning, too, was being goaded by the London press which had rushed to the defense of Berkeley. Once more Canning refused to treat on these terms, the matter of reparations reached a stalemate instead of redress being accorded while the incident was fresh in the public mind. In fact on both sides the will to conciliate was lacking and, in spite of the brilliance of the master minds of Canning and Jefferson, the two countries were permitted to drift farther apart.

After what had occurred Monroe's usefulness in London was clearly at an end and he was recalled, Pinkney succeeding him as Minister. Canning promised that the British Government would send a commissioner to Washington to continue negotiations over the *Chesapeake* affair. Berkeley was recalled, but that was as far as Canning was willing to go. There was no court-martial.

As the year 1807 was growing to a close, several events took place in quick succession that made the American position even more untenable. When Napoleon issued the Berlin Decree the French Minister of Marine, Decrès, as we have seen, assured the American Minister that the decree did not apply to American ships. Nevertheless there had been seizures. On October 7 Champagny, Duke of Cadore, French Foreign Minister, reversed what Decrès had said a year before and admitted that American ships were included. His excuse was that this had been made necessary by the British orders in council. Actually Napoleon here saw an opportunity to embroil the United States in a war with Great Britain. Besides, he was badly in need of funds and seizure was merely a step toward confiscation.

On November 11 Great Britain issued a new order in council. It reasserted a blockade of all the ports and places of France, or her allies, and of all countries from which British ships were excluded. All trade in articles produced or manufactured in such countries was forbidden and ships engaged in it were declared subject to search and seizure along with their cargoes. However, on the same date another order appeared permitting neutral ships to carry goods from the enemy's ports to the ports of Great Britain upon payment of duties, and to re-export from the British ports subject to British regulations. In other words, while ostensibly laying down a blockade, Great Britain was insisting upon a control of American trade as strict as that which had existed in the days of the colonies. She was demanding that a sovereign country should proceed with its trade only by having its vessels enter a British port, pay a duty to the British Government and continue the voyage under British regulations. And, to cap the climax, the British Government had issued a proclamation recalling all of its sailors and announcing that those who did not obey the order would be hunted out from the ships on which they had taken refuge. The proclamation not only closed the doors to any compromise on impressment but was, in fact, a reassertion of the right.

When Napoleon heard of the order in council requiring neutral ships to touch at British ports and pay a duty he immediately retaliated. From Milan, on December 17, he issued another decree declaring that any ship which, in obedience to the order, should enter a British port and pay a duty would be regarded as denationalized and, in effect, British property.

American ships trading with Europe found themselves on the horns of a dilemma. If they obeyed the decrees of Napoleon they were subject to seizure by Great Britain. If they obeyed the orders in council they were subject to seizure by France. Under such circumstances neutral trade was well-nigh impossible. As Napoleon had, through his military conquests, forced all the countries of Western Europe to enter into a compact not to trade with Great Britain, he now hoped to accomplish the same end with the United States through his decrees. Great Britain might have been expected to thwart his purpose by courting favor with the United States. Instead she adopted a course which could not fail to annoy, irritate and estrange the United States.

These several events of the last months of 1807 were not immediately known to Jefferson, for news traveled slowly across the ocean. But he knew enough to realize the critical position of American commerce and sense that it was becoming more critical. It gave him an opportunity to try an experiment which was close to his heart, a substitute for war in the guise of peaceable coercion. At his instigation, during the last days of the dying year, Congress passed the Embargo Act, forbidding all American vessels to depart from American ports and excluding all foreign ships from the same ports. Such was his answer to the decrees and orders. American ships would be kept at home so that they would run afoul of neither. Great Britain and the Continent would be denied cotton and other American products which they sorely needed. As soon as they began to feel the force of their deprivations, Great Britain and France would adopt a more conciliatory attitude, and without striking a single blow the United States would achieve her ends. That was what Jefferson hoped and prayed for.

CHAPTER FOUR

A Noble Experiment Fails

To JEFFERSON the Embargo was a magnificent experiment; to Timothy Pickering it was a magnificent opportunity. Pickering had had a distinguished career. The son of a prominent New England family, he had been educated at Harvard. During the Revolutionary War he had served first as Adjutant General, then as Quartermaster General of the American Army. He had been successively Postmaster General, Secretary of War and Secretary of State under Washington. He had carried on the last office under Adams until, intriguing with the enemies of the administration, he had been asked to resign. In 1803 he had been elected to the Senate.

An irreconcilable Federalist, Pickering was the prime mover in that little band of die-hards known as the Essex Junto, named after the Massachusetts county in which it originated. The French Revolution was as loathsome to him as it had been to Pitt and the British Tories; and, because Jefferson had been a friend of France, the Virginian was to Pickering as loathsome as the French Revolution. Having held the highest post in the cabinet, enjoyed the confidence of the great Washington, Pickering saw himself and his party hopelessly overwhelmed while power fell into the hands of men whom he distrusted and hated. The disappointment was more than he could stand, and he allowed his prejudices to produce a mania which warped his judgment and led him to commit acts against his government that were treasonable, if not actually treason. At the time of the purchase of Louisiana, which he saw only as a factor in increasing the preponderance of the West and the South, he even went so far as to suggest the destruction of the Union and the setting up of a confederation composed of New England and New York, a pro-

41

posal which Alexander Hamilton, with greater vision, promptly rejected.

Had Pickering been obscure, his hallucinations might have been ignored. But as a political leader and a senator he was in a position to sway the minds of many of his fellow New Englanders, particularly those of wealth and prominence, until disloyalty to the government became fashionable in that section of the country. It was unlucky for Jefferson that his Embargo came into operation in a presidential election year when the Federalists were in need of a popular issue. No sooner had the bill passed Congress than Pickering seized upon it and turned it to political ends. Ignoring completely Jefferson's aims to avoid war he advertised the Embargo as designed to support Napoleon's Continental System and a subtle means of destroying New England while benefiting the Southern and Western States.

The cry was taken up by the pulpit and the press. The *Chesapeake* affair and impressment were forgotten while the Federalists extolled England. Pickering exclaimed in a letter made public, ". . . although England, with her thousand ships of war, could have destroyed our commerce, she has really done it no essential injury." William Cullen Bryant, a rising young poet of thirteen years, took the cue from his elders, damned the Jefferson administration as a "weak ruler's philosophic dreams" and, twanging his lyre, sang on:

> Curse of our nation, source of countless woes,
> From whose dark womb unreckoned misery flows,
> The Embargo rages, like a sweeping wind—
> Fear lowers before, and Famine stalks behind.

It is true the Embargo worked immediate hardships on the country. Ships lay idle at their wharves. Sailors were thrown out of employment. In New York the Commandant of the Navy Yard hired 300 of them who were glad to work for rations only. Many of them somehow found their way to the British colonies and enlisted in the British Navy. Republican newspapers declared that the bulk of them returned to farming and other industries while Federalist newspapers insisted as strongly that they had taken the only course open to them and submitted to impressment. Within six months few of them were to be found. In September of that year the New York *Evening Post* was lamenting, "Is it not notorious that not a seaport in the United States can produce enough seamen to man three merchant ships?"

Wages were cut in half and laborers were deprived of the ordinary necessities of life—sugar, salt, tea, coffee, molasses and rum. In the Middle Atlantic States, for want of a market, wheat fell from $2.00 to 75 cents a bushel. If Jefferson wished to advance the interests of the South, he took a poor means of accomplishing it. His native state of Virginia fared worse than the rest of the country. Her tobacco crop could not be sold and yet her planters had to support in idleness 400,000 slaves. Many of her wealthiest people were ruined. Farther South the wharves were piled high with cotton. While the South found no market for her produce, she had to pay more for manufactured goods which attained scarcity values. No people ever suffered more for party loyalty than did the Republicans of the South in the last year of Jefferson's administration.

New England made the loudest complaints, yet actually she was better off than the South. Her fishing and her shipping interests, of course, suffered, but no loyalty to the administration restrained her. Under the circumstances there was every temptation to smuggle and a thriving illicit trade sprang up on the Canadian border, with Boston as a center. To New England, though she was not aware of it, the Embargo brought a permanent blessing in disguise, for it turned peoples' thoughts from the sea to the factory, laying the foundation for New England's commercial supremacy. John Randolph of Roanoke saw it when, speaking of New England, he exclaimed, "she has forsaken the trident for the distaff."

Jefferson realized the machinations of his enemies and their results in the rising tide of popular condemnation of his pet measure. Yet he stuck firmly to his purpose and endeavored to strengthen the Embargo by supplementary acts. Too many vessels with certificates for the coasting trade reported that they had been "blown out to sea" and wound up in foreign ports. To halt these evasions of the law Jefferson enacted restrictions that seriously impaired the trade and virtually closed the route of traffic on the sea between North and South that in those days was far more important than the routes by land. Distasteful as it was to a Republican who had protested

43

similar action in the administration of the Federalists, the President called upon the army and the navy to enforce the laws against smuggling.

America suffered, yet the European countries against whom the Embargo had been laid gave no appreciable evidences of distress. Napoleon applauded the act as a measure adding the final touch to his Continental System. Before the Embargo went into effect many American vessels put to sea to escape it. Others that were in foreign ports remained away from home. Many of them, under British certificates, made their way to France. Napoleon promptly took advantage of the opportunity on April 17 to issue the Bayonne Decree under which he ordered the seizure of American vessels and their cargoes in French ports to the value of $10,000,000. Similar seizures took place in the harbors of Holland and those now under his control on the Baltic Sea. When Minister Armstrong protested, the Emperor replied that the vessels were either British or American. If they were British they belonged to his enemy; if they were American they were in France in violation of the Embargo Act and the American Government should thank him for helping to enforce its law. Knowing Napoleon's need for money, Armstrong despaired of the return of such valuable property.

Great Britain, too, accepted the Embargo with apparent indifference. A revolt in the Spanish colonies which followed the crowning of Joseph Bonaparte as King of Spain opened to Great Britain a new source of trade that compensated for losses in the United States. When Minister Pinkney suggested to Canning that the Embargo might be removed in exchange for a repeal of the orders in council, Canning refused the offer, adding in his most sarcastic manner that he imagined the Embargo was an inconvenience to the American people.

Pinkney, however, was not deceived by what he divined to be a magnificent bluff. From London he wrote to Madison, Secretary of State, "The Embargo and loss of our trade are deeply felt here, and will be felt with more severity every day. The wheat harvest is likely to be alarmingly short, and the state of the continent will augment the evil. The discontents among the manufacturers are only quieted for a moment by temporary causes. Cotton is rising and will soon be scarce." He urged Jefferson to stick to his policy.

Yet at home the situation was growing more tense. The enforcing acts instead of putting an end to violations of the law only served to arouse its opponents to greater fury. Massachusetts lawyers now fell back upon the familiar expedient of questioning the constitutionality of the law. The Boston *Gazette* in its editorial columns openly proposed secession from the Union. "It is better," said the editor, "to suffer the amputation of a limb than to lose the whole body. We must prepare for the amputation."

A handbill distributed in Newburyport illustrated the temper of the opposition. "Let every man," it read, "who holds the name of America dear to him stretch forth his hand and put this accursed thing—the Embargo—from him. Be resolute; act like the sons of liberty, of God, and of our country; nerve your arms with Vengeance against the Despot who would wrest the inestimable gem of your independence from you, and you shall be conquerors!"

Canning, it will be recalled, offered to send to the United States a minister plenipotentiary to settle the matter of the *Chesapeake*. The minister arrived early in the year in the person of George H. Rose. Once more Rose began with the Secretary of State an argument as to whether withdrawal of the President's proclamation forbidding British men-of-war to enter American ports should precede announcement of British reparations for the attack on the *Chesapeake*. By this time Jefferson was ready to yield if he could find the means gracefully to do so. Rose had been instructed by Canning not to divulge the details of the reparations Britain would grant, but at last he yielded to persuasion. Then, to their astonishment, the President and Secretary of State discovered that Canning set forth as a condition that Commodore Barron should be disciplined for having refused to admit a British officer to search his ship! This was, indeed, adding insult to injury. Immediately the conversations came to an end.

There was, however, at least one man in Washington in whom Rose found a friend and kindred spirit. He was none other than Timothy Pickering. Pickering expressed himself as enchanted with Rose's personality and intelligence. He went even further than that. Years before, as Secretary of State, Pickering had been responsible for a law imposing fine and imprisonment on any American who conducted a correspondence with the agents of a foreign power. Ignoring the law which he had himself devised, he now proposed a plan for conducting a correspondence with Rose upon the latter's return to England. To such extremes had Pickering been brought by his hatred of Jefferson and the party in power!

The Federalist agitation bore fruit in the November election. All of New England returned to the Federalist ranks. Senator John Quincy Adams, running for re-election as a Republican, was cast out of office—a potent object lesson to men of Massachusetts who violated party tradition. In New York the Federalists made large gains in the legislature. But the Federalist tidal wave was stopped abruptly in Pennsylvania which remained in the Republican column. Her industries, it seems, had profited by the Embargo. The Federalist candidates for President and Vice-President, Charles Cotesworth Pinckney of South Carolina and Rufus King of New York, were defeated, and James Madison of Virginia and George Clinton of New York rode into office. The Virginia Dynasty was saved from a revolution but with considerable loss of prestige. The Electoral College, which had given Jefferson 162 votes in 1804, gave to Madison only 122.

Whether William Pinkney was correct in his estimate of the increasing strength of the Embargo in Great Britain was beyond the point. In the United States it had already failed. Weary, disappointed, and with a sigh of relief, Jefferson prepared to retire to Monticello, leaving little James Madison and his faithful Treasurer, Albert Gallatin, to reap the whirlwind he had sown. "Never," he declared, "did a prisoner released from his chains feel such relief as I shall on shaking off the shackles of power. Nature intended me for the more tranquil pursuits of science by rendering them my supreme delight."

With distress throughout the land, rumors of rebellion in New England, and a report showing that in that year customs had declined from $16,000,000 to $8,000,000—a condition, as Gallatin put it, equivalent to war—something had to be done and done quickly. Peaceable coercion had failed, miserably failed. On February 27 the Embargo Act was repealed, the repeal to take effect on March 4, Inauguration Day, as a happy omen of the new administration. Heaven knows, the new administration needed one!

CHAPTER FIVE

President Madison Inherits Trouble

DAVID MONTAGUE ERSKINE was a well-intentioned young man who believed in his soul that blood is thicker than water. Eldest son of Great Britain's Lord Chancellor, he had set out upon a diplomatic career, owing his first appointment to Charles James Fox. In the year 1800 he had had the boldness to wed an American, the daughter of General John Cadwalader, thus allying himself to an illustrious Philadelphia family.

In 1809 Erskine was British Minister to the United States and it pained him to observe the strained relations existing between his own people and those of his wife. He proposed to do something about it. What a feather it would be in his cap if he could bring the two branches of the English-speaking world into harmony, an ideal which he had symbolized by his own marriage! Who could have been in a better position than he to see the right on both sides?

Upon the repeal of the Embargo, Congress passed the Non-Intercourse Act, under which the commerce of America was declared open to all the world, with the exception of those two irritating countries—Great Britain and France, whose ships were excluded from American ports. No sooner had Madison's administration been organized than Erskine entered upon negotiations with the Secretary of State, Robert Smith, and the President. Smith, a Marylander and a man of limited intellect and talent, had been foisted upon Madison by a political clique that was jealous of Albert Gallatin who, by every measure of training and ability, should have had the post. As a result, Robert Smith was a mere figurehead while Madison performed the functions of Secretary of State as well as those of the chief executive.

With a willingness on both sides to arrive at a happy conclusion, the negotiations proceeded swiftly and without hitch. Erskine inquired of the President if, should the orders in council be withdrawn, the United States would reciprocate by opening American ports to British trade. Having been assured upon this point, on April 9 Erskine addressed a message to the Secretary of State which read: "I am authorized to declare that His Majesty's Orders in Council of January and November, 1807, will have been withdrawn, as respects the United States, on the tenth of June next." Immediately the President issued a proclamation to the people informing them that on the same date American ports once more would be open to British commerce.

The President's proclamation was received with a delirium of joy. The shipping men envisioned their vessels once more filled with rich cargoes; the merchants in the seaboard towns saw their shops once more displaying British goods to a trade-starved people. All credit was owed to the energetic little man who had brought it about. Madison at once became a popular hero. Even the Federalists raised their glasses in toasts to him. The visionary Jefferson, thank heaven, was safe in Monticello where, without injury to the republic, he could proceed with his research into the theories of government. But at last the country had in the White House a sane, sensible, practical man who would leave business alone; who had achieved the impossible by persuading Great Britain to withdraw her obnoxious orders.

News traveled slowly across the Atlantic in those days. Through May and June the country exulted, meanwhile preparing for the resumption of trade on a colossal scale. Then, suddenly, on July 31, the bubble burst. David Montague Erskine, His Majesty's Minister to the United States, notified the President that his government had repudiated the agreement!

In the fervor of accomplishment, David Montague Erskine had exceeded his instructions. At least that is what Canning declared, although there were some who hinted that old King George III, reviving temporarily from his insanity and recalling old scores, had put his foot down on any concessions to the American people. Be that as it may, His Majesty's Government had spoken, His Majesty's Minister was in disgrace and not even his father, the Lord Chancellor, could save him. Along with the message of repudiation came the order for Erskine's recall. David Montague Erskine was a well-intentioned young man, but good intentions meant nothing to Canning. To him a blunder was a blunder.

Erskine's embarrassment was as nothing compared to that of Madison. The honeymoon which the American people grant their newly elected presidents was definitely over. Alas! there was never to be another one for him. On August 9 Madison was compelled to issue a second proclamation rescinding the first. While loyal Madisonians cursed England for her perfidy, loyal Federalists bemoaned the toasts they had drunk and condemned Madison as an unconscionable blunderer no better than his predecessor. The prospects for peace had been so bright, and now the two countries once more were poles apart.

The year 1809 dragged on to its weary close. In England the Portland ministry fell, giving way to that of Spencer Perceval. Canning was succeeded in the Foreign Office by Lord Richard Wellesley, fresh from his triumphs in India and brother of the Wellesley who was making history on the Spanish Peninsula. Wellesley was capable, but the Perceval Ministry, its leader a weakling, was shot through with intrigue and it was as much as its members could do to keep their skins whole. Minister Pinkney found his task in London even more hopeless than it had been when he had to deal with Canning.

The new Ministry dispatched to America Francis James Jackson to resume the now old, time-honored negotiations over the *Chesapeake* affair. The new envoy was better known as "Copenhagen" Jackson, he having acted as messenger in delivering the ultimatum which resulted in the rape of the Danish fleet. He arrived with a titled German wife, a coach and four and a retinue of servants to show the crude American backwoodsmen how civilized people lived. The mushroom village of Washington, with its muddy roads and its miserable climate, was a sorry descent for a man who was accustomed to consort with royalty in the capitals of Europe, previous experiences of which he was quick to relate to all who came within earshot. A more useless person for the work in hand could hardly have been found. One thing at least he condescended to praise. He found the horseback riding in the environs of the capital city agreeable.

Madison he described as "a plain and rather mean looking little man" and Jackson could not help but "contrast this audience with others I had had with most of the sovereigns of Europe."

When Jackson got down to business he proceeded at once to lecture the President and the Secretary of State on the art of diplomacy. He intimated that both of them must have known that Erskine was exceeding his instructions in the previous negotiations. As unschooled as they may have been in diplomacy Mr. Madison and Mr. Smith had no intention of letting Mr. Jackson scold them. When, in a second letter, he renewed his insinuations, they requested his recall. And thus another envoy added fuel to the flame.

It was now obvious to all save the Federalists that negotiations with Great Britain were a waste of time. Having no better recourse the Administration undertook to see what it could do with France. Early in 1810 M. de Champagny, Duke of Cadore, French Foreign Minister, had informed General Armstrong that if the British were to withdraw the orders in council, Napoleon would withdraw his Berlin Decree. This conciliatory attitude on the part of the Emperor was, however, overshadowed a month or two later when he published the Rambouillet Decree, ordering the sale of the American vessels seized under the Bayonne Decree of the previous year. What went into the imperial maw was not likely to come out while the Emperor was straining every effort to finance his military campaigns. Yet the American Government tried to make itself believe that Napoleon might, if only by accident, sometime be guilty of sincerity.

Non-intercourse had proved to be quite as ineffective as the Embargo in bringing Great Britain and France to terms; therefore the administration tried a new combination. On May 1, 1810, Congress repealed the non-importation and non-intercourse laws. In their stead it passed the act known as "Macon's No. 2," after the gentleman from North Carolina who had sponsored it. "Macon's No. 2" stipulated that if either Great Britain or France should revoke or modify respectively their orders or decrees before March 3, 1811, then within three months the United States would revive non-intercourse against the other.

Little did Congress realize, when it passed the act, that it was dealing a hand that Napoleon would be delighted to play. What, for example, was to prevent a gentleman possessing an easy conscience like Napoleon from informing the United States that he had revoked the Berlin Decree, then demanding that she revive non-intercourse against Great Britain? How could he more easily embroil the blood cousins? As a matter of fact, while the British fleet swept the seas, the Berlin Decree was nothing more than a scrap of paper. It was the Bayonne and Rambouillet decrees that did the damage when American ships ventured into the ports of France. Napoleon knew Britain's stubbornness too well to believe that she would withdraw her orders. Corsican shrewdness could count on winning the day while the two stolid Anglo-Saxon countries butted their heads together. The cards having been dealt, Napoleon proceeded to play his hand.

On August 5, 1810, Champagny addressed a note to Armstrong officially declaring that the Berlin and Milan decrees had been revoked as far as they affected the United States, upon the understanding that Great Britain would now revoke her orders in council. If Britain did not revoke her orders then, the note concluded, "the United States will cause their rights to be respected by the British." What could this mean except that Napoleon expected the United States to go to war with Great Britain as part of the bargain?

Yet Napoleon refused to issue a public announcement of the revocation of the decrees; and, for lack of such announcement, Great Britain refused to believe that the decrees had actually been revoked. No arguments on the part of the Secretary of State or of Minister Pinkney in London could persuade her. On the other hand, her ministers pointed out that at the very moment when the decrees were supposed to have been revoked, the United States was protesting the seizure of her vessels by France. To this the Americans replied that the seizures complained against had been made under the Rambouillet and Bayonne decrees, which were no concern of Great Britain's. As a matter of fact the United States Government had hoped that Napoleon would restore the American vessels, but instead he held on to them waiting to see what action the United States would take against Britain. On November 2 President Madison issued a proclamation reviving non-intercourse against Great Britain to take effect in February, 1811, if Great Britain had not by that time rescinded her orders.

At last Pinkney concluded that all overtures to the Perceval Ministry were hopeless and early in 1811 departed from London. Not only did Great Britain retain her orders, but she added insult to injury by sending men-of-war to the American coast to prey upon outgoing merchantmen and, not infrequently, to impress sailors from them. Her only concession was to designate Augustus John Foster, former secretary of the British Legation in Washington, as minister plenipotentiary to resume negotiations on the *Chesapeake* affair. His appointment was announced on February 15. Some two months later the American public was again aroused when, almost within sight of New York, a British frigate believed to be the *Guerrière*, under the command of Captain James R. Dacres, halted the American merchantman *Spitfire* and removed from her deck a sailor whom her captain claimed to be a native of Maine.

On May 6 the frigate *President*, 44 guns, pride of the American Navy and Commodore John Rodgers' flagship, was lying at anchor in Chesapeake Bay, off Annapolis. Near midnight a messenger arrived from Washington bearing orders to the frigate to put to sea at once and investigate the British man-of-war lying off New York. Commodore Rodgers was not aboard the *President*, having gone for a visit to his estate, Sion Hill, near Havre de Grace, 70 miles distant at the head of the bay. He must be notified of the order at once.

At midnight there put out from the *President* one of her boats commanded by Midshipman Matthew Calbraith Perry, who in later years was to win fame for his voyage to Japan. Inspired by the importance of his mission, young Perry zealously urged his men forward. All through the night and all of the next day the little boat pressed on without a pause, the sailors taking turns at the oars, fresh men replacing those that fell exhausted. By nightfall the boat had reached Havre de Grace and Perry leaped out and raced up the hill to report to the Commodore. Apprised of his orders Rodgers joined the party for the return journey, and this time they were fortunate to have a favorable breeze and raised a sail. By 3 P.M. on May 8 the boat with the Commodore aboard drew alongside the *President*. The trip of seventy miles each way, or a total of 140 miles, had been made in the average time of 3.6 miles an hour. The story is said to have been preserved in the annals of the Perry and Rodgers families.

It seems odd that with a good road all the way from Annapolis to Havre de Grace, and in a state famed for its horsemen, no one thought of carrying the news to the Commodore by mounted courier, a means both swifter and less exhausting to the messenger. But then, of course, these were sailors. It is said that in later life Matthew Perry never mentioned the incident. Could it have been that, upon reflection, he concluded that it might not enhance his reputation?

On May 11 the *President* set sail from Annapolis and, on her way down the bay, took ammunition aboard. On the 16th she passed out of the capes and at noon sighted a sail to the eastward. At 2 P.M. the stranger approached and the *President* displayed her standard and the Commodore's pennant. Without replying to the *President's* signals, the stranger altered her course and bore away to the south.

The *President* at once took up the chase which continued throughout the afternoon. It was not until 8:15 P.M., as darkness was closing in, that the *President* came within hailing distance. According to his testimony at the court-martial which followed the incident Rodgers at once inquired, "What ship is that?" From the stranger came the reply, "What ship is that?" Rodgers made no reply, considering that as he had made the first inquiry he had a right to receive the first answer.

Again, according to Rodgers' account, a shot suddenly was fired by the stranger which struck one of the masts of the *President*. Almost immediately a gun from the *President* responded, and the stranger countered with a broadside and musketry. The engagement now became general and, within a few minutes, the guns of the stranger were silenced. Rodgers kept his battle lights lit and cruised in the vicinity throughout the night. At dawn he discovered his adversary a mile away, evidently badly injured. He approached her and dispatched Lieutenant Creighton in a boat with offers of assistance. The vessel proved to be His Majesty's sloop *Little Belt*, 18 guns, under the command of Captain A. B. Bingham. The Briton refused help and set sail for Halifax, where Bingham told his story, which differed in all the important details from that of Commodore Rodgers.

Bingham, it seems, had a rendezvous with the frigate *Guerrière* and ran into the *President* by mistake. He asserted that he had been the first to hail and that the *President* had been the first to fire. Furthermore, he declared that the engagement had lasted more than an hour.

Mr. Augustus J. Foster sidetracked his negotiations over the *Chesapeake* momentarily to demand satisfaction from the United States Government for the behavior of the *President*. He found it strange that as early as 8:15 P.M., on an evening in May, in a southern latitude, Commodore Rodgers had not had light enough to see that his adversary was a mere sloop and no match for a frigate. He protested that a British vessel on a friendly mission should have been subjected to such ill treatment. Monroe, who had succeeded Smith as Secretary of State, replied curtly that the United States had a perfect right to investigate men-of-war near her shores that acted suspiciously and pointed out that nobody was more jealous of that right than Great Britain herself. The argument must have been conclusive, for the British Government let the matter drop.

News of the engagement was received with joy throughout the country, save in Federalist circles in New England. For in the popular mind at last the navy had avenged the insult to the *Chesapeake*. Upon his arrival in New York Commodore Rodgers was wined and dined and given the freedom of the city while President Madison, without waiting to receive a report, wrote him a letter of congratulation. Great Britain contented herself with blowing off steam through her press. The London *Courier*, which publisher Niles of Baltimore's *Niles' Register*, described as being "controlled by Perceval, Wellesley & Co.," thus took the United States to task:

"The account given by the American is anything but a true one. The American government having published Rodgers' account and approved of his conduct, thereby precluding all negotiation, Captain Bingham's letter having placed it beyond a doubt that the hostile conduct of the American was unprovoked, and that being coupled with Admiral Sawyer's previous instruction, demonstrative of the anxiety of our government not to give the least provocation or cause of offense to the United States, *there is but one course left to us to pursue.* The blood of our murdered countrymen *must be avenged* and WAR MUST ENSUE. The conduct of America leaves us no alternative; and therefore it is idle, if not worse, to treat the subject as if it were an 'inconvenient dilemma which ministers,' according to the opposition 'have solely to attribute to their own folly in not confirming Mr. Erskine's sensible arrangement. Of *Mr. Erskine's sensible* arrangement we have so often expressed our opinion that it were unnecessary to repeat it. *We have behaved toward America with* UNEXAMPLED FORBEARANCE, but the forbearance has produced INSOLENCE, AND THAT INSOLENCE MUST BE PUNISHED! !"

The London *Gazette,* official organ of the government, added the comment: "We have now the word of honor of Captain Bingham, that the firing was commenced by Rodgers; and who will put the veracity of an American captain in competition with that of an honorable British officer!"

The comments of the *Courier* and the *Gazette* were picked up by the Republican press in the United States and given conspicuous place, thus keeping the pot boiling; and useless was it for the extreme Federalists to protest in their journals that Bingham was right and Rodgers wrong. So the two great English-speaking countries continued to pursue their divergent ways as Napoleon had intended them to do. Well might the little Corsican sneer at Anglo-Saxon intelligence. His diplomacy was working magnificently.

CHAPTER SIX

Tecumseh and Tippecanoe

VOL. I, Number 1, of *The Weekly Register,* published in Baltimore and edited by Hezekiah Niles, late editor of the Baltimore *Evening Post,* appeared on September 5, 1811. Subscribers to the first issue might have turned to the department headed "The Chronicle" and read:

"There has lately occurred no important event in Spain or Portugal; the French emperor is said to be reinforcing his army; and Wellington, with his strongholds, appears able to make a formidable resistance. The ultimate expulsion of the British is a probable event, but whether Bonaparte will shortly obtain quiet possession of these countries, is at least problematical—he has taught the people to fight, and supposed to have lost in the bloody contest not less than *six hundred thousand men.* 'Ye Gods! What havoc does ambition make.'

"Our accounts from England, to use the language of Consul O'Brien, are 'squally'! The affair of the *President* frigate and the *Little Belt* has excited much sensibility in England. A squadron of ships under the command of Rear Admiral Sir Joseph York, consisting of four vessels of 74 guns and 2 frigates, has been dispatched for our coast, and may be daily expected. Some of the London newspapers say the Admiral has orders to commence immediate hostilities unless our government shall disavow the conduct of Commodore Rodgers. It also appears that some important dispatches have been received from England—'A king's messenger,' the first *officially* acknowledged as such in the United States, passed through this city on Wednesday last to the British Minister, Mr. Foster, at Washington. In the meantime the British ships of war are making captures on our coast. Important events may be expected, but at present all is rumor and uncertainty.

"From France our accounts are less gloomy than heretofore; several American vessels have been released; rather effected, it would seem, by a whim of the government than in consequence of any material change in its policy. But the present enormous duties on American produce in France forbids all hope of a profitable and extensive trade until they are reduced, of which a prospect is held out."

Thus Editor Niles' customers obtained news of the doings in the world about them. In Portugal, behind the impregnable line of Torres Vedras, Wellington had held off the superior French army of Masséna. Masséna, his men unable to support themselves in a devastated country, had appealed to Napoleon for reinforcements and provisions; but the Emperor, recruiting an army for an attack upon Russia, would send him neither. And so Masséna had been forced to retreat, with Wellington at his heels.

The invasion of Spain had brought about a national uprising in that country, yet neither the world nor Napoleon realized that this was the beginning of the end. To the casual observer Napoleon was at the height of his power. His mighty empire extended from the Atlantic to the Adriatic Sea; the German principalities were its satellites. Prussia and Austria were crushed. Belgium and Holland were integral parts of France and the Grand Duchy of Warsaw, a French creation, was thrust into the side of Russia.

Except for Russia all the countries of the Continent, including Scandinavia, had unwillingly consented to his Continental System, designed to exclude all trade with Great Britain. And now the United States, also out of necessity, had fallen into line, refusing the admission of British goods.

If there was ever a time when Great Britain appeared to need an ally, it was at that moment. And if her statesmen had been able to display even a reasonably conciliatory spirit, she could have had the United States. Half the nation was with her in spite of orders and impressments, and the other half would have welcomed a break with Napoleon who, in spite of professing to have withdrawn his decrees, still held millions of dollars' worth of American property. Yet at that moment Britain lacked the leaders with the courage and the foresight to abandon an ancient custom upon the maintenance of which she imagined her salvation depended. Her men-of-war hovered near our coasts, she continued to impress our seamen. As for the orders in council, Perceval, the Prime Minister, was one of their most ardent supporters, and protests against them were useless.

And why, after all, should Great Britain fear the United States? The best advices indicated lack of preparedness and division of public opinion in America. Even after the action of the *President* and the *Little Belt* His Majesty's Ministers were unconvinced that the American people would fight. The absence of American cotton and other raw commodities was bringing distress to Britain's manufacturers and the loss of the American market was provoking protests from her merchants; her currency had depreciated and her harvest had failed, yet Perceval, Wellesley & Co. pursued their chosen course relentlessly and undeviatingly. The more the opposition criticized, the more adamant became the ministry.

Turning from the foreign to the domestic scene "The Chronicle" goes on to say: "At a meeting held at Vincennes, Indiana territory, at which were present a large number of very respectable gentlemen, it was agreed among other resolves, as the opinion of the assembly, 'that the persons and property of this frontier can never be secured, but by breaking up of the combination formed by the Shawnee prophet on the Wabash.' It is generally believed in the western country that the outrages committed by the Indians are brought about by 'British influence.' A war, however, is not expected; the Indians fearing the Americans too much to engage in it."

Vincennes was the capital of Indiana Territory which had been established in 1800 and which included the present states of Indiana, Illinois and Wisconsin. General William Henry Harrison, a young Virginian less than thirty years of age, had been appointed its first governor. Within ten years the white population of the territory had increased from 2,500 to 25,000 persons, the principal settlements being at Louisville and Vincennes. In 1805 a territorial legislature had been established and, through treaties with the Indians, the Americans had acquired title to 46,000 acres of land.

The method through which land was obtained lay in debauching the Indians with liquor. Governor Harrison in one of his reports stated: "I do not believe that there are more than 600 warriors on the Wabash, and yet the quantity of whiskey brought here annually for their consumption is said to amount to 6000 gallons." Encouraged to drink and run into debt, the chiefs were told that they could absolve themselves by giving title to the land. But this they had no actual right to do since, under Indian custom, title to land resided not in the chiefs but in the tribe.

At this point there appeared on the scene two Indians of remarkable personality. They were Tecumseh and Elkswatawa, better known in history as the Prophet. Tecumseh and the Prophet were brothers, being two of a set of triplets born of a Creek mother and a Shawnee warrior. Tecumseh was a man of distinguished appearance, great personal courage, and considerable dignity and oratorical ability. The Prophet, on the other hand, was a drunkard whose generally depraved features were made even more forbidding through the lack of an eye. Tecumseh furnished the brains, the Prophet the mysticism. The latter claimed to hold converse with the Great Spirit and attributed to himself the power of performing miracles. His claims were accepted by many Indians, save those of his own tribe, thus bearing out the old Biblical saying.

Jefferson in his day had advised the Indians to settle down to farming. Tecumseh took him at his word, with somewhat embarrassing results for the white settlers. At Tippecanoe, on the Wabash, he and the Prophet established a town, prohibited the use of liquor and set to work to till the soil. Furthermore, Tecumseh put himself relentlessly to the task of preventing continued sequestration of the land. As a last desperate effort to stem the rising tide of white settlers he contemplated a federation of all the Indian tribes, both north and south, throughout the entire Valley of the Mississippi. As complimentary as this was to Tecumseh's foresight and statesmanship, and as admirable as it was from the standpoint of the Indians, it was highly annoying and detrimental to continued extension of the white frontiers.

Besides this major conflict of interests there were other factors which widened the breach between the Indians and the frontiersmen. When the Indians were drunk they not infrequently murdered each other, and now and then they murdered white settlers. White settlers, on the other hand, now and then murdered Indians. When a white man was accused of murdering an Indian he was brought to trial by the whites. When an Indian was accused of murdering a white man he was brought to trial not by his fellow Indians, but by the whites. Such a system necessarily led to suspicion that the punishment of the accused Indian was more certain than that of the accused white. The Indians had lived peaceably with the French settlers, but an occasional Frenchman in Indian territory was far different from the thousands of Americans with many more thousands behind them.

A climax was reached when, on September 30, 1809, at Vincennes, Governor Harrison concluded a treaty with the Delawares, Pottawattomies, Miamis, Kickapoos, Wea and Eel River Indians by which he obtained no less than 3,000,000 acres of the finest hunting grounds on the Wabash. The price agreed upon was $8,200 in cash and $2,350 in annuities. Realizing the hopelessness of the Indians' position if this deal were permitted to go through, Tecumseh, abetted by the Prophet, vehemently protested it. It made little difference to him that the land in question was not that of his own tribe.

Through an interpreter Governor Harrison invited Tecumseh to visit him at Vincennes to discuss the matter. Tecumseh accepted the invitation. He was told to come alone, but on August 12, 1810, he appeared at the capital with 300 armed warriors at his back. The settlers were greatly alarmed at the display of force and a massacre might have taken place had not Governor Harrison faced the situation calmly and cowed the Indians by parading two companies of militia. He ordered Tecumseh to withdraw, after the latter had spoken with great bitterness of the behavior of the whites. On the following day Tecumseh, who admired courage, reappeared in a more friendly frame of mind, and it was agreed that Governor Harrison would refer the complaint to the President. On this visit Tecumseh promised that if the lands were returned he would ally himself with the Americans.

War seemed imminent and, as a precautionary measure, Governor Harrison ordered up to Vincennes a detachment of regulars which had been stationed in Kentucky, and combined them with three companies of militia infantry and a company of dragoons. The rest of the summer, however, was passed in relative quiet. But the spring of 1811 saw parties of marauding Indians on the Wabash who plundered the houses of the settlers and the wigwams of friendly Indians, stole horses and committed other depredations. Stirred to action by reports of the conduct of the Indians, Harrison sent a warning to them that he was ready to attack. This brought Tecumseh once more to Vincennes. He protested his friendship but still demanded return of the lands. Shortly after his departure it was learned that he had gone on a trip to the South in the hope of encouraging the Creeks, Choctaws and Chickasaws to join his confederation.

No sooner had the people of Vincennes heard of Tecumseh's absence than they urged Governor Harrison to strike. The Governor had received from the Secretary of War a rather broad order instructing him to attack the Indians at Tippecanoe, if he should deem it advisable. With that authority from his government and encouraged by the settlers Harrison determined upon invasion of the Indian country. He assembled at Vincennes a force of about 900 men, including 250 regulars of the 4th U. S. Infantry under Colonel John P. Boyd, 60 Kentucky volunteers, 600 Indiana militia and 270 mounted dragoons and riflemen.

On September 26 the expedition set out from Vincennes and marched through the Wabash Valley. For a week they proceeded without molestation, pausing at the present site of Terre Haute to erect a fort which they named Fort Harrison in honor of their commander. On October 10 the first blood was shed when a sentinel was wounded by a Shawnee warrior. Harrison at once dispatched a message by some friendly Miamis to Tippecanoe ordering the Prophet to restore the horses and other property stolen during the spring and to surrender certain Indians who had been accused of murder. The Miamis never returned.

On November 5 the expedition arrived within eleven miles of Tippecanoe, and now Indians were constantly appearing, but without offering resistance. Governor Harrison took precautions against surprise by conducting his infantry in two separate columns with mounted men in advance, on the flanks and in the rear. The following day the little army came within sight of the Prophet's town. They were met by Indians who asked for a parley, as the result of which the Indians promised to refrain from hostilities and suggested a

61

camp site for the Americans on a bluff about a mile from the town. Two of Harrison's officers inspected the site, reported it to be satisfactory, and there the troops pitched their tents and prepared to spend the night. The General disposed them in a rough parallelogram, with the baggage and supplies in the center, and posted guards and sentinels.

All was quiet until shortly before dawn on November 7 when the camp was awakened by the firing of a rifle by one of the sentinels who had made out a savage approaching him through the darkness. In a few minutes the Indians were attacking at two separate points and making as good use as they could of the confusion in the American camp. General Harrison mounted a charger and moved from place to place encouraging the defenders. The encounter was sharp and bloody, but at last the Indians were repulsed. As the sun rose the Americans proceeded to count their losses. Out of the 900 men no fewer than 61 had been killed or mortally wounded and 127 wounded. Among the casualties were an aide-de-camp, a major, three captains and two subalterns.

It was believed at the time that the early morning attack by the Indians was accidental. The story had it that the Prophet intended to hold the council in the town as he had promised the previous day, proffer friendship and then fall upon the Americans and massacre them. But in the course of the night he conducted a ceremonial, assuring his hearers that he had charmed the white men's bullets so that they would not injure the Indians. The story of the charm won their confidence so effectually that he could not keep the young warriors in check and they proceeded at once to the attack. The Prophet himself observed the battle from a safe distance and, as a result of its outcome, lost considerable prestige.

On November 8 Harrison entered the town to find it deserted. He devoted the day to burning all the supplies and the houses, leaving it in the afternoon a mass of charred wood and ashes. But, what is more to the point, in the town were found firearms of British manufacture. This was sufficient to confirm the suspicion that the British Government was behind all the Indian unrest and to add one more indictment to the long list of wrongs charged against His Majesty's Government. So far as the West was concerned all other contributing causes were forgotten. And this was important, for as the Indians and Americans were meeting in battle on the banks of the Wabash, the Twelfth Congress was convening at Washington. What happened at Tippecanoe had much to do with what was about to take place at the nation's capital.

CHAPTER SEVEN

The War Hawks Swoop Down

THE Twelfth Congress convened on November 4, 1811, one month ahead of the usual time of meeting. The voice of the people had been heard in the spring congressional elections again clamoring vociferously for Mr. Jefferson's party. The result was a Republican landslide. In the Senate were 28 Republicans and six lonely Federalists; in the House, 107 Republicans, 36 Federalists and John Randolph of Roanoke.

Randolph was an annoying fellow who could not be counted on to stay regular. He had first gained distinction in the Republican councils; but he did not like the Yazoo scandals, and liked even less the apparent willingness of Jefferson and Madison to offer a bribe to the venal French Foreign Minister, Talleyrand, to negotiate the purchase of the Floridas. Eccentric was the best way to describe him. Randolph called himself a "Tertium Quid." *Niles' Register,* which printed the names of Republicans in italics and Federalists in Roman letters, solved the problem ingeniously by printing Randolph's half in italics and half in Roman.

Seventy new members were on the rolls of the Twelfth Congress and among them were a number of young men who were impatient with the way the elder statesmen had been running the country. The old Republicans were opposed to a large standing army, a large navy, imperialistic ambitions and the levying of internal taxes, all of which they regarded as Federalist measures. They had let Great Britain bully and browbeat them. They had neglected to keep their ears to the ground so that they had not heard the talk about "manifest destiny." Here were Florida and Canada ripe for the plucking, ready to be annexed at the drop of a hat. Why, boasted Henry Clay, the Kentucky militia alone could take Canada! Yet

64

the old fogies wasted time in arguments and did nothing about it. The young men meant to change all that.

The ring leader was Clay, former Virginian "mill boy of the slashes," now a rising statesman of Kentucky, who at the age of 34 had already sat for a brief space in the United States Senate before being elected to the House. There were John C. Calhoun, South Carolinian aristocrat and scholar, who had been educated at Yale; and, from the same state, Langdon Cheeves, William Lowndes and David R. Williams. There was handsome young Peter B. Porter, another Yale graduate, native son of Connecticut and now of western New York. There were Felix Grundy of Tennessee and Richard M. Johnson of Kentucky. Not one of them was over 40. The elder statesmen had dillydallied too long. The younger statesmen knew what they wanted—empire and war. John Randolph, who had a knack for coining apt expressions, mocked the young gentlemen from the South and West by christening them the "War Hawks."

Randolph, older in experience, might laugh at them. Let him laugh. The War Hawks proceeded straight to the business at hand. They elected Henry Clay, Speaker, snowing under William Bibb, the representative of the Peace party, by a vote of 75 to 38. They took command of the Committee on Foreign Affairs, making Peter B. Porter the chairman and giving him Calhoun for moral support. In the membership of nine there was only one Federalist. Somehow Randolph, too, slipped in. By the evening of the 4th the Twelfth Congress had been organized and its members were ready to give ear to what the President should say in his message.

The President covered considerable ground. He recited the outrageous damage inflicted by the British orders in council; he took a dig at the French, too, for their restrictions on American trade; he touched upon the state of the national finances; he bemoaned the extent to which smuggling and trading under false papers had increased in defiance of the non-importation laws, and he called for an increase in the nation's armed forces.

The schoolboy inevitably associates the War of 1812 with Stanley M. Arthur's immortal painting of the proud American youth on the deck of a merchantman just as he is about to be delivered up to the tender mercies of a British press gang. If there is one issue the average person links with the War of 1812 it is impressment. Yet, in his message to this momentous meeting of Congress, of impressment Madison said not a word. In fact the President and a good part of the public had of late been so occupied with the turmoil caused by the British orders and the French decrees and the American non-importation laws and the material matter of trade that they had temporarily forgotten the poor American seaman. Between 1807 and 1811 impressment had become a dead issue and had to have the breath of life blown into it.

That task was performed by the Committee of Foreign Affairs. The Committee's report, like the President's message, went fully into the orders in council. It pointed out that Great Britain had refused to withdraw them; while, on the other hand, Napoleon had rescinded his decrees as regards the United States, and reminded that the United States had a promise to keep with Napoleon in the matter of resenting the behavior of Great Britain. Having dealt to its satisfaction with these high affairs of state, the report at last got down to the business of impressment.

"And while we are laying before you the just complaints of our merchants against the plunder of their ships and cargoes," said the report, "we cannot refrain from presenting to the justice and humanity of our country the unhappy case of our impressed seamen." Warming to the subject the report lamented that the "cries of their wives and children . . . have, of late, been drowned in the louder clamors at the loss of property." Then, in a sweet appeal to reason, it continued: "If it be our duty to encourage the fair and legitimate commerce of this country by protecting the property of the merchant; then, indeed, by as much as if life and liberty are more estimable than ships and goods, so much more impressive is the duty to shield the persons of our seamen."

The War Hawks were intent upon war. Could this almost apologetic mention of impressment have been the result of a search for a moral issue? Apparently the Maryland Legislature suspected it, for after the war was ended it went on record as declaring that impressment was a matter for negotiation and never had been a cause of war.

The Committee's report concluded, ". . . we must tamely submit, or resist by those means which God has placed within our reach." The Deity had been somewhat shortsighted in His provisions, for the Committee augmented the divine preparations by proposing that:

The military establishment be filled up.

An additional 10,000 regulars be raised to serve three years.

The President accept not more than 50,000 volunteers.

He be authorized to order out the militia.

The naval vessels not now in service be repaired and commissioned.

The merchant vessels be permitted to arm.

The six resolutions were the excuse for what so delighted statesmen and populace—a full-dress debate on the general subject of the war. First to take the floor was the Chairman of the Foreign Relations Committee. Mr. Porter likened the country to a young man just entered into life who, if he submitted to one cool, deliberate, intentioned indignity, might safely calculate upon being kicked and cuffed for the remainder of his life.

How was the war to be waged? That this country could contend with Great Britain on the sea, continued Mr. Porter, it was folly to pretend. But within six months we could have privateers to harass her commerce and destroy her fisheries. Then he played the War Hawks' trump card. We could deprive her of Canada! Why the exports of Quebec alone were worth $6,000,000 a year. The seizure of Canada would enable us to compensate ourselves tenfold for all the spoliations committed on our commerce.

Having thus expressed himself, Porter yielded the floor to his fellow War Hawk, Mr. Grundy, of Tennessee. The speaker reminded his hearers of Britain's violation of the freedom of the seas, the iniquities practiced under her system of impressment and of the unmistakable evidence found at Tippecanoe of her base intrigue with the Indians. He recalled the sacred pledge made to France; and, like Porter, held out the pleasant prospect of the acquisition of Canada. As a representative of Tennessee and with his eye on his constituents, who were only mildly interested in Canada, he added what was nearer to their hearts, the conquest of the Floridas.

On December 10 the expected happened. John Randolph of Roanoke entered the debate. Randolph was forever on his feet, and the man never knew when to sit down. "Mr. Randolph spoke for three hours." "Mr. Randolph spoke about two hours and a half against the

bill and against war." "Mr. Randolph spoke two hours and a half."
The reports of the Twelfth Congress are punctuated with such
weary comments. Impatient members fled the chamber. The more
conscientious settled back in their seats to await the ordeal. To the
comfort of his fellow members, Randolph was indifferent. He was
fully aware of the superiority of his talents, and this occasion found
him in his most brilliant and sarcastic mood.

"The question," began Randolph, in his shrill voice, "is one of
peace or war—a war not of defense, but of conquest, of aggrandizement, of ambition." He looked accusingly at the young members
as he added, "a war foreign to the interests of this country, to the
interests of humanity itself."

With studied malice he recalled the earlier repugnance of the
Republican party to acts of aggression and chided them for forsak-
ing their principles. "I know not how gentlemen calling themselves
Republicans could advocate such a war!" He paused to let the shaft
sink in. "To whom will you confide the charge of leading the flower
of our youth to the Heights of Abraham? Will you find him in the
person of an acquitted felon?" There was not a member of the House
who did not know that this remark was aimed at Brigadier General
James Wilkinson, commanding the New Orleans district, who had
been charged with accepting bribes from the Spaniards but who, in
spite of the suspicions, continued to hold high position in the army.
So they criticized Randolph for withdrawing from the Republican
party; it was the party, not he, which had changed. "Those who oppose are upheld as the advocates of England, those firm and un-
deviating Republicans who now dare to cling to the ark of the
Constitution!" He next referred to the preceding speaker's mention
of Tippecanoe. "Has Mr. Grundy any proof that the massacre of the
Wabash was instigated by the British? It is mere surmise and suspicion. It is our own thirst for territory that has driven these sons
of nature to desperation!" Randolph, at any rate, refused to be impressed by the British arms found in the Indian village.

Then, in a flight of sarcasm and fancy: "I could not but smile at
the liberality of the gentlemen in giving Canada to New York,
while at the same time he warned her that the western scale must
preponderate. I could almost fancy I saw the capital in motion to-

wards the falls of the Ohio; after a short sojourn taking flight to the Mississippi, and finally alighting in Darien."

There was the suggestion of a sneer as he continued. "But, it seems, this is to be a holiday campaign. There is to be no expense of blood or treasure on our part. Canada is to conquer herself. She is to be subdued by the principles of fraternity. The people of that country are first to be seduced from their allegiance and converted into traitors, preparatory to making them good citizens. We are to succeed in the French mode. How dreadfully it might be retorted on the western and slave-holding States." The sneer gave way to scorn as he exclaimed. "No! If we must have them, let them fall by the valor of their arms."

It was now the turn of his Southern colleagues to receive a verbal lashing. "I am not surprised at the war spirit of the gentlemen from the South. By impolitic and ruinous measures they have knocked down the price of cotton to seven cents and tobacco to nothing, raising the price of blankets and every other necessity 300 to 400 percent.

"But is war the remedy? Who will profit? Speculators, a few lucky merchants, commissioners and contractors. Who must suffer? The people! It is their blood, their taxes that must flow to support it." Cold and relentless, Randolph pursued his quarry. "I am gratified to hear acknowledgment that the non-importation law is destructive. Are you ashamed to repeal it? The French Emperor stands in the way." At this the Federalist members pricked up their ears and smiled maliciously at their Republican opponents. Randolph, of course, was a long-winded bore, but he did occasionally hit the nail on the head. Too bad he was so erratic. There was the making of a good Federalist in him.

Then the tall, gaunt orator, the large dark eyes accentuated by the pallor of his face, stood before his colleagues and, like a Cassandra, warned them of what was to come. "We have so increased the trade and wealth of Montreal and Quebec that at last we cast a wistful eye at Canada. Go! March to Canada! Leave the broad bosom of the Chesapeake and her hundred tributary rivers; the whole line of seacoast, from Machias to St. Mary's, unprotected. You have taken Quebec. Have you conquered England? Will you seek for the deep foundations of her power in the frozen deserts of Labrador?

"Our people will not submit to be taxed for the war of conquest and dominion. I am unwilling to embark on a common cause with France and be dragged at the wheels of the car of some Burr or Bonaparte. Consider the defenseless state of our seaports. And what of the situation of our slave-holding states and the danger of insurrection?"

The speaker paused to draw breath and mop his brow, then continued: "The heart of the English people is with us. It is a selfish and corrupt ministry and their servile tools to whom we are not more opposed than they are. And shall Republicans become the instrument of him who has effaced the title of Attila to the Scourge of God?"

His argument was at an end. And no one knew better than Randolph of Roanoke himself that he had delivered a capital speech. Yet with becoming modesty he apologized for his "very desultory manner of speaking." He regretted that his bodily indisposition—he was a confirmed hypochondriac—had obliged him to talk perhaps somewhat wildly, yet he trusted some method might be found in his madness.

The War Hawks were not lacking in gifted orators. Doubtless they had foreseen Randolph's outburst for, to guard against any effect it might have, they had saved their champions, Calhoun and Clay for the rebuttal. Calhoun pooh-poohed the likelihood of an insurrection of the slaves, and declined to treat the other arguments in detail. "The question," he insisted, "even in the opinion and admission of our opponents, is reduced to this single point. Which shall we do, abandon or defend our commercial and maritime rights, and the personal liberties of our citizens in exercising them? These rights are essentially attacked, and war is the only means of redress. . . . He [Randolph] dared not deny his country's wrongs, or vindicate the conduct of her enemy."

Calhoun yielded the floor to Clay, the little fellow with the big mouth who met eloquence with eloquence. Clay began with a rhetorical question. "What would be gained by war? Sir, I ask in return what will you not lose by a mongrel state of peace with Great Britain? Look at the treasury reports—$6,000,000 of revenue as against $16,000,000 before the orders in council. Some people suggest repeal of the non-importation law. That would be an act of perfidy. You would present the strange phenomenon of an import without an export trade. By a continuance of this peace, then, we should lose our commerce, our character and a nation's best attribute, our honor!"

Laying responsibility for the orders not upon fear of French subjugation, as the British asserted, but upon British fear of commercial rivalry, he declared: "She sickens at your prosperity; she is jealous of you, she dreads your rivalship on the ocean. She saw in your numberless ships, whose sails spread on every sea; she perceived in your hundred and twenty thousand gallant tars the seeds of a naval force which, in thirty years, would rival her on her own element. She therefore commenced the odious system of impressment."

After Randolph, Calhoun and Clay had been heard, the debate gradually wasted itself away among the remarks of the rank and file. It is doubtful if many votes were altered by the arguments presented on the floor. The resolution asking an increase in the military establishment was passed by a handsome majority. The action of the House was amended by the Senate under the leadership of William B. Giles of Virginia. Eventually it was the Senate's bill which President Madison signed on January 11. It increased the regular army to 35,000. Supplementary bills appropriated $1,000,000 for arms and ammunition, camp equipment and quartermasters' stores, $400,000 for ordnance, powder and small arms for the navy. Even the acid Federalist leader, Josiah Quincy, voted for the bills, defending his action on the ground that it would have been unpatriotic to oppose the administration in its efforts to provide national defense. Next came the question of the 50,000 volunteers who must necessarily be recruited from the organized State militia, ordinarily under orders of the governors. Should the President be granted the right to call the organized militia into service? If so, to what extent could it be used? Would the President have the right to command it to operate outside the country; in other words, in Canada? Congress had discussed the conquest of Canada as the major operation of the proposed war. But when it came to a question of sending militia there, Congress hemmed and hawed. Members were not so sure as to how such an infringement of States' rights would be received in their bailiwicks. They voted the President the authority to call to arms a force of volunteers not exceeding 50,000 men, but

71

on the matter of foreign service they dodged, leaving that highly important but delicate issue to the President's discretion.

Voting to raise the regular army to 35,000 men was one thing, recruiting it was quite another. Under the law every able-bodied man was a member of the State militia. Consequently before a man could enlist in the regular army he had to be released from the militia. And how many, pray, would elect to sign up for a term of five years as Giles' bill directed, when they could serve their country gallantly on a two months' enlistment? At the moment only a few thousand were with the colors. As for the use of the militia for foreign service at the President's discretion, that meant going over the heads of the governors, promised certain protests from those opposed to the war and the administration and provoked a serious constitutional question. There was grave danger of the war being fought out in the courts rather than on the battlefields.

The absurdity of the situation was manifested when, a few days after the passage of the bill, Representative Porter proposed the raising of a provisional force of 20,000; for, said he, "We have made a parade in passing laws to raise 25,000 regular troops and 50,000 volunteers, but in truth and in fact we have not given him [the President] a single man."

The raising of the army having been thus doubtfully disposed of, the next question that presented itself was how the men were to be paid, fed, equipped and armed. Money obviously was needed. Equally obvious was the fact that it had to come from the people. This was a matter which Congressmen would have liked to ignore, but the Secretary of the Treasury, Albert Gallatin, was constantly reminding them of it. Gallatin, a bald-headed little foreigner with an accent, a merchant who could only think in terms of dollars and cents! What if he had been the only man in the Republican party able to meet the gifted Hamilton in debate over fiscal matters? A member of the upper class, he ought to have been a Federalist. But for some strange reason he preferred to consider himself a liberal. If he couldn't put up with the American way of doing things, why didn't he go back to the Switzerland from which he had come? When his colleagues had blocked his aspirations to be Secretary of State they thought they were done with him, and here he was turning up in the worst of all positions as holder of the purse strings, interfering with the preparations for a war by insisting that it would cost money! The truth of the matter was, according to the war party, that Gallatin didn't want war any more than did the other merchants to whose class he belonged. Wright, Republican from Maryland, openly charged him with as much.

As early as November 22 Gallatin called attention to the condition of the Treasury, suffering from declining revenue as a result of the non-importation laws. In the event of war he suggested that the customs duties be raised 50 per cent. If this did not prove sufficient he proposed increasing the duties still more and restoring the import on salt and moderate internal taxes to defray the cost of a loan. The loan, he thought, should be $40,000,000 at eight per cent. Again in January Gallatin raised the grim specter of expense. This time his plan called for a loan of $10,000,000, the doubling of existing duties, a stamp tax, a salt tax, taxes on distilled spirits, refined sugar, licenses to retailers, on auctions and carriages. Internal taxes, the invention of the devil and the Federalists, and now brought forward by a member of the Republican party! A whole month passed before Congress could get up its courage to tackle the problem. At last it authorized a loan of $11,000,000 at six per cent. It did not get up its courage to pass the other tax measures until after war had been declared.

Quite as difficult as raising an army was raising money to pay for it. Thanks to the Embargo and other restrictive trade measures, most of the specie in the country had taken flight from the South and West to the manufacturing centers of New England. It lay in the coffers of New England banks to the credit of New England capitalists, Federalists almost to a man, violently inimical to the war and the administration. And now, by this odd turn of affairs, New England Federalists were invited to finance a policy that was not of their choosing.

New England editors fairly foamed at the mouth at the mere suggestion. The Boston *Gazette*, Federalist organ, thundered a denunciation. "Nothing," exclaimed its editor, "is now wanting to the perpetuation of the system of commercial restriction but that the Federalists should lend government the money which they are obliged to withdraw from commerce. Mr. Gallatin calculates that they will come fluttering round his books like pidgeons round a handful of corn. The opinion entertained by the statesmen of the backwoods of our merchants is the same once expressed by the Dutch—'that they would make a voyage to h—l, if they were sure of not burning their sails!' But they will find themselves mistaken. Our merchants constitute an honorable, high-minded, intelligent and independent class of citizens. They feel the oppression, injury and mockery with which they are treated by their government. They will lend them money to retrace their steps, but none to persevere in their present course. Let every highwayman find his own pistols."

Inexorable, too, were the Federalists of New York. There the editor of the *Evening Post* thus greeted the government's appeal: "We have only room this evening to say that we trust no true friend to his country will be found among the subscribers to the Gallatin loan. Some observations on this subject will be submitted to the public in a day or two, proving that it is not even for the interest of monied men to subscribe on the terms proposed."

The press and the bankers prevailed. Up to May 14, within a month of the declaration of war, New England, the wealthiest section of the country, had subscribed less than $1,000,000; New York a little over $1,000,000, Philadelphia a like amount; Baltimore, where Editor Niles of *The Register* beat the drums for the administration, as much as all of New England, and the country as a whole $6,102,-900, or barely more than half the amount authorized. The despised foreigner, Gallatin, had to fall back upon the issuance of Treasury notes. The heroic little man was unruffled, as usual treating his adopted fellow countrymen with a patience bordering upon the sublime.

Next something had to be done about the navy, a matter particularly obnoxious to the old-line Jeffersonian Republicans who regarded a big navy as a badge of imperialism. There was not a single capital ship in the establishment and, for lack of attention, several of the frigates were out of commission. Jefferson had put his faith in gunboats as being the only craft that could not possibly act offensively, disregarding the possibility that they might prove to be almost as useless on the defense.

The South Carolinian, Langdon Cheeves, as chairman of the Naval Affairs Committee, shocked fellow Republicans of the House by proposing the laying down of 25 ships of the line and 40 frigates at a cost of several millions of dollars. He argued that, in view of the distance from the home base, Britain would have to meet every American ship with three of her own; one for active service, one to hold in reserve and one to ply back and forth across the Atlantic with supplies and men. Construct a navy of 65 ships and Great Britain would have to find 195 to oppose them, a considerable burden considering the vast expanse of water her squadrons had to patrol and her troubles nearer home.

To such a proposal Congress was cold. Where were the millions to be had to pay the cost? Besides, it had been generally agreed that Canada was the chief objective, and no navy was needed for that. This was to be a land war. The Republicans turned down Cheeves' ambitious program, made an appropriation to recondition the ships already in existence and, in a final fling at their old *bête noir*, the Navy, cut that appropriation in half.

At this point a suspicion took form among the War Hawks that the gallant little Madison was not displaying the enthusiasm for the struggle becoming to a commander-in-chief. The President's first administration was in its last years and party nominations were imminent. It was rumored that a delegation of Republicans had taken it upon themselves to call upon him and arouse his military ardor by stating that if war were not declared before the election he would certainly be defeated by the Federalists; indeed if he did not act quickly, he could not rely even upon his renomination. The incident in later years was attested to by one James Fisk, Republican from Vermont, who claimed to have been a member of the committee.

Yet another event occurred to add to the perplexities of the administration. We have noted how the report of the House Committee on Foreign Affairs and Henry Clay in his war debate speech alluded to the solemn pledge made to France in return for Napoleon's withdrawal of the Decrees of Berlin and Milan, and how the fulfillment of that pledge was used as an argument for going to war. Imagine, then, the pained surprise of the administration when there arrived in port the American brig *Thames*, whose master, Samuel Chew, brought with him a heart-rending tale of French double-dealing. In mid-Atlantic, reported Chew, he had come upon a French squadron which had just burned two American ships, the

Asia and the *Gershorn*. Upon inquiry the French commodore had informed Chew that he had orders to destroy all American ships going to or from enemy ports. So, whatever Napoleon may have promised, the decrees were in actual fact still in operation! Other American ships returning from overseas confirmed Chew's report.

Secretary of State Monroe rushed to the French Minister Serurier, laid the facts before him, reminded him how the United States had cooperated with France against Great Britain until the country was on the very threshold of war and, in a burst of justified passion, exclaimed, "It is at such a moment that your frigates come and burn our ships, destroy all our work, and put the Administration in the falsest and most terrible position in which a government can find itself."

What was there for the representative of a man like Napoleon to do? Serurier could merely shrug his shoulders, assume an expression of sympathy and report Monroe's complaints in his dispatches to his imperial master in the Tuileries. As the news spread through the country, friends of the administration cursed the perfidy of Napoleon, declared that France and Britain were tarred with the same brush. Hotheads even proposed going to war against both, while Federalists rejoiced. Hadn't they said all along that this was what would come of having traffic with the Corsican blackguard? The rascal was now revealed in his true colors. The administration was convinced of only one thing. It refused to take on two adversaries at once. France was several thousand miles out of reach, and the administration was now too far committed to turn back. The party nomination and the election were staring it in the face, and this was no time to procrastinate. It stuck to the war with Great Britain.

CHAPTER EIGHT

Two Clever Rogues and Other Intrigues

IN THE winter of 1812 Mr. Madison's administration was in considerable need of fuel to feed the flickering war spirit. Impressment, as we have seen, though valid, had become rather a stale issue. The orders in council were still a thorn in the flesh, but the merchants were of two minds about them. The New England merchants were definitely and actively hostile to war as a remedy. The country as a whole was not sufficiently aroused to give serious thought to preparation for the conflict. Something new, startling and dramatic was needed to turn the trick. And, by a lucky chance, fate placed that most desirable weapon in Mr. Madison's hands, a weapon calculated to confound his enemies both at home and abroad.

To explain the situation one must needs return to the year 1808-09 when the public was in an uproar over the *Chesapeake* affair and war with Britain seemed but a matter of days. It was the desire, nay even the duty, of Sir James Craig, the then Governor-General of Canada, to know the temper of the American people at firsthand, particularly that of the New Englanders who might prove useful to the British cause in an emergency. To undertake the delicate mission of confidential agent for Sir James a gentleman bearing the name of John Henry offered himself. Sir James accepted Mr. Henry's services and to Boston, the seat of Federalism, Mr. Henry went. From there he kept up a lively correspondence with Sir James.

Sir James seems to have imagined that Mr. Henry was inspired by purely patriotic motives and would scorn anything so debasing as pay. In this surmise Sir James was in error. Upon returning to Canada Mr. Henry presented his bill. Sir James protested it and the Governor-General and his emissary failed to reach an agreement. Meanwhile Sir James died and Mr. Henry sailed for England to carry his claim to the Foreign Office. There he stated his case and is reported to have valued his services at $160,000. The Foreign Office proved to be as unsympathetic as had Canada's Governor-General. In consequence it was a disappointed, perplexed and embittered agent who left England in the autumn of 1811 on a packet boat bound for Boston.

Aboard ship Henry fell in with a personable fellow traveler, a young Frenchman bearing the impressive name of Count Edouard de Crillon. As acquaintance blossomed into friendship the attractive young count unbosomed himself to Henry while they paced the decks or sat during long evenings in the cramped cabin. The young man was, according to his story, a son of the Duc de Crillon, member of an ancient and noble family of France. By marriage, he explained, he was connected with Bessières, the Maréchal Duc d'Istrie, a favorite of Napoleon. Count Edouard, too, had stood high in the estimation of the Emperor, until an innocent enough escapade removed him temporarily from the good graces of his master. He had, in consequence, deemed it advisable to retire to America until the unfortunate incident had had time to blow over.

Having received Count Edouard's confidences, it was only natural that John Henry should, in turn, give an account of himself. In Crillon he discovered an interested and sympathetic listener. Henry, Crillon agreed, had been treated shabbily by the officers of the Crown, so shabbily indeed that patriotism and loyalty to his former employers were no long matters of consideration. Thus encouraged, Henry exhibited to Crillon the Boston correspondence which he had in his possession and announced that he had thought of offering it to the government of the United States.

After one look at the letters Crillon expressed himself as convinced that here were documents of great political importance that ought by all means to be in possession of the authorities in Washington. What was more, Crillon suggested that he could be of great assistance in approaching the Washington government through his connection with the French Minister, Serurier. Henry expressed himself as most grateful to his new friend and accepted the offer.

In the course of their conversations, Henry had disclosed a desire to retire from a world that had treated him so shabbily, and to seek out some remote but pleasant spot where he might pass the remainder of his days. In this aspiration, too, Crillon thought that he might be of help. He had spoken to Henry of St. Martial, his country estate at Le Beur, situated on the Spanish border not far from the ancient seat of his family at Crillon. As a matter of fact, Crillon had the title to St. Martial with him. Now if Henry were interested he would willingly turn over the title to St. Martial to him, taking in return the cash the United States Government would undoubtedly be willing to pay for possession of the Henry correspondence. Henry was delighted at the prospect of owning St. Martial and the bargain was struck.

Upon the arrival of the ship at Boston Crillon at once wrote to Serurier. Having waited a reasonable time without receiving a reply from the French Minister, Crillon suggested that Henry remain in Boston while he set out with the letters for Washington to handle the matter in person. So, while Henry waited, Crillon arrived at Washington and presented himself to Serurier. The French minister received him coldly, but soon was thawed by the charm of his young countryman; and, impressed with the documents he carried, introduced him to Secretary Monroe who, in turn, presented him to President Madison.

Incriminating evidence against the Boston Federalists was most welcome to the two Virginians at that moment, and such evidence the Henry documents purported to give. The President and his Secretary of State jumped at this opportunity to discredit the opposition. A young nobleman, French or otherwise, was a welcome addition to the drab and provincial capital, and seldom indeed did the provincial capital have a chance to entertain a nobleman with the grace and courtliness of Crillon. He was a frequent guest at the White House during the months of January and February. Hostesses in search of a new sensation for their teas, receptions and balls overwhelmed him with invitations and all the women lionized him, the maidens no doubt wondering what a figure they would cut as the Comtesse de Crillon.

Delightful as the social interlude might be Crillon could not forget that he was in the capital on important business. The President and Mr. Monroe had examined the letters carefully and were satisfied with their contents. Eventually the time came to settle the matter of their disposition. How much did Crillon want for them? He set the price at $120,000. The President and the Secretary of State gasped. They could imagine what that sum would sound like to their tight little Treasurer, Gallatin. No, no. As much as they wanted the letters the sum of $120,000 was out of the question. They offered $50,000. Crillon replied that he would have to consult with Henry, and a summons was sent to Henry to hurry down from Boston. After discussion Henry accepted the offer, but upon the express condition that the letters were not to be published until he had left the country. He had no desire to be confronted by a group of angry Federalists, whom he had delivered into the hands of their archenemies. To this reasonable request the President and the Secretary of State consented. Henry departed from Washington taking the title to St. Martial with him. Crillon handed over the letters to Monroe, and Monroe handed over to Crillon the sum of $50,000 which he had taken from the contingent fund.

On March 9, having assured himself that Henry was on the high seas, President Madison set off the dynamite. He forwarded the letters to Congress and with them a statement in which he charged that the British Government had been guilty of the high crime of sending an agent to foment disaffection against the constituted authorities of the nation and to engage in intrigues with the disaffected for the purpose of bringing about resistance to the law and, eventually, in concert with a British force, of destroying the union and forming the eastern part thereof into a political connection with Great Britain.

When the President's statement reached Congress, Federalists were in a dither. Of what indiscretions had their colleagues in Boston been guilty? How deeply involved were they in plots against the government? Examination of the letters promptly relieved their anxiety. The name of not a single individual appeared in the correspondence. The important information that Henry had forwarded to Sir James Craig was, in fact, no more than he might have obtained from the Federalist newspapers. Here and there Henry had filled spaces with asterisks indicating that the spaces might have included matter too vital to be consigned to paper. And, to cap the climax, it was revealed that the letters were not the originals, but only copies.

The shoe was now on the other foot. The emboldened Federalists demanded of Monroe that he give them the names of the persons who, Madison charged, had intrigued with Henry. To this demand Monroe could only reply that he knew no more than was in the letters. Crillon was then summoned to appear before Congress and testify to what he knew of the affair. But Crillon, too, could shed no further light. The Federalists immediately turned the incident to their own advantage, scoring the President and the Secretary of State for having wasted $50,000 of the public money on worthless documents!

At that juncture Crillon grew restive. He had learned of Napoleon's projected expedition into Russia. Such a momentous affair, he declared, could not be permitted to occur without Crillon having a share in it. He would return to France, throw himself upon the mercy of his imperial master, beg forgiveness and ask leave to take part in the campaign. And so the gallant young nobleman said good-bye to the President, the Secretary of State and the many friends he had made during his visit and departed from Washington. As a favor he willingly consented to carry with him diplomatic correspondence destined for the American Minister in Paris, Joel Barlow. Serurier, too, seized the opportunity to intrust to Crillon letters for the French Foreign Minister.

Crillon had hardly left the shores of America when a dispatch arrived in Washington from Barlow, who had been busy investigating Count Edouard. To the chagrin of Madison and Monroe he announced that there was no Duc de Crillon, there was no Le Beur, there was no St. Martial. Count Edouard de Crillon was an impostor. The only thing about him that was real was the $50,000 of government money he had in his pocket!

Unfortunately for the administration the embarrassment caused it by Henry's letters led to embarrassment in another quarter. Part of the manifest destiny envisioned by the young empire builders in Congress were the Floridas, East and West. West Florida was that territory lying between the Mississippi and the Perdido Rivers, which today constitutes the southern portions of the States of Mississippi and Alabama. East Florida comprised the territory that is the present State of Florida. In the Louisiana Purchase agreement the disposition of the Floridas was left vague by Napoleon, intentionally, no doubt, to embroil the United States in a dispute with

Spain. The United States claimed West Florida, though the Spaniards continued to control it.

In the summer of 1810 the citizens of the Baton Rouge district of
West Florida, chiefly of American and British descent, revolted
against the Spanish rule, raised a flag with a single star, declared
the district to be an independent state and appealed to the United
States Government for aid and protection. The independence,
however, was short-lived, for the United States Government responded to the appeal by claiming the district as part of the Louisiana Purchase and sending troops to enforce the claim.

Meanwhile Napoleon had conquered Spain, the Spanish royal
family had fled and Great Britain had begun to exhibit an alarmingly solicitous attitude toward His Catholic Majesty, the King of
Spain. Suspicious as always of Britain, Congress in January, 1811,
passed a secret resolution in which it declared "that the United
States, under the peculiar circumstances of the existing crisis, cannot,
without serious inquietude, see any part of the said territory [the
Floridas] pass into the hands of any foreign power." The resolution went on to say that if any foreign power threatened to seize the
Floridas or if the citizens themselves expressed a desire to be annexed, the United States would take possession.

During the spring West Florida was in turmoil and by summer
the United States had taken over all of it except Mobile, which remained under the control of Folch, the Spanish Governor. President
Madison appointed as commissioners Colonel McKee, an Indian
agent, and Brigadier General Mathews, a distinguished Georgia
statesman who had served his country in the Revolutionary War
and his state as its governor, to treat with Folch. The Spaniard declined to confer with the commissioners and the question of West
Florida was delegated to Governor William Claiborne of Louisiana,
while Mathews and McKee were directed to turn their talents toward East Florida.

The problem of East Florida was difficult because the people of
that benighted land preferred their barbaric existence to citizenship
in the United States. In the course of the operation of the embargo
and the non-importation laws the town of Fernandina, on Amelia
Island across the St. Mary's River from Georgia, had become vir-

tually a free port. Fernandina was the center of a thriving, though illicit, trade in slaves and other contraband. To win them over to a right way of thinking General Mathews needed something more than patriotic phrases. Mathews journeyed to Washington to discuss the matter with Madison and the President obliged by ordering Captain Hugh G. Campbell, commanding the United States naval forces in the southeast to hurry five gunboats to the St. Mary's River, together with the sloops *Wasp* and *Nautilus*. Campbell also was directed to ship to St. Mary's, Georgia, 20 barrels of gunpowder and 500 pounds of lead. Simultaneously Captain T. A. Smith was ordered by the War Department to move a force to Point Petre, on the St. Mary's River, near St. Mary's, Georgia.

There seems to have been some hitch in the arrangements for the State Department received from its distinguished representative in the field, General Mathews, a letter which read:

"On my arivil hear, I found the Gentilmin hows [whose] names I give you well disposid to sarve our Government. But thare has not one solder arived or one armed vesil or a Gun Boat in this rivar, from this cause its thought not propar to attempt Enething at present."

Monroe received this impressive state paper but appears to have considered no answer necessary. In fact the Secretary took care to engage in no correspondence that would reveal official participation in the intrigue.

Foster, the British Minister at Washington, was beginning to take cognizance of the doings in the Floridas and to prod the State Department for an explanation. On July 2 Foster addressed a note to Monroe bringing to mind the "intimate alliance subsisting between His Majesty [George III] and Spain." He referred specifically to the military occupation of West Florida. He announced that the Prince Regent, acting in behalf of His Majesty, was "still willing to hope that the American government has not been urged to this step by ambitious motives or by a desire of foreign conquest, and territorial aggrandizement." The alleged affection of the Prince Regent and the mad King, his father, for their fellow monarch, the deposed King of Spain, was most touching. If the occupation continued, said Minister Foster, he was commanded to present the solemn protest of His

Royal Highness against an attempt "so contrary to every principle of justice, good faith, and national honor, and so injurious to the alliance between His Majesty and the Spanish nation."

To this ultimatum Monroe replied that the President of the United States could not admit of the right of Great Britain to interfere in any question relating to West Florida. He cited the many and grave injuries inflicted upon the United States by Spain, recalled his country's claim under the Louisiana Purchase and finally clinched the argument by asserting that the inhabitants had themselves asked aid of the United States. So much for West Florida.

In East Florida the kettle continued to simmer. In August Mathews wrote to Monroe asking 200 stand of arms and 50 horsemen's swords. There is no record of a reply. On September 5 came a note from Minister Foster. Foster, it seems, had it from the Spanish Minister, Chevalier d'Onis, who had it from the Governor of East Florida, that on August 14 General Mathews had been at Newton, on the Spanish side of St. Mary's River, treating with the inhabitants to deliver the town to the United States, "using every method of seduction," promising to each white man "fifty acres and a guarantee of religion and property." Shocked to the core Foster declared himself "wholly unable to suppose that Governor Mathews can have orders from the President."

It took the Secretary of State two months to compose an answer. On November 2 he replied: "With equal frankness I shall now communicate the part they [the United States] have acted with respect to East Florida." Again he recited the wrongs inflicted upon the United States by Spain. To Foster's charge of dishonor he retorted that it would be "equally unjust and dishonorable in the United States to suffer East Florida to pass into the possession of any other power." He then made known officially the secret resolution which Congress had passed on January 15. But of the good General Mathews' mission Mr. Monroe said not a word.

In November Paul Hamilton, Secretary of the Navy, ordered Captain Campbell to take command of the flotilla at St. Mary's. T. A. Smith, now promoted to lieutenant colonel, was with the soldiers at Point Petre. The year 1811 drew to a close without further action. Then, on March 11, 1812, Mathews advised Campbell that the time was ripe for delivering the stroke. He also sent word to Point

Petre, but here the empire builders hit a snag. Lieutenant Colonel Smith was away and Major Jacint Laval, in temporary command, for reasons best known to himself, flatly refused to cooperate. Mathews' most persistent appeals could not move him. The plot stood still in its tracks until Lieutenant Colonel Smith returned. On March 14 Mathews took the bull by the horns and gave orders to proceed. His best efforts had resulted in the winning over of only 250 "patriots," including but a few dozen Spaniards. At Rose's Bluff, on the south side of the river opposite St. Mary's, the pathetic little band unfurled its flag. Two days later the revolutionists moved on Fernandina and demanded the surrender of the town, on which the guns of Campbell's flotilla were trained.

The secret resolution of Congress had called for an appeal by the people of Florida to the United States on a threat of foreign invasion. Mathews had his revolutionists and, to give the proceedings a further air of legality, a renegade Englishman was now engaged to appear upon the scene and announce that Great Britain was on the point of occupying the peninsula.

Justo Lopez, the Spanish Commandant, might have defied the patriots but he did not like the look of the guns of the United States Navy frowning upon the town. Before replying to the ultimatum he took the precaution to inquire of Campbell whether, if he resisted, the flotilla would open fire. Campbell answered, in effect, that the United States was far from intending to take aggressive action against a nation with which it was at peace; but on the other hand, it could not close its ears to the appeals of the patriots. In other words, he would fire.

Under the circumstances Lopez could do nothing but surrender. The Spanish flag was hauled down, and in its place went up the standard of the patriots, a flag bearing the words "Salus populi, suprema lex." The populi, 250 in all, whose safety was being preserved by the might and power of the United States Navy, stood by to receive their salvation while the grandiose sentiment expressed by the flag caused a ripple of laughter among those who understood Latin. Flushed by this initial success Lieutenant Colonel Smith and his regulars hastened to the outskirts of St. Augustine and demanded the surrender of that town.

But here the imperial design came to an abrupt end. The events in

Florida coincided with the revelation of the Henry letters in Washington. Federalists wanted to know what moral difference there was between Henry's activities in Boston and Mathews' intrigues in Florida. If the administration supported Mathews, then the whole force of its charges against the nefarious British was lost. Monroe was quick to appraise the situation. It was a question of the government or Mathews. Monroe, as Secretary of State, chose to abide by his solemn oath to uphold the government. He wrote to Foster disavowing Mathews' conduct in Florida, asked Foster to inform D'Onis, the Spanish Minister, and dismissed Mathews. The American troops, however, were permitted to remain on Amelia Island.

The old general, unschooled in the niceties of diplomacy, was stunned by the sudden turn of events. He had performed his mission efficiently and successfully. East Florida was as good as a part of the United States. And all he received in reward was dismissal and disgrace! Mathews at first was too shocked to act; he accepted dismissal in silence. But as the shabby treatment he had received dawned upon his reviving consciousness, he resolved to go to Washington and defend himself. And what a nice scandal that would have created!

The excitement had, however, been too much for the old man; he died on the journey, his lips forever sealed. In this supreme sacrifice he served the administration as magnificently as he had ever served his country during his long and distinguished career. Let it be hoped that he received his just deserts upon his "arivil" in the Promised Land.

CHAPTER NINE

As Britain Yields, We Declare War

JAMES MADISON celebrated his 61st birthday on March 16, 1812. That is an age at which most men are thinking of retirement. But not a president of the United States who has served only one term. The Henry letters might cause a tempest, trouble might be brewing in Florida, war was obviously on the way, a large and important section of the country hated his administration, the treasury was short of funds—chaos seemed to be just around the corner. None of these considerations discouraged Mr. Madison. He was a victim of that strange fascination for the job that grips all presidents and his hat with the big cockade was in the ring.

With the War Hawks spurring him on Mr. Madison's only hope lay in the possibility that Great Britain might back down. But all the information the President received was to the contrary. News came from England that the old King had now been declared by his doctors to be insane past all recovery and the Regency had been set up in the person of his son. On March 28 the British Minister, Foster, stated definitely and finally that the Prince Regent would never consent to a withdrawal of the orders in council. This opinion was confirmed by Mr. Jonathan Russell, our Chargé d'Affaires in London. The matter had been debated in Parliament. Whitbread became the champion of conciliation with America, attacking the ministry for its recalcitrant attitude; Alexander Baring, the banker, who was a friend of Gallatin, added his voice to that of Whitbread. Even George Canning, who had done little enough to appease the United States when he was Foreign Minister, now changed his tune, questioned the advantages accruing from the orders and spoke for conciliation. The government's attitude, however, was stoutly defended by James Stephen and Prime Minister Perceval.

So impressed was Russell by the firmness of the government that, the day after the debate, he wrote to Secretary Monroe, "If anything was wanting to prove the inflexible determination of the present Ministry to persevere in the orders in council, without modification or relaxation, the declarations of leading members of the administration on these measures must place it beyond the possibility of a doubt. I no longer entertain a hope that we can honorably avoid war."

Had Russell been a more astute observer he would have paid less attention to the windy orations in Parliament and more to what was going on outside of London. He might have found significance in the epidemic of "frame-breaking" riots, the destruction of looms, that spread in 1811 and 1812 from Nottingham to the chief industrial centers of the North and the Midlands. The ministry interpreted them as Jacobin demonstrations. Actually they were the result of the Non-intercourse Act which cut off trade with the United States. This, combined with bad harvests, brought misery to the agricultural and artisan classes.

Frame-breaking was added to the list of capital offenses and 16 Luddite frame-breakers were executed by special commission. The Prince Regent, Castlereagh, and Sidmouth, who were believed responsible for the Government's foreign policy, achieved widespread unpopularity. At last the merchants, who depended for a livelihood upon American trade, became articulate and outcries reached Parliament from Birmingham, Liverpool, Nottingham and Hull. If Russell was aware of these incidents he did not deem them of sufficient importance to be reported to his superiors in Washington.

Uninformed of the changing situation in England Madison proceeded upon the assumption that war was only a matter of days. But before war came, it was essential that the United States merchant marine be held in a place of safety. The merchant marine was to supply the privateers that were to harass British commerce and it would never do to have it spread over the high seas where it would fall prey to British men-of-war the instant hostilities were commenced. The logical step, therefore, preceding a declaration, was an embargo to keep the ships at home.

This proposal was turned over to the Committee on Foreign Relations. The embargo, originally designed for 60 days, was extended to 90 and became law at midnight on April 4. It was intended to keep the proposal secret but, no sooner had it reached the committee, than Calhoun notified Josiah Quincy. Quincy, in turn, notified his fellow Federalists, Senator Lloyd of Massachusetts and Representative Amott of New York. These two gentlemen at once engaged an express service to carry the news to the Eastern ports. When the merchants learned what was in store for them, disregarding the patriotic purpose of the embargo and intent only upon escaping its restrictions, they set to work with every dray and every longshoreman they could mobilize. Day and night, from Tuesday, March 31, the labor of loading ships went on until the following Sunday morning. From New York alone 48 vessels cleared; from Baltimore, 31; from Philadelphia; Alexandria, Virginia; and Boston, still others. It was estimated that in those five days, even in the adsence of labor-saving devices, there went out of the country 200,000 barrels of flour and great quantities of grain to the total value of $15,000,000. And the skippers knew that most of these foodstuffs were destined for the army of the prospective enemy at that moment under Wellington on the Spanish Peninsula! "In this hurly-burly to palsy the arm of the Government," lamented Editor Niles of the Republican *Register*, "all parties united."

As though this lack of cooperation were not discouragement enough to the administration, Massachusetts heaped insult upon injury by slipping back into the Federalist column, Caleb Strong defeating Elbridge Gerry for re-election as Governor, and in the May elections it chose a general court that was strongly Federalist while New York followed suit by voting in a Federalist assembly.

On May 18 Madison achieved his ambition by being renominated by the Republicans, with the lame-duck Gerry as his running mate, George Clinton having died in office. If the opposition imagined that the numerous evidences of internal dissension were going to reduce the incentive to war it was greatly mistaken. On the contrary, the administration and the War Hawks took the attitude that a good, stiff dose of hostilities was just what was needed to unite and solidify the country.

As the crisis approached, even so stalwart a little man as the Commander-in-Chief of the armed forces of the United States might have cringed at the prospect. At the head of the War Department was Secretary William Eustis, a political doctor, who owed his appointment primarily to the fact that he had been an ardent Republican in the Federalist stronghold of Boston. To assist him in the strenuous duties of administration attendant upon the organization of the new army he boasted a modest staff of seven clerks. But even these appeared sufficient to do the work immediately at hand; for, though bills enough had been passed for the raising of a regular army of 35,000, by May 1 less than 7,000 had actually "flocked to the colors," in spite of cash bonuses and promises of grants of land. In April Congress had authorized the President to call out 100,000 militia. The Governors of Massachusetts, Connecticut and Rhode Island refused to obey the order. Nobody, said they, had a right to call out the militia of Massachusetts, Connecticut and Rhode Island except the governors of those states. The disaffected militia numbered 14,500, about one-seventh of the force called out.

If the ranks were slow in filling, Dr. Eustis could at least while away the time selecting the high command. Congress had authorized him to appoint two major generals, nine brigadiers, a quartermaster general, an inspector general, an adjutant general and four colonels. Naturally, the good Doctor wanted experienced men and it was not his fault that the army's last battles had been fought a matter of 31 years before. The gallant warriors of the Revolution to whom he turned in his extremity were, for the most part, white-haired old gentlemen. For his senior officer, Dr. Eustis selected Henry Dearborn, like himself a worthy Republican who at the moment was serving the nation as Collector of the Port of Boston. Dearborn was 62 years old. Thomas Pinckney, the South Carolinian, appointed second in command, outranked his superior officer in age by one year. His military experience was confined to guerrilla warfare in his comparative youth, under Marion and Sumter. Wilkinson, senior brigadier, and already in active service, was suspected of having accepted bribes from the Spaniards. William Hull, Governor of Michigan and James Winchester of Tennessee, also numbered among the brigadiers, might have been fittingly described as venerable.

If the United States Army was scarcely an impressive military

90

array, the Canadians were no better served. British sources gave the regular strength in Canada at 4,500 effectives. American authorities estimated it at 7,500. This was augmented by 40,000 militia and Indian allies, the whole covering a front extending from Detroit to Quebec. Indeed, in view of Canada's limited resources, Clay's assertion that the Kentucky militia alone were needed for her conquest seemed not altogether a boast.

Paul Hamilton, a former Governor of South Carolina, headed the Navy Department. His plantation was hardly an appropriate place in which to acquire knowledge of men-of-war. Randolph of Roanoke, in his inimitable way, paid his respects to Hamilton when, rising in the House to offer an estimate of Dr. Eustis, he declared: "I will say this much of the Secretary of War—that I do verily believe, and I have grounds to believe it to be the opinion of the House, that he is at least as competent for the exercise of his duties as is his colleague who presides over the Marine."

In the matter of commanders the Navy had an advantage over the Army. In the war with Tripoli its officers had seen active service under the most trying conditions, and those in the higher grades were in the prime of life. Commodore Rodgers, ranking officer, was but 41. Decatur, Isaac Hull, Porter, Lawrence and Perry were all young men. The Navy's weakness lay, not in the officers or the men, but in the ships. There was not a single ship of the line. Of the nine frigates, several were in the docks for repairs. The rest of the fleet consisted of three sloops and five brigs, not to mention the less than 200 gunboats that were so top-heavy they were in danger of capsizing if they ventured into rough water away from shore. As there were not enough ships to go around, the officers remedied the situation by the simple expedient of taking turns at command.

To meet this pitiful naval force the British had on the American station alone, at Halifax, Newfoundland, Jamaica and the Leeward Islands five ships of the line, 19 frigates, 41 brigs and 16 schooners. There were as well four armed vessels on the Great Lakes. And, of course, behind this force was the full power of the British Navy numbering over 1,000 vessels and including 150 ships of the line, 164 frigates and 134 sloops. With such odds against it nothing much was expected of the United States Navy. This in the opinion of the amateur strategists, from Jefferson down, was to be a landsman's war, except for what damage the privateers could do.

On May 19 the sloop *Hornet* arrived from England with the announcement that Castlereagh had supplanted Lord Wellesley at the Foreign Office. But there was no suggestion of a British proposal of peace. It was, therefore, high time that the President put the war in motion by sending a war message to Congress and informing that austere body and the American people what the war was to be about.

In previous discussions of the issues statesmen had made conspicuous reference to the solemn obligations of the United States to France. But, after the burning of the American ships by the French in the spring, that argument was definitely out. The orders in council were a primary provocation, but it was hard to work up the war spirit of the people merely by citing the losses of ships and goods which were the property of the wealthy. Obviously the President's best bet was impressment.

Even in the matter of impressment there was no unanimity of opinion. Ever since the opening of the Twelfth Congress Republican and Federalist editors had debated the question with great heat, but without either side achieving a decisive victory. The Philadelphia *Aurora*, the Boston *Patriot* and the Baltimore *Whig* had thundered that impressment was quite as important as a matter of trade. Coleman, Federalist editor of the New York *Evening Post*, had thundered back that such sentiments merely proved the Republican editors to be the tools of France, dismissing Duane of the *Aurora* and Irvine of the *Whig* as "a pair of cut-throat French hirelings." The New York *Morning Post*, owing allegiance to neither party and purely on humanitarian grounds, came out against impressment, but all the editor got for his pains was denunciation by Federalist editors as a "damned Democrat."

In his message to Congress in November Madison, as we have seen, had overlooked impressment. In his war message delivered on June 1 he made amends by giving it a leading position. He included in his bill of complaints the orders and added a suggestion of British responsibility for the Indian troubles. As to France, the President concluded, he had no recommendations to make at this time. As to Great Britain, he proposed war!

Meanwhile a series of events had materially altered the attitude of the British Government. Parliament had been deluged with petitions from merchants pointing to their distress and urging a resumption of trade with the United States. Then on May 11 Prime Minister Perceval, as he entered the House, was shot dead by a lunatic. This temporarily threw the ministry into confusion while at the same time it removed one of the most stalwart champions of the orders.

The ministry's potent argument against rescinding the orders had been its unwillingness to believe, as the United States claimed, that Napoleon had actually rescinded his decrees. Thus far, while assuring the United States that the decrees had been withdrawn, the Emperor had refused to verify the fact by proclamation. He was determined, first, to see what the United States was going to do. Now at last Serurier convinced him of the obvious determination of the United States to go to war, and at the same time Minister Barlow in Paris was pressing the Duke of Bassano to make a public announcement. Finally, in May, Napoleon yielded and caused Bassano to issue the proclamation. It was dated April, 1811, to give it the appearance of having been promulgated the year previous, though the fraud was perfectly apparent to everybody. Thus at last was removed the chief obstacle to Britain's withdrawal of the orders.

The President's war message was delivered to Congress in secret session and, after being read, was referred to the House Committee on Foreign Relations. On June 3 Chairman Calhoun brought in a report recommending an immediate appeal to arms. Josiah Quincy, as leader of the anti-war forces, arose and moved that the discussion be made public. He was promptly voted down. Randolph then, in the hope that delay would reduce the temperature of the members of the House, suggested adjournment until November. He fared no better than had Quincy. The War Hawks were in the saddle and riding hard.

The following day the war bill was put to a vote. It was carried by 79 to 49. Of the 79 members voting for war, 48 were from the South and West, 14 from Pennsylvania and only 17 from the states north of Pennsylvania. Of the 49 members voting against war, 34 were from the North, only two from Pennsylvania and 13 from the South.

Obviously, it was to be both a party war and a sectional war. Impressment had now become the chief issue and of the men impressed the majority came from New England. As one commentator aptly phrased it, "the war was one insisted upon by the South and West in defense of the North which didn't want to be defended." But then the War of 1812 was full of anomalies.

On June 18, after several days' debate, the Senate passed the bill by a vote of 19 to 13, the division again following sectional lines. The same day President Madison signed it and the momentous news was announced to the nation in a proclamation composed by William Pinkney, late Ambassador to Great Britain, who now held the office of Attorney General.

The public rejoicing was not of an impressive nature. Quincy and the other opponents, having been refused a public debate, presented their side of the case in an open letter in which they enlarged upon the unpreparedness of the country and the folly of the action taken. In New England a day was set aside for humiliation, fasting and prayer, the church bells tolled, flags were flown at half mast, and William Ellery Channing and other distinguished orators of the pulpit joined in the general lament. Willie Cullen Bryant, now grown to 17 years, seized upon the occasion for another ode:

> Lo! Where our ardent rulers
> For fierce assault prepare,
> While eager "Ate" awaits their beck
> To "slip the dogs of war."
> In vain against the dire design
> Exclaims the indignant land.
> The unbidden blade they haste to bare,
> And light the unhallowed brand.
> Proceed! another year shall wrest
> The sceptre from your hand.
>
> The same ennobling spirit
> That kindles valor's flame
> That nerves us to a war of right,
> Forbids a war of *shame*.
> For not in *Conquest's* impious train

94

> Shall Freedom's children stand,
> Nor shall in guilty fray be raised
> The high-souled warrior's hand;
> Nor shall the *Patriot* draw his sword
> At Gallia's proud command.

Perceval had been assassinated on May 11. It was not until June 8 that Lord Liverpool succeeded in forming a new ministry. Then the action of the government was swift. On June 16 Castlereagh announced to Parliament that the orders had been withdrawn. Thus, two days before President Madison issued his declaration, one of the two major causes of the war had ceased to exist.

The dogs of war, to borrow Bryant's poetic terminology, had been "unslipt." But they stood, as it were, with their tails between their legs.

CHAPTER TEN

General Hull's Martyrdom

THERE had been no more gallant soldier in the Revolutionary War than young William Hull. He had taken part in several pitched battles and acquitted himself as a gallant soldier should. Now, in 1812, the same William Hull was approaching the close of his career. He was 59 years old and a grateful country had rewarded him for his services by making the old soldier Governor of Michigan.

In the winter of 1812 official business carried Hull to Washington where he conferred with President Madison over the situation in the Northwest. From the President he obtained an outline of the grand strategy to be executed by the American forces in the event of war with Great Britain. Canada, as almost every orator in the Twelfth Congress had made clear to the world, including the prospective enemy, was to be the first objective. Canada, according to the plan, was to be spitted on a three-pronged fork. Prong number one, on the right, was to project from Lake Champlain toward Montreal. Prong number two, in the center, was to extend from Niagara and neatly sever the connecting cord between Lower and Upper Canada. Prong number three, on the left, was to penetrate from Detroit. To serve as generalissimo over the entire Northern front, except Detroit, and also to command the right wing of the embattled American forces, the President designated Major General Henry Dearborn, like Hull an aging and rheumatic warrior.

To Hull the President offered the honor of commanding the left flank with the rank of brigadier general. Hull was, no doubt, flattered by the confidence placed in him by Mr. Madison, but his satisfaction was considerably impaired by his sense of the responsibility the post entailed. For what the President calmly asked of him was that he go to Detroit and leave behind him a line of com-

Scale of Miles

0   25   50   75   100

········· Designates Boundary of
          Black Swamp

Lake St.Clair

DETROIT

Sandwich

Malden
Amherstburg

River Raisin

Chatam

River Thames

Moravian Town

Dolson's

Put-in-Bay

LAKE ERIE

Frenchtown

Ft.Miami

Ft.Deposit

Maumee R.

Ft.Meigs

Ft.Stephenson

Sandusky Bay

CLEVELAND

Ft.Wayne

Ft.Defiance

Ft.Seneca

AuGlaise River

Upper Sandusky

To Pittsburg

OHIO

Urbana

Scioto River

Springfield
Franklinton

Dayton

Chillicothe

CINCINNATI

OHIO RIVER

ddef

Map I. Northwest Front

munications two hundred miles long, part of it through a wilderness full of hostile Indians and part of it bordering on Lake Erie which was then controlled by a British fleet. What the President held out to him was the imminent prospect of getting himself into an untenable position which could only lead to disaster. Not only that, but the President proposed that he should still further extend his line of communications by invading Canada. (See Map I)

True enough, Upper Canada was sparsely settled and little opposition was to be expected from the Canadians. A young and more audacious man might have jumped at the opportunity to take the risk and perhaps achieve glory, but Hull was long past the imaginative age. He saw only the insuperable obstacles. These he took pains to point out to the President, but Mr. Madison was persistent. He refused to take no for an answer. And so, at last, Hull was persuaded to accept the commission. He confessed that he was not so sure about the invasion of Canada, but he promised to do his level best to help Michigan.

Ever dear to the hearts of soldiers are the firesides which they must abandon on the way to meet the foe. In this particular matter Hull displayed an ingenuity that was not to prove characteristic of his military plans. He solved the problem by taking his fireside with him to the front. Accompanying him on this doubtful venture were his son, who was to serve as an aide, and his daughter and two of her children.

Every day war was growing nearer and if the grand strategy was to succeed the army of the left must be in its jumping-off place before the official declaration. Preparations were considerably expedited by the zeal of the Governor of Ohio, who bore the intriguing name of Jonathan Return Meigs. On April 5, 1812, Governor Meigs ordered the Ohio militia to rendezvous at Dayton. Enthusiasm for war was high in the West and, on the day appointed, 1,500 patriotic Ohioans responded to the call.

On May 25 General Hull arrived at Dayton and took command. "His gray locks," says a historian, "commanded reverence and respect." Nevertheless history records that the unruly Ohio militia were not sufficiently awed by the old man's presence to refrain from riding one of their officers on a rail. The assumption of command was attended by due ceremony and speechmaking on the part of

Governor Meigs and the General. On June 1 the column set out from Dayton and marched by way of the Miami River first to Staunton and then to Urbana where it was joined by the 4th Regiment of regulars under the command of Lieutenant Colonel James Miller. The joining of the two forces was made the occasion of more celebration. A triumphal arch was raised bearing the words "Tippecanoe—Glory" and again Hull treated his command to a flow of oratory.

"The General," said he, "is persuaded that there will be no other contention in the army but who will most excel in discipline and bravery. . . . The patriots of Ohio, who yield to none in spirit and patriotism, will not be willing to yield to any in discipline and valor."

Reverence and respect for the gray locks of their commander and discipline and valor, all were soon in great need, for at this point the expedition entered a wilderness whose distinguishing feature was the Black Swamp. Immediately trouble began and the Ohio militia began to discover that a military expedition is something more than triumphal arches and oratory. There was no road and the first task of the patriots was to build one sufficiently sound to carry the supply wagons and other impediments. For two solid weeks the men labored and sweated in the heat of the summer sun and by June 16 were rewarded by seeing the road extended to Kenton, in Hardin county, a distance of about 40 miles. The column was advancing at the rate of three miles a day. On June 22 the struggling army reached Blanchard's Fork on the Au Glaize. Here heavy rains began to fall and, to make matters worse, the army met its first attack; not by the British, but by what at the time seemed even worse—black flies and mosquitoes. The morale of the troops was at a low ebb and, as though to add insult to injury, two days later Hull received a dispatch from the War Department in Washington ordering him to hasten forward. As though he were not already making as much haste as swamps, rains, black flies and mosquitoes would allow!

Had war been declared? On that point the dispatch was silent. The expedition had now somehow struggled to the falls of the Maumee River which flows into Lake Erie. And there, at the falls of the Maumee, before their eyes lay peacefully riding at anchor on the bosom of the river the sturdy schooner *Cuyahoga*. To the weary, footsore troops the *Cuyahoga* appeared as a godsend, for here was an easy means of transportation for much of the heavy equipment which had been weighing them down and delaying them on the march. Into the spacious hold of the schooner went the officers' baggage, the hospital stores and the entrenching tools. On board her, too, went two lieutenants and 30 men as guards for the precious baggage, not to mention the wives of three other officers who had followed their commander's good example by taking their domestic establishments with them. Assisted by the river's current and favorable winds the *Cuyahoga* should be in Detroit with its cargo unpacked well before the head of the column reached the town.

But that was not all. According to Hull's later testimony there was added to the *Cuyahoga's* cargo by mistake a trunk in which were the muster rolls of the army, containing complete data on the number and character of his force, and also his official orders in which the plan of his campaign was duly set forth. On July 1 the *Cuyahoga* dropped downstream with her miscellaneous and precious cargo. The army, relieved of so considerable a part of its burden, took up the march with revived spirits.

The relief, alas! was not for long. The following day, as the expedition approached Frenchtown it was overtaken by a courier, who in great excitement demanded to see the General without delay. The courier was the bearer of an important dispatch. Hull received him, took the letter, broke the seal and hastily read its contents. It was the official announcement of the declaration of war, bearing the signature of Secretary Eustis.

Good Doctor Eustis had employed an ingenious method of informing the commander of an expeditionary force that hostilities had commenced. He had sent the letter through the regular mail to the postmaster at Cleveland with the request "please forward!"

Hull knew all too well that on her way to Detroit the *Cuyahoga* must pass under the guns of Fort Malden on the Canadian shore. He immediately dispatched a messenger in the hope of catching and warning the *Cuyahoga* before she put out into Lake Erie. But, alas! the schooner had met with ideal weather, made excellent time and was already beyond recall. On that very day she was sailing up the Detroit River, and, when she came abreast of Fort Malden, a shot was fired across her bow, an armed vessel put out from shore and the British officer in command announced to the surprised passengers on the *Cuyahoga* that war had been declared, that they were prisoners and that the schooner, the intrenching tools, the hospital supplies, and the precious muster rolls and official orders were prizes of war.

The declaration was a shock to the American commander of the left wing, but not to the Canadians. In those days John Jacob Astor, the fur merchant, had agents throughout the country and had lost no time in notifying them of the action of the United States Government. Astor was a business intimate of Albert Gallatin, the detested alien, and at once the enemies of the Secretary of the Treasury spread the rumor that Gallatin had been responsible for sending the news to Canada. Gallatin, not good Dr. Eustis, was blamed for the disaster and came in for a full share of public opprobrium.

The rest of the journey proved uneventful. On July 5 the long, weary column wended its way into Detroit, then a town of 800 inhabitants. Before setting out Hull had expressed certain reservations with respect to the invasion of Canada, but now that he was on the scene he resolved to make the attempt. His information indicated that Fort Malden was held by a garrison of only 200 men, and his decision to attack was no doubt considerably stimulated by the arguments of several young and adventurous officers in his command. So the order for invasion was issued and the necessary scows assembled for the crossing.

On July 12 Hull's command, except for some 100 members of the Ohio militia who stood on their constitutional rights not to be employed outside the United States, was ferried to the Canadian shore to a point north of Fort Malden and the town of Amherstburg. The General issued a high-sounding proclamation to the inhabitants announcing that he had come as their liberator. This manifesto was well received and many persons evidenced a desire to go over to the American side which, for the moment, seemed the safest and most bloodless course to pursue.

Having won this moral victory Hull proceeded to send reconnoitering parties in the direction of Fort Malden which lay 18 miles to the south, while the main body followed at a more leisurely pace. As a matter of fact the garrison at Malden was so weak that it despaired of successfully defending the fort and was on the point of abandoning it. Of this, however, Hull was ignorant. He concluded that it would be folly to attack the stronghold until he could bring over cannon and, in consequence, valuable time was lost. Several days were consumed by brushes with the Indians who were allied with the British, followed by successive advances and retirements. Meanwhile the *Queen Charlotte,* a British armed vessel of 18 guns, anchored in the Detroit River near the port and served as a support to the garrison.

Upper Canada was greatly alarmed by the presence of the Americans at Detroit, at Niagara and other points along the frontier and many of the inhabitants were ready to capitulate. But, at this critical moment, Canada was fortunate in having the services of an experienced, energetic soldier and capable administrator in the person of General Isaac Brock, Governor of Ontario. Brock, who was 43 years of age, acted with vigor. He suppressed the defeatist party, dispatched Colonel Henry Proctor to Malden, hastily collected a force of militia and followed. The reinforcements arrived while Hull remained at a safe distance, unable to make up his mind whether to risk an attack.

Hull was soon to experience another shock to his already overtaxed nervous system. On July 17 news reached him of the fall of Mackinac Island, which lies in the straits between Lake Huron and Lake Michigan. Mackinac was regarded as the Gibraltar of the Lakes and to Hull its collapse was interpreted as releasing all the Indians in the north country to descend in a deluge upon him. His worst fears were realized when a letter from an agent of the Northwest Company was intercepted—possibly it was intended to reach Hull—in which the writer reported that the Indians in the neighborhood already numbered some 1,700 and, within a day or two, were expected almost surely to reach a total of 5,000.

This blow was too much for the old man to endure. On July 21 he returned to Detroit where he remained more or less in seclusion for four days, leaving his expeditionary force in Canada to its own devices and arousing the suspicion of his subordinates that he was either a coward or a traitor. In his dilemma Hull sent an urgent appeal to the governors of Ohio and Kentucky for reinforcements, and a few days later received the welcome news that Captain Henry Brush was at the River Raisin, 30 miles south of Detroit, with 200 volunteers, 100 head of beef cattle, provisions, and mail. Fearing an attack from the British and Indians, Brush asked for a guard to see him over the rest of his journey. Hull promptly responded by sending out Major Thomas Van Horne and 200 men. But at Brownstown Van Horne and his force were ambushed by the British and Indians, under the leadership of the redoubtable Tecumseh, and were defeated. In the engagement Van Horne lost dispatches from Hull to the War Department in which Hull complained to his superiors of the defection prevailing in the American Army. When Hull heard of Van Horne's defeat he abandoned all hope of an offensive against Fort Malden and recalled his forces to Detroit.

Thanks to the capture of the orders and dispatches, General Brock now knew as much about the Americans as they knew about themselves and was fully aware of the weakness of the leader opposed to him. He lost no time in playing upon the old fellow's fears. Brock dressed newly recruited Canadian militiamen in the red tunics of British regulars and paraded them where they were sure to be seen by the enemy. He planted a letter so that it could be readily captured by the Americans. This one purported to be from Colonel Proctor to the British officer commanding at Mackinac and in it Proctor directed him not to send down any more Indians for the present as there were at Malden "already 5,000!"

Hull took the bait, hook, line and sinker. He made an estimate of the situation. According to the information he had received, there was in front of him on the Canadian shore a large body of soldiers, the majority of them regulars, accompanied by 5,000 Indians, while many thousand more were merely awaiting the word of command to swoop down from Mackinac. He was 200 miles from his base and his line of communication had been cut. He was responsible for the lives and safety of several hundred civilians, including old men, women and children. Not the least of his considerations were his own daughter and grandchildren. And to defend his post against the almost unnumbered hosts that were assembled against him he had not more than 1,000 men. Actually, the British and Indians were only slightly superior in number to Hull's own force which was protected by a fort. To such an extent had Brock played successfully upon the old general's fears and gullibility.

On the same day he ordered the withdrawal from Canada Hull

sent out another party, this time one of 600 men under Lieutenant Colonel Miller in the hope of forming a junction with Captain Brush. This force, too, had a battle with the British and Indians in which Miller was wounded, though the enemy was driven back. But Miller failed to get through to Brush with the result that Hull felt his situation was even more desperate.

What, meanwhile, had happened to the other features of the grand strategy—the thrust by way of Niagara and the thrust by way of Lake Champlain and on to Montreal under the personal supervision of Generalissimo Dearborn? Hull appealed to the army of the center to create a diversion only to receive the reply from Niagara that the army was not ready to move.

As for Dearborn, through some unaccountable failure to receive instructions, or to construe them correctly if he ever received them, Dearborn did not understand that he was commander-in-chief over the Niagara as well as the Champlain front. As late as July 28 he was writing to Secretary Eustis inquiring, "Who is to have command of the operations in Upper Canada? I take it for granted that my command does not extend to that distant quarter." What hope could Hull expect of Dearborn relieving the pressure by attacking at Niagara when Dearborn did not know that he commanded there?

Aside from the hazy notion of his duties, Dearborn was deterred for another reason. After the declaration of war Augustus J. Foster, the British Minister, had received his passport in Washington and departed for home. Upon the arrival of his ship at Halifax, however, he received news of the withdrawal of the orders in council. Since the orders were one of the principal issues of the war Foster quite naturally thought that their withdrawal might serve as a basis for the cessation of hostilities. Foster immediately communicated with Dearborn, informed him of the change in the situation and proposed an armistice until the matter could be examined. This seemed reasonable enough to Dearborn who, though he had been uncertain about the extent of his authority in the field of operations, now did not hesitate to agree to an armistice without first consulting Washington. When President Madison heard what Dearborn had done he promptly advised him that he had no business to be making an armistice when the administration was intent upon making war. The interchange between Dearborn and the President consumed valuable time. From August 9 to August 29 this false armistice paralyzed American operations on the Niagara at the very time they might have relieved the pressure on Detroit.

Meanwhile Captain Brush and his reinforcements and 100 head of cattle remained just beyond reach. Hull stuck to his task of sending out rescue parties from Detroit. The third party went out on August 14 under the joint command of Colonel Cass and Colonel McArthur. Hull, no doubt, was glad to be rid of those two gentlemen, for they had been his severest critics. With them went 350 men.

The following day, August 15, Brock and his cohorts, consisting of 330 regulars, 400 militia and 600 Indians appeared in sight on the Canadian shore opposite Detroit. Brock pointed his guns in the direction of the town and, having assumed this threatening attitude, requested a parley.

In the war of nerves Brock was now ready to play his trump card. He drew attention to the Indians, terrible in feathers and war paint. As an English officer and a gentleman he found it incumbent upon him to warn General Hull that, once the battle had commenced, he would not be able to restrain the savages; and, therefore, could not be responsible for their conduct. To prevent this tragic episode Brock demanded the immediate and unconditional surrender of the town, its fort and garrison. To this bold demand Hull returned an equally bold refusal. The parley came to an end.

From the Canadian shore Brock proceeded to bombard the fort whose guns replied. Throughout the night the artillery duel continued while, under cover of darkness, Tecumseh and 600 Indians crossed the river to the American side, taking station in the woods below the town. At dawn Brock followed with the rest of his force.

Hull placed several of his guns, shotted with grape, outside the fort and these were trained on the advancing enemy with every prospect of accomplishing great destruction. But when he saw the British and Indian forces on his own side of the river, Hull's caution overtook him and he called his troops inside the fort. As the attacking party approached, the British batteries across the river maintained a lively bombardment and, at the crucial moment, a shell exploded inside the fort, killing several officers, terrifying the women and causing temporary confusion.

From the fort, guards reported that the Indians could now be seen in the tanyard at the edge of the town. The bloodshed that had already occurred, the thought of the old men, the women and children, including his own daughter and his grandchildren, and what might happen if the Indians stormed and took the fort, was too much for the commander. Even if the first attack was unsuccessful, his line of communications had been cut and no relief was in sight. The fort could be starved into submission before help arrived.

A young and bold commander might have taken the risk, for Hull was only slightly, if at all, outnumbered by the enemy. Protected by the fort he might reasonably expect his losses to be much smaller than those of his adversaries. But Hull was neither young nor bold. He had never wanted the command. He had foreseen exactly what was now happening. The roar of the guns across the river was dinning in his ears. Hull could stand the strain no longer. Without firing a shot he ordered a white flag to be raised!

Cass and McArthur with their 350 men had set out in search of Captain Brush but had somehow managed to get lost in the wilderness. However, a courier dispatched during the night by Hull found them, explained the imminent peril of the garrison and handed them an order from Hull to return at once. The men immediately turned their faces toward Detroit, Cass and McArthur urging them on. Had Hull held out the detachment might have taken the Indians in the rear. As it was it arrived just in time to hear of the surrender. And, to the anger and disgust of Cass and McArthur, they were informed that Hull had included them in the capitulation.

Thus ignominiously ended the first attempt at an American invasion of Canada.

Brock held the United States regulars as prisoners of war but, whether from compassion or from scorn of their ability as soldiers, he permitted the captured Ohio militiamen to return to their native state. General Hull was released on parole and went home to face an enraged public and, two years later, a court-martial. In North Carolina they burned the old man in effigy. In Baltimore Editor Niles of *The Register* exclaimed, "Gen. Hull went into the army with high popularity—so did Arnold; that both were purchased there is too much reason to believe."

The court-martial, which oddly enough was presided over by General Dearborn whose own inactivity had had much to do with the disaster, did its duty nobly. Responding to public opinion, it found Hull guilty of cowardice and condemned him to be shot. Madison, fortunately, had the humanity to extend clemency, using Hull's fine record in the Revolution as an excuse. Hull himself for the rest of his life defended his action, declaring that if he had to do it over again he would do exactly the same thing.

Henry Clay, it will be recalled, had boasted that the Kentucky militia alone could conquer Canada. There was no Kentucky militia at Detroit, but at Vincennes was a fine body of 4,000 Kentucky volunteers, including 2,000 expert mounted riflemen, under another venerable commander, General Samuel Hopkins. Orders came to Hopkins to take the horsemen on a punitive expedition into the Indian country on the Illinois River and annihilate the Kickapoo and Peoria villages.

On October 14 Hopkins crossed the Wabash. No sooner had the expedition set out than the men began to murmur and complain and give other evidences of lack of discipline. Five days had passed when a major rode up to the General and demanded that he march the party home. A prairie fire in the distance served further to alarm and demoralize the detachment. Next day a council of officers met to discuss the situation and arrived at the conclusion that the men were unmanageable and advised a retreat. As a last resort Hopkins assembled his men, addressed them eloquently and called for 500 volunteers to save the expedition from disgrace. Not a man came forward. Hopkins had led the Kentucky volunteers out; he had to follow them back.

Still another disaster befell the Americans. At Chicago, Captain Nathan Heald and a detachment of 54 men with their wives and children were established in Fort Dearborn, a blockhouse on the south side of the Chicago River. Relations with the Indians were friendly up to the battle of Tippecanoe, but after that they began to deteriorate. When General Hull retired from Canada he sent orders to Captain Heald to evacuate the post at Chicago. The order arrived on the very day of the fall of Detroit.

Through Tecumseh the Indians at Chicago learned of the disaster to the American arms and their attitude became more threatening. Members of the garrison urged Heald to disregard Hull's order and remain in the comparative safety of the blockhouse, but Heald insisted upon following his instructions. Even when some friendly Miamis arrived at the fort and warned Heald that if he attempted to get away he would be attacked en route, the Captain stuck to his purpose.

Small arms and ammunition which could not be carried along were destroyed and the whiskey at the post was poured into the river. Other supplies were distributed among the Indians as a gesture of appeasement. On August 15 the garrison, accompanied by their women and children, set out from the fort on a road that ran through the dunes on the shore of Lake Michigan. With it as a guard went the friendly Miamis.

The party had gone only a few miles when they were set upon by a band of 500 Pottawattomies. While the Miamis fled the field, the Americans battled for their lives, some of the women fighting as gallantly as the men. But the odds against them were too great. Under the determined assault of the Indians two-thirds of the Americans were killed or wounded. Those who survived were taken back as prisoners to Chicago where the Indians burned the fort. Among the victims were a dozen children. With the loss of Fort Dearborn the Americans now had not a post left in the Northwest beyond the Ohio and the Maumee rivers.

The left prong of the trident that was to be thrust into the side of Canada had been badly blunted. But General Dearborn on the right and New York's militiaman, Van Rensselaer, at Niagara in the center were still to be heard from. There was yet time for glory to crown the American arms and, as the writers of the day expressed it, "to redeem the American character."

CHAPTER ELEVEN

Disaster on the Niagara Front

THE bluest of blood flowed in the veins of Stephen Van Rensselaer. He was the fifth in lineal descent from William Van Rensselaer, the earliest and best known of the American patroons. His education was the finest that money could buy and he bore the distinction of having attended both Princeton and Harvard. From his father he inherited a vast estate. With such an enviable background of wealth and breeding he was, virtually by necessity, a Federalist. Though opposed to the war he sacrificed his political beliefs to his patriotism and, in spite of a lack of military training and experience, accepted a commission as major general of the New York militia.

The summer of 1812 found him in command on the Niagara front. His deficiency in the military arts he counted upon overcoming by attaching to himself his nephew, Colonel Solomon Van Rensselaer, who had seen considerable active service in the Revolution. As has been previously mentioned, while Hull was engaging and being engaged by the enemy at Detroit the central theater of the war was inactive save for a few unimportant forays on Lake Ontario and the upper St. Lawrence. The Americans raided towns on the Canadian shore and the Canadians were driven off in raids on Ogdensburg and Sacketts Harbor in New York. General Dearborn's unauthorized armistice served to delay the American effort.

Nor was Dr. Eustis, War Secretary, successful in speeding the machinery of national defense. Volunteers and militia were slow to take the field. So it was that on September 1, more than two months after the declaration of war, General Van Rensselaer at his headquarters at Lewiston, on the American bank of the Niagara a day's march below the falls, could count less than 700 men. These were

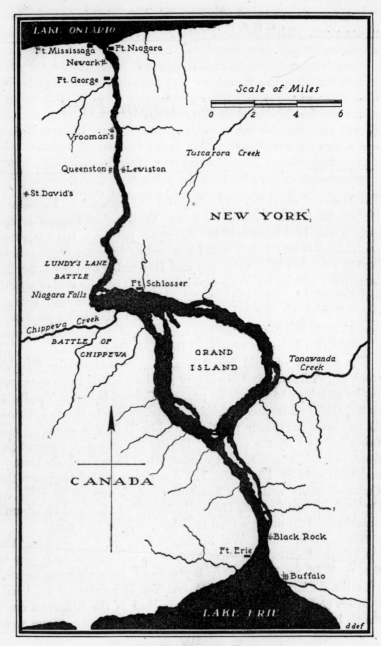

Map II. Niagara Front

ill-equipped, ill-fed, many of them without shoes and all of them clamoring for pay. (See Map II)

These circumstances the public ignored. What it had not overlooked was that Van Rensselaer was a Federalist and that he had been opposed to the war. The ugly rumor was spread that, because of his politics, he was being deliberately lukewarm in his military efforts. His situation was in no way improved by the fact that he was a candidate to succeed New York's Governor Tompkins, who was a Republican. The General was overwhelmed with letters from patriotic citizens far from the battle front and goaded by editorials in the Republican press urging a swift and decisive stroke to wipe out the stain of Detroit.

During September the situation improved materially. At last arms and men were on the way and by the first week in October Van Rensselaer's command grew to some 6,000 men distributed along the Niagara from Buffalo to Fort Niagara at the river's mouth. General Alexander Smyth, a Virginian of Irish birth and an officer of the regular army, had arrived at Buffalo, then a village, with 1,650 regulars and 386 militia. At Lewiston was Brigadier General William Wadsworth with 1,700 New York militia and Brigadier General Miller with 600 militia. At Fort Niagara there were 1,350 regulars.

Opposing this force and covering thinly a line 35 miles long were only 1,500 of the enemy, including British regulars, militia and Indians. Thus the Americans enjoyed a superiority of about four to one. However, as at Detroit, the British had an incalculable advantage in the person of the resourceful Brock who had hastened back from the scene of his victory over Hull to meet the new threat as lieutenant to General R. H. Sheaffe.

Still further to weaken the American effort there developed an instance of the traditional feud between the regular army and the militia. After Smyth had established his headquarters at Buffalo he refused to report in person to Van Rensselaer and, though unfamiliar with the ground, proposed a line of attack contrary to that already chosen by the commander in the field. When, on October 5, Van Rensselaer invited Smyth to a council of war, the latter did not even condescend to reply. The meeting therefore was abandoned and Van Rensselaer determined to proceed on his own.

For a brief moment fortune smiled on the Americans. On the

night of October 9, Lieutenant Jesse D. Elliott, of the Navy, leading a force of 124 men, slipped across the river from Black Rock, boarded and captured the British brigs *Detroit* and *Caledonia,* which were lying under the guns of Fort Erie. The *Detroit,* formerly the *Adams,* had been surrendered by Hull and renamed by the British. The *Caledonia* was brought safely off; but the *Detroit* ran aground and, after being fought over for several hours, had to be burned by the Americans to prevent her recapture. This bold enterprise, accomplished in the face of strong enemy resistance, gave impressive evidence of the valor of which the Americans were capable when properly led. A volunteer member of the expedition was a stalwart young lieutenant colonel of the regular army, standing six feet four inches and conspicuous for his Virginia accent. That day he was receiving his baptism of fire and he was to be heard from many times in this and other wars. His name was Winfield Scott.

Van Rensselaer's men, in their camp at Lewiston, had been chafing under their inactivity. Lieutenant Elliott's victory made them even more impatient to share in the glory. In response to this popular appeal Van Rensselaer determined to make his long-awaited attack.

Lewiston and Queenston face each other across the Niagara River where it breaks through a narrow, rocky gorge. The stream at this point is only 600 feet wide but has many treacherous eddies. The village of Queenston lies on a plateau and above it are the heights rising over 200 feet from the river bank and presenting a precipitous front to the stream. Halfway up the heights on the more gradual slope facing Queenston the British had constructed a redan, a v-shaped fortification mounting a battery, which commanded Queenston and the American shore. The Americans also had erected a battery on the heights above Lewiston with the guns directed toward the Canadian heights.

The cliffs and the rocky shore, combined with the river barrier, offered an uninviting prospect to the attackers, as General Smyth had pointed out in proposing an alternate plan. However, during the false armistice in August some of the Americans had had an opportunity to visit the Canadian shore under a flag of truce and discovered that Queenston was lightly held. They counted upon a surprise attack to seize the heights, thus turning the British flank. After that they proposed to sweep down the Canadian bank carrying everything before them until they reached Fort George, at the mouth of the river opposite the American Fort Niagara.

General Van Rensselaer placed his nephew, Colonel Solomon Van Rensselaer, in immediate command of the expedition, a choice which led to a charge of favoritism. The hour for the attempted crossing was set for 3 A.M. on October 10. On the evening before, 13 large boats were brought down on wagons from the falls and, after dark, launched from the Lewiston landing. The men embarked in preparation for the assault. Rivermen familiar with the currents were assigned to getting the boats across, under the direction of a Lieutenant Sims who had been selected as being especially fitted for the job. A storm set in which drenched the party while they waited patiently for the order to proceed.

Promptly at the appointed hour the order was given and the first boat, with Lieutenant Sims in it, moved out into the darkness. The others were about to follow when the discovery was made that there were no oars. Sims had taken all of them with him. In consequence the attack had to be called off, and the attackers returned to camp to dry themselves as best they could and curse whoever was responsible for the fiasco. When day dawned it was learned that Sims had dropped down the river, tied his boat to a tree and decamped. Thus disgracefully he passed out of history and thus dismally ended the first attempt to carry the American flag across the Niagara. Contemporary accounts give no explanation for Sims's strange and disloyal behavior.

General Van Rensselaer rather hoped that this humiliating experience would dampen the ardor of his men sufficiently to give him time to hold a council of war and perfect his future plans. But, in spite of the tragicomic prologue, the men were as impatient as ever to get on with the job. The element of surprise might, of course, have been regarded as lost since the arrival of the boats and the activity in the American camp were now apparent to the British. On the contrary, the very ineptitude of the Americans proved to be the most perfect deception. The British could not believe that so apparent a plan was to be taken seriously and assumed that it was a feint to mask a real attack on Fort George. They therefore did nothing to strengthen their force at Queenston, which consisted of one lone company of Canadian militia, a small body of Indians and 60 grenadiers of General Brock's 41st Regiment of Regulars.

The second attempt was set for 3 A.M. of the 13th. Meanwhile Lieutenant Colonel John Chrystie, commanding the 13th U.S. Infantry at Four-mile Creek, to the east of Fort Niagara, asked General Van Rensselaer for command of the expedition. But the General refused to displace his nephew, though he consented to Chrystie taking part with his regiment in the attack. Chrystie and his men made their way to Lewiston by a back road, unseen by the British. With him came Lieutenant Colonel Fenwick and a detachment of artillery.

This time the attacking party was composed of 300 regulars and 300 militia, but since the regulars had been only a short period in the service the distinction was not great. This time also the boats were put in charge of a reliable man to prevent a repetition of the Sims episode. And, since the regulars got to the boats ahead of the militia, they were the first to embark. Once more a storm came up in the night to add to the men's discomfort. And once more at the appointed hour the order to proceed was given.

The second attack proved more successful than the first. Within a few minutes the prows of 10 of the boats touched the Canadian shore while the artillery on the Lewiston heights covered the landing. But the British were on the alert, and, while the attackers were still in the boats, they poured a deadly fire into them, killing and wounding a number of the Americans. Three of the boats went astray in the darkness and in one of them was Lieutenant Colonel Chrystie, so that as the battle opened the 13th Infantry was without its leader. The command fell to John E. Wool, the regiment's senior captain, a young man in his early twenties who had recently entered the service.

Though he was receiving his baptism of fire, Captain Wool possessed the instincts of a true soldier. He at once organized his men and led them from the beach to the plateau where he formed them in line of battle. He was shortly joined by Colonel Van Rensselaer and the militia who formed beside him. The preparations were made none too soon for the British counterattacked fiercely. In the exchange of fire Van Rensselaer was wounded in five places while Wool received a ball through both his thighs.

So vigorous was the British attack that Van Rensselaer ordered a withdrawal to the protection of the rocks on the riverbank, though even here the Americans were not altogether free from enemy fire. Day had now dawned, and Van Rensselaer made an estimate of the situation. His wounds were so severe that it was clear he could not continue on the field. On the other hand, if nothing were done the Americans would soon be driven back across the river; or, more likely, they would be captured where they stood.

The only apparent solution was to offer the command of what seemed a forlorn hope to Captain Wool, young and inexperienced and wounded though he was. Wool without hesitation accepted the mission which involved the capture of the heights. Two choices lay before him. He might lead his men to the plateau from which they had retreated and attack the British head on. Or he might undertake to scale the steep side of the heights which faced the river and reach his objective without being seen. Wool selected the latter route. Fortunately he had with him several officers who knew the way. In some places the approach was so steep that Wool's men had to drag themselves up by the branches of trees growing out of the rocks. But as they struggled toward the summit they discovered a path which had been left unguarded and which greatly expedited the last stage of the climb.

Meanwhile at Fort George, seven miles down the river, General Brock received warning of the attack. He at once mounted his charger and, accompanied by an aide, galloped to Queenston. He arrived to find that the first American attack had been beaten off and that the British defenders were now massed defiantly around their redan. Brock inspected the fortifications and apparently was satisfied with the situation.

But at that moment a noise attracted the attention of the British to the heights, and to their chagrin they discovered Wool and his men swarming over the summit. One look was enough. Thy turned and retreated toward Queenston. Brock did not even have time to mount his horse. The Americans rushed exultantly down the hill, seized the redan and raised the Stars and Stripes.

Brock, however, was not a man to give in easily. He quickly reorganized his force and marched it back up the hill, attacking so fiercely that Wool and his men were driven to the summit and almost over the cliff. One of Wool's men, in fact, was about to raise a white flag and another, before retreating, spiked one of the British guns. But Wool, disdaining surrender, rallied his little band, ordered a charge and once more drove the British past the redan and back to the protection of Queenston, where Brock chided his grenadiers of the 41st Regiment for giving way.

Just then two companies of York militia, under Lieutenant Colonel McDonnell, arrived in Queenston from Fort George, and with these reinforcements Brock determined to have another try. A second time he turned his men toward the heights and, to encourage them, led the column himself on horseback. The forces were hardly engaged when Brock, who presented a conspicuous target, fell from his horse with a bullet through his chest. He lived only long enough to warn his aide not to let the men know of his death. McDonnell now took over the command, but the American fire was so accurate that he had scarcely assumed his duties when he, too, fell mortally wounded. With both leaders gone the British attack faltered, then stopped and the men turned and retired in confusion, leaving the Americans masters of the field.

It was now the middle of the morning and reinforcements were moving steadily from the American shore, the boats providing a shuttle service across the river. Among them came General Van Rensselaer, General Wadsworth, of the New York militia, Lieutenant Colonel Scott and other officers. Scott had arrived from the falls the night before and, like Chrystie, had offered to take command and been refused. But with Solomon Van Rensselaer wounded, no further conflict over rank remained. Scott, as superior officer, took over while General Wadsworth graciously withdrew in his favor. Scott at once put Lieutenant Totten, of the Engineers, to work throwing up fortifications. The lost Lieutenant Colonel Chrystie had by this time recovered his bearings and appeared on the scene to resume command of the 13th Infantry, Captain Wool being relieved to return to the American shore to have his wounds dressed. He had done more than enough fighting for one day, had conducted himself superbly and richly deserved a rest.

The work of entrenching and making the proper disposition of the forces continued until two o'clock in the afternoon. At that hour a band of Indians under their handsome young chieftain, John Brandt, debouched from the woods to the west of the Americans' position. Frightful in their war paint, brandishing tomahawks and uttering blood-curdling cries, they set upon the outposts and drove them back on the main body. Under the force and surprise of the attack the left of the American line gave way. Scott, seeing the danger, rushed to the spot, boldly exposing his full stature to the enemy, rallied his men and soon had the Indians retreating to the woods. Calm once more fell over the battlefield.

But it was the calm before the storm. A mile to the north, at Vrooman's Point, below Queenston, a long column of British soldiers in their red coats appeared in view. It was General Sheaffe bringing reinforcements from Fort George. Instead of advancing directly on the heights, Sheaffe made for the village of St. David's, several miles to the west. There he was joined by Chief Brandt and his Indians and another British force that had marched north from Chippawa. Sheaffe's force now numbered upwards of 1,000 men, exclusive of the Indians. To oppose him Scott had, or thought he had, only 350 regulars and 250 militia.

The little band of Americans on the heights, however, was encouraged by the knowledge that on the opposite shore were more than 1,200 militiamen who had not been engaged and who could be quickly transported across the river in the boats. But the flow of reinforcements was slowing down and General Van Rensselaer recrossed the river to hurry them up. Imagine his surprise when he reached the American camp to learn that the militiamen would not move! The General pleaded, threatened and cajoled. Several other prominent men in the community harangued the warriors, who the day before had been so impatient to do battle. The speakers pointed to the handful of their fellow countrymen on the heights across the river in imminent peril and besought the militiamen to go to their rescue.

The militiamen were unmoved. They didn't need to have the danger pointed out to them. They had heard the war whoops of the Indians and the fire of the musketry; they had seen the wounded and learned from eyewitnesses details of the carnage. They were in no mood to leave a safe spot for a dangerous one. Many of the accounts state that they invoked the Constitution, contending that nobody had the right to send them outside the national boundaries. On that point General Van Rensselaer's report is silent. He is content to say simply that they would not go. The best he could do was to send word to Scott that if worst came to worst the boats would be there to bring his force off.

Around 4 P.M., having marshaled his troops, Sheaffe launched his attack. Scott had counted 700 men in his command in all, but it was later estimated that not more than 250 stood their ground to meet the oncoming host. They received the first shock bravely and warded it off, but when Sheaffe brought his artillery to bear on the center and attacked both flanks simultaneously, the American line gave way.

Defeat quickly turned into rout as the Americans tried to save themselves by seeking the most convenient line of retreat to the riverbank, fighting their way by the plateau above Queenston or scrambling down the sheer side of the heights and taking refuge in the caves at the bottom. To make the tragedy complete the boatmen took fright and refused to bring the survivors off.

The Americans made several efforts to surrender but those who raised the flag of truce were killed by the Indians. At last Scott, in desperation, ripped a white cravat from the throat of Lieutenant Totten, attached it to the end of his sword and waved it in the air. This attracted the attention of the British and the Indians were called off. Thus disastrously for the American cause ended the battle, and the rounding up of the prisoners began. Though not more than 250 Americans had fought on the heights, those taken by the British were found to number 900. Save for several hundred who had been captured in an attempted landing at Vrooman's Point, the vast majority after reaching the Canadian shore had skulked in the caves by the river and had seen no fighting at all.

In the several engagements during the day the British lost in killed and wounded 130 officers and men. The estimated loss of the Americans was 90 killed and 100 wounded, in addition to those made prisoner. Among the captured were Lieutenant Colonel Scott, General Wadsworth and several other high-ranking officers. Detroit had not been avenged and the score now stood at two to nothing against the Americans.

To one person the outcome was no surprise. General Smyth might well flatter himself that he had had the foresight to stick to his tent at Buffalo instead of sharing the shame of defeat under the leadership of a militiaman. That was what came of failing to give the command to a regular. But time and patience correct many errors. After the defeat at Queenston, General Van Rensselaer, the militiaman, resigned his commission and Smyth, the regular, succeeded to his place.

It has been said many times that the pen is mightier than the sword. Smyth brought both his pen and his sword along with him, but he used his pen to better advantage. No sooner had he taken over command than he sat down at his desk to compose a proclamation to the people of New York designed to stir their patriotism and at the same time to congratulate them upon the sort of man they now had to lead them. Reminding them of the traditional valor of the American people, he added: "That valor has been conspicuous, but the nation has been unfortunate in the selection of some of those who directed it. One army has been disgracefully surrendered and lost; another has been sacrificed by a precipitate attempt to pass it over at the strongest point of the enemy's lines with most incompetent means. The cause of the miscarriages is apparent. The commanders were popular men 'destitute alike of theory and experience' in the art of war!"

Having thus neatly disposed of Hull and Van Rensselaer, the General proceeded in logical order to give an intimation of what the New Yorkers might expect from him. "In a few days," he wrote, "the troops under my command will plant the American standard in Canada. They are men accustomed to obedience, silence and steadiness. They will conquer or they will die."

Would the New Yorkers stand by with folded arms? Would they force him to appeal for aid to the Six Nations and "suffer the ungathered laurels to be tarnished by the ruthless deeds of the Indians"? Here the General evidently dipped his pen in ink as he turned a phrase over in his mind. The result of his reflection must have gratified him as he read it over. "Shame, where is thy blush!

No. Where I command, the vanquished and peaceful man, the child, the maid and the matron shall be secure from wrong. If we conquer, we will 'conquer but to save.'"

Then at last, oblivious to his own recent conduct during the battle of Queenston, he arrived at the exhortation:

"Men of New York, the present is the hour of renown. Have you not a wish for fame? . . . Then seize the present moment. If you do not you will regret it and say 'the valiant have bled in vain; the friends of my country fell and I was not there.' Advance then to our aid. I will wait for you a few days. I cannot give you the day of my departure. I will organize you for a short tour. But come on. Come in companies, half companies, pairs or singly. Ride to this place if the distance is far, and send back your horses. But remember that every man who accompanies us places himself under my command and shall submit to the salutary restraints of discipline."

So eloquent was the appeal, so ringing the challenge that the patriotic New Yorkers could not ignore it. They came "in companies, half companies, pairs and singly." Smyth's army, for the space of one month, was increased to 4,500 men. It included not only New Yorkers under Congressman Peter B. Porter, now wearing the star of a brigadier, but regulars, volunteers from Baltimore under General William H. Winder and Pennsylvania volunteers under General Tannehill. The troops were ordered to rendezvous at Black Rock on the New York side of the river, a few miles from Buffalo and opposite Fort Erie. Smyth's plan was to attack between Fort Erie and Chippawa, which lay several miles to the north of the fort.

When the army had been assembled the General stiffened its morale with a windy address which closed with another blast of inspired prose in his most florid style:

"Rewards and honors await the brave, infamy and contempt are reserved for cowards. Companions in arms! You come to vanquish a valiant foe. I know the choice you will make. Come on, my heroes! And when you attack the enemy's batteries, let your rallying word be 'The cannon lost at Detroit, or death!'"

Orders were issued for the embarkation to take place, under the direction of General Winder, at the navy yard below Black Rock early on the morning of November 28. Silence and stratagem were not among Smyth's distinguished qualities. So noisy was his camp that the enemy had become fully aware of his plan and made preparations to meet it. A thousand men were spread out along the Canadian shore which fairly bristled with artillery.

The season in that part of the country was now far advanced and the day selected proved to be cold and stormy. While it was still dark the advance guards put out in the boats. Some of them reached the Canadian shore and captured a battery. But there was great confusion in the darkness, and though members of the party displayed rare courage, no advantage was gained and those who did not get back to the American shore were taken prisoner by the British. At this critical moment the commanding general was nowhere to be seen. Having delivered the exhortation and assigned the problem he left its solution to his subordinates. From early morning until late afternoon the men of the main body were allowed to sit exposed and shivering in the boats in a cold rain that soon turned to sleet and from sleet to snow.

The original plan had failed, but nobody knew what other plans, if any, were in the General's mind. The men's patriotism was sorely taxed. Smyth had promised them the chance for valor and glory, but there was little of either sitting in open boats which were by now coated with ice and rapidly filling with water. At last, when their endurance was almost at an end, an order came through. It was a cheerful message from the commander enjoining them in his most graceful language to "disembark and dine." The army by this time was beginning to realize the sort of man that had been assigned it as a leader. As for Peter B. Porter, he disembarked his New Yorkers and, without waiting to "dine," marched them off home.

Undismayed by his failure, Smyth ordered a renewal of the attack on the morning of November 30 and again set himself to the task of raising the flagging spirits of his men by applying his pen to the composition of still another literary masterpiece. As though addressing an army of postmen he exclaimed, "Neither rain, snow or frost will prevent the embarkation." Then, having noted that the previous attack had lacked an element of gaiety, he took pains to see that the same error should not occur again. "While embarking," he announced, "the music will play martial airs. Yankee Doodle will be the signal to get under way. . . . The landing will be effected despite of cannon. The whole army has seen that cannon is to be little dreaded . . . Hearts of War! Tomorrow will be memorable in the annals of the United States."

And the morrow was memorable, though not in the sense that Smyth had meant. The "Hearts of War" were now thoroughly disgusted with their commander. Reluctantly and after much persuasion from their company officers they again took their places in the boats. Ugly rumors began to fly about that the Pennsylvanians were on the point of asserting their constitutional rights and refusing to set foot outside of the United States. Even the officers were beginning to question the wisdom of undertaking so risky an expedition under a leader who gave every impression of being either a coward or a madman. Every minute the temper of the men was growing worse. At this point the regular officers in the army took matters into their own hands and hurriedly called a council of war. There was little debate over what should be done. From the council was issued an order that all troops were to debark at once and return to camp. It was announced further that an invasion of Canada was to be abandoned for the time being; the regulars were to go into winter quarters, the volunteers were to go home.

Now that the suspense was broken and it was known that the war was over for the time being, the men lost all sense of discipline and behaved like schoolboys at the end of a term. Muskets were discharged at random and at the risk of life and limb. The camp was turned into a bedlam. In the course of the celebration the commander was not forgotten. A double guard had to be placed before Smyth's tent to protect him from his own men. Even this precaution was insufficient and the General had to move his headquarters several times to escape the insults hurled at him.

General Porter lost no time in expressing publicly his sentiments of Smyth in no uncertain terms, and Smyth defended his somewhat tarnished honor by challenging Porter to a duel. The two men met and exchanged shots at twelve paces, but neither was hit. Three months later Smyth retired permanently from the Army, "unwept, unhonored and unsung." But his gift for oratory was not to be wasted. He returned to Virginia, took the stump and made such good use of his eloquence that he was elected to Congress.

While these operations had been taking place at Detroit on the left, and at Niagara in the center, the grand strategy on the right had been even less eventful. Dearborn, the reluctant generalissimo, headed a force of nearly 6,000 men in the vicinity of Lake Champlain. His only accomplishment was to make a desultory advance toward Canada, capture a blockhouse and fall back to his original position. Feeling that he had done his bit for the time being he went into winter quarters.

So ended the campaign of the year 1812. Henry Clay had promised to subdue Canada with the Kentucky militia alone. Thomas Jefferson, from his lofty lookout at Monticello, where all the world seemed to lie at his feet, had turned military critic and written to a friend abroad that "the acquisition of Canada this year [1812] as far as the neighborhood of Quebec, will be a mere matter of marching." The muster rolls of the United States Army show that during that year militia called into service numbered 49,187. To this must be added 15,000 regulars. Thus, during 1812, no less than 65,000 men were called to active service, yet so widely were they distributed that nowhere had there been more than a few thousand men on a single field. Three attempts at the invasion of Canada had been repulsed and not an inch of Canadian soil was in American hands, while the flag of Britain flew exultantly over Detroit. No wonder the New England Federalists, who hadn't wanted the war anyway, charged that the failure of the Canadian effort was deliberate, that the South was afraid of the inclusion of Canada in the Union, and that the last thing Mr. Madison desired was a brilliant victory in that zone of operations. And, indeed, it almost passed belief that an honest effort could have failed so dismally.

CHAPTER TWELVE

Our Frigates Make History

THE engagements between British and American frigates did little or nothing to settle the final issue of the war. As sporting events, testing the skill and courage of the combatants and arousing the emotions of the supporters of the ships engaged, they were without equal.

Not infrequently opposing commanders addressed challenges to each other through the newspapers. Typical of these challenges was one directed to Captain David Porter, of the U. S. frigate *Essex*, by Sir James Yeo, commanding His Majesty's ship *Southampton*. Having heard that Porter had maltreated a British subject serving under him, Sir James caused the following letter to be published in an American paper:

"A passenger of the brig Lyon, from Havana to New York, captured by the brig Southampton, Sir Yeo, commander, is requested by Sir J. Y. to present his compliments to Capt. Porter, commander of the American frigate Essex. Would be glad to have a tête-à-tête anywhere between the Capes of Delaware and the Havanna, when he would have the pleasure to break his own sword over his damned head and put him down forward in irons."

To this challenge Captain Porter promptly replied: "Capt. Porter, of the U.S. Frigate *Essex*, presents his compliments to Sir James Yeo, commanding his Britannic Majesty's frigate *Southampton*, and accepts with pleasure his polite invitation. If agreeable to Sir James, Capt. Porter would prefer meeting near the Delaware, where Capt. P. pledges his honor to Sir James that no other American vessel shall interrupt their tête-à-tête.

"The *Essex* may be known by a flag bearing the motto 'Free Trade and Sailors Rights.' And when that is struck, Capt. Porter will deserve the treatment promised by Sir James."

In this instance the meeting did not take place. Sir James's bark was considerably worse than his bite as he was to prove later by cruising Lake Ontario for months on end without bringing on a major engagement with the squadron under Commodore Isaac Chauncey who, on his part, was equally competent at producing good reasons for not fighting.

Under the prevailing rules of the game, warships approaching each other at sea were at liberty to conceal their true identity by flying the flags of other nations and employing similar subterfuges while they studied each other at a safe distance. If one ship judged herself inferior to her adversary she was free to run away without sullying her honor. At the beginning of the war British commanders, contemptuous of American ships, seamanship and fighting qualities ignored this vital consideration and thereby invited disaster.

Frigates carried on their gun deck some 44 carronades, short 42- or 32-pounders, used for firing broadsides; and several long guns of greater range on their bows and sterns. As the vessels approached for combat, the long guns first came into action while the adversaries maneuvered for position. The object was, if possible, to get the advantage of the wind and also to "cross the T," coming into range at a right angle to the enemy so that a broadside could rake his deck from bow to stern or stern to bow before he had time to bring his own broadside to bear. When one broadside had been fired, the vessel would endeavor to come about and fire a broadside with the guns on the opposite side of the deck while the first guns fired were being reloaded. These intricate maneuvers were conducted by a sailing master who stood at the wheel on deck throughout the engagement or until a sharpshooter, perched in the enemy's fighting tops, picked him off or grape shot or canister got him.

The first phase of an engagement consisted of a desperate effort to shoot away the enemy's masts, rigging and steering gear so that he could no longer maneuver, while marines in the fighting tops aimed their rifles at the officers and vital members of the crew on the enemy's deck below. Broadsides were hurled at each other until sometimes the muzzles of the opposing guns almost touched.

The combat reached its climax when the ships ran afoul of each other, the command "Boarders away!" was given, and the crews, armed with pikes, cutlasses and axes, leaped to one or the other deck and fought it out in hand-to-hand combat. The sign of surrender was striking, or lowering, the flag. Bold commanders often nailed their flag to the mast to make striking impossible, a gesture of bravado that sometimes proved most inconvenient to them.

The battle ended, a prize crew was put aboard the defeated ship. If she was too badly damaged to be salvaged, her officers and men and the prize crew were removed and the ship was set afire. Victor and vanquished then forgot their differences, fraternized over kegs of rum and had a royal good time on their voyage back to port where the prisoners were generally exchanged or released on parole and permitted to return home on a cartel ship.

Nobody seriously considered standing up to the British Navy with its vast array of ships of the line, frigates, brigs and auxiliaries. Our pitifully few frigates and our privateers were to act merely as commerce raiders. The administration and the Congress had ordained that this was to be a land war. Yet, in keeping with the anomalous character of war, it turned out that the only American claims to glory in the year 1812 rested upon the brilliant achievements of the naval captains and their crews.

Unlike the generals, the naval commanders were men in the prime of life. Practically all of them had seen active service and achieved distinction in the war with Tripoli and they were eager to try their mettle against the ships of the greatest navy in the world. When, during Jefferson's administration, the Navy was neglected, it proved necessary to cut the roster of officers from 500 to 200. This drastic pruning greatly improved the quality of the survivors.

No sooner had war been declared than, on June 23, Commodore Rodgers set sail from New York in the *President*, one of the new frigates of 44 guns, in command of a squadron which included the frigate *United States*, 44, Captain Stephen Decatur; the frigate *Congress*, 38, Captain Smith, and the *Argus*, 16, Lieutenant Commander St. Clair. Rodgers had learned that a large fleet of Jamaica-men was sailing for England under convoy and his purpose was to intercept them.

Off the New England coast the Commodore sighted a British frigate which proved to be the *Belvidera*, 36, Captain Richard Byron, and immediately gave chase. The *President*, piling on all her canvas, gradually gained on her quarry, but in doing so she outdistanced the rest of the squadron which was lost to sight. As soon as the *Belvidera* came within range Rodgers ordered his long bow guns to fire. The gunners took their time, aimed carefully and the first gun bellowed as the round shot left the muzzle and went hurtling over the water to smash straight through the *Belvidera's* stern frame. The Americans set up a shout. Two more shots were fired and both of them found their mark. The gunners worked furiously ramming a new charge home. The engagement had begun auspiciously and a wave of confidence spread among officers and crew. A few more shots from the long guns, a broadside or two and the *Belvidera* would be a prize. The gun was ready, the fuse lit. The Commodore himself was standing near by observing the gunners and their work. Suddenly a terrific explosion rent the air, the deck was enveloped in smoke and the men were hurled about like tenpins. One of the long guns had blown up. When some degree of order was brought out of the confusion it was found that 22 sailors lay dead or wounded. Rodgers himself sustained a broken leg. By the time the wreckage had been cleared away and the wounded carried below deck to the surgeon the *Belvidera* had made good her escape. She proceeded to Halifax where Captain Byron reported the engagement to Rear Admiral Sawyer.

Rodgers had lost his squadron and, not knowing where to find it, proceeded alone in search of the Jamaica convoy. Jetsam served as an occasional clue and encouraged him in the hunt. He sailed all the way across the Atlantic and approached the English coast but failed to come up with the convoy. He then turned southward, cruised in the neighborhood of Madeira, overhauled and captured seven British merchantmen, including 120 members of their crews, and finally returned to New York after an absence of 70 days.

While he was away other interesting events had been taking place in the waters nearer home. When Rear Admiral Sawyer heard Captain Byron's report of the encounter between the *Belvidera* and the *President* he organized a squadron to set out in search of Rodgers. This British squadron was commanded by Captain Philip Broke and included the *Shannon*, 38, flagship; *Guerrière*, 38, Captain James Dacres; *African*, 64; *Aeolus*, 32; *Belvidera*, 36; the brig *Nautilus* and a schooner. It was a force more than sufficient to meet anything the Americans could pit against it.

Ignorant of what had taken place and pursuant to the general order to take to the high seas and harry British commerce, Captain Isaac Hull, nephew of the ill-starred General William Hull, set sail from Annapolis in the frigate *Constitution* on July 12. He passed through the Virginia Capes, cruised northward and in five days reached New England waters. About twilight of the fifth day he sighted a frigate which he identified as British and followed her all night.

When day dawned on the 18th Hull, to his surprise and confusion, made out no fewer than three sails on his starboard quarter and four astern. Unwittingly he had taken the bait held out for the *President* and had been lured straight into Captain Broke's squadron. Attack against such odds would have been suicidal; Hull's only possible hope was to run. But, to his great embarrassment, a dead calm set in. Fortunately, the *Constitution* lay just out of range of the British men-of-war.

There was one more way of escape and it did not take Hull long to find it. He ordered his boats lowered and manned, hawsers were run from the boats to the *Constitution* and the sailors set to work with might and main at the oars. Thus, so to speak, generating its own power, the *Constitution* began to move. At the same time Hull mounted two long 18-pounders, one on the forecastle to hold off attack from that quarter, the other on the stern to meet a threat from behind. His stratagem was undertaken none too soon for by now the *Shannon,* which lay nearest the *Constitution,* had opened fire.

Two could do the trick as well as one and Broke, whose ships had also been becalmed, was not to be robbed of his prey. He, too, ordered his boats lowered, hawsers run, and in a few minutes the whole of his squadron was being towed in a pursuit which was "hot," so far as the oarsmen were concerned. Here, on the broad bosom of the Atlantic the ships—but not the oarsmen—rested while American brawn and sinew were pitted against British. Here sweated at their oars throughout the day Americans whose battle cry was "Sailors' Rights" and Britons whose boast was that they "never would be slaves." In the long annals of rowing it is doubtful if there was ever a more unique contest, each of the entrants in the race hauling a full-rigged man-of-war behind him!

Hull knew still another trick. Soundings showed only 20 fathoms. The American commander collected all the spare rope he could find, spliced it together, attached a small anchor known as a "kedge," carried the kedge half a mile ahead and let it take hold of the bottom. Then the men who were left on deck trudged astern with the rope and so pulled the *Constitution* along until she had caught up with the kedge, when the performance was repeated.

However, in spite of the towing and the kedging, Hull noted with concern that the *Shannon* had made a slight gain. He discouraged her by letting her have a shot from his stern chaser. And then, as if in answer to prayer, a light breeze sprang up. It was now 9 A.M. and the men had been rowing since dawn. Hull called in his boats and took immediate advantage of the breeze to increase his lead. The breeze, however, died away as suddenly as it had come. There was nothing to be done but order the boats out again. All that day and all the succeeding night the sailors bent to the oars or gave a hand at kedging. The Britons, with their customary bulldog determination, hung on. It was a triumph of endurance for the two great branches of the English-speaking race.

When the morning of the second day dawned the men were still at their oars, but exhaustion was rapidly overtaking them. Whether through superior oarsmanship, more powerful muscles or greater fear of the cat-o'-nine-tails that might await the laggards, three of the five British frigates crept up within long cannon-shot range. It looked as though the jinx which had attended old Uncle William had descended upon his nephew Isaac. At that crucial moment up sprang another breeze and it turned out to be a good one. Again Hull called in his boats, crowded on all canvas and, bringing to bear all the ingenuity of his trade, he outmaneuvered and outsailed his pursuers. At 4 P.M. the *Belvidera*, nearest British ship, was four miles away. At 7 P.M. a squall came up and rain clouds brought with them a welcome darkness. Under its cover Hull made good his escape. When the third day dawned not a British vessel was to be seen; and, unmolested, the *Constitution* put into Boston where her men had a chance to nurse their blisters, work the kinks out of their backs, and tell of their miraculous escape.

129

The respite was not for long. Hull's beard may have been singed, but he had not yet felt the fire. On August 2 the *Constitution* again set sail, and this time Hull kept his weather eye open against such a snare as he had blundered into on his previous voyage. Nothing of importance happened until he reached latitude 40° 41′, longitude 50° 48′, which is to say in the landsman's parlance about midway of a line drawn between New York and the Azores. There, on August 9, the lookout in the masthead reported a sail on the horizon. Hull promptly gave chase and, at 3:30 P.M., identified the vessel as a British frigate. Hull ordered the *Constitution's* deck cleared for action, beat the men to quarters, hoisted the American colors and with sails set proceeded to bear down gallantly on the enemy.

As the *Constitution* neared, the enemy frigate, which proved to be the *Guerrière*, 38, Captain Dacres, which had sailed in Broke's squadron, met the challenge boldly by hoisting three ensigns, giving the *Constitution* a welcoming broadside of grape, coming about and firing a second broadside on the other tack. Dacres, however, misjudged his distance. The shots fell short. For three quarters of an hour the sailing masters of the two ships tried every trick they knew, each one attempting to get his frigate on the stern of the other and in a position to rake. Neither was successful, and at length the *Guerrière* sailed off followed by the *Constitution* which fired an occasional shot from her long guns.

For an hour and a half the ships sailed on the same course. By 6 P.M. the *Guerrière* was responding briskly; her shots were well aimed and began to tell on the *Constitution*. Hull had not yet ordered a broadside though his guns were shotted and ready. Hull's men began to grow impatient under the punishment their ship was receiving without making a commensurate return. But Hull stood on the quarter-deck, calm and imperturbable, measuring the distance to the *Guerrière*. Lieutenant Morris, second in command, thought he would see what suggestion might do and asked permission to fire. "Not yet," snapped Hull. The vessels were drawing nearer and every moment the *Constitution* was getting worse punishment. Shots were ripping through her rigging, cutting splinters from her masts and spars and making things generally unpleasant for the crew. Morris was beginning to wonder if a madman was in command. In no other way could he account for Hull's inaction in the face of so determined an attack. Again he approached Hull and for the second time asked permission to fire. And again, as curtly as he had done before, Hull replied, "Not yet."

Then, as though suddenly coming to life, Hull made a couple of full bends to the deck and at the same time shouted, "Now, boys, you may fire!" Hull was stout and his breeches fitted like a glove. The strain of the full bends was too much for them; his breeches split neatly from waistband to knee. Though partially unbreeched, Hull stood his ground. His broadside rent the air. Fired at half pistol-shot range it plowed into the *Guerrière*, which shivered from stem to stern. As fast as the men could reload the guns, broadside followed broadside, literally tearing the *Guerrière* to pieces. Within fifteen minutes her mizzenmast had been shot away, her hull had been riddled and her spars and rigging were a mass of shattered wreckage. All the while volleys of musketry played a treble accompaniment to the deep bass of the guns.

In spite of the punishment she had received and though she lacked the weight of metal of her adversary, the *Guerrière*, under the capable leadership of Captain Dacres, fought gallantly on. For a moment the bow of the *Constitution* touched the *Guerrière's* port side and the parties on both ships prepared to board. The *Constitution* caught fire, but the blaze was promptly extinguished.

Before the order "Boarders away!" could be given the *Constitution's* sails filled, she freed herself and shot forward just as the *Guerrière's* mainmast and foremast fell, leaving the once proud British frigate a helpless, drifting hulk, her guns forever silenced. But the Union Jack still waved from the stump of her mizzen. Having ordered his own guns to cease fire, Hull lowered a boat and dispatched an officer to the *Guerrière* to inquire if she had struck her colors. The officers found Captain Dacres on deck, dazed by the misfortune that had so swiftly overtaken him. The question was a hard one for a British commander to answer, and one that was seldom put to him. Dacres stood puzzled for a moment. "Well," he replied reluctantly, "I don't know. Our mizzenmast is gone, our mainmast is gone; and, upon the whole, you may say we *have* struck our flag."

Hull, having just finished pouring shot and shell into the *Guerrière* and doing all he could to slaughter her crew, now graciously offered Captain Dacres the services of a surgeon or a surgeon's mate to patch up some of the damage he had inflicted. Upon hearing the offer Dacres remarked that he imagined Hull's surgeons had about as much as they could do to handle their own wounded. It was a surprise to him when he was informed that the *Constitution's* casualties amounted to no more than 14 killed and wounded out of a total crew of 456. That, of course, was exclusive of the Captain's breeches! Hull himself at the moment had more need of a tailor than a surgeon. On the other hand, out of a crew of 272 the *Guerrière* had lost 79 killed and wounded.

Through the night the frigates rode beside each other. Early in the morning the *Guerrière* began to fill with water and the ship's carpenters announced she was too far gone to be saved. In consequence, the prize crew and prisoners were removed. The *Guerrière* had fought her last fight. A torch was applied to her and when the flames reached her magazine there was a loud explosion and all that was left of her sank slowly under the waves.

Victors and vanquished now proceeded in company to Boston where they arrived on August 30. For the time being Republicans and Federalists forgot their differences and sat down together at the same banquet table to do honor to the first hero of the war. From Boston Hull, according to the custom of the day, proceeded upon a triumphal tour which took him first to New York, where he and his officers were presented with swords and granted the freedom of the city delivered in a gold box suitably inscribed; then on to Philadelphia to receive a piece of plate. Congress capped the climax by voting Hull a gold medal and $50,000 prize money for the crew. The victory was made the occasion for the drinking of toasts throughout the country, a welcome event since suitable toasts had been rather rare and patriots' throats were parched.

The *Guerrière's* tonnage was only 1,338 compared with the *Constitution's* 1,576; her broadside weighed 570 pounds as against the *Constitution's* 736. Mahan estimates the *Constitution's* physical superiority at 30 per cent and the disparity between the crews was even greater. The conclusion is that Dacres fought his ship well against a more powerful foe. But there was no room for excuse in the opinion of the fiery editor of the London *Times* who refought the battle on paper in his cozy London office. The editor lamented that for the first time in history a British man-of-war had struck to an American, conveniently overlooking the earlier achievements of the American Navy under John Paul Jones.

Hull, having displayed to the full his unusual gifts as a commander, now turned the *Constitution* over to Captain William Bainbridge. There were more commanders than ships and it was the Navy's custom, regardless of performance, to give each commander in turn a go at a ship. Whatever the results might be the Navy was determined to be eminently fair.

Over two months passed before men-of-war again engaged in combat. However, early in October, the U. S. sloop *Wasp*, 18 guns, under the command of Captain Jacob Jones, set sail from Delaware Bay on a cruise designed to intercept merchantmen in the West India trade. The *Wasp* proceeded without incident until about midnight on October 18, at a point due north of Bermuda, when her lookout sighted several vessels. Unable to determine their nature, Captain Jones steered a course parallel to them throughout the night. At daylight he discovered before him six armed merchantmen which were being convoyed by the sloop *Frolic*, 18, Captain Thomas Whingates.

It was a Sunday morning. The sky was cloudless, the air balmy and a brisk wind was blowing up white caps. No sooner had the convoy seen the American sloop than the merchantmen clapped on sail and hastened out of harm's way. The *Frolic*, on the other hand, stood her ground and showed fight. Both ships shortened sail and at 10:30 A.M. the first shots were exchanged. The vessels were now running along side by side in a choppy sea at a distance of 50 yards, using their broadsides for all they were worth. There was one difference; while the *Frolic* fired when she was in the trough of the waves, the *Wasp* fired from the crest.

The combat was significant because the two ships were so evenly matched. They were of approximately the same tonnage, carried the same number of guns and threw the same weight of metal. The *Wasp* had a slight advantage over the *Frolic* in that her crew numbered 135 men as against the *Frolic's* 105. On the other hand the day before the *Wasp* had been damaged in a squall. In fact it would have been difficult to devise a more accurate test of the relative quality of British and American seamanship and fighting ability. The *Frolic* displayed considerable superiority in the speed with which the crew worked her guns. So rapid was her fire that her shots seemed to outnumber those of the *Wasp* by three to two. But what they gained in speed they lost in accuracy, for many of the shots went wild. Jones's technique of firing from the crest of the waves proved to be far more effective.

Within the space of a few minutes the *Wasp* had demonstrated her superiority. The *Frolic's* masts and rigging were shot away while the *Wasp* suffered chiefly in her hull. At this point the two ships ran afoul of each other and the *Wasp* was in position to send over a broadside which swept the *Frolic's* deck. Immediately the cry of "Boarders away!" went up from the *Wasp* and at the command her sailors, brandishing their pikes, cutlasses and axes, leaped to the deck of the *Frolic* ready to settle the issue in a hand-to-hand fight. But they found no opposition. The terrific fire of the *Wasp* had driven the whole of the *Frolic's* crew below. There remained on deck only a few officers and a man at the wheel who kept defiantly at his station. Without further resistance the officers offered their swords while an American sailor lowered the colors.

The entire engagement lasted less than three quarters of an hour, during which the British lost 90 men, killed and wounded, out of their total of 105. The Americans got off with only five killed and five wounded. The battle was as decisive as it had been brief. Captain Jones placed a prize crew on the *Frolic* and was about to set off for Charleston when a sail appeared on the horizon and rapidly grew in size. Scenting danger Jones tried to steal away but what with his prize and the injuries he had received in the fight he could make little speed. The stranger was now close on, and through his glass Jones recognized her as a British ship of the line. She proved to be the *Poictiers,* whose 74 guns frowned down upon the sloop as she demanded the *Wasp's* surrender which Jones was unable to refuse. Thus hardly had his victory been won than it was snatched from his grasp and he found himself, his ship and his prize all prisoners of the newcomer.

The three vessels put into Bermuda and there the prisoners were exchanged to make their way home. In spite of this misfortune, a generous public recognized Jones and his men for the heroes they were. Though he had lost his ship, Jones was voted a sword by the city of New York while a grateful Congress appropriated $25,000 as prize money for the crew.

Within less than a week yet another blow was struck at England's pride. On October 25, near Madeira, the frigate *United States,* 44, in command of the redoubtable Captain Stephen Decatur, encountered His Majesty's frigate *Macedonian,* 38, Captain John S. Carden. As soon as the ships sighted each other they cleared for action and came full on. At 9 A.M. the *United States* fired her first broadside and was repaid in kind. For half an hour the ships stood off and pounded each other, but the *United States* had the greater weight of metal and her shots were well aimed, while those from the *Macedonian* did little or no damage. Her mizzenmast shot down, and the rest of her masts tottering, the *Macedonian* struck her colors. She had received no less than 100 round shot in her hull and had lost 36 men killed and 68 wounded out of a complement of 300. The *United States,* whose crew outnumbered the *Macedonian's* by 178 men, lost only five killed and six wounded. British commanders were taking some time to learn that they could not with impunity engage American ships of superior power.

The fight ended, the rival commanders met and Carden offered his sword. With a grace becoming his fame, and in the best copybook manner, Decatur replied, "Sir, I cannot receive the sword of a man who so bravely defended his ship. But I will receive your hand." Officers and men of both ships now mingled freely while the men-of-war proceeded across the Atlantic. More fortunate than Jones, Decatur brought both ships safely to port. He reached New York just in time to share with Hull and Jones the honor of an official banquet, to receive the freedom of the city and to have a medal struck to commemorate his victory. Though he had won a victory he lost his command. For it was now Jones's turn to have a frigate and the *United States* was nearest to hand.

The Navy's quaint custom might have proved disastrous had not all the commanders been tried men. Thus, when Isaac Hull relinquished the *Constitution* to Captain William Bainbridge, the frigate fell into the best of hands. Bainbridge was not long in making a score. Setting sail from Boston on October 26 he arrived off Brazil on December 13. Three days later he espied two sails. The larger of the ships, by her actions, indicated she was spoiling for a fight and Bainbridge obliged.

At noon the *Constitution* and her adversary showed their colors. The latter proved to be the British frigate *Java*, 38, Captain Henry Lambert. In spite of the fact that her tonnage was only 1,340 to the *Constitution's* 1,576 and that she had fewer guns and a lighter weight of metal, the *Java* swiftly bore down on the *Constitution* to rake her. The *Constitution* skillfully maneuvered to escape danger and opened with a single gun to which the *Java* replied with a broadside. A general cannonade ensued in which the *Constitution's* wheel was shot away. But even with this serious handicap Bainbridge displayed fine seamanship by getting into position to rake. The *Java* attempted to close but before she could do so the *Constitution* fired two broadsides into her stern at point-blank range, which shot the *Java's* mainmast clean away. After another exchange of broadsides the *Java's* guns were silenced and she struck. The engagement had lasted three hours. At its close the *Java* was too badly damaged to be salvaged, so her crew was removed and she was set afire. The *Java's* loss was 60 killed and 101 wounded out of a crew of 426, not including a detachment of 100 soldiers who happened to be aboard and rendered service during the fight. The American loss was nine killed and 25 wounded out of a total of 475.

One American victory might have been blamed upon the inefficiency of a British captain, but when four American victories came in quick succession London editors who gave inefficiency as an explanation ran the risk of accusing far too large a part of the British Navy of that failing. A new excuse was devised. London editors found it in the physical superiority of the American frigates. They charged that, as a matter of fact, these were not frigates at all but actually ships of the line disguised as frigates! The new explanation was much more in keeping with the popular British conception of the perfidy which distinguished the American character.

When the results of the operations at sea for the year 1812 had been tabulated it was revealed that the insignificant little navy of the United States had captured or destroyed British men-of-war to the total of 4,330 tons as against a loss to themselves of only 820 tons. In addition, 46 prizes had been safely brought to port. These did not include the numerous prizes taken by the privateers. The British Admiralty was humiliated, but the British Navy was far too large to have been seriously affected. The United States Navy had employed virtually all of its available power; the British Navy had used only a small fraction of its own. There had been glory enough and the establishment of a splendid naval tradition. As for immediate results, however, the gallant frigates had done little more than stir up a hornet's nest.

CHAPTER THIRTEEN

Harrison Has His Problems

THE year 1812 drew to a close on a bleak American scene illuminated only by the victories at sea. Detroit had fallen, the British center at Niagara had not been pierced and on the right flank Dearborn had wasted useful time without seriously engaging his army. New England continued to stand aloof, her political leaders more sympathetic toward the enemy than toward their fellow citizens of the Republic.

As though all the fates were against her, the United States' only possible ally in Europe was in serious trouble. For a decade victory had crowned the arms of the French Empire and Napoleon had been the undisputed master of the Continent. Now reports of an alarming nature reached the United States. Napoleon set out in the spring to conquer Russia. The summer passed with a succession of the customary triumphs and the Emperor entered and occupied Moscow. But he failed to catch and crush the Russian Army. Through the early autumn Napoleon lingered in Moscow, for the first time in his career uncertain what course to pursue. To advisers who warned him of the approach of a Russian winter with all its dangers he showed indifference, even suggesting that he found the climate not unlike that of France.

When at last the truth dawned upon him and Napoleon reluctantly gave the order to retreat, it was too late. Winter and the Cossacks fell upon him and within a few weeks the Grande Armée became a mob of freezing, starving men. This greatest of military disasters marked the decline of Napoleon's star. Now, at last, the War Hawks were brought to a realization of the significance of John Randolph's words when he protested against being "dragged at the wheels of the car of a Bonaparte." No longer could Napoleon be counted upon to create a diversion in Europe that would keep Britain's thoughts and attention from her war in America.

Though the American war was six months old the West had not brought to bear the power of which Henry Clay had boasted. Yet Ohio and Kentucky seethed with a desire to wipe out the shame of Detroit. And they believed that they had in William Henry Harrison, the hero of Tippecanoe, the leader who could turn the trick.

The son of Governor Benjamin Harrison of Virginia, William Henry while little more than a boy had accompanied "Mad Anthony" Wayne on his campaign against the Indians in the Northwest. He closed that episode as the general's aide. At the comparatively early age of 24 he had been appointed Secretary of the Northwest Territory; and when, in 1801, the Territory of Indiana was created, he was named as its first governor. A man of distinguished bearing and proven courage he was popular with the frontiersmen and feared by the Indians. The battle of Tippecanoe, costly as it had been, had enhanced his reputation as a soldier. All important from the Virginian point of view he was a Harrison and, as such, could wear his hat in the presence of Lees, Carters, and Randolphs.

When the fall of Detroit was imminent Harrison had been the most active man in the West in the organization of a force to go to Hull's rescue. After news of the disaster had removed all chance of assistance he exerted all his energy in building blockhouses, ordering reinforcements to threatened points and otherwise protecting the frontier from an Indian invasion. Kentucky wanted him to lead its militia, but a state law reserved that distinction for a native son and Harrison was not a Kentuckian. The stout Kentuckians, however, were not to be put off by a legal technicality. In fact they had an instrument known as a "caucus" to meet just such an emergency. The caucus in this case consisted of Henry Clay; Charles Scott, governor of the state; and Isaac Shelby, the governor-elect. These three distinguished gentlemen met together on August 25, constituted themselves a body to speak and act for all the people of the state and assumed the responsibility of naming Harrison major general of the Kentucky militia. Three days earlier in Washington Secretary of War Eustis had bestirred himself and commissioned Harrison as brigadier general in the United States Army and ordered him to take command of all the forces in Indiana and Illinois.

There was, however, one other impediment that stood in the way of Harrison's military career in the West. The impetuous Dr. Eustis had, it seems, already given command in the Northwest to Brigadier General James Winchester, of the regular army. For a moment it looked as though there would be two suns on the Western horizon. Winchester, a veteran of the Revolution, was 61 years old; Harrison, now at the age of 39, was in the prime of life. Winchester was a man of wealth and, some said, of much too aristocratic a bearing; Harrison was a popular hero. When the rough-and-ready soldiers of the frontier learned that their idol, Harrison, might be snatched away from them they began to whisper mutiny. Their fears, however, proved groundless. Between two such unequal adversaries there could be but one decision. When Eustis heard of the Kentucky caucus he relieved Winchester of the command of the Northwest, turned it over to Harrison and placed Winchester under him. To Harrison he gave as full authority as a commander in the field could wish for. "Exercise your own discretion," Eustis wrote him, "and act in all cases according to your own judgment."

Dr. Eustis might instruct Harrison to act according to his judgment, but that was more discretion than it was in his power to give. Far more powerful than that of the Secretary of War and of the commander in the field was the judgment of the people of the West. Harrison knew that only too well and he was soon to be brought to regret it. In fact it might be questioned as to which had been the victor, Winchester who was relieved of command or Harrison who accepted not the command alone but the responsibility of doing what the people wanted. What they wanted was clear enough. It was swift and immediate action to clear Indians and other interlopers away from the frontier and the recapture of Detroit both as a safeguard and as a means of wiping out the stains of the late defeat.

Winter was now coming on. Harrison was familiar enough with the country and with military strategy to realize the rigors and uncertainties of a winter campaign, waged with a line of communications 200 miles long through a bleak and desolate wilderness inhabited by unfriendly Indians and containing the well-nigh impassable swamp with which old Hull had contended six months before. Harrison could not plead lack of support in Washington. The government overwhelmed him with a promise of 10,000 men and gave him a free hand to collect supplies and equipment. Harrison's judgment cautioned him to use discretion; the voice of the people clamored for boldness and so did that of the Commander-in-Chief. Mr. Madison's administration was greatly in need of a ringing victory to silence the many critics of the war. There is a note of pathos in Harrison's letter of October 13 to Secretary Eustis. "I am fully sensible," he wrote, "of the responsibility invested in me. I accepted it with full confidence of being able to effect the wishes of the President, or to show unequivocally their impracticability."

". . . or to show unequivocally their impracticability." The alternative Harrison had left himself was unpleasant to contemplate. He was supposed to have in his command 10,000 men including regulars and militia and volunteers from Kentucky, Ohio, Western Pennsylvania and Western Virginia. Actually his force was about 6,500 men. Yet this was two or three times as large as the British and Indian army gathered together at Amherstburg under Colonel Henry Proctor and guarding the approach to Detroit. Harrison was imbued with the idea of guarding the whole of the frontier and so, at the very outset, he sacrificed his numerical superiority by making a division of his army the key to his plan of campaign. The advance upon Detroit was a small-scale reproduction of the strategy that was to have conquered Canada. Three columns were to be set in motion. The first was to be directed toward Sandusky, the second to the rapids of the Maumee River above the present city of Toledo and the third to Fort Defiance. The distance from Sandusky to the rapids was 60 miles; from the rapids to Fort Defiance higher up the river was some 30 miles, and the country between them was exceedingly difficult for the transportation of arms and supplies. Connecting roads were few and far between and of inferior quality made worse by heavy rains which turned them into quagmires, impeding the march and holding up the columns while the men put their shoulders to the wheels of supply wagons that were up to their axles in mud. Finally, to add to Harrison's embarrassment, the British held command of Lake Erie. (See Map I, p. 97)

In a letter written to the Secretary of War on October 22, Harrison indicated the difficulties into which he had run. "I am not able," he said, "to fix any period for the advance of the troops to Detroit. It is pretty evident that it cannot be done upon proper principles until the frost shall become so severe as to enable us to use the rivers and the margin of the lake for transportation of the baggage and artillery upon the ice."

Shortly thereafter Eustis resigned and returned to his drugs while, temporarily, James Monroe took over the War Office. To Monroe Harrison restated his problem, suggesting that unless it was deemed absolutely expedient to take Detroit at once, the attempt might with profit be postponed until spring and the money the government was now pouring into supplies, transportation and equipment be better expended on the construction of a fleet to take possession of Lake Erie. This was the proposal Hull had made six months before, but it had met with no cordial response from Washington. Harrison was more fortunate. Monroe, who had had a bit of practical military experience in the Revolution, quickly fell in with the suggestion. However, like Eustis, he enjoined Harrison to do as he thought best which left the decision to the commander in the field and still subject to popular opinion. Only a few weeks before Harrison had lamented to his friend ex-Governor Shelby, "I wish to God the public mind were informed of our difficulties, and gradually prepared for the course [abandonment of a winter campaign]. In my opinion, we should in this quarter disband all but those sufficient for a strong frontier guard, convoys, etc., and prepare for the next season." But the public mind was not informed. It was confident that its idol and its hero was not to be deprived of new laurels by such minor matters as mud, rain, ice, sleet and snow and a bitter wind blowing off the lake.

Early in December General Simon Perkins, with an Ohio brigade, battled through physical obstacles more terrifying than redcoats and redskins and reached his objective at Lower Sandusky. He was joined shortly by the Pennsylvanians and Virginians. General Edward W. Tupper, with more Ohio militia, plowed his way over Hull's old road to the rapids of the Maumee where he had a brush with the Indians and retreated. Winchester, who was at Fort Defiance with the Kentuckians, was suffering most of all. His line of communications was little more than a slender thread. His supplies were exhausted, his men suffering intensely from starvation and cold. As though this were not enough, an epidemic of typhus fever broke out in camp. The only comfort his men could claim were rude huts which they had painfully erected to serve as winter quarters.

In spite of his own misgivings Harrison still toyed with the idea of attacking Detroit at once. Pursuant to that plan he ordered Winchester to advance from Fort Defiance to the rapids and there build huts as though he were going to remain for the winter. It was a stern order for Winchester to fulfill when his men were in such wretched condition but, like a good soldier, he obeyed it promptly and ten days after New Year's had his whole command at the designated spot. On January 13, before his men had had time to settle in their new camp, alarming news reached him from the village of Frenchtown 30 miles to the north. A messenger from the 33 white families dwelling there reported that they were in imminent peril of an attack by the Indians and begged Winchester to come to their aid as quickly as possible.

Frenchtown was 18 miles from the British stronghold at Malden. Consequently response to the appeal meant that Winchester would place himself within a day's march of the main body of the enemy. Harrison was 60 miles away at Upper Sandusky. By the time a message could be got to him and Harrison could reply, Frenchtown might already have been captured and its people murdered. So Winchester decided not to take the matter to Harrison, but to act upon his own initiative. A council of officers was called and, after due consideration of the urgency of the appeal and the dangers involved, it was unanimously agreed to respond to the appeal. Winchester directed Colonel William Lewis to march at once with 550 men and Colonel John Allen to follow with 110 men.

There was some delay in getting the expedition ready and the wretched condition of the road made marching difficult and slow. In addition, precautions had to be taken to avoid ambush since it was suspected that many hostile Indians were in the country through which the expedition had to pass. It was not until January 18 that Lewis reached the outskirts of the town. He then discovered that the enemy had arrived ahead of him and were already in possession. Informants put the number at 200 Canadians and 400 Indians. Lewis assumed that his 550 men and the 110 men under Allen were enough to justify an attack, so after he had seen that his force was supplied with ammunition and properly disposed, he gave the order for the assault. The Americans moved forward with a shout. The

143

Canadians and their allies were taken by surprise and offered little resistance before beating a hasty retreat. In a very few minutes Lewis was in complete control of the town. His position was precarious and he felt considerable relief when, three days later, Winchester himself arrived with 300 reinforcements bringing the aggregate to 960 men.

Winchester now assumed command, making his headquarters in a house on the south bank of the river opposite the village and a good half mile from the lines. His arrival lulled the Americans into a false sense of security. There was every reason to believe that, at any time, Proctor would advance from Malden with a stronger force and attempt to drive them out. Yet they failed to take the simplest precautions against attack. No one was sent out to reconnoiter, no provision was made for strengthening the lines and no ammunition was distributed. Rumors began to spread that the British were on the way. Winchester ignored them. He was satisfied to accept the word of a resident of the town, who later proved to be a British agent, that the rumors were false.

On the evening of January 21 the Americans retired early and proceeded to get a good night's rest, little realizing that for many of them it was to be their last night on earth. Promptly at 4 A.M. reveille sounded and the soldiers, still half asleep, began to turn out. "Night," says one chronicler, "had not yet yielded its gloomy sceptre to Day." Suddenly and without previous warning a crash of artillery and the rattle of small arms turned the silence of the village into an unearthly, terrifying din. The Americans leaped for their rifles, while officers shouted confused orders. Nobody knew what had happened or what to do. In the darkness it was impossible to assemble companies or to distinguish friend from foe. Men fired blindly and were themselves shot down. Mingled with the sound of cannon and rifle were the blood-curdling war whoops of Indians.

What had happened was that Colonel Proctor, leading a force of 500 whites and 600 Indians, had approached within a short distance of the town without his presence being suspected. Selecting his own time he had fallen upon the settlement with terrible effect. What followed was hardly deserving the name of battle. Rather it was a massacre. As the sun came up its light revealed a scene of horror. Where the American lines had been dead men lay strewn about on the cold ground, while here and there the cries of the wounded added to the picture of desolation. General Winchester himself was taken prisoner. His army, without having a chance to defend itself or to strike a telling blow, was completely overwhelmed. When the firing had ceased, it was found that the Americans had lost 397 men killed, 27 wounded and over 500 taken prisoner. Of the 960 who answered the roll the day before only 33 men escaped. They fled the town to report the disaster they had witnessed and in which they had had a part.

Proctor was quite satisfied with what he had accomplished. A caution that was to prove characteristic of him led him to abandon the town and retreat in haste toward Malden for fear of being attacked in turn by a larger American force. Perhaps some secret messenger had warned him that Harrison was on the way. A similar caution, however, did not restrain the Indians from returning to Frenchtown. There the American wounded had been left without protection. Giving Proctor no inkling of what they were about to do the Indians, on the night of the battle, slipped into the town, celebrated the victory with a drunken debauch and, as a fitting climax, murdered and tomahawked the American wounded as they lay in their beds.

Before Winchester left the rapids he notified Harrison of his plans. Harrison immediately recognized the danger of Winchester's position and set out posthaste for the rapids where he arrived January 20. He succeeded in getting together 900 men to add to the force at Frenchtown. Before they reached the scene the blow had fallen. Upon receiving news of the tragedy Harrison supposed that Proctor would take advantage of his victory and advance to destroy all American forces that lay within reach. To save them he ordered the relieving party to retreat. And so, while Proctor hurried northward, the Americans retreated as fast as they could to the south, each army fearful that it was in immediate danger of being destroyed. Only a few hours after the engagement they were miles apart.

Harrison had been as good as his promise. He had endeavored to effect the wishes of the President by undertaking a winter campaign. The frozen American corpses in the lines at Frenchtown showed "unequivocally its impracticability." Whatever might be said Harrison had justified the frontiersmen in their belief that he was a man of action. But the massacre of Frenchtown was a high price to pay for the demonstration. At least it provided a brand-new battle cry. After the bloodshed at Frenchtown the fall of Detroit was almost forgotten. The earlier defeat was swallowed up by another even more tragic. From then on not "Detroit" but the "Massacre at Frenchtown" was the American watchword.

Though Harrison abandoned for the time being an attack on Detroit he kept within striking distance at the rapids of the Maumee. In February his force at that point consisted of 1,800 Virginians and Pennsylvanians and these he set to work constructing a fort which he named Fort Meigs in honor of the Governor of Ohio. His most immediate problem resulted from the prevailing system of short enlistments. There was no such thing in those days as enlistment in the militia for the duration of the war, so that at the most inconvenient time a general might find his command melting away. The enlistment of the troops at the rapids was due to expire in April, just when Harrison should be putting the last touches on them in preparation for the spring campaign. General John Armstrong, former minister to France, who had now relieved Monroe as Secretary of War, directed Harrison to dispense with militia and employ only the regiments of regulars in the vicinity. But Harrison maintained that there were not sufficient regulars to guard the half million dollars' worth of property at the rapids and in other exposed positions, which were in constant danger from Proctor. He disregarded Armstrong's order and appealed to the governors of Kentucky and Ohio to send him more men.

Once during the month Harrison halted work on the fort long enough to undertake a bold expedition against the British fleet which was frozen in the ice on Lake Erie. The winter, it so happened, was unusually mild, and the lake was not entirely frozen. On the way the expedition ran into open water before it reached the fleet and was forced to return with nothing accomplished. Harrison now granted himself a furlough to visit his family in Cincinnati. The officer he left in charge was incompetent, the men took advantage of Harrison's absence to halt construction of the fort and, even worse, used the pickets for firewood. Their period of service was almost at an end and they were indifferent to what might happen to the fort after they were gone. At last the day came for them to depart and, for a time, the garrison at Meigs was reduced to 500 men.

Fortunately Proctor, who was lacking in initiative, did not take the opportunity to strike. He was working hard throughout the winter attracting the Indians to his cause. By April 1 he had assembled at Malden 1,500 of them under the capable leadership of Tecumseh and his brother, the Prophet. In addition to the Indians, before the end of the month he had under him 522 British regulars and 461 Canadian militia. During the same time Harrison's appeal for recruits brought results. He succeeded in increasing his force at Meigs to 1,100 effectives, while at Fort Defiance, within supporting distance, General Green Clay appeared with 1,200 newly recruited Kentuckians.

Proctor now felt that he was strong enough to strike a blow in United States territory. Collecting boats and scows he embarked his little army, crossed the lake and on April 26 appeared at the mouth of the Maumee, 12 miles below Fort Meigs. On the 28th he approached a few miles nearer. Harrison had received warning of Proctor's presence and at once dispatched a messenger to General Clay ordering him to drop down the river and join his forces with those at Meigs. This Clay proceeded to do, distributing his men in boats for the 30-mile journey down the river.

Fort Meigs was on the south side of the river. Harrison did not have to wait long for Proctor who soon appeared on the north bank opposite the fort and placed two batteries in position to shell it. On May 1 the siege commenced with a bombardment of the fort, while a detachment of white troops accompanied by Indians under the personal command of Tecumseh crossed the river to attack the fort from the rear. Harrison, however, had foreseen this possibility and constructed a traverse behind the fort to protect it from that quarter. Consequently when, on the following day, a British battery that had crossed the river opened fire the American garrison was under cover and little damage was inflicted. Having virtually surrounded the fort Proctor ceased fire, requested a parley and demanded the fort's surrender. The demand was refused and the bombardment resumed.

On May 4 a messenger slipped through the British lines. He came from Clay and brought word that the force from Fort Defiance was on the way down the river, would arrive shortly and that Clay was awaiting further orders. No news could have been more welcome to Harrison. He sent the messenger back directing Clay, when he arrived a mile and a half above the fort, to detach 800 of his men, land them on the north bank of the river and attack the British batteries that were shelling the fort in front. Clay received the order and detailed Colonel William Dudley to carry out the mission. Dudley started off well. He landed his force in a concealed spot and pressed forward eagerly. The British, who had not expected an attack from that direction, were unprepared to meet it. In short order Dudley stormed and captured the battery and spiked the guns while the enemy retreated in confusion. Harrison witnessed the assault from the other side of the river and, when the batteries had been taken, he signaled to Dudley to recross the river and join him in the fort.

Dudley and his men, however, had tasted victory, their blood was up, and they were in no mood to retire. Like a pack of hounds in full cry, and indifferent to Harrison's order, they dashed off in pursuit of the British, losing all sense of discipline and organization, and throwing caution to the winds. Their enthusiasm was fatal. Hidden in the woods and underbrush around the British camp was a large force of Indians. As Dudley's men struggled toward the camp the Indians leaped out with savage yells. In an instant the Indians were everywhere, in the front, on the flanks and in the rear, some brandishing their tomahawks, others pouring in a deadly rifle fire. The Americans now tried to extricate themselves, but the slaughter was terrible. Of the 800 who entered the engagement, 170 managed to cut their way out and flee back to the battery and across the river to the fort. The rest, 630 of them, were either killed or captured.

While this painful scene was being enacted, Clay arrived at the fort with 50 men. Encouraged by this reinforcement the garrison boldly sallied forth, captured the British batteries in the rear of the fort and routed the Indians. More fortunate than Dudley's expedition and more intelligently led, they contented themselves with this success and retired safely to the entrenchment. This bold stroke was all that was needed to raise the siege. The faint-hearted Proctor concluded that he had had enough. Breaking camp he retreated hastily to Amherstburg on Canadian soil. Successful invasion apparently was as difficult of achievement for the British as for the Americans. On the way home he was careless and permitted 20 of his prisoners to be tomahawked and scalped by the Indians. Even more of them would have been murdered if Tecumseh had not ridden up and peremptorily put an end to the sport. The Americans, naturally, had objected strenuously to the British use of Indians, but now even the opposition newspapers in Great Britain took up the cry. Such practice, they declared, was "injurious to the British character." But that did not stop it. The commanders in the field defended themselves on the ground of stern necessity. The Americans, too, at times employed Indians.

Gratified by the relief of Fort Meigs Harrison left General Clay in command and rode to Lower Sandusky where he arrived on May 12. There he was met by Governor Meigs with a large body of Ohio militia who had come to share the dangers and glories of the campaign. So confident was Harrison that he had dealt effectively with Proctor and was in no danger of immediate attack that he called the Ohioans together, formally thanked them for their fine spirit and then dismissed them to their homes.

In this Harrison was mistaken. Proctor, ordinarily, was not greatly to be feared but he was the recipient of a new and unexpected inspiration. Upon his arrival at Malden he found encamped there a host of Indians which had descended from all parts of the Northwest. They were in sufficient numbers to increase his command to a total of 5,000 men. Even then Proctor might have hesitated, but what he lacked in decision was more than balanced by the audacity of Tecumseh. In fact in this strange partnership, which lasted for more than a year, it was the King's officer who held back and the Shawnee warrior who counseled action. It was Tecumseh now who urged Proctor to use this fresh force for a second attack on Fort Meigs before the Americans should have had time to recover from the first.

Tecumseh also proposed a snare for Clay. According to his plan, when Proctor's force had arrived within sound of Fort Meigs the British and Indians were to engage in a noisy sham battle. Clay, Tecumseh contended, upon hearing the noise of the battle would assume that another American force was being attacked and would venture out of the fort to go to the rescue. The rest would be a mere

149

matter of counting the Americans killed, wounded and captured. The proposal had sufficient originality to appeal to Proctor, who accepted it.

Harrison's forces guarding the frontier were now disposed in three areas. Clay was at Fort Meigs. At Fort Stephenson, situated at Lower Sandusky, was a garrison of 160 regulars under the command of a youth of 22, Major George Croghan of the United States Army. At Seneca Town, nine miles up the Sandusky River from Fort Stephenson, Harrison made his headquarters in order to be within supporting distance of both Fort Meigs and Fort Stephenson, whichever might be attacked. By the middle of July he had 1,000 men under his command.

On July 20, pursuant to Tecumseh's plan, Proctor once more appeared at the mouth of the Maumee. Again his presence was reported to the Americans. Clay received the first warning and immediately communicated with Harrison. He then awaited eventualities. When Proctor's force had arrived near Fort Meigs whites and Indians proceeded to engage in a sham battle that had all the earmarks of realism when heard from a distance. Cannons roared, the rattle of small arms grew in intensity, and during occasional lulls in the fire, the Indians made the air hideous with their cries. As Tecumseh had designed, all of this was heard by the garrison at Fort Meigs; and, as he had hoped, a good many of the Americans were completely fooled. In fact some of Clay's officers came to him and urged him to go out and join the fight. But something aroused Clay's suspicions. As impressive as the noise was, it did not quite resemble that of the battles he had been in. So, in spite of the entreaties of his officers, Clay persisted in staying inside the fort with the gates tight shut, compromising with his subordinates by firing a few desultory shots in the direction from which the uproar was coming. After this performance had gone on for some time and Clay showed no indication of moving, Proctor and Tecumseh were forced to admit that the plan had failed.

As Proctor did not mean to risk another assault on Meigs, Fort Stephenson was selected as the next objective. In addition to infantry, Proctor had with him one five-and-a-half-pound howitzer and five 6-pounders on a gunboat. He re-embarked his expedition and sailed from the Maumee to the mouth of the Sandusky. Believing that Fort Stephenson was too weak to resist artillery fire, Harrison directed Croghan to abandon the fort if the British brought artillery with them. He now learned of Proctor's guns and sent word to Croghan to obey his previous instructions. But by this time the Indian warriors of Proctor's force were showing up in large numbers on all sides of the fort and Croghan concluded that an attempt to escape would be even more desperate than an effort to hold the fort. With the impetuosity of youth he sent word back to Harrison, "We have determined to maintain this place; and, by heavens! we can."

Old campaigner that he was, Harrison was not the man to accept quietly such arrant disobedience from a callow lad of 22. As quickly as he could put pen to paper he wrote out an order relieving Croghan of command, designating another officer in his place and commanding Croghan to report himself in person at once to Seneca Town to answer for his conduct. But when Croghan put in an appearance he so impressed his commanding officer with his earnestness and the justification for the decision he had made that Harrison yielded and not only forgave him for the tenor of his letter but returned him to his post.

Having made his boast it was now Croghan's task to live up to it. The only artillery the young man had in the fort was a single 6-pounder. Croghan studied the situation to determine how it might best be used. A careful inspection convinced him that the fort's weakest spot was an angle and that consequently this was the point that was most likely to be singled out for an attack. Behind this angle he placed the 6-pounder, carefully masked.

On July 31 Proctor arrived by water in front of the fort. According to the plan he had mapped out, the assault was to be made by 400 British regulars and several hundred Indians, while Tecumseh with 2,000 more Indians was to guard all approaches and cut off any reinforcements that might endeavor to reach Croghan. When these dispositions had been made, Proctor dispatched a messenger to Croghan demanding the surrender of the stronghold. He called attention to his overwhelming force of Indian warriors, pictured in the most impressive way the hideous treatment the Indians were accustomed to inflict upon their prisoners and admitted that, once they had had a taste of blood, it would be completely beyond his power to restrain them. It was the same familiar war of nerves that had proved so effective against Hull.

Croghan, however, was made of sterner stuff. In spite of the tremendous odds against him he disdained the offer, replying that he would hold out or die in the attempt. On the afternoon of August 1 Proctor's artillery opened on the fort and continued the bombardment for several hours. Having put Croghan's little group of defenders through this softening-up process, Proctor at 5 P.M. ordered Lieutenant Colonel Short to lead an assault party into the ditch that protected the fort. Short responded eagerly and, with a cry of "Cut away the pickets, my brave boys, and show the damned Yankees no quarter!" he urged his men forward.

As Croghan had anticipated, Proctor selected the weakest point in the fortifications, just opposite the masked 6-pounder, for the attack. Croghan waited until the redcoats arrived within easy range. His single cannon had previously been charged with grape. Suddenly he unmasked it and delivered a fire that ripped a hole in the scarlet line, which wavered and yielded ground. But the retreat was only momentary. Short rallied his men, the gaps were closed, and again the line advanced. Once more the crash of the 6-pounder rent the air, the grapeshot scattered and embedded itself in human flesh. When the smoke cleared the anxious watchers on the ramparts of the fort were able to judge the deadliness of their aim. On the slope below them lay more than 100 men, some of them convincingly still, some writhing in their last death struggles, and others less seriously wounded crying out in pain. The officers shouted encouragement to those who were alive and urged them forward, but the single 6-pounder frowned ominously upon them, ready to deliver another devastating charge. All the fight had gone out of the redcoats. Nobody was in the humor to brave the gun again. The attackers, sullen and cowed, drew off while the Americans raised a cheer.

Proctor now determined to make use of his more than 2,000 Indians. Tecumseh's warriors could hold their own against rifle fire, but artillery struck terror into the Indian heart. It was a weapon with which they were not familiar. In spite of the entreaties of Proctor and Tecumseh the Indian warriors skulked in the rear. Neither threats nor entreaties could induce them to cross that stretch of bloody ground that lay between them and the fort.

In contrast to the severe losses among the attackers, Croghan had protected his men so well that the fierce bombardment of the fort had left them practically unscathed. When the young commander checked his garrison he found to his satisfaction that, in the course of the whole engagement, only one man had been killed and seven wounded. Night had now fallen and Croghan lost no time in taking the necessary precautions to meet an attack in the darkness. The preparations, however, proved unnecessary. Disheartened by the failure of the assault and the cowardly behavior of his Indian allies, Proctor admitted defeat, recalled his men to the boats and during the night set sail for Malden. Croghan and his little garrison were left in complete command of the situation and reaped the reward of public acclaim that their heroic conduct so richly deserved.

The attack on Fort Stephenson was Proctor's last attempt at an invasion of American soil. Thereafter it became his policy to sit at Malden and wait for the Americans to find him. Some eight months had elapsed since Harrison, at the behest of the Westerners, had undertaken his punitive expedition. In the course of it he had had at his disposal over 10,000 men. Thousands of dollars had been expended on their supplies and equipment. Contractors had waxed fat on the needs of the Army. But Harrison had not put foot on Canadian soil. He had been lucky in that the British did not stay on his own. Nevertheless the General continued to hold the affection and confidence of the people of Ohio and Kentucky. Even they seemed to realize at last, and too late, the impossibility of the task they had set him.

One thing now had been made clear to everybody—though it had been quite apparent to Hull more than a year before. There was no chance of making a successful attack on Detroit or of invading Upper Canada until the American Navy gained undisputed control of Lake Erie.

CHAPTER FOURTEEN

We, Too, Burn a Capital

As a young man of 24, fresh from the New Hampshire hills, Henry Dearborn had his first taste of battle at Lexington. That was the beginning of a distinguished military career in the Revolutionary War. At Bunker Hill he headed a company. He was with Benedict Arnold on the bold and arduous expedition up the Penobscot River and through the Maine wilderness to Quebec. In the fight which ensued there he had the misfortune to be captured, but managed to arrange his exchange. Once more in active service with the American Army he was promoted to major and behaved with such gallantry at Saratoga that he was made a lieutenant colonel. He took part in the battle of Monmouth and he was with Washington when Lord Cornwallis found himself trapped at Yorktown and surrendered his army. Thus, at the age of 32, Dearborn had done more fighting than most men do in a lifetime, and everywhere he had conducted himself so magnificently that he earned a merited reputation as a warrior of high degree and one who deserved the recognition of a grateful country.

Dearborn, however, did not immediately capitalize on his fame. Instead he beat his sword into a plowshare and retired modestly to a farm on the Kennebec River. But such distinction as he possessed could not go forever unnoticed. In 1789 his old chief, George Washington, called him to government service as marshal of the district of Maine; and so pleasant did Dearborn find public life that he entered politics and was elected to Congress. When the statesmen of the day, having no longer a foreign foe to fight, split into two parties in order the better to fight among themselves, Dearborn forsook Washington and gave his adherence to Thomas Jefferson and the Republicans. When Jefferson was elected President, Dearborn was rewarded by being elevated to the cabinet as Secretary of War, a post he held for eight years. Upon the succession of Madison Dearborn was named Collector of the Port of Boston, a particularly juicy plum reserved for deserving Republicans in the Federalist stronghold. Dearborn was happy in his surroundings and, no doubt, would have been glad to remain there. At the outbreak of the War of 1812 he was 61 years of age and beginning to succumb to the inevitable aches and pains of that period of maturity. He was so stout that a special vehicle had to be designed to carry him. The vehicle, bearing his name, later became for years a favorite with farmers.

However, a generalissimo had to be found. Madison looked far and wide but he could discover no one better qualified for the post than Dearborn. His career in the Revolution and his eight years of experience in the War Department marked him as a military man. More to the point, his politics were right. Besides, a New Englander at the head of the Army would serve to refute the Federalist libel that this was a war, not of New England, but of the South and the West. Dearborn's age was a handicap, yet Madison may have recalled that Cincinnatus was reputedly an elderly man when he saved his country and that Frederick the Great presented a more recent example of a warrior who continued his career with considerable success in spite of advancing years. When duty called it was not the part of Dearborn, any more than it had been of William Hull, to decline. And so, once more, painful as it may have been for him, he found himself enduring the hardships and rigors of the camp.

Dearborn appears to have been dazzled by the honor thrust upon him by Madison, so much so that he did not quite take in the extent of the authority vested in him, as has been previously mentioned. Even when his position had been clarified he did nothing about it. He let the summer and autumn of 1812 slip by without striking a blow commensurate with his position, his past record and the size of the force he had with him on the right flank. But if Dr. Eustis had, perhaps sympathetically, permitted Dearborn to take things easy, his successor in the War Department, General Armstrong, was of a different mind. Hardly had Armstrong taken over the reins than he began to consider how he might get action out of Dearborn. The

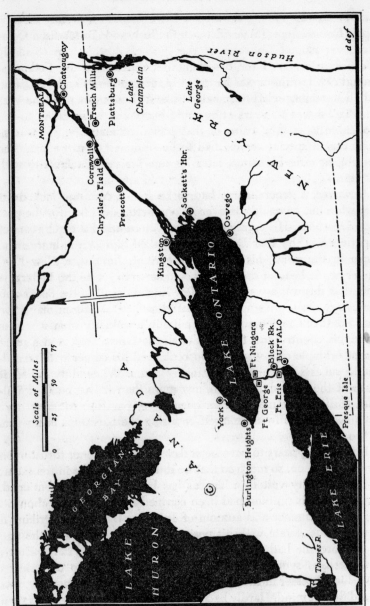

Map III. Northern Front

result of his cogitations was a plan that involved a combination between Commodore Isaac Chauncey's fleet and Dearborn's command.

In the early months of 1813 Commodore Chauncey succeeded in temporarily bottling up the British fleet of Sir James Yeo at Kingston and thus gaining control of Lake Ontario. Kingston stands on the Canadian shore of the lake not far from the head waters of the St. Lawrence River. Armstrong regarded this auspicious circumstance as an opportunity to strike a telling blow at Canada. Pursuant to this object, orders were given to concentrate an impressive force of 7,000 regulars and volunteers at Buffalo and at Sackett's Harbor, an important naval depot at the eastern end of the lake, 3,000 men at the former, 4,000 at the latter. (See Map III)

According to the plan proposed, the troops at Sackett's Harbor were to cross the ice to Kingston, capture the town, destroy all shipping and then proceed to York, the capital of Upper Canada and today better known as Toronto. There they were to seize the army stores and destroy two frigates that were building. When Dearborn received the order on February 10, he was at Plattsburg with 2,500 men. Before he could carry out this ambitious plan a report came to him that Sir George Prevost, Governor-General of Canada, had forestalled him by sending heavy reinforcements to York. Dearborn considered the prospects of the expedition in the light of this new intelligence. The report appeared reasonable, for the defeat of Napoleon in Russia had improved the situation of the Allies on the Continent and it was generally known that several veteran regiments of British regulars had arrived at Halifax and were only waiting for the ice in the St. Lawrence to break before proceeding inland to the relief of their countrymen in Upper Canada. Dearborn, therefore, did not see fit to make a further check on the report of reinforcements at Kingston before accepting it as truth. The news, as it turned out, was premature; Kingston and York were lightly garrisoned. And so the Generalissimo stuck to his comfortable campfire on good solid American soil; passed up the prospect of a dreary march across the ice and, along with it, an opportunity.

The only winter operation of the Americans was a modest raid from Ogdensburg, New York, across the St. Lawrence to Elizabethtown, the expedition being under the command of Major Benjamin

Forsyth who rescued a handful of prisoners from the village lockup. The British retaliated in kind by raiding Ogdensburg and plundering the town. It was, in fact, this British attack that was responsible for the report that reached Dearborn of large reinforcements at Kingston. The rest of February and the whole month of March passed without further activity.

By April, however, the Americans had succeeded in concentrating at Sackett's Harbor 5,000 regulars and volunteers, 2,000 militia and 1,500 sailors, an unusually large number of troops to be gathered together in one place according to War of 1812 standards. As little as they had shown themselves to be distinguished for initiative, even Dearborn and Chauncey were brought to realize that something ought to be done and done quickly, too, before the veteran regiments at Halifax had time to march and reverse the advantage. Between them they devised a new plan. In this Kingston was left out of consideration. Instead the expedition was to sail across the lake direct to York. Having destroyed the military and naval objectives there, it was to recross the lake and reduce Fort George which stood on the Canadian shore near the mouth of the Niagara River directly opposite Fort Niagara on the American side. Simultaneous with the attack on Fort George, the troops at Buffalo and Black Rock were to pass over the river to Canadian territory and overwhelm Fort Erie and Fort Chippawa, thus driving the British back along the line of the Niagara all the way from Lake Erie to Lake Ontario.

On April 25, when all the preparations were complete, the flotilla under Chauncey, loaded with 1,700 men of Dearborn's command, set sail from Sackett's Harbor. The food or the climate, or both, were constantly affecting the health of the American army in the lake region. On this occasion the commanding general became so ill that he was confined to his cabin and was quite incapable of conducting the operations. While Dearborn was dosed by the doctors, General Zebulon Pike took his place and gave the orders. The expedition met with no resistance on the lake and on the morning of April 27 it arrived off York.

York, with its valuable army stores and government buildings, was defended by Major General R. H. Sheaffe and only 800 men, not including the usually untrustworthy contingent of Indian allies.

The odds were hopelessly against him but Sheaffe was obstinate and determined not to surrender the town without a struggle. Anticipating the attack he had constructed a mine and artfully concealed it, planning to set it off upon the arrival of the Americans, throw them into confusion and thus to some extent equalize the strength of the two contending forces.

By 8 A.M. all was in readiness among the Americans for the attack. Equipment was checked, officers and men were given their final instructions and the vessels put in as close to the shore as they dared go. At word of command the soldiers leaped into the shallow water and struggled toward the beach. They were immediately met by a volley from the defenders but pushed bravely on. It was not, however, Sheaffe's intention seriously to contest the landing. As soon as the Americans appeared in force the British began to fall back upon the town, firing as they retreated and luring the Americans on to the trap which Sheaffe had prepared for them.

Dearborn was still indisposed and remained aboard ship. General Pike however led the attack in person and set a brave example to his men by exposing himself in the forefront of the battle. In their enthusiasm over having broken down the British resistance the Americans pressed forward toward the town. Suddenly a great explosion was heard, shattered human bodies, equipment and debris hurtled through the air and the surroundings were obscured in a heavy acrid pall of smoke. The British mine had been set off.

The explosion had been timed so clumsily that the British were unable to get their own men out of danger and inflicted almost as much damage on themselves as upon the Americans. Forty-two of the British were killed outright. The Americans lost 52 killed and 180 wounded. Unfortunately, among those fatally wounded was the brave General Pike. A heavy stone dislodged by the explosion fell on him and crushed his chest and he died within a few minutes.

As Sheaffe had anticipated, the mine created temporary confusion but the Americans quickly recovered from it and Colonel Cromwell Pearce succeeded to the command and continued to push on. As soon as Sheaffe realized that the Americans had not been completely demoralized by the unpleasant surprise he prepared for them, he called in his regulars and withdrew from the town. So hasty was his departure that he left behind his official papers and

his personal baggage, including among other trifles a musical snuff-
box that delighted the Americans who already had established the
national tradition for collecting souvenirs.

Finding themselves without defenders and at the mercy of the
Americans, the civilian authorities and the militia officers who had
not run away with the regulars now advanced under a flag of truce
and offered to surrender the town. General Dearborn had by now
sufficiently recovered from his indisposition to land and resume the
command. He accepted the surrender of 290 prisoners, naval and
military stores and the two frigates that were building. The blowing
up of the mine, however, and the death and wounding of so many
of the Americans put them in a vindictive mood. Not only did they
destroy the military objectives, but some unknown person or persons took it upon themselves to set fire to the public buildings which
were burned to the ground. The American authorities did not con-
done this act of vandalism but explained that some of the men had
been infuriated when they found a human scalp, recently taken,
hanging on the wall of one of the buildings. The British, for their
part, retorted that the scalp was that of an Indian and that the scalp-
ing had been done by no less a person than Commodore Chauncey
himself.

For four days the Americans made themselves at home in the
town. After having removed all the public property they wanted
and made sure that the rest had been destroyed they withdrew to
the ships, while Sheaffe and his regulars, who had been lurking outside, reoccupied the town. This brief sojourn on Canadian soil cost
the Americans 66 killed and 220 wounded. The British loss was
60 killed, 89 wounded and 290 prisoners. The unfinished frigates
and other military property had been destroyed, but the destruction
of the public buildings was a precedent that was later to bring re-
grettable retaliation upon Washington.

Having completed the first phase of its operations the expedition
was now ready to proceed with the second. Hoisting sail the fleet
soon left York behind, recrossed the lake and anchored offshore
four miles east of the mouth of the Niagara. While the troops de-
barked to reorganize, Chauncey set off for Sackett's Harbor to replen-
ish his supplies. The excitement of the operations at York, limited
as his participation in them had been, proved too much for Gen-

eral Dearborn. He had a relapse and became quite ill; age proved to be his most dangerous enemy. Luckily for the expedition he had as his adjutant young Winfield Scott who not only was hale and hearty but loved nothing so much as a good fight. While Dearborn's military career was drawing rapidly to a close, Scott's was just beginning. So far as the proposed campaign was concerned Dearborn's physical incapacity was a blessing in disguise. Another valuable recruit, who left off building vessels at Erie when he smelt the smoke of battle, was Oliver Hazard Perry, a rising young naval officer. Perry's arrival was just the force needed to stimulate the somewhat hesitant Chauncey. The Commodore soon returned from Sackett's Harbor with his supplies and all was in readiness for the attack on Fort George.

The American force consisted of 4,000 men fit for duty. Opposing them were 1,800 British regulars under Brigadier General John Vincent. The engagement opened on May 26 with a spirited artillery duel between Fort Niagara on the American side of the river and Fort George on the Canadian side. This was merely a diversion to keep the British occupied until night came. As soon as it was dark the American troops embarked on the *Madison,* the *Oneida,* the *Lady of the Lake* and small vessels and boats that had been collected together to receive them. During the night a heavy fog set in and though this served to conceal the flotilla from the British it at the same time rendered much more difficult the posting of the vessels. This task was placed under the immediate direction of Perry who displayed the professional ability that might have been expected from him. As dawn broke on May 27 all the ships and boats were in their proper order, lying near the mouth of the river and facing the Canadian shore where the landing was to be made. (See Map II, p. 110)

Colonel Scott had accepted the office of adjutant to General Dearborn on the express condition that he be permitted to lead his regiment into action. He now elected to go with the vanguard of 500 men who preceded the main body. As the hour designated for the attack approached a wind came up, dispersing the fog and at the same time raising a choppy sea. This created a new and unexpected problem which Perry handled with great skill, keeping the fleet in formation while it approached the shallow water near shore.

Vincent's regulars, accompanied by Indian warriors, lay concealed in a ravine and wood opposite the landing place and awaited the Americans. As soon as the boats had arrived within wading distance of the beach the 500 men led by Scott and Perry plunged into the lake with all their heavy battle equipment and made for land. Fortunately, the shore at this point rose to a height of from six to 12 feet, making a natural entrenchment which afforded excellent protection while they were getting themselves together for the strenuous effort which lay ahead. By way of welcome the British discharged a volley of musketry, but the bullets passed harmlessly overhead.

Now that the vanguard had gained a foothold, the main body followed as fast as the boats could put them ashore and in short order the beach was dotted with men. The British and Indians, 1,000 strong, advanced to the attack and the Americans scrambled up the embankment to meet them. For 20 minutes the battle raged. Three times the Americans moved forward and three times they were driven back to the beach at the point of the bayonet. Throughout the engagement the guns of the American schooners roared as they hurled grape and canister into the ranks of the enemy. Scott and Perry, both conspicuous for their splendid physiques, were in the thick of the fight giving aid and encouragement to the men. For a time the situation was in doubt. Then the scarlet line of the British regulars faltered. The deadly fire of the American infantry accompanied by that from the ships was taking a heavy toll of their numbers, and the Americans were pressing relentlessly forward. It was more than even British regulars could stand. They broke and withdrew, leaving the Americans in possession of the field.

Seeing his army defeated and in full retreat Vincent ordered the guns of Fort George to be spiked, the ammunition destroyed, and the garrison to withdraw immediately. Similar orders were issued to the garrisons of Fort Chippawa and Fort Erie. Vincent selected as a rallying point Beaver Dams, 18 miles to the west, thus leaving the Americans in complete control of the Niagara River. However, before the order at Fort George could be carried out, the American forces took possession and saved much of the munitions and stores. In the engagement the British lost 863 men killed, wounded and taken prisoner. The American loss was comparatively light, amounting to no more than 40 killed and 100 wounded.

In the full flush of a fine victory against British regulars, Scott was all for pursuing Vincent's beaten army and destroying it before it had time to reorganize. But Scott was no longer in a position to make the decision. The operations had now come within the province of General Morgan Lewis, who commanded at Fort Niagara and who outranked Scott. Lewis, adopting a policy of caution in marked contrast to Scott's audacity, recalled the Americans just as they were coming up with the stragglers from Vincent's army. Scott, who had won the victory, was forbidden to touch its fruits. He obeyed the order like a good soldier, but with considerable reluctance.

Two days later, on May 29, General Lewis himself, accompanied by the brigades of General William H. Winder and General John Chandler, set out in pursuit of Vincent who had now retired farther west to Burlington Heights at the western end of Lake Ontario. But the expedition failed to come up with the enemy and returned to camp. Meanwhile Lieutenant Colonel James P. Preston commanded a force which crossed over from Black Rock and occupied Fort Erie. Thanks to Lewis' caution several more days were wasted during which Vincent had time to receive reinforcements from York. Then, at last, General Winder was dispatched to search for him, but with a force of only 800 men. Winder, upon approaching the heights, learned of the reinforcements and sent back for help to Dearborn, who had recovered and resumed command. He was soon joined by Chandler with 500 men, bringing the total American force to 1,300. The Americans now boldly advanced until they came within sight of Vincent's camp. They were content to drive in the British pickets and then retired 10 miles to Stony Creek where they pitched camp for the night, throwing out pickets and patrols and sleeping with their arms by their sides in anticipation of an attack.

In this they were not disappointed. A British reconnoitering party discovered the American camp and returned to Vincent to urge a night assault. Vincent approved and at midnight set out with 600 men for Stony Creek, halting his force a mile from it. By good fortune he ran into a deserter who gave him the American countersign. Armed with this information Vincent's men approached the American pickets, whispered the magic word in their ears and, having been passed as friends, returned the compliment by capturing the pickets before they had time to give the alarm.

Vincent then ordered his men to charge. The Americans, sleeping peacefully in the assurance that their pickets were watching over them, were taken completely by surprise. Before the attack was well under way their first line was broken and their guns captured. As usual with night attacks, great confusion reigned on both sides. British and Americans fought among themselves as much as they fought each other. Even General Vincent, when he was thrown from his horse, lost his way. He turned up next day miles from the scene of the conflict. An even worse fate befell the two American commanders. Winder and Chandler ran into the enemy and submitted to ignominious capture. It was, on the whole, not a glorious display of American military prowess which took place that night of June 5 at Stony Creek. Yet, oddly enough, it was to enhance the military reputation of one of the American victims and give him an opportunity for undying glory, if it did not give him the glory itself. Though the British won the victory they lost 23 men killed, 100 wounded and 55 missing in contrast to the American loss of 17 killed, 38 wounded and 99 missing.

When day came what was left of the American host, disheartened by the loss of its leaders, broke camp and began an unhappy march back home by way of the lake shore. Hardly had it started when Sir James Yeo's squadron put in an appearance and attacked the column with such spirit that twelve boatloads of baggage and camp equipment were lost. To add to the Americans' discomfort and depress their already dampened spirits they were chased most of the way to Fort George by Indians and Canadian militia.

Vincent now advanced from Burlington Heights to Beaver Dams. Dearborn, who unfortunately for the American cause continued to enjoy a period of good health which enabled him to resume command, sent out another expedition of 570 men, including infantry and artillery under Lieutenant Colonel Charles G. Boerstler, to dislodge the enemy. Not far from Beaver Dams the road over which Boerstler and his column was marching passed through a dense wood. In the very middle of the wood the Americans were ambushed by a band of Indians who let them pass and then fell upon their rear. Boerstler immediately disposed his men for the fight, and for three hours held off the Indians. But after this exertion he concluded that his force was too small to undertake an engagement with the British while at the same time it ran the risk of being harassed by Indians. He therefore prepared to retire. Hardly had he made the decision when he saw a detachment of the British approaching under a flag of truce. Boerstler granted a parley and the officer in command introduced himself as Lieutenant James Fitzgibbon. He stated that his was an advance party of a strong force composed of 1,500 British and 700 Indians, who already were within a few minutes' march. It was obvious, he said, that Boerstler's men stood no chance whatever against such odds, and pointed out that it was now too late for the Americans to hope to escape. He realized, of course, that a man of Colonel Boerstler's courage would welcome a trial at arms. But before Colonel Boerstler came to that decision, he would like to remind him that the Indians were a bloodthirsty lot and that if the Americans attempted to resist, a horrible fate awaited them. He suggested that the sensible course for Colonel Boerstler to adopt was to admit the hopelessness of his situation and spare his men the suffering and bloodshed.

Boerstler was duly impressed by the horrors painted by Lieutenant Fitzgibbon. However, his pride revolted at abject and unconditional surrender. He replied that he would yield, but on the express condition that the officers be permitted to retain their sidearms and that the members of the militia in his force be granted parole. To these stipulations Fitzgibbon courteously consented. The agreement having been made Boerstler turned over to Fitzgibbon 542 prisoners, all the muskets, two guns, all the ammunition they had brought with them and a stand of colors. Having completed these operations, the Americans looked for the arrival of the main British force. But no force appeared. When inquiry was made Fitzgibbon confessed that there wasn't any main force. There were no 1,500 British soldiers and no 700 Indians. The only force in the neighborhood was the 250 men Fitzgibbon had with him. To a mere lieutenant and 250 men an American lieutenant colonel had surrendered a force over twice its size!

While these events were taking place at York and along the Ni-

agara, the British forces at Kingston were not idle. Sir George
Prevost learned that, after the departure of Dearborn's expedition,
Sackett's Harbor across the lake from him had been left virtually unprotected. Its garrison, he was informed, consisted of no more than
60 artillerymen and 100 infantrymen and most of these were either
invalids or raw recruits. So Sir George, though he had little reputation for enterprise, found this opportunity too good to ignore. He
determined upon an attack with the assistance of Sir James Yeo and
the fleet.

On May 27 word reached the Americans at the harbor that Sir
George had put to sea. They had not entirely overlooked the possibility of such an attack during Dearborn's absence and General
Jacob Brown, a capable officer of the New York militia and a
Quaker, had been counted upon to take command in an emergency.
Brown was immediately notified and called out the militia. The following day the British squadron, consisting of 12 ships and 40
bateaux, bearing 1,200 troops and a contingent of Indians, was
sighted off the harbor. With all sails set, the ships made an impressive picture. But just as the Americans at the harbor sighted the
British squadron, the British observed 19 American gunboats bringing up reinforcements. So the squadron departed in haste.

Bright and early next day the British were back again. Off the
harbor the fleet was becalmed so that the larger vessels could not
come close to land. Sir George, however, got his party into boats and
came along himself. The militia at the harbor had never been under
fire before and at sound of the first shots they fled in disorder. On
the other hand the regulars and volunteers put up stiff resistance
and, though outnumbered, fought a delaying action for more than
an hour.

Nevertheless the situation was desperate. With the limited force
at his disposal General Brown saw little hope of driving the British
off. His only possible reinforcements were the militia and they, thoroughly frightened, were keeping at a safe distance from the engagement. But Brown had an inspiration. He sent a messenger speeding
after the militia to announce that the day had been won and urging
them to share in the victory!

To be on the losing side was one thing, to take part in a victory
was quite another. Frightened though they were, 300 of the militia

accepted General Brown's bait and returned boldly to the field to take their part in administering the *coup de grâce* to an already vanquished enemy. Fortunately they did not have time to discover the deception or else they might have scampered off again. If the American militiamen were timid, so was the British commander. Sir George, seeing the new force on his flank mistook the militia for regulars and imagined that he was about to be caught in a trap. So he ordered his men to retreat to the boats. Or, as he preferred to express it in his official dispatch, "I reluctantly ordered the troops to leave a beaten enemy." At noon Sir George's "victorious" squadron set sail for Kingston, leaving the "beaten enemy" in full possession of the field and of the objective which Sir George had failed to reach.

Sir George's "victory," however, was not altogether fruitless. From behind the lines Lieutenant Woolcott Chauncey, of the United States Navy, had watched the battle. When he saw the American line fall back and the militia in flight, he came to the very natural conclusion that the Americans were beaten. To prevent the spoils from falling into British hands, he set fire to the *General Pike*, which was building, and to all the naval stores. Luckily, the *General Pike* was too green to burn; but the stores were not. Lieutenant Chauncey's prompt action cost the United States Government a matter of $500,000.

Late in July, Colonel Scott and Commodore Chauncey paid another surprise visit to York, burned the barracks, the public storehouses and their contents and eleven transports, and captured five cannon. That just about completed the activities of the army of the center for the summer. It attempted no conquest of Canada and was content to hold the line of the Niagara. Meanwhile every day's delay saw the arrival at Halifax of veteran regiments released from the European war.

General Dearborn's leadership had now been tried and found wanting. The spirit may have been willing, but the flesh was weak. So he was permitted to retire. It was only fair to the aging warrior.

CHAPTER FIFTEEN

Marauders on the Chesapeake

"FREE TRADE AND SAILORS' RIGHTS" was the battle cry of the United States Navy. The "Free Trade," sad to relate, was interpreted by many Americans as trade with the enemy. During 1812 and 1813 the British army under Wellington on the Peninsula was in constant need of flour, grains and other provisions, and the United States was a convenient source of supply. Though their country was at war with Great Britain, American merchants who had passed through lean years, could not resist the temptation to turn a penny that, under the strictest construction, could not be called honest.

The British themselves were a willing party to this business. British consular officers readily granted licenses to American ships allowing them free passage with supplies destined for Wellington's men. The records show that during the year ending September 30, 1813, American home products exported reached a total of $25,-008,152 of which provisions to the value of $15,000,000 went direct to Spain and Portugal. This trade could not be blamed on the disgruntled Federalist opposition; for when, in February, 1813, Admiral Warren announced a commercial blockade of the coast as far north as New York and abandoned the practice of issuing licenses, in the loyal port of Baltimore, where Republicans predominated, the price of flour immediately dropped $2 a barrel.

Warren's blockade resulted from the fact that Wellington's army had entered France and no longer needed the provisions. But there was still a British army in Canada to be fed and for that reason Boston and other New England ports were excluded from the blockade so that no obstacle would stand in the way of the profitable business the New Englanders were doing, and had been doing in that field since the commencement of hostilities. As early as November, 1812, an American in Halifax reported that within the brief space of two weeks he had seen landed there 20,000 barrels of flour by vessels under Spanish and Swedish flags. The flour had come chiefly from Boston.

What the vessels transported was only a part of the trade. Droves of cattle were constantly being herded across the New England border into Canada. In December, 1813, Governor-General Sir George Prevost wrote to his home government: "Two thirds of the army in Canada are at the moment eating beef provided by American contractors. . . . This circumstance, as well as that of the introduction of large sums of specie in the province being notorious in the United States, it is expected Congress will take steps to deprive us of those resources, and under that apprehension large droves are daily crossing the lines coming to Canada."

The United States Government was quite aware of the illicit trade being conducted by its own citizens but was incapable of stopping it. All that President Madison could do was to berate the wicked British for putting temptation before his people. In his message to Congress in February, 1813, he charged the enemy with having made "an unfortunate progress in undermining those principles of morality and religion which are the best foundations of national happiness." His indignation rising the President charged that, by encouraging the New Englanders to deliver supplies to Canada, Great Britain had introduced into her modes of warfare a system "equally distinguished by the deformity of its features and the depravity of its character; having for its object to dissolve the ties of allegiance, and the sentiments of loyalty in the adversary nation, and to seduce and separate its component parts the one from the other!" The attempted seduction of Canada from her allegiance to Great Britain, the President tactfully overlooked. In spite of the President, New England yielded gracefully to a seduction that brought her a handsome return in cash. While the rest of the coast was blockaded the ports north of Narragansett Bay were left open. New England became the distributing center for virtually all imports. Money poured into her coffers from all the other states which could obtain only there the goods from abroad that were so much in demand. It is estimated that by 1814 the total specie in the country was $17,000,000 and that of this the Boston banks held $10,-

000,000. With part of it the bankers purchased British drafts at a discount while to their own government's war loans they contributed a niggardly $3,000,000.

President Madison might protest that "these demoralizing and disorganizing contrivances will be reprobated by the civilized and Christian world, and the insulting attempt on the virtue, the honor, the patriotism and the fidelity of our brethren of the eastern States will not fail to call forth their indignation and resentment, and to attach more and more all the States to that happy union and constitution, against which such assiduous artifices are directed." To these noble sentiments of their stout little President, the reply of the American merchants was "Business as usual," or if anything a little more than usual even though it might be conducted with the enemy to his advantage and to the disadvantage of their own arms.

It will be recalled that in one of his most inspired passages in his speech before the Twelfth Congress, John Randolph exclaimed: "Go march to Canada! Leave the broad bosom of the Chesapeake and her hundred tributary rivers; the whole line of seacoast, from Machias to St. Mary's, unprotected." The words proved prophetic. The march to Canada had been made. And now, as Randolph had predicted, the broad bosom of the Chesapeake was to feel the rough hand of the invader. Stung by the defeats of their frigates, the attacks on Canada and the burning of the capital at York, and with their forces partially released by Napoleon's retreat from Moscow and the rapid disintegration of the Corsican's empire, the British public became impatient to launch a punitive expedition against the presumptuous Yankees and show them just what the British lion was like when aroused. Chesapeake Bay offered the most convenient field for the demonstration, and the British Navy had just the man to strike terror into the hearts of the planters and townspeople along its shores.

George Cockburn was a hard-bitten sailor. He had entered the Navy at the tender age of nine years and been cuffed about until he was good and tough. In the course of his career he sailed the seven seas, took part in the battle of Cape St. Vincent and in the defense of Cadiz and passed so successfully through the hardening process that a grateful sovereign bestowed a knighthood upon him and raised him to the rank of rear admiral before he had passed his

42nd birthday. In response to public appeal at home an order in council was issued on December 26, 1812, declaring the Chesapeake and Delaware Bays blockaded, and an expedition under the command of Admiral John B. Warren was organized at Bermuda with the object of invading the two bays and giving the neighboring inhabitants a taste of real war. Cockburn was at the moment free, and to him was intrusted the actual chastisement as second in command. There is no record of his having protested the unpleasant assignment and he executed it with efficiency and dispatch. Where there was looting and destruction, there was Sir George. Where the war assumed its harshest aspects it was a good guess that Sir George was around. So thoroughly did he go about the business of harassing and terrifying the civilian population that within a few months his name was the most feared and hated of all His Majesty's officers on service in America.

On a crisp morning in early February, 1813, lookouts at Cape Henry, Virginia, sighted enemy sails and immediately messengers were dispatched posthaste to the military authorities at Norfolk and throughout the countryside to announce the dreaded news of the arrival of a British fleet. Looming large and menacing were four ships of the line, of 74 guns each, every one of them more powerful than any American ship afloat. They were accompanied by a large number of smaller craft and aboard them was a land force of 1,800 men, fully equipped with surfboats for landing, and the very latest models in bomb ships and rocket ships to deliver bombshells and the terrifying Congreve rockets.

Norfolk had long been preparing for just such a descent and full precautions had been taken. The town itself was defended by two forts. At the mouth of the Elizabeth River, which separates Norfolk from Portsmouth, was a line of gunboats that reached all the way from Norfolk to Craney Island at the far end of the river's mouth. On the island was a strong force of regulars, volunteers and Virginia militia, including both infantry and artillery. In support of the gunboats was the frigate *Constellation*, 38 guns, which was in the navy yard for repairs, had not gone to sea, and was now anchored to serve as a battery.

Arrived in Hampton Roads, the invaders reconnoitered the defenses and concluded that Norfolk was too strong to attack. For the time being they turned their attention elsewhere. Cockburn, in the *Marlborough,* was ordered to Lynnhaven Bay, near Cape Henry, while Captain J. B. Beresford, commanding the *Poictiers,* was detached with his ship and the *Belvidera* and directed to proceed to Delaware Bay and commence operations in that vicinity.

Pursuant to his orders Beresford hoisted sail and passed out of the Capes, appearing next off Lewes, Delaware, where he anchored and dispatched a boat to land to demand supplies for which he offered to pay. The request was refused and the town prepared to defend itself. In response to this inhospitable reception Beresford proceeded to bombard the town, but his fire did little damage. The Du Ponts got news of the arrival of the British ships and rushed to Lewes a generous supply of powder from their factory at Wilmington. Spent cannon balls from the guns of the *Poictiers* were now lying about Lewes and the townspeople, upon examining them, were delighted to find that the balls exactly fitted their own guns. So, with the assistance of the Du Pont powder, they sent the British cannon balls flying back at the *Poictiers* as quickly as they arrived.

After a while Beresford grew tired of this exchange, called off the bombardment and attempted a landing below the town for the purpose of filling his water casks. This effort, too, was defeated and, concluding that the Delawareans were too hard a nut to crack, Beresford upped anchor and sailed away to Bermuda, leaving the good townspeople of Lewes once more in peace.

Cockburn, however, was more persevering. He terrorized the countryside around Lynnhaven Bay, sending out marauding parties to plunder and burn the farmhouses, arm the slaves and make off with the cattle, pigs and poultry. Sir George justified his unseemly behavior on the ground that extreme measures were taken only where resistance was offered. Indeed, throughout his entire expedition the people were forced to an unhappy choice. Submission carried with it a certain amount of disgrace and, besides, the Americans could not be quite certain that Sir George would live up to his promise not to molest them. On the other hand, if they offered resistance by appealing for protection to the local militia, they could not be sure that, at the first sound of a musket, the militia would not scamper to safety and leave them to the tender mercy of Sir George.

Finally, having reached the conclusion that he had taught the people of the Lynnhaven Bay country enough for one lesson, Cockburn weighed anchor and sailed off up Chesapeake Bay. On the way he made a feint at Baltimore, but knowing it to be well defended, he continued northward until he reached the Elk River at the head of the bay. As a result of the blockade the coastal trade had been interrupted and the route now passed inland up the bay. Frenchtown, on the Elk, had become an important commercial center, for there freight was removed from the bay boats and placed in warehouses to await shipment by wagon to Philadelphia and other Northern markets.

On April 29 Cockburn's flotilla, consisting of two brigs, several tenders and a complement of land troops aboard, entered the river and lay off Frenchtown. The Admiral met with no serious opposition and set to work pillaging the storehouses, after which he set fire to them and burned them to the ground. It was admitted that he spared the private houses, treated the women and children with respect and gave receipts for all property commandeered from noncombatants. Having completed the devastation of Frenchtown, Cockburn next turned his attention to Havre de Grace, a few miles distant. This town was unfortunate in that it was allegedly protected by a battery and a detachment of militia and, consequently, was classified as "armed" and subject to the use of force. It also bore the distinction of being the home of Commodore Rodgers whose estate, Sion Hill, was situated on the outskirts.

On May 2, in the middle of the night, Havre de Grace received the first warning of Cockburn's approach when the inhabitants were awakened from sleep by the noise and light of rockets which came whistling through the air to fall on rooftops and start a number of fires. The rockets were followed by a shower of bombs. The terrified populace lost no time fleeing the town and along with them went the raw militia. There was, however, in the town one John O'Neil, an elderly Irishman. O'Neil had seen service in the Revolution and enemy fire was nothing new to him. His Irish blood was up. Making his way through the militia that was flying in the opposite direction O'Neil hastened to the battery. He looked for officers and men but found nobody there. Even that did not discourage him. He had some knowledge of ordnance and singlehanded he manned one of the heavy guns, rammed home the charge and the ball, trained the gun on the British ships in the harbor, then lit the fuse and stepped back as the gun boomed and the shot went hurtling toward the enemy craft. O'Neil stuck courageously to his post until at last he failed to step back quickly enough, the gun rebounded, struck him on the side and put him out of action. Cockburn had by now dispatched a strong force from the boats to assault and take the battery at the point of the bayonet. The men rushed forward expecting to encounter at least a company. To their astonishment, as they leaped over the ramparts, they discovered one old and disabled Irishman who alone had undertaken to defend a town against a whole flotilla. O'Neil was captured and taken aboard one of the ships as a prisoner. But O'Neil's pluck appealed to Cockburn who treated him handsomely and, a few days later, let him go.

Commodore Rodgers was on the high seas, but Mrs. Rodgers was at Sion Hill. So was her sister-in-law, Mrs. William Pinkney, wife of the Attorney General. The ladies, in spite of all the terrible stories they had heard of Cockburn, dared to approach him and appeal to him to spare the town. Thanks to their efforts Cockburn was persuaded to leave some of the houses untouched and, among them, Sion Hill. He insisted, however, upon searching the house for important papers and took possession of the Commodore's mahogany writing desk, through which his men plunged a saber in the hope of finding a secret drawer. Not satisfied with that they took the desk off with them to one of the ships. According to family tradition the desk was later recovered when it was found by the Commodore on a British ship he had captured.

While his brigs lay at Havre de Grace Cockburn sent out a party which destroyed an ironworks and cannon foundry situated farther up the Susquehanna River. Pleased with the success he had achieved Cockburn next crossed the bay to the Eastern Shore and entered the Sassafras River. There he met with opposition from the defenders but drove them off and requited himself for the trouble they had given him by burning the villages of Fredericktown and Georgetown. Having terrorized the head of the bay as successfully as he had terrorized the Lynnhaven country, Cockburn now returned triumphantly to rejoin the fleet in Hampton Roads.

On the first day of June Admiral Warren entered the Capes with the grandest fleet that had yet been assembled in American waters.

174

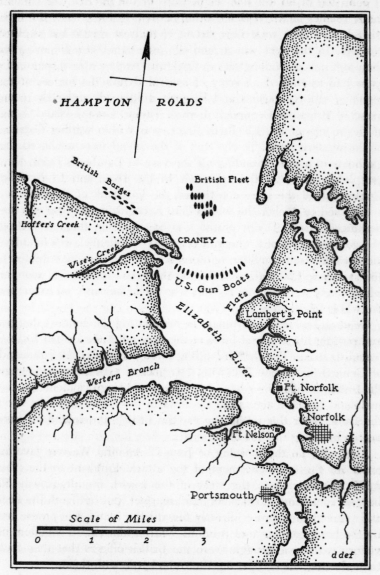

Map IV. Battle of Craney Island

It consisted of no less than eight ships of the line, 12 frigates and many smaller boats. With these impressive reinforcements the British felt that they were now strong enough to attack and capture Norfolk. In the fleet was a landing force of 5,000 men, many of them veterans of Wellington's campaigns. To oppose them the Americans had assembled an army of several thousand men, including regulars, sailors, marines and Virginia militia, all under the command of Brigadier General Robert B. Taylor. Craney Island, lying at the mouth of the Elizabeth River, was within wading distance of the western shore. To the east of the island were anchored the gunboats in a line extending all the way to Lambert's Point, thus completely covering the approach to the river and to Norfolk. Craney Island therefore constituted the left flank of the defenses and served to anchor the whole line. Recognizing its strategic importance General Taylor posted a strong garrison there consisting of two companies of artillery, a company of riflemen, 416 infantrymen of the Virginia militia, reinforced by 30 regulars, 30 volunteers, 150 sailors and 50 marines, bringing the grand total to 737 men, of whom many were veteran fighters who might be expected to temper the whole force. (See Map IV)

General Taylor was fortunate in penetrating the enemy's designs and putting his strongest force at the very point the British had selected to strike. The British landing force was under the command of General Sir Sidney Beckwith. His plan of action was to engage the fort in front while part of his force was being dispatched to the mainland to wade across the shallows to the island and take it on the flank. After this initial success the British anticipated an easy task in breaking the line of gunboats.

At sunrise on the morning of June 22 Admiral Warren gave an order for the commencement of the attack. Pursuant to the plan 2,500 men landed to the west of the island. Simultaneously 50 barges, containing 1,500 sailors and marines, put out from the fleet and pointed their prows directly toward the island. They were led by the big green barge of Admiral Warren himself. So confident of victory without a struggle were the British officers that they took their shaving kits and pet dogs into the battle with them.

The 50 barges, loaded to the gunwales with men, created no alarm among the Americans. The sailors and marines had faced broadsides at point-blank range from the decks of men-of-war and their calm and self-possession spread among all ranks and steadied the whole force. Quietly the gunners trained their pieces on the approaching barges and awaited the order to fire. That order was not long in coming. Suddenly the American batteries blazed away with a tremendous roar that shook the surroundings while the smoke from the guns clouded the clear morning sky. The barges made perfect targets. One of the first to receive a direct hit was the barge of the Admiral, which filled with water and sank, carrying down all aboard it. Seeing the Admiral's barge go down, the whole attack was thrown into confusion. Men went overboard in heavy equipment and were drowned while the Americans poured a relentless fire into the struggling masses. Hardly had the attack begun when the few barges that had miraculously escaped the storm of shot and shell put about and scurried back to seek protection under the guns of the fleet. The attack on the flank was no more successful. This, too, the Americans had foreseen and posted men and guns in position to drive it off. When the British land force saw what had happened to the sailors and marines in the barges they, too, retreated, leaving the Americans in continued possession of the island. This spirited defense served as sufficient warning. Once more the invaders abandoned the idea of taking Norfolk.

Stung by the unexpected defeat and the loss of many of their comrades in the waters before Craney Island, the British now looked for a spot where they might wreak vengeance on the Americans for what had just occurred. Their eye lit upon the little town of Hampton across the Roads. Hampton was defended by a body of Virginia militia that, from all accounts, was not too strong and consequently seemed a likely prey. Thither the British sailed on June 24 and anchored opposite the town. To oppose them was a little band of 450 militiamen under Major Stapleton Crutchfield. Commanding the British flotilla was the redoubtable Admiral Sir George Cockburn.

On the morning of the 25th Sir George made a demonstration with the fleet before the town while General Beckwith, who commanded the military, dispatched a force of 2,500 men in surfboats to land below it. Conspicuous in this force was a detachment of French prisoners who had preferred action to the boredom of Dartmoor Prison and had volunteered for service in the American campaign. These French troops, uniformed in green, bore the name of Chasseurs Britanniques.

For a short time Crutchfield and his handful of men resisted the landing but he soon realized that the odds were hopelessly against him. His retreat quickly became a rout, every man looking to his own safety. The American loss was 30 killed and wounded, while the British lost 50 killed and wounded. The victors now proceeded without further molestation to make themselves at home in the town. Admiral Cockburn and General Beckwith landed and established their headquarters in the home of a Mrs. Westwood. A British officer killed in the action was interred with due religious ceremony in the Westwood yard.

The night passed quietly and the people of Hampton began to assume that they would escape without great annoyance. Next day, however, witnessed a sudden change in the temper of the invaders. In spite of the presence of the two commanding officers the soldiers engaged in a wild orgy that had no counterpart in the whole war. Houses were looted from ground floors to attics, several women were ravished and an aged bedridden man was deliberately murdered and his wife wounded in her effort to protect him from the fury of the soldiers.

When the news of the disgraceful happenings at Hampton became known a wave of indignation swept over the whole country. General Taylor, in Norfolk, promptly addressed a letter of protest direct to Admiral Warren. "The world," he said, "will suppose these acts to have been approved, if not executed, by the commanders, if suffered to pass with impunity; I am prepared for any species of warfare which you are disposed to prosecute. It is for the sake of humanity that I enter this protest."

The United States appointed two commissioners, Thomas Griffin and Robert Lively, to investigate the Hampton outrage. The commissioners having heard witnesses and collected the evidence, put their findings into a report in which they declared:

"We are sorry to say, that from all information we could procure, from sources too respectable to permit as to doubt, we are compelled to believe that acts of violence have been perpetrated which have disgraced the age in which we live. The sex hitherto guarded by the soldier's honor escaped not the rude assaults of superior force."

Against the charges of disorder General Beckwith defended his men on the ground that they were exacting reprisals for the shooting of the helpless crew of a British barge as it went down in the fight at Craney Island. As for the "assaults of superior force" upon the "sex hitherto guarded by the soldier's honor," he protected the British character by laying that to the Chasseurs Britanniques. As a result of their conduct at Hampton the French soldiers were made the scapegoats and dismissed from the service.

During the last few days of June the British fleet left Hampton and continued the reign of terror by sailing for the Potomac. On July 1 seven ships of the line, seven frigates, and a complement of smaller vessels entered the river and threw Washington and Alexandria into a panic. They came no closer than 70 miles from the capital. The fleet then returned to Chesapeake Bay and threatened Annapolis and Baltimore in turn, but departed without launching an attack. Cockburn then devoted his attention to the coasts of the Carolinas and Georgia, raiding the country about Pamlico Sound, seizing cattle, slaves and any other property that could be carried off. Not until the following year did he return to ruffle the accustomed calm of Chesapeake Bay.

If the summer of 1813 was the most distressing and painful one the delightful Chesapeake Bay country has ever had to endure, on the other hand it was not without its pleasant and amusing moments and many stories of the times have been handed down to become a part of local tradition.

There is, for example, the story that has to do with one Jacob Gibson, a well-to-do planter who owned Sharp's Island and an estate known as Marengo, on the mainland of the Eastern Shore of Maryland not far from the little town of St. Michael's. Gibson was one of those who believed that the best policy was to deal peaceably with the invaders. When Cockburn came up the bay he did not spare Sharp's Island but replenished his stores with its cattle, sheep and hogs. Nothing daunted Mr. Gibson boarded the Admiral's flagship, was hospitably entertained and received payment for his commandeered property. While this action squared him with Cockburn it aroused bitter criticism among his neighbors who spread the report that he had sold out to the enemy. Gibson heard of the gossip and determined to avenge himself.

St. Michael's, on the Miles River, was in constant fear of attack and prepared to meet it by raising fortifications, mounting a battery of guns and posting sentinels who were directed to give the alarm if the British fleet should put in an appearance. One fine day a lookout sighted offshore what looked to him like a barge with the British ensign flying from the masthead. His worst fears seemed justified when, over the water, came the sound of the martial beats of a drum. The sentinel immediately gave the alarm and, in a few minutes, the whole town of St. Michael's was in an uproar. Women and children fled to safety, taking along with them what possessions they could carry, while the men rushed to man the guns of the battery. Soon all was in readiness for an attack, and the gunners awaited the first hostile move of the barge which was approaching rapidly with its crew straining at the long oars.

Arrived opposite the town the barge shifted its course and passed by; and then, for the first time, the people of St. Michael's realized its true nature. For in the stern sat Jacob Gibson. The "drum" was an empty rum keg resting between his legs. The "British ensign" was his red bandanna handkerchief. The crew were his slaves, rowing him to his home at Marengo!

When they recovered from their fright the people of the town were outraged by the practical joke Gibson had played on them and threats were made against his life. In fact feeling ran so high that Gibson's only means of appeasing his neighbors was by presenting the town with a couple of cannons to add to its defenses.

The cannons proved useful a short time later when the British fleet did actually put in an appearance in the night and bombarded the town. But, according to local tradition, the defenders adopted the ruse of hanging lanterns in the trees. The British trained their guns on the lanterns and so overshot the town. The only blood shed in the attack was that of a chicken which had selected a bad night to roost in one of the trees.

One great annoyance to the people of the Chesapeake Bay country—who then, as today, were most sociably inclined—was the interruption caused to the social season. Eastern Shoremen who accepted invitations from their kinsmen in Baltimore never knew whether they could keep their engagements without being over-hauled and captured by a British man-of-war. Baltimoreans contemplating a quiet week end with relations on the Eastern Shore were similarly incommoded. To obviate this difficulty swift packets were employed. These smart little boats outsailed anything double their size and consequently could generally be counted upon to show their heels to an annoying stranger.

Such a packet was the *Messenger,* commanded by Captain Clement Vickers, which had succeeded many times in running the blockade. One fine summer morning the *Messenger* was on just such a trip, returning from Baltimore to Talbot with some dozen passengers aboard, a mixed and lively company of men, women and children and several colored servants to look after their comfort. Among them were a Mrs. Edith Dawson and her two little daughters. Off Poplar Island Captain Vickers sighted the British ship of the line, *Dragon,* 74 guns, under the command of Captain Barrie of the British Navy. Ordinarily Captain Vickers would have clapped on all sail and sped away, but on this occasion a calm set in and there was no escape. While the guns of the *Dragon* pointed threateningly at the *Messenger,* a barge put out from the man-of-war and was shortly alongside the *Messenger.* In the barge was a British naval officer who introduced himself as Lieutenant Pearson and informed Captain Vickers that the *Messenger* and all persons aboard were his prisoners.

Men, women and children, in a great state of alarm and not knowing what dreadful fate awaited them, were taken aboard the *Dragon.* Captain Barrie, however, proved to be a perfect gentleman. He apologized for the inconvenience he was causing them, explained that his orders forced him to hold the men and promised to release the women and children at the first opportunity. Then, still further to relieve their anxiety, he invited the whole party to dine with him in his cabin. A short time later all were seated at a sumptuous repast while Captain Barrie presided at the head of the table with all the consideration of a gracious host. Noticing that one of Mrs. Dawson's little daughters was eating with a pewter spoon, the gallant Captain sent a mess boy to his private lockers for a silver spoon to replace it.

When the meal was over and while arrangements were being

181

made for the departure of the women and children, Captain Barrie presented the silver spoon to little Miss Dawson and insisted that she keep it as a memento of her captivity. Mrs. Dawson in a few well-chosen words accepted the gift on behalf of her daughter, and the now historic spoon became a treasured possession of the Dawson family, to be handed down to succeeding generations.

The incident, unimportant in itself, is evidence that all of His Majesty's naval officers were not Cockburns. There were Barries as well who could hold their own with the Bay country people on the score of courtesy and social decorum.

CHAPTER SIXTEEN

"Don't Give Up the Ship"

IF JAMES LAWRENCE's father had had his way, James would have been a lawyer. But the youth from Burlington, New Jersey, early developed a longing for the sea. To a boy of 14 the lawbooks in his brother John's office at Woodbury seemed dull stuff and James displayed little aptitude for the tedious pursuit of Coke and Blackstone. So, after the death of the elder Lawrence, Brother John yielded to the boy's persuasion and helped him obtain the instruction needed as the foundation for a naval career.

At the age of 18 James entered naval service as a midshipman, took part in the Tripoli campaign as a lieutenant and exhibited such zeal in his profession that he was mentioned in dispatches by Decatur. Returning to the United States he served as first lieutenant on the *Constitution* for a time and then commanded in turn the *Vixen, Wasp, Argus* and *Hornet*. Between voyages he found time to woo and win a New York girl, and by the outbreak of the War of 1812 he had risen to the rank of master commandant.

January, 1813, found Lawrence in command of the *Hornet*, a sloop of 18 guns, which was cruising off San Salvador. In the harbor lay the British merchantman *Bonne Citoyenne* laden with a rich cargo, and Commodore Bainbridge ordered Lawrence to seize her when she came out while he sailed for New York in the *Constitution*. A few days later, however, the British ship of the line *Montagu*, of 74 guns, appeared on the scene and the *Hornet* had to seek refuge in the harbor. But, under cover of darkness, Lawrence managed to sail his ship safely past the guns of the *Montagu* and made good his escape. He then resumed his cruise northward along the coast keeping a sharp lookout for any quarry that came his way.

The *Hornet* on February 24 arrived off the mouth of the Demerara River, where she ran in with another sloop which proved to be His Majesty's *Peacock*, of 18 guns, under the command of Captain William Peake. Judging that the *Hornet* was a fair match for her, Lawrence determined at once to give battle, called the men to quarters and cleared the decks for action. The *Peacock* displayed an equal disposition to fight.

At 5:25 P.M. the two sloops had maneuvered until they were within half pistol-shot range of each other and Lawrence opened the engagement with a broadside from his larboard batteries. The *Peacock* shivered under the impact and Peake endeavored to bring her into position to rake. Lawrence, however, outwitted him, came about and brought his starboard battery to bear and delivered another devastating broadside. The *Peacock* was now severely damaged. She continued to fight gamely but the deadly broadsides of the *Hornet* were too much for her. As fast as the American gun crews could load and fire they continued to pour shot into the *Peacock* at close range. Within the brief space of 15 minutes the *Peacock* was a shambles and she struck her colors. Her commander had been slain; and of her crew of 130, five had been killed and 90 wounded. The *Hornet*, on the other hand, had come through the battle with the loss of only one man killed and two wounded. Lawrence now sent a party aboard the *Peacock*, which was sinking, to rescue the survivors. But before they could be got off the sloop went down, taking with her nine of her own men and three Americans.

The speed with which the victory had been won at so little cost was all the more surprising because the two vessels were so evenly matched. There were no extenuating circumstances. Lawrence had accomplished the feat through his own genius and the skill of his men in handling the guns. This was Lawrence's first encounter with the British and it very naturally inspired him and his men with an abounding confidence in themselves and scorn for British seamanship. It led to overconfidence that very soon was to prove disastrous.

As soon as news of the engagement between the *Hornet* and the *Peacock* reached the United States the country rang with the victory. The names of the two sloops lent themselves particularly well to the cartoonists who on this occasion outdid the poets in glorifying the victors. Lawrence arrived at Martha's Vineyard on March 19, crossed to the mainland and proceeded on a triumphal journey to

New York where he was treated to a sumptuous banquet attended by all the local dignitaries and given the freedom of the city. President Madison did him the honor of mentioning him in his message to Congress and even the British prisoners joined in the praise, if not the thanksgiving, expressing their admiration for the kindness and courtesy with which Lawrence had treated them. Sir Charles Napier, who happened to be in Bermuda, went so far as to say that "these Yankees, though so much abused, are really fine fellows."

Just about the time the *Hornet* and the *Peacock* were fighting it out, the frigate *Chesapeake*, of 38 guns, under the command of Captain Samuel Evans, set sail from Boston. Superstitious sailors whispered that there was a jinx on the *Chesapeake*. It was she, it will be recalled, that had suffered in the engagement with the *Leopard* several years before. Ill luck pursued her on this voyage. She crossed the Atlantic, cruised around the Canaries and the Cape Verde Islands, skirted the coast of South America and returned to Boston after a voyage of two months and for all her pains could claim no more than the capture of four merchantmen. Captain Evans was in bad health and had to be relieved of his command and the crew was in a very bad humor and on the verge of mutiny as the result of a dispute over the division of the prize money. At this juncture Lawrence was ordered to assume command.

In the month of May, blockading the port of Boston, was His Majesty's frigate *Shannon*, of 38 guns, with the *Tenedos* as consort. Commanding her was Captain Philip Bowes Vere Broke, as gallant an officer as his name suggests. Hearing that Lawrence had been promoted to the command of the *Chesapeake*, which was in Boston harbor, Broke took his pen in hand and composed the following challenge:

"As the Chesapeake appears now ready for sea, I request you will do me the favor to meet the Shannon with her, ship for ship, to try the fortunes of our respective flags. To an officer of your character it requires some apology for proceeding to farther particulars. Be assured, sir, it is not from any doubt I can entertain of your wishing to close with my proposal, but merely to provide an answer to any objection which might be made, and very reasonably, upon the chance of our receiving any unfair support."

Broke then obliged by revealing to his chosen adversary a de-

185

tailed account of his strength in personnel and weight of metal and the disposition of other British vessels. He concluded by designating the place of combat and indicating the signals his ship would fly.

Broke's invitation was, no doubt, quite sincere. He probably had no idea that he was asking Lawrence to accept odds. He·could not have known of the dissatisfaction among the *Chesapeake's* crew, or that the itemized list of personnel and armaments of the *Shannon* gave her a clear superiority over the *Chesapeake*, or that the first and second officers of the *Chesapeake* were ill and on leave. Had he been aware of all these handicaps a man of Broke's character would certainly not have couched his challenge in such terms as to make refusal a virtual admission of cowardice.

There were plenty of valid excuses had Lawrence cared to make use of them, but Broke had accurately gauged his man. Once Lawrence read the challenge the thought of declining it never entered his mind. Doubtless Lawrence, still flushed by his victory over the *Peacock*, imagined that Broke would prove to be as delicate a morsel as Peake had been.

June 1, 1813, was as rare a day as was ever sung by a New England poet. The people of Boston were up betimes, for the news spread rapidly that Lawrence had accepted Broke's challenge. The peace advocates and the Federalist leaders might grumble but the humbler citizens knew a good show when one was offered. This was the greatest opportunity that had come their way since Bunker Hill and they had no intention of letting their New England consciences interfere with the gratification of their sporting instincts. Early in the morning the spectators began to line the waterfront and climb to the housetops and other vantage points. They came in thousands, bringing their lunches with them. The principals were already on hand. In the harbor rested the *Chesapeake*, her tall slender masts towering above those of smaller craft, her hull bright with new paint, her guns frowning from the ports, her decks and rigging trim. She looked for all the world like a black panther ready to spring on her prey. All the while outside the harbor in the vicinity of Boston Light, the *Shannon*, with her sails set, darted back and forth like some monstrous bird of the sea.

Aboard the *Chesapeake* was Captain Lawrence, keeping his counsel. He had taken the precaution to dispatch a pilot boat to reconnoiter and make sure the *Shannon* was alone and, upon the boat's return, he received assurance from her master that Captain Broke was as good as his word. Despite appearances, things were not in the best of shape aboard the *Chesapeake*. The crew was still grumbling and, in a final effort at conciliation, Lawrence distributed among them checks for the disputed prize money and hoisted a white banner bearing in big letters the inscription, "Free Trade and Sailors' Rights." He was only partially successful. A rumor reached him that a Portuguese sailor was still active sowing dissension among the crew. But it was now too late to investigate the rumor or to call a court-martial.

In the absence of the first and second officers, Lawrence took with him as first officer Lieutenant Augustus Ludlow who had been third officer under Evans. Ludlow had a good record and there was no question of his courage, but he was very young. Lawrence was beginning the game with a crippled team. Yet the memory of the *Peacock* was still vivid and Lawrence relished the opportunity of repeating the performance before a gallery worthy of it.

The morning hours passed away, nothing happened and the crowd was beginning to grow restless. Then, promptly at noon, the *Chesapeake* raised anchor, set her sails and, as they filled, glided gracefully away from her mooring and gained speed rapidly as she put out into Massachusetts Bay amidst the cheers of her well-wishers on shore.

There was disappointment for the crowd, however. Even the best of naval antagonists cannot exactly stage their battles for the benefit of the onlookers. Before the frigates met they were well out of sight. Fate ordained that the populace of Salem were to have the best seats; the Bostonians had to be content with the distant boom of the guns.

As the *Chesapeake* sailed away Lawrence ordered her decks cleared for action and beat his crew to quarters. The opposing frigates bore away to a position 30 miles from Boston Light between Cape Cod and Cape Ann, each seeking the weather gauge. It was now midafternoon. At 4 P.M. the *Chesapeake* commenced the action by firing a single gun. The *Shannon* hove to and awaited the *Chesapeake* which swiftly bore down upon her. At 5:45 P.M. the frigates stood yardarm to yardarm at pistol-shot distance. The crucial moment had come and it was evident that this was to be a battle to the death; not a series of skillful maneuvers, but a trial of brute force, gun against gun and man against man.

The *Shannon* first fired her cabin guns, then followed with the rest from aft forward. As soon as the *Chesapeake's* guns bore she replied with a broadside. In a few moments the afternoon sun was blotted out by the smoke from the guns. For eight minutes the frigates lay side by side pouring shot into each other without either seeming to gain an advantage. Broke was a competent officer and he knew his crew. For weeks as the *Shannon* cruised along the coast he had rehearsed his men in their parts until they were perfect. Gradually the skill of the crew and the extra weight of the *Shannon's* metal began to tell. After 12 minutes much of the *Chesapeake's* sail had been shot away and she refused to answer to her helm. To make matters worse her mizzen rigging fouled the *Shannon's* forechains, exposing her to a raking fire.

Lawrence himself was slightly wounded. As the ships touched, he ordered his boarders up. As luck would have it, his regular bugler was not at hand. The substitute was so pale with fright that he couldn't get his wind up to blow. At last he managed to produce a blast, but it was so pathetically feeble it could not rise above the din of battle. The boarders didn't hear him. Verbal orders were then attempted, but they were misunderstood.

At this most critical moment the *Chesapeake's* reputation for bad luck asserted itself. Just when his indomitable will was most needed Lawrence dropped to the deck, mortally wounded. Loyal men picked up their captain and, with all the gentleness at their command, carried him below. There in the shadow, as the battle still raged above him, Lawrence gave his last order that has been passed down to generation after generation of men of the United States Navy in those immortal words, "Don't give up the ship."

But it was now too late. The gunners, in the absence of their officers who were stunned by the loss of Captain Lawrence, had fled to safety below decks. At the very moment that Lawrence gave his order, Captain Broke leaped upon the deck of the *Chesapeake* with 20 boarders behind him. He found nobody there to meet him. Lieutenant Ludlow made a desperate effort to rally the crew but before he succeeded he was struck down by a saber and critically wounded.

Broke called up 60 marines to reinforce him, but he didn't need them. The battle was already won. A British officer set to work hauling down the *Chesapeake's* colors and while doing so was killed by grapeshot fired from his own ship. In the engagement the *Chesapeake* lost 48 killed and 98 wounded. The *Shannon's* loss was little more than half of that, 26 killed and 58 wounded.

The victorious *Shannon* now set out triumphantly for Halifax with her prize in tow. Her celebration was subdued out of consideration for Captain Lawrence and Lieutenant Ludlow, both of whom had been transferred to her and now lay desperately wounded below. Lawrence died on the voyage and the body of the 32-year-old commander, at the order of Captain Broke, was draped with an American flag and laid reverently on the quarter-deck. Upon arrival in Halifax Ludlow's spirit followed that of his commander. The bodies of both officers were treated with full military honors and given a splendid funeral in which all the dignitaries of Halifax and 300 sailors and soldiers took part.

Having paid their own tribute the British authorities graciously granted the request for the return of the bodies to the United States. On August 18 they were landed at Salem where another state funeral was held. From there they commenced a journey to New York which consumed a whole month. At last, on September 17, the third and final obsequies were held and there in Trinity Churchyard the now much-honored but weary bodies were consigned to their final resting places.

While England exulted over the victory with bonfires and illuminations throughout the kingdom, the United States mourned its dead and paid tribute to the glory they had left behind them. Now that the battle was over and almost before the corpses of Lawrence and Ludlow were cold the leaders in New England took occasion to rebuke the populace for the unseemly interest it had displayed in the engagement. Josiah Quincy sponsored a resolution which was pushed through the Massachusetts Senate by his fellow Federalists and which read:

"Resolved, as the sense of the Senate of Massachusetts, that in a war like the present, waged without justifiable cause, and prosecuted in a manner which indicates that conquest and ambition are its real motives, it is not becoming a moral and religious people to express any approbation of military or naval exploits which are not immediately connected with the defense of our sea coast and soil."

That resolution, denying to American heroes the recognition of deeds well done, stands as a lasting illustration of the lengths to which political prejudices and partisan feeling can drive otherwise reasonable and intelligent persons. This was "Mr. Madison's War," not New England's.

On June 18, three days after the passage of the Massachusetts Senate's resolution and 18 days after the encounter between the *Chesapeake* and the *Shannon*, the United States sloop *Argus*, of 18 guns, under the command of Lieutenant William Henry Allen, of Rhode Island, set sail from New York bearing the Honorable William H. Crawford, of Georgia, as Minister to France to succeed the late Joel Barlow. Three weeks later she put into Lorient where Mr. Crawford was landed. While in that port Lieutenant Allen learned that no British naval forces were at the moment in the English Channel or in the Irish Sea. He seized this auspicious occasion to carry the war into the enemy's waters.

Departing from Lorient the *Argus* rounded Land's End and for the next thirty days struck terror into the heart of British shipping. In the course of that brief space of time she captured and destroyed 20 merchant vessels and their cargoes to the total value of $2,000,-000. The ships were burned, the crews permitted to keep their personal belongings. The prisoners being too numerous for the limited accommodations of the *Argus* they were landed and released on parole. When the news got abroad that an American raider was at large within sight of the shores of England itself, insurance rates leaped to excessive figures and a storm of protest arose against the government which not only had not won the war but, apparently, was incapable of protecting shipping in home waters. The Admiralty bestirred itself and sent out men-of-war to scour the seas in search of the marauder.

August 13 proved to be unlucky for the *Argus*. For on that day she came up with and captured a merchantman that was on its way home from Oporto laden with a cargo of potent and palatable wine. After their strenuous month at sea the crew of the *Argus* were unable to resist such an inviting opportunity. In spite of Lieutenant Allen's efforts to prevent it, the captured wine was smuggled aboard the *Argus* and an orgy followed, lasting well into the night.

The cold, gray dawn of the "morning after" was breaking and many members of the crew were nursing headaches or sleeping off the effects of the party when a sail loomed on the horizon. The stranger was His Majesty's sloop *Pelican*, of 18 guns, commanded by Captain J. F. Maples. Allen aroused his men and by the sheer force of his will drove them stumbling to their stations. The decks were somehow cleared for action, the cannons loaded and all was made ready for battle.

There was not much time. At 6 A.M. the ships closed and delivered broadsides into each other. In the first exchange of fire Lieutenant Allen's leg was shot away and he was carried, bleeding, below. He was succeeded in command by his first officer who almost immediately was disabled. There remained on deck only one commissioned officer. For 30 minutes the *Argus* fought her adversary. The wine may have given her crew courage but it played havoc with their skill and their accuracy. The *Argus* was outmaneuvered and outshot until there was no more fight left in her and she had to strike her colors. Her wounded commander was transferred to the *Pelican* and given as considerate care as if he were a British officer; but he had lost much blood and died the next day. His body was landed at Plymouth and there interred with full military honors. The career of the *Argus* was brief, but the tough sloop and her resourceful commander had given the British Admiralty as good a scare as it had had in a number of years.

The third duel of the year between rival ships took place on September 1 off the coast of Maine. The adversaries were the United States *Enterprise*, 14 guns, Lieutenant William Burrows, and His Majesty's *Boxer*, 14 guns, Captain Samuel Blyth. The two men-of-war met near Pemaquid Point, closed to within half pistol-shot range at 3:20 P.M. and proceeded to pound each other in the accustomed manner. At 3:30 P.M. the *Enterprise* ranged ahead, crossed the *Boxer's* bow and raked her from stem to stern. By 4 P.M. the *Boxer* had received all the punishment she could take, but her colors were still flying. At this point in the engagement a British officer raised a trumpet and shouted through it that the *Boxer* was ready to strike. She couldn't because, as an act of bravado before she went into action, somebody had nailed her colors to the mast.

In this spirited contest between two small but evenly matched ships, the *Enterprise* lost two killed and 10 wounded; the *Boxer*, several killed and 17 wounded. Among the dead were the two commanders, Burrows and Blyth. Their bodies were brought ashore at Portland. They were given a joint and spectacular funeral, and buried side by side.

As the days grew shorter and winter approached in this second year of the war the superiority of the British Navy was beginning to tell. Only three United States frigates remained at sea—the *President*, 44; the *Congress*, 38; and the *Essex*, 32. The *Constitution* was in port under repair; the *United States* and the *Macedonian* were in the Thames River, Connecticut, blockaded by a British squadron. The *Adams* was under repair; the *John Adams*, the *New York* and the *Boston* had been declared unfit for further service. Of the brigs, all except the *Enterprise* had been captured.

Of the frigates at sea the *Essex* was the most successful. Her career as a commerce raider took her halfway around the world on a cruise that has become a classic in the honorable history of the United States Navy. Under the command of Commodore David Porter she set sail from Delaware Bay on October 28, 1812. Porter's orders were to join the *Constitution* and the *Hornet* which were cruising in southern waters under the command of Commodore Bainbridge. The *Essex* carried a crew of 319 men and was provisioned for a long voyage.

The *Essex* missed her rendezvous with Bainbridge's squadron, crossed the equator, and took a valuable prize in the capture of the British packet *Nocton*, which carried $50,000 in gold. A prize crew was put aboard the *Nocton* and she set sail for the United States but was recaptured before she arrived there. Porter, however, had stowed the $50,000 away on the *Essex*, thus providing himself with working capital for his enterprise.

The *Essex* next put in at the island of Fernando de Noronha. There Porter found waiting for him a message from Bainbridge, written in sympathetic ink, directing him to cruise to Cape Frio, north of Rio de Janeiro. Porter obeyed the order but, again failing to find Bainbridge, he set sail on January 26 for Cape Horn. On the

14th of February the *Essex* rounded the Cape, entered the Pacific and cruised up the coast of Chile. On March 5, the lofty, snow-clad peaks of the Andes came into view and, for the first time since entering the Pacific, the *Essex* dropped anchor, while her boats put ashore and returned with wild hogs which provided the crew with a welcome ration of fresh meat.

On March 14 the *Essex* entered the harbor of Valparaiso. A frigate flying the Stars and Stripes was a rare sight in that distant port and the officers and crew were welcomed and royally entertained with a series of banquets, balls and excursions. It was a pleasant contrast to the long, bleak voyage around the Horn and the monotony of life at sea. Porter, however, was not a man to waste his time on idle frivolities at the expense of the mission with which he had been intrusted. Within the space of a few days he revictualed and again put to sea.

The *Essex* had scarcely left Valparaiso behind when she came up with an American whaler whose captain reported that two other whalers had been captured by a Peruvian corsair that was cruising in the neighborhood. Porter went in search of the corsair, found her, released the American prisoners aboard her and recovered one of the whalers which he converted into a consort for the *Essex*. He was told that 20 British whalers were at work in the vicinity of the Galápagos Islands and set off in quest of this valuable game.

British whalers were vessels of from 300 to 400 tons, well armed and bearing letters of marque. From April to September Porter devoted his attentions to running them down and demoralizing the British whaling industry in that quarter. In the course of the summer he captured 12 of the whalers, 360 seamen, whale oil and other property to the estimated value of $2,500,000, a considerable sum in that day. He virtually lived off the enemy. Some of the ships he dispatched with their cargoes of oil to the United States to be sold as prizes. Others he converted into men-of-war until he had quite an impressive flotilla under his command. The best of them, the *Atlantic*, which mounted 18-lb. carronades, he converted into a cruiser and rechristened the *Essex Jr.*

Having succeeded in destroying the whaling fleet Porter determined next to cross the Pacific to the Marquesas, refit and return home. He set sail on October 2 and reached the islands on October

23. There he came upon a bitter war that was being waged between a tribe on the coast and a tribe in the hills. Forgetting for the time being the unpleasantness with Great Britain Porter embraced the cause of the coastal tribe which was being hard pressed. Thanks to the arrival of this powerful and unexpected ally, the coastal tribe soon won a decisive victory over the hill men. The gratitude of the tribesmen to Porter and the *Essex* was unbounded. With true Marquesan hospitality they presented their deliverers with their wives and daughters. There followed a highly romantic interlude.

But, as ever, Porter's call to duty transcended all mundane joys. All too soon the Commodore announced that it was time for the festivities to break up and for the sailors to go home. While Porter shepherded his crew aboard the *Essex,* the seductive Marquesan matrons and maids stood on the beach beating their breasts and uttering cries of lamentation. Their distress was too much for the gallant American seamen and an ominous grumbling spread among the crew and reached the ears of the Commodore. Porter faced up to the situation. He called the men on deck, told them of his authority over them and their duty under the articles of war. He then demanded that those who were ready to obey him stand on one side of the deck, those who were against him to take the other side. Of the whole crew only one man had the courage of his convictions. Porter directed this seaman to be put ashore, then gave the order to weigh anchor and sail. When last seen by his shipmates the lone American sailor, apparently content with his lot, was surrounded by the Marquesan matrons and maidens. What eventually became of him history fails to record.

The *Essex* recrossed the Pacific and again entered the port of Valparaiso on February 3, while the *Essex Jr.* cruised outside on guard against the enemy. The precaution was not misplaced for the news of Porter's escapades had spread abroad and the British Navy had received orders to run the *Essex* down and put an end to her career. Shortly after the arrival of the *Essex* at Valparaiso the *Essex Jr.* reported a British man-of-war approaching. She proved to be the frigate *Phoebe,* of 36 guns, under the command of Captain Hillyer, and she was accompanied by the *Cherub,* a sloop of 20 guns, Captain Tucker. The two ships entered the habor.

194

Valparaiso was ostensibly a neutral port and, therefore, no naval engagement could take place in the harbor without a violation of Chilean neutrality. Nevertheless, as the *Phoebe* entered she sailed close to the *Essex* in a decidedly threatening manner. She carried a complement of 329 men and boys, while the *Cherub* had a crew of 180. The *Essex* had by now been reduced to 225 men, the *Essex Jr.* to 60. The weight of metal, too, was on the side of the British. However, as the *Phoebe* approached Porter cleared for action and shouted through his trumpet to Hillyer that if the *Phoebe* so much as touched the *Essex* he would fire. Hillyer luffed and his jib boom was thrown across the *Essex's* forecastle. In that position the *Essex* had the *Phoebe* at her mercy. Hillyer apologized in the nick of time declaring that the maneuver was accidental. Porter, against his better judgment but out of respect for Chilean neutrality, accepted the apology. He was destined never again to have such an opportunity.

The *Phoebe* obtained the supplies for which she had come and then left the harbor, cruising outside in wait for the *Essex*. By way of entertainment she hoisted a large banner inscribed "God and Our Country. British Sailors' Best Rights, Traitors Offend Them." Porter, not to be outdone, mobilized the literary talent aboard the *Essex* and produced two banners, the first reading, "Free Trade and Sailors' Rights," the second, "God, Our Country, Liberty; Tyrants Offend Them."

Pleased with his handiwork, Porter hoisted the banners; and, with these and all flags flying, he weighed anchor and sailed proudly out with the intention of running the blockade. Scarcely had the *Essex* reached open water with all sails set when a squall struck her, sweeping away her main topmast and the men on it who were reefing. The *Phoebe* at once gave chase while the *Essex*, badly crippled, endeavored to regain the safety of the neutral port.

Porter made the shelter of the bay while the *Phoebe* bore down upon him, followed by the *Cherub*. It was apparent that, regardless of the respect owed the Chileans and of Porter's consideration previously shown him, Hillyer this time meant business. The disabled *Essex* cleared her decks for action. The *Phoebe* took up an advantageous position and at 5 P.M. opened fire. The *Cherub* meanwhile joined the *Phoebe* in the attack. It was some time before the *Essex*, crippled as she was, could get her guns to bear in order to reply. At last Porter managed to train three of her stern guns on the enemy and drove them off. The relief was only temporary: the *Phoebe* and *Cherub* shortly returned to the attack.

Porter, in desperation, tried to close with the *Phoebe* in order to board her, but she drew away, the while pouring a murderous fire into the *Essex*. He next endeavored to run ashore and land his crew but, as luck would have it, the wind shifted, subjecting the decks of the *Essex* to a severe raking. The dead and dying were strewed about him and the cries of the wounded rose above the din of battle; still Porter marshaled the survivors and fought on. A whole hour passed while Porter clung to the vain hope that something might turn the tide of battle. For one hour more the *Essex* shuddered and shook under the terrific pounding of the guns of the *Phoebe* and *Cherub*. The defenders now numbered only a handful. Reluctantly Porter admitted that he could ask no more of his men. He struck his colors. Of the men of the *Essex* who had gone into battle, 58 were killed outright, 66 were wounded and 31 were missing. Only 75 effectives remained. Evidence of the one-sidedness of the engagement lay in the fact that the British loss amounted to only five killed and 10 wounded.

Thus, disastrously but gloriously, ended the cruise of the *Essex*. Porter and the survivors were immediately paroled, the *Essex Jr.* was turned into a cartel ship and set sail for home. Upon the arrival in the United States the public generously overlooked the loss of the frigate and recalled only the feats the *Essex* had performed. The Commodore and his men received a welcome that befitted returning heroes.

Hindsight is easier than foresight. Had the United States naval officers of the day been able to look a little farther into the future they might have possessed a new weapon which, if not decisive in its effect, would at least have been more valuable to them than to the British. At the turn of the century an inventor, bearing the name of Robert Fulton, had conceived the idea of blowing up ships from beneath the water, and he proceeded quietly to work on the idea. By the year 1805 he had made so much progress that he felt prepared to give a demonstration of his invention. As the British Navy was the greatest sea power in the world Fulton journeyed to London and made his offer to the Admiralty. The Admiralty consented to the demonstration which took place in English waters on October 15, 1805.

For his experiment Fulton used the Danish brig *Dorothea*. His new weapon consisted of two torpedoes attached to each other by a 70-foot rope. The torpedoes were suspended 15 feet underwater from rowboats. Each of the torpedoes was filled with a charge of 180 pounds of powder to which was connected a time clock set to go off in 18 minutes. The rowboats were floated by the tide in the direction of the spot where the *Dorothea* rode at anchor. The connecting rope struck the *Dorothea's* hawser and stopped, while the rowboats and the torpedoes beneath them continued on until they were respectively alongside and under the *Dorothea*. In exactly 18 minutes there occurred a violent explosion and when the smoke cleared the *Dorothea* was seen to have been blown in two and to be sinking rapidly.

The demonstration was a complete success. In fact, from the Admiralty's standpoint, it was too great a success. The torpedoes had almost as devastating an effect upon the Admiralty as they had had upon the *Dorothea*. For the power of the British Navy rested primarily upon the preponderance of its men-of-war over all other navies. And here was a simple device, a couple of rowboats, a 70-foot length of rope and a few hundred pounds of powder, capable of blowing the most magnificent and costly man-of-war to kingdom come in a matter of minutes. The Earl of St. Vincent had good reason to remark that William Pitt would be a fool to encourage a mode of warfare which they, who commanded the sea, did not want and which, if successful, would deprive them of it. The Earl's view prevailed and Fulton and his torpedoes were sent packing.

Discouraged, but not hopeless, Fulton next appealed to the United States Government. Jefferson, Madison and members of Congress listened sympathetically to his proposal and a sum of $5,-000 was voted to defray the costs of a demonstration in New York harbor. The experiments were to be made under the joint supervision of a commission and Commodore Rodgers and Commodore

Chauncey, representing the United States Navy. This time Fulton directed his torpedoes against the sloop *Argus* and, unfortunately, the experiment failed.

The commissioners, nevertheless, returned a favorable report, but not the representatives of the Navy. They did not have the same excuse as the Earl of St. Vincent, but doubtless as naval commanders they felt that they had about all they could do in an engagement to maneuver against the enemy, contend with his raking broadsides and dodge the shots of sharpshooters aimed at them from the tops. Probably they did not relish the added risk of being blown up from underwater. Whatever their motives they obstructed further progress by declaring Fulton's scheme to be wholly impracticable, thus "damning the torpedoes" as successfully as a distinguished admiral was to do some 50 years later.

What Fulton's torpedoes might have accomplished had he received encouragement and means to perfect his invention is a matter of conjecture. Even without encouragement they had considerable nuisance value. There were various instances of patriotic experimenters who endeavored to row alongside anchored British men-of-war and blow them up. Some of the experiments were almost successful. Captain Hardy, of the *Ramillies*, while blockading New London, was so annoyed by these machinations that at last he lost patience and announced that if the Americans did not stop this cruel and unheard-of mode of warfare he would retaliate by destroying their towns and desolating their country.

The peace party, as usual, accepted the British viewpoint and added the torpedoes to their long list of outrages attributed to the Madisonian war. They refused to listen to the arguments of the editor of the pro-administration Philadelphia *Aurora* who inquired: "We would respectfully solicit the pious men to explain to us the difference between waging war with submarine machines and with aerial destructive weapons—fighting under water or fighting under air." A generation was to pass before torpedoes became as eminently respectable as pistol bullets and cannon balls.

Though the American operations on the sea in 1813 were not without many instances of individual glory, they failed to approach the achievements of 1812. British war vessels, sunk or captured, reached a total of only 754 tons as against American naval losses of

1,711 tons. In the matter of merchant prizes, the score was considerably better. The American Navy captured a total of 79 merchantmen as compared with 46 in 1812. Most of the American frigates were now bottled up in port. The business of harassing British mercantile trade was being confined more and more to the privateers, as had originally been intended.

CHAPTER SEVENTEEN

Perry on Lake Erie

GENERAL WILLIAM HULL's surrender at Detroit in 1812 and General William Henry Harrison's costly and ineffectual efforts to reach the town during the winter of 1813 had one salutary effect. The commanders in the field, the War Department, where General John Armstrong had replaced Dr. Eustis as secretary, and an impatient public smarting for revenge at last were convinced that there was no hope of taking and holding Detroit until the Americans should have assured their line of communications by gaining control of Lake Erie. (See Map I, p. 97)

At this very critical moment a young officer, ambitious to have a part in the glorious deeds of the American Navy, was eating his heart out in comparative obscurity and inactivity as commander of a flotilla of gunboats at Newport, Rhode Island. At the age of 15 Oliver Hazard Perry entered the Navy as a midshipman. He saw service with Preble at Tripoli, and though by accident and to his keen disappointment he missed most of the fighting, he had abundant opportunity to learn the art of his profession from that fine old sailor as well as to broaden his outlook by extensive travel in Italy and other countries bordering on the Mediterranean. In 1810 he had been promoted to the rank of lieutenant. Now 27 years old, handsome, bold, and a natural leader, he was ripe for any daring exploit. With rare discernment the Navy Department, looking for a man to do the job on Erie, chose Perry. On February 17, 1813, he received orders to report to Commodore Chauncey at Sackett's Harbor and to take his best men along with him.

Perry lost little time bidding farewell to his gunboats. He selected 150 of his most capable seamen and most promising officers for service on the Lakes. In two days' time the detachment, split up into three parties of 50 men each, had left Newport. Perry followed after them, making the trip over the snow-covered roads of a New England winter by sleigh.

Perry's first objective was Lebanon, Connecticut, where his father and mother were living in retirement. There, too, was Perry's younger brother, Alexander, a boy 13. The elder Perry was himself an old Navy man so that Mrs. Perry was quite accustomed to brief reunions and hurried leave-takings. Nevertheless, this one-night visit of Oliver Hazard was probably the most difficult she had ever had to face. When Alexander saw his brother and heard from his lips the prospect of adventure, he was impatient to go along.

Boys as young as Alexander frequently left home to begin their careers at sea, but Mrs. Perry must have hesitated when she reflected upon the long journey through a frozen wilderness, possible encounters with hostile Indians on the way and, finally, the inevitable battle to wrest Lake Erie from the British. On the other hand, she must have reflected that Alexander could not have a more zealous and trusted protector than Oliver Hazard.

What arguments may have been presented and what objections raised to the proposal we do not know. But when, in the morning, Oliver Hazard was ready to resume his journey, Alexander was in the sleigh with him. The elder Perrys were to have days of anxiety and suspense no doubt, but they had the gratification of knowing that the younger generation of Perrys were breeding true to the old stock.

From Lebanon the brothers journeyed to Hartford where they changed to a mail coach which carried them to Albany. There they awaited the arrival of Commodore Chauncey from Sackett's Harbor and Oliver Hazard met for the first time his new commander. The two men found themselves mutually agreeable and the meeting was entirely amicable, giving no indication of the misunderstandings that were to follow. The worst stretch of the journey still lay ahead of them, from Albany to Sackett's Harbor. It took the travelers through dense forests and over trails and frozen lakes with the temperature well below zero. February had given way to March when they arrived at their destination and Perry had his first dreary view of one of the Great Lakes with which his name was to be forever after associated. There he remained for two weeks before he received his final instructions from Chauncey and set out for Presqu' Isle (now Erie, Pennsylvania) which, his orders told him, was to be his headquarters.

Presqu' Isle was situated on the south shore of Lake Erie. It had a good harbor lying behind the peninsula which gave the place its name. The entrance to it was protected by a sand bar which, while it was effective in keeping large hostile ships out, also provided a serious problem in getting large ships into the open lake. The base had been chosen through the instrumentality of Daniel Dobbins, an experienced lake captain, who made a trip to Washington to convince President Madison that this was the logical place for the building of a fleet. Thanks to the energy of Captain Dobbins two brigs and three gunboats were already on the ways.

Having inspected his new base Perry realized the immensity of the task that lay before him. There was timber in abundance in the neighboring forests, but all other supplies and equipment that go into the building, rigging and arming of ships and the men to do the building had to be transported at great expense from miles away. Most of the materials to be had were at Pittsburgh, a four days' journey.

To add to his difficulties Perry knew that the British had a fleet on the lake under the command of Captain Finnis and that they knew what was going on at Presqu' Isle. No telling when they might descend on the place, which was virtually defenseless, and destroy it. Perry organized a guard but, because of lack of arms, its effectiveness was highly doubtful. Eventually he obtained the services of some Pennsylvania militia, but the men were undisciplined, ignored the commands of their officers and did a faltering job.

Nevertheless, in spite of all the handicaps and because of the driving power of Perry and Captain Dobbins, work went on apace. Early in May the three gunboats were launched. Finally, on May 24, the two large brigs took the water. Perry, however, was not there to attend the launching for he had gone to join Dearborn on the Niagara front and to handle the flotilla in the landing of the troops and the successful attack on Fort George. His important part in that engagement has already been described. It tested him under enemy fire and gave him other valuable experience.

The capture of Fort Erie in the same campaign was vitally important from Perry's standpoint because it released five vessels which were on the Niagara River below Black Rock, and which were unable to pass into Lake Erie under the guns of the fort so long as the stronghold was in British hands. One of these five ships was the schooner *Caledonia* which, six months before, had been taken from under the guns of Fort Erie in the night attack led by Lieutenant Jesse D. Elliott. With the greatest exertion these vessels were warped up the swift waters above the falls to Buffalo. Perry embarked on the *Caledonia* and the flotilla set sail for Presqu' Isle, keeping a sharp lookout for Captain Finnis and his British squadron on the way.

Finnis would have found Perry's flotilla easy prey. Perry was beginning to get a reputation for good luck and surely it was with him on this occasion. For not until his ships had reached Presqu' Isle and were safely over the bar did Finnis put in an appearance and then he was too late to do any harm. Perry was pleased to find that during his absence construction had gone speedily forward and all the ships building were nearing completion. By July 10 the little fleet was ready. The two 20-gun brigs were christened respectively the *Lawrence,* in honor of the heroic commander of the *Chesapeake* who had been a personal friend of Perry's, and the *Niagara.*

Now came the question of manning the fleet. The government in Washington and General Harrison at his headquarters at Seneca on the Sandusky River began to grow impatient and wrote to Perry demanding action. Little did they appreciate Perry's predicament. The trouble lay in the fact that men destined for Perry were sent by way of Chauncey at Sackett's Harbor. Chauncey, who was attempting to build up his naval force to wrest Lake Ontario from Sir James Yeo, the British naval commander in that quarter, was reluctant to send any men on to Perry. Perry wrote Chauncey beseeching letters. In return he got a handful of men who, apparently, were the dregs of Chauncey's forces, without experience and most of them sick into the bargain.

Meanwhile the British had been active assembling a fleet at Fort Malden, on the Detroit River. There the *Detroit*, a brig of 17 guns which was designed to be the flagship, was nearing completion. In command of the fleet and supplanting Captain Finnis was Captain Robert H. Barclay, a capable officer of the Royal Navy, 32 years of age. He had served under Nelson in the battle of Trafalgar and, like his famous commander, had lost an arm in the service. Perry knew that he had a worthy adversary and one who had had more practical experience than he. Barclay several times cruised with his squadron off Presqu' Isle, challenging Perry to come out and fight, but without the necessary complement of men Perry could not accept the challenge.

By the end of July Perry counted only about 300 officers and men, and he needed at least 500. Those he had were a motley group and he was especially short of experienced officers. Nevertheless he concluded that he could wait no longer. On August 1 he learned through spies that Barclay had been invited to attend a dinner given in his honor, and the disappearance of the British fleet from off Presqu' Isle seemed to confirm the report. Perry decided to seize this favorable opportunity to undertake the perilous task of getting his fleet over the bar and into the lake. No difficulty was anticipated in getting the smaller ships across, but the *Lawrence* and *Niagara*, when laden, drew nine feet of water and there were but six feet over the bar under normal conditions. On the day chosen an offshore wind sprang up driving the waters of the lake toward the Canadian shore and reducing the depth over the bar by an extra foot or so.

Perry, however, refused to abandon the attempt. Two of the gunboats were crossed and took up a defensive position outside the harbor. It was decided to try the *Lawrence* first while the *Niagara* stood by inside the bar with her decks cleared and guns shotted, ready for instant action if the British fleet should appear. But, halfway across, the *Lawrence* stuck in the mud. Releasing her entailed the laborious task of removing all her guns and ballast. Even that expedient failed to bring the desired result and as a last resort use was made of "camels," airtight floats which were placed on each side of the brig and lifted her when the water in them was pumped out. During this operation the ropes holding the camels broke and the whole operation had to be repeated. Four days were consumed in this laborious work and all the while Perry felt grave anxiety over the imminent possibility that Barclay would reappear and catch his fleet in this embarrassing situation.

The next task was to get the *Niagara* over and this was accomplished with less difficulty and delay. Not until then did Barclay arrive on the scene. Seeing the two brigs at the mouth of the harbor and mistakenly assuming that they were ready for battle and about to attack him he hurriedly made off and missed a splendid opportunity. Barclay was reluctant to fight until the *Detroit* was with his fleet.

Perry's luck once more asserted itself. On August 10 the long-awaited reinforcements arrived from Sackett's Harbor under Elliott, who now had the rank of captain. The party numbered in all 102, including a half dozen or so officers of whom Perry was in particular need. Perry at once named Elliott as his second in command and gave him the *Niagara*, permitting him also to select his own personnel from the men he had brought with him.

The fleet set out on a trial cruise to the west end of the lake to try out the ships and give the crews experience in handling them and firing the guns. This practice was to continue for a whole month and it probably had much to do with the eventual outcome of the battle. Perry claimed that he had in his whole company less than 100 first-class seamen and of these only 40 knew anything about guns. But among them were some veterans of the *Constitution* who were of vast help in leavening the lump.

This period of training was enlivened by a spirited correspondence with Chauncey. As we have seen, Perry complained bitterly of the difficulty of getting men from the Commodore and of the quality of the men sent him. In a letter dispatched by Elliott the Commodore answered Perry in kind, Perry lost his temper and offered to resign then and there. He probably would have done so had not the Secretary of the Navy urged him to remain while Chauncey wrote another and more sympathetic letter which removed the sting of the first.

At Seneca General Harrison had assembled a force of 8,000 men. He and Perry met and discussed the plan of operations for the invasion of Canada. The proposal was made that the army be put aboard the fleet but this Perry was unwilling to hazard until he had disposed of Barclay. He did, however, agree to make Put-in-Bay his base. It lay off what is now Port Clinton, Ohio, and afforded close communication between the fleet and the army.

On August 25 Perry located the enemy fleet in the Detroit River. But at this point he was stricken with what the doctors of the day described as "bilious remittent fever" and his plans for immediate attack had to be abandoned. The disease was widespread throughout the fleet. A week later, though still weak from his illness, Perry sailed toward Fort Malden prepared to give battle. But the *Detroit* was not yet completely fitted so Barclay refused the challenge and retired to the protection of the fort's guns. Perry was now strengthened by 100 Kentuckians, loaned him by Harrison. They had never seen ships of the size of the *Lawrence* and the *Niagara* and only a few of them had had experience even with river boats. But they brought their famous rifles with them and were prepared to serve as marines.

Barclay was having even greater trouble than Perry in arming and manning his ships. Sir James Yeo, Barclay's superior on Lake Ontario, followed Chauncey's example by saving the best men available for himself and sending only the castoffs to Barclay. According to Barclay he never had more than 50 regular seamen in his force of a total of about 450. The remainder were composed of Canadian volunteers and 240 regular soldiers from General Proctor's command. His fleet was composed of six ships of which the four largest were the *Detroit*, 19 guns; the *Hunter*, 10 guns; the *Queen Charlotte*, 17 guns; and the *Lady Prevost*, 13 guns. The two smaller ships were the *Chippawa*, one gun and two swivels, and the *Little Belt*, 3 guns. Because of the difficulties of transportation, similar to those that had handicapped Perry, heavy ordnance was scarce in Upper Canada and Barclay was driven to the extremity of arming the *Detroit* with land guns stripped from the fort at Malden. The fleet carried a total of 63 guns.

To oppose Barclay, Perry counted primarily on the *Lawrence*, 20 guns, and the *Niagara*, 20 guns. His force was completed by the *Caledonia*, 3 guns, the *Ariel*, *Scorpion*, *Somers*, *Porcupine*, *Tigress* and *Trippe*. His fleet mounted altogether 54 guns to Barclay's 63. Perry enjoyed a superiority in tonnage of about 8 to 7. His broadside at close range was 900 pounds against the British fleet's 460. At long range the respective batteries were more nearly equal though here, too, Perry had an advantage of 288 pounds to the enemy's 195. But that was assuming he could bring all his ships into action at once.

While the *Lawrence* and *Niagara* were armed chiefly with 34-

pound carronades which could throw a heavy broadside at close range, they were no match at all for the *Detroit* and *Queen Charlotte* at long range since the latter were armed chiefly with long guns. Realizing his overwhelming superiority at close range, Perry planned to come to immediate grips with the enemy and endeavored to impress his strategy upon his subordinates. Barclay, realizing his own strength and weakness, was equally determined to fight the battle at long range.

Through a friend in Malden, Perry came into valuable information. He learned how Barclay planned to dispose his ships and, consequently, could dispose his own accordingly. He also learned that the food supply was growing scarce at Malden, where Proctor had to issue 10,000 rations a day to the Indian warriors and their families. The only way supplies could be brought to Malden was by the lake so Barclay would have to come out and force a decision. Every indication led Perry to the belief that the battle for which he had waited so long was imminent. He continued to keep on the alert in Put-in-Bay.

On September 9 Perry called his lieutenants into conference, outlined in detail what each ship would be expected to do and issued written orders. He reserved for his own ship, the *Lawrence*, the honor of opposing Barclay's flagship, the *Detroit*. To the *Hunter* he assigned the *Caledonia*, to the *Queen Charlotte* the *Niagara* and to the *Lady Prevost* and *Little Belt* the *Somers, Porcupine, Tigress* and *Trippe*. Since he had been told that the *Queen Charlotte* would lead the British line he directed Elliott to take the corresponding position in the American line. The gunboats *Ariel* and *Scorpion* were to flank the *Niagara* so as to use their long guns until the *Niagara* could close with the enemy and bring her carronades into play. All the ships were to keep in close order, half a cable length apart.

Perry had seen to the making in Presqu' Isle of a large square flag of blue muslin bearing in large white letters Lawrence's last words, "Don't Give Up the Ship." Before the conference broke up he displayed it before his officers and explained that when it was hoisted to the mainmast on the *Lawrence* they were to take it as the signal for the whole fleet to go into action.

Shortly after dawn of September 10 a lookout at the masthead of the *Lawrence* gave the warning, "Enemy in sight." As the sun rose Barclay's fleet was discovered in line of battle silhouetted against the sky at a distance of from five to six miles. A light morning shower cleared the air and was followed by a perfect September day with hardly more than enough wind to ripple the waters of the lake. Perry weighed anchor and tried to pass the islands in the bay and still keep the weather gauge. But when he was told by his sailing master that this might take all day he decided to surrender the advantage to the enemy and sailed boldly out into open water.

Here again the proverbial Perry luck came to the rescue for the wind shifted in his favor and he proceeded to bear down upon the British fleet which, still in line, awaited his coming. Perry then perceived that Barclay had changed his order of battle and that the *Detroit* was leading the British line. He promptly directed the *Niagara* to shift position accordingly and placed the *Lawrence* in the American van. Barclay now moved forward to meet the Americans.

Perry realized that the engagement would likely take place about noon, the hour of the midday meal. With rare thoughtfulness in this moment of excitement and suspense he ordered food to be served his men so that they would fight on full stomachs. When the crews had completed this hasty repast they stood to their guns and awaited the battle.

The suspense did not last long. The fleets now approached to within a mile and a half of each other. At 11:45 A.M. the Americans heard from their stations a bugle on the *Detroit* sounding the call to action. Immediately thereafter a gunner on the *Detroit* directed a 24-lb. shot from one of the long guns at the *Lawrence*. It fell short. Five minutes later a second shot struck the *Lawrence*, killing a member of the crew. Perry ordered the *Scorpion* and the *Ariel* to fire their long guns, but though the shots reached the *Detroit*, they were unable to penetrate her stout timbers and did little damage.

Owing to the lightness of the breeze the smaller ships, the *Somers*, *Porcupine*, *Tigress* and *Trippe*, which brought up the end of the line, had fallen behind until a mile lay between them and the *Lawrence* at the head of the column. Through his trumpet Perry gave the command to close up and it was relayed from ship to ship. Yet, according to Barclay's later account of the battle, the *Caledonia* and the *Niagara*, in disregard of Perry's order, continued to fight at long range, the *Niagara* using only two guns while her powerful broadside of carronades remained idle.

Meanwhile the British fleet, disregarding all the other American ships, centered its fire on the *Lawrence*. Perry fired one broadside but it fell short. At 12:15 P.M. the *Lawrence* was within pistol-shot range of the *Detroit* and her guns began to bear. Alone and unaided save by the *Scorpion* and the *Ariel,* which fought valiantly, the *Lawrence* battled the *Detroit* and the *Queen Charlotte*. For two solid hours Perry continued the unequal struggle, pounding the two enemy ships but receiving terrific punishment himself. Throughout the conflict young Alexander remained steadfast beside his brother. He was struck by some flying object but escaped serious injury.

Every minute brought the destruction of the *Lawrence* nearer. The *Queen Charlotte* had moved out of line and closer to the *Detroit* the better to direct her fire on Perry's flagship. But the *Niagara* did not follow. The *Lawrence's* rigging was shot away, her sails torn to ribbons by grape and canister, her spars splintered and many of her guns torn from their mountings. Of the crew of 103 which entered the battle, 22 lay on the decks, dead or crying out in their last agonies; 61 were nursing their wounds. The ship's bay was above water and shells tore through it, killing men as they lay on the operating table. All of Perry's officers were killed or wounded. He alone appeared to lead a charmed life. Though with his usual courage he exposed himself freely to enemy fire, not so much as a splinter touched him. The *Lawrence* was fast becoming a useless, unmanageable hulk. Only 20 whole men remained to work the guns. Defeat appeared inevitable.

At last the *Lawrence's* guns were silenced. Throughout the heat of battle Perry's men had asked each other what had become of the *Niagara* and why she had not moved in to the rescue. Now, when hope had all but vanished, they got an answer. From the deck of his ship Elliott had seen the destruction wrought on the *Lawrence*. As the flagship lay helpless and silent and no orders came from her he must have assumed that Perry was dead. At any rate Elliott acted as though he thought so. He ordered the *Caledonia* to close with the *Hunter* and he himself moved the *Niagara* toward the front of the line.

Even then Elliott did not go to the rescue of the *Lawrence* but put the flagship between him and the enemy. He was to have a startling surprise, for he had reckoned without true knowledge of his superior. As the two ships came abreast at a distance of half a mile a rowboat put out from the *Lawrence*. Five men were in the boat. Four of them labored at the oars while the fifth stood in the stern. That fifth man was Perry.

Seeing the *Niagara*, fresh and unscathed, entering the conflict Perry was suddenly seized with an inspiration indicative of his genius and his indomitable will. He would undertake what few commanders before or since have done—transfer his flag to another ship in the very midst of the battle. Perry ordered a boat over the side. One account has it that he fought the engagement in a dark-blue undress uniform; another that he wore a red flannel shirt. However that may be, he now had on his full-dress uniform and boarded the rowboat which took off for the *Niagara*. He carried, folded over his arm, the blue flag bearing Lawrence's last words.

When the *Lawrence* ceased fire Barclay assumed that Perry was about to surrender and chivalrously withheld the fire of his own ships. But, seeing the boat put out, he at once divined Perry's intentions. Immediately the fire of the British fleet was directed against the boat. Though a hail of shells and bullets fell about them, the brave little group made the perilous trip to the *Niagara* without harm and clambered aboard. There Perry met Elliott face to face.

Whatever may have been Perry's feeling of indignation at Elliott's failure to come to his rescue he did not show it. Elliott suggested bringing up the lagging gunboats and Perry told him to do so. Elliott repeated Perry's gallant action by transferring to the *Somers* and fought the ship well throughout the rest of the battle.

On leaving the *Lawrence* Perry turned over the command to Lieutenant John J. Yarnall with authority to do as he saw fit. Since the guns had been silenced and only a handful of men had survived the carnage Yarnall could see no other course but to surrender. Just as the poor, battered *Lawrence* struck her colors, Perry in his new ship bore down upon the British line and smashed his way through. To his left lay the *Lady Prevost* and the *Chippawa*, to his right the *Detroit*, the *Hunter* and the *Queen Charlotte*. As Perry passed between them his carronades poured broadsides to right and left. The *Niag-*

ara came about and repeated the performance. Inspired by the gallantry of their leader the smaller American ships entered the fray. In maneuvering the *Queen Charlotte* her sailing master misjudged his distance and ran his ship afoul of the *Detroit*. At last, after two and a half hours of fighting, Perry succeeded in carrying out his original plan. With the exception of the *Lawrence,* which was too far gone to take part, he was using the whole of his striking power at close quarters. The Americans now pounded the British more mercilessly than the British had, a short while before, pounded the *Lawrence.*

Confusion seized the British fleet. Barclay was wounded and his ships were badly crippled by the superior weight of metal hurled against them. Once the tide of battle turned it continued with a rush. Eight minutes after Perry broke the line the *Detroit* struck her colors. When the rest of the fleet saw the flagship surrender, they too gave up the struggle. That is, all of them except the *Chippawa* and the *Little Belt* which tried to escape. They were hotly pursued and soon overhauled and captured.

The battle ended, Perry returned to the *Lawrence* to receive the surrender. His first question as he put foot on the deck now slippery with blood and strewn with the dead and the wounded was for his young brother. Alexander could not be found and it was feared that he might have been swept overboard. A search of the ship was made and, according to contemporary accounts, the boy at last was found sound asleep in a bunk, completely exhausted by the excitement of the day. He was destined to accompany Oliver Hazard on his triumphal return to Newport and later to pursue a career in the United States Navy.

When the British officers came aboard Perry received them graciously and, with a consideration worthy of a hero, declined their swords. He inquired solicitously for Captain Barclay, the prelude to a lasting friendship between the two men. Then, taking an old letter from his pocket, he scrawled with a pencil the note to General Harrison that has become immortal:

"We have met the enemy and they are ours; two ships, two brigs, one schooner and one sloop. Yours with great esteem and respect. O. H. Perry."

Soon the news of the victory had passed from one end of the

211

country to the other; and, as usual, served as the occasion for more banquets and illuminations, more oratory, more drinking of toasts and the customary outpouring of song and verse from scores of bad rhymesters. The Legislature of Pennsylvania voted its thanks and a gold medal to Perry, a silver medal to every man who was with him in the battle. Congress, not to be outdone, voted its thanks and ordered medals struck to both Perry and Elliott.

The captured fleet was appraised at $225,000, and an equivalent amount of prize money was distributed among officers and men. Perry and Elliott received $7,140 each and all the other officers and hands were rewarded according to rank down to the humblest seaman whose portion was computed at $209. In addition, Congress made a special grant of $5,000 to Perry. To Commodore Chauncey, who wasn't there at all, went a generous slice. As commander on the Lakes he received $12,750.

In his official report of the battle, written in the exultation of victory, Perry spoke well of Elliott and made no direct reference to his failure to support the *Lawrence* which almost lost the battle. Elliott, however, was not satisfied and commenced a controversy which went on for years and would have resulted in a duel between the two officers had not Perry refused a challenge. Elliott's defense of his action was that he had stood strictly by his orders to keep a half cable length behind the next ship in line. This argument was a poor excuse for his refusing to come to the help of the *Lawrence* when he saw that ship in trouble.

Before the battle Elliott's reputation was greater than that of Perry. He might well have expected to receive the command of the fleet. When, at the last minute, the order of battle was changed, he was denied the place of honor in the van which might have served further to excite his Irish temperament. Whatever his design may have been it is hard to believe that his actions were not in some part dictated by personal pique. As it turned out they merely provided an opportunity for the enhancement of Perry's glory. It has been remarked that never was there a victory which was owed so much to the will and determination of a single man.

The effect of the victory of Lake Erie was immediate. At last, command of those waters was in the hands of the Americans. We shall see what use they made of it.

CHAPTER EIGHTEEN

A Victory in Canada at Last!

LAKE ERIE being controlled by the Americans as the result of Perry's victory, it was the Army's turn to act. And Harrison was ready. The regulars promised him had not come up to expectations; nevertheless he had two brigades, totaling 2,500 men respectively, under the commands of Brigadier General Duncan McArthur and Brigadier General Lewis Cass. Harrison still had to depend in part upon Kentucky militia and the state responded nobly.

Earlier in the summer Harrison appealed to Governor Isaac Shelby to send him 1,500 men. Not only that but he invited the Governor, a veteran of the Revolution and known affectionately throughout Kentucky as "Old King's Mountain" for the distinguished part he had played in that battle, to join the expedition. "Scipio," he reminded the Governor, "did not disdain to act as the lieutenant of his younger and less experienced brother, Lucius." The classical allusion had the desired effect. Shelby, in spite of his 66 years, responded cordially to the invitation, and his example inspired his countrymen and stimulated recruiting. The Kentuckians flocked to his banner and, in the end, he brought with him, not 1,500, but 4,000 men.

Included in the number was a regiment of mounted riflemen, 1,000 strong, under the command of Colonel R. M. Johnson, a spirited and competent leader. Colonel Johnson's troop already had been active patrolling the Indian country and proved most successful in keeping the savages subdued. The whole Army of the Northwest now was encamped near the shores of Lake Erie between Sandusky Bay and Port Clinton. The ranks were further swelled by a band of 260 friendly Indian warriors. (See Map I, p. 97)

On September 20 a picked force of 4,500 men, which was to invade Canada, was embarked on Perry's fleet and other vessels at Put-in-Bay to be concentrated on Middle Sister Island, which lay about 12 miles from the Canadian shore. The volunteers who had brought their mounts with them were disappointed when they were told that there would be no room aboard ship for the horses; not even for the general's charger. The animals were penned up on a peninsula behind a corral a mile and a half long and left in care of a guard. Colonel Johnson's troopers were an exception. They were ordered to march to Detroit by land and join the main force in Canada.

The movement of the army to Middle Sister Island was successfully accomplished. While the men rested there, Harrison and Perry, who commanded the ships, sailed in the schooner *Ariel* to reconnoiter the mainland. Satisfied that all was in readiness, Harrison ordered the re-embarkation of the troops on September 27. Nine armed vessels and 80 miscellaneous ships had been assembled to transport the army; and, as they departed with all sails set, they made a splendid and awe-inspiring spectacle. Never before in American history had such an armada been brought together for the invasion of a foreign shore.

The crossing proceeded according to plan. At 4 P.M. the first boats touched at Hartley's Point, and as they reached the shallow water the men plunged in and waded to shore where they formed in line of battle on the beach, prepared to meet any opposition the British might raise against them. The precautions, however, were unnecessary for the Americans found the place deserted.

Colonel Proctor, who after his several forays into American territory earlier in the summer had retired to Malden, had there and at Detroit approximately 1,000 regulars and a force of Indians under Tecumseh estimated at about 3,500. Of the Indians he could not be too sure. He had not dared tell them of Barclay's defeat on the lake. During the battle Tecumseh paddled far out from shore in the hope of observing the engagement but he did not get close enough to see the result. After the battle Proctor explained that the British fleet had gone to Put-in-Bay for refitting, which was true enough. He neglected to add that Barclay and his men had gone as prisoners.

When Proctor learned of the host that was preparing to descend upon him he determined to evacuate Malden and Amherstburg, but the great question was how to do it without estranging his Indian allies. He and his men were fearful that the Indians, disillusioned at the turn events had taken, might set upon and massacre them. Tecumseh urged Proctor to make a stand on the beaches; and, when Proctor refused, the Indian chieftain likened him to a whipped cur dog who crawls away with his tail between his legs. Proctor could appease the Indians only by promising to make a stand farther to the rear. His men, watching the Indians suspiciously, proceeded with their packing. On September 24, three days before the landing, Proctor burned all the public buildings at Malden and what stores he could not take with him, and retreated to Sandwich opposite Detroit. His object was to reach the line of the Thames River, which ran inland, enabling him to transport his provisions by boat while his troops and the Indians marched by the road which paralleled the river. His progress was greatly impeded by the fact that the warriors were accompanied by their squaws and children.

Thus it was that when Harrison's army reached Malden, Proctor was already many miles away. The only human beings to meet the invaders were a group of weeping women who came forward to beg for mercy. They were greatly relieved when the venerable Governor Shelby, who was with the advance guard, mustered all of his Kentucky chivalry to assure them that not a hair of their heads would be touched.

The Kentuckians had hoped to find mounts in Canada to replace those that had been left behind. But not a horse was to be had. A pony was somehow obtained and assigned to the Governor in deference to his seniority and his consequently uncertain legs. Having invested what remained of Malden the army proceeded toward Sandwich. A British rear guard was surprised in the act of setting fire to the bridge over the Aux Canards River, and the structure was saved. Yet, in spite of this piece of luck, the march of some 13 miles to Sandwich took the better part of two days. The army reached it on September 29, and on the following day Colonel Johnson's mounted regiment arrived in Detroit across the river. The appearance of the Kentucky cavalrymen was hailed with delight by those

215

Americans who had remained in the town ever since Hull's surrender the preceding year. And, after the festivities were over, a detachment of troops was left to protect and reorganize the settlement.

Yet another day was consumed while Johnson's troopers were crossed over to Sandwich. At last, on October 2, Harrison was ready for the pursuit of Proctor up the Thames. After leaving garrisons at Malden, Amherstburg and Detroit, he still had a force of 3,500 men. By that time Proctor was at Dolson's, 50 miles to the east. Once the trail was taken up it was pursued in earnest. While Perry continued with Harrison as an aide, several of his ships carried supplies for the army up the Thames until the shallowness of the water and the height of the banks, from which Indian sharpshooters could operate, made the undertaking both impractical and dangerous. In his haste to get away, or in the belief that Harrison would not follow, Proctor neglected to burn the bridges or to place obstacles in the road. And, since Johnson's troopers set the pace, the distance between pursuer and pursued rapidly grew less. Soon the Americans began to find smoldering campfires, abandoned supplies and other evidences of Proctor's haste.

On October 4 the Indians attempted a stand at Chatham, three miles east of Dolson's; but, at the first exchange of fire, they fled. It now became apparent to Proctor that, encumbered as he was with the squaws and babies, he had no hope of escaping from the Americans. His choice lay between either deserting the Indians, which he had promised faithfully not to do, or of turning and fighting. He elected the latter course. On October 5, while his baggage and the Indian domestic establishment withdrew to Moravian Town, a missionary settlement, he halted his troops and his Indian warriors and formed a line of battle a mile and a half to the west of the town.

The position selected was far from ideal, since the ground was level at that point and the only protection was a grove of trees and some swampland. Proctor rested his left on the river, his line extending to a large swamp on his extreme right. In the middle of his front was a smaller swamp. His force of regulars had now been reduced to about 400 infantrymen and a few dragoons. These he formed in two lines in open order, as he did not have enough men for closed ranks. On the road which paralleled the river he posted a 6-pounder gun. This gave his line a menacing appearance, but that was all. The gun could not be fired because there was no ammunition. The Indians under Tecumseh continued the line to the right, taking station on the edge of the large swamp.

When Harrison learned from his scouts that the British were preparing to make a stand he advanced with Perry, Colonel Johnson and other members of his staff and reconnoitered the position. It was determined that Johnson's troopers should form the first line and that they should be followed by the infantry in three succeeding lines. One brigade at the left flank was to be "refused," that is to say, faced at an angle to the front in order to guard any attempt of the Indians to penetrate the American flank or rear. On the extreme right, between the road and the river, a small body of Americans and friendly Indians was to attempt to slip by the British line, get in on the rear and give the British the impression that they were being attacked by their own allies. When the order was given by Harrison for the engagement to begin Johnson and his troopers were to withdraw to the rear, leave the assault to the infantry, and then come in at the end.

At the last minute the plan underwent a drastic change. Seeing the British in open order Johnson ventured the opinion that his troopers alone could break the line and asked the right to try. This meant that the battle would open with a cavalry charge. Though Harrison said later that he did not know of any military precedent for such a maneuver he nevertheless agreed to it. The troopers accordingly took their places in the front line and awaited the word of command.

When all was ready the charge was ordered and the Kentuckians dashed forward under the leadership of Colonel Johnson's brother, James. They were met by a fire from the British line which temporarily threw the horses into confusion. Quickly recovering they made a second try, broke through the first line and continued on to the second, spreading to right and left, cutting down those who resisted and taking prisoners. The British regulars were the remnants of the 41st Regiment, which had behaved so gallantly and suffered so severely in the frontal attack on Fort Stephenson. The 41st also had provided men for Barclay's fleet. After all they had endured it was asking too much of them to stand up and be cut to pieces by a force several times their size. By now they had lost confidence in their leader and were in a mutinous state. Consequently, finding themselves surrounded by the Kentucky troopers, they surrendered for the most part as soon as opportunity offered. Within a few minutes the fight was over on this part of the field.

Colonel Johnson, however, had made another last-minute change of his own without previously consulting General Harrison. As the regiment formed for the initial charge he discovered that the ground between the little swamp and the river did not afford sufficient room for the maneuvering of all his mounted men. He therefore took it upon himself to detach half of his regiment, 500 men, and lead them around the small swamp to attack the Indians.

Here the situation proved more difficult. The trees and undergrowth were thicker, the ground broken and the larger swamp did not allow solid footing for the horses. The Indians, too, numbered in the neighborhood of 1,000 and Tecumseh was at their head. When Colonel Johnson attacked he was met with a heavy fire from behind trees and underbrush. It immediately became apparent that the fight could not be continued on horseback and the order was given to dismount. Kentuckians and Indians engaged in bitter hand-to-hand combat. Colonel Johnson was personally assailed by a warrior who was shot down. He himself sustained a painful wound but continued in the fight. The Kentuckians had old scores to settle and raised the cry of "Remember the Raisin" as, for a time, the battle swayed back and forth.

Governor Shelby, "Old King's Mountain," had taken post at the angle between the first line of infantry and the brigade turned to the flank. From that vantage point he saw the difficulty Johnson and his troopers were in and ordered up the infantry. How far the infantry got became later a matter of dispute. For at this moment the tide of battle turned. Tecumseh, bravely leading his warriors, was struck down. The Indians, seeing their chieftain fall, lost heart, gave up the battle and fled, being hotly pursued by the Kentuckians. Proctor had taken station on the road at the rear of his regulars and there observed the battle. Seeing how the day was going he leaped into his carriage and deserted. The battlefield and the country behind it now presented a scene of bloody confusion. Some of the Kentucky horsemen, learning of Proctor's flight, followed behind him and the chase became so hot that Proctor abandoned his carriage and hid in a wood until he was lost to his pursuers. The carriage and his private papers were captured and brought back in triumph by the troopers.

The squaws in Moravian Town, hearing news of the defeat, gave way to panic and many of them threw their babies into the river. On the battlefield the victors came upon the body of an Indian warrior which was identified as that of Tecumseh. True to the American souvenir tradition the Kentuckians cut strips of skin from the body to be made into razor strops. But there is doubt that they actually wrought this personal vengeance on the man who had given them so much trouble. Indians who survived the battle later testified that the mutilated corpse was not Tecumseh's and that during the night after the conflict the body of the chieftain was recovered and spirited away to be given a decent burial by his own people.

Tecumseh died a noble death as he had wanted to do, facing his enemies and fighting to the last. "Tippecanoe," "Detroit," "The Raisin"—all were associated with his name. It would have consoled him had he known that his activities had caused the United States Government to raise 20,000 troops and spend a fortune conservatively estimated at $5,000,000. That was the price he had made the Americans pay for the lands wrested from his people, not to mention the American blood that had been shed on the frontier.

With Tecumseh's death ended the Indian opposition in the Northwest. After the battle of the Thames, Detroit was again safely in American hands, Lake Erie was under American control, and from Detroit to the western end of Lake Ontario British influence virtually ceased to exist in Upper Canada save for the small post at Mackinac Island. Now at last it appeared that Clay's dream had come true. The Kentuckians of whom he had boasted were all inside Canadian territory, Proctor's army had been destroyed and the way lay open to strike hard at the British flank and rear in cooperation with the American forces on the Niagara front. That, in any other war, would have seemed the obvious move to make in order to reap the full rewards of the victory. But the War of 1812 followed no such rules.

The victory had been cheaply won. The American loss in the engagement was 15 men killed and 30 wounded. Evidence of the

British lack of resistance was their record of 12 killed, 36 wounded and 477 captured. This, apparently, was satisfaction enough for the Kentuckians. The weather was beginning to grow unpleasantly cold. No provision had been made for feeding the army on an extended march through Canada. So, instead of going forward, Harrison retired with his army to Detroit. There he released the Kentuckians and sent them home.

Harrison and the regulars shortly after boarded ships and sailed across Lake Erie to join forces with General McClure's New York militia which were stationed on the Niagara front around Fort George. A campaign to drive the British from that area was contemplated. Meanwhile, however, Secretary of War Armstrong had centered his attention on Wilkinson's campaign down the St. Lawrence against Montreal. Sackett's Harbor was threatened and Harrison and his men were ordered there. Then Armstrong suggested to Harrison that, after his strenuous service in the field, the General might like to return home to visit his family.

The suggestion aroused in Harrison the suspicion that Armstrong was indifferent to his services. Indeed the Secretary of War was of the opinion that Harrison's military skill was greatly overrated. Another star was rising in the West in the person of Andrew Jackson; and, between Harrison and Jackson, Armstrong preferred the latter. The Secretary took occasion to issue orders over Harrison's head and inflicted other similar indignities that led to the General's offer of his resignation. Acceptance would leave a single vacancy among the regular major generals. Acting in the absence of President Madison, Armstrong accepted Harrison's offer and gave his commission to Jackson.

Thus, at the very height of his career and while the laurels of victory were still fresh on his brow, Harrison retired from the military scene, not to return during the rest of the war. He was not to reappear before the public until many years later and then as a candidate for President of the United States.

CHAPTER NINETEEN

Wilkinson in Quest of Laurels

"To whom will you confide the charge of leading the flower of our youth to the Heights of Abraham? Will you find him in the person of an acquitted felon?"

At last John Randolph's prophetic utterance before the Twelfth Congress was to come true. Perhaps, after all, the prophecy was not surprising for General James Wilkinson was a warrior of no mean distinction. Like Dearborn and Hull, he had seen active service in the Revolution. For a time he enjoyed the confidence of Washington, but his love of intrigue got the better of him. When he was discovered taking part with Conway in the cabal against the Commander he lost his position in the field. Wilkinson next assumed the office of Clothier-General to the army only to retire once more when serious shortages were found in his accounts. Nevertheless, after the war he was back again in the regular army, and as Federal commander in the Southwest he had the honor of raising the Stars and Stripes in New Orleans. In that same capacity he became involved in the conspiracy of Aaron Burr. It was rumored that Burr counted upon him to seize New Orleans. But if that charge was true Wilkinson neatly cleared himself by appearing as chief witness against the Vice-President. He received a pension from the Spanish Government, presumably for services rendered, and his name appeared on the Spanish account books as "Spy No. 13."

It is said that where there is smoke, there must be fire. Wherever Wilkinson happened to be there was always smoke, but it never quite burst into flame. He faced a Congressional court of inquiry and a court-martial, but so far as conviction was concerned he led a charmed life. "Not guilty" was invariably the verdict, though in one instance Madison accepted the decision of the court "with regret."

When it became apparent that old Henry Dearborn was no longer capable of commanding the army on the Canadian border Secretary Armstrong began to look about for a successor. There were two possibilities in the Southwest; one was Wilkinson, the other Andrew Jackson. But Jackson's military genius was then unknown. Besides, he too was suspected of connivance with Burr, though later events proved how baseless the suspicion was. While Armstrong knew Jackson chiefly through the insults he had hurled at the administration, he was personally acquainted with Wilkinson with whom he had served in the Revolution. So it was that the invitation went to Wilkinson, who was none too keen to accept it, and not to Jackson, who was impatient to go. Had Jackson been selected by Armstrong in place of Wilkinson history might have contained a glorious chapter in place of one that records the shameful failure of American arms.

So it was to Wilkinson in New Orleans that the Secretary of War wrote inquiring, "Why should you remain in your land of cypress when patriotism and ambition equally invite you to one where grows the laurel?" An offer couched in such florid language could hardly be refused. The invitation went out in March; but seldom has a commander proceeded more casually to his post. It took Wilkinson until July 31 to reach the national capital. He had the excuse of having been ill on the way. Wilkinson was another of the numerous veteran leaders of 1812 who enjoyed bad health.

In Washington Wilkinson lingered, conferring with Armstrong on plans for the contemplated campaign. Armstrong proposed first an attack on Kingston and then an expedition down the St. Lawrence against Montreal. This was not ambitious enough for Wilkinson, at least while he was still some thousand miles from the front enjoying the comparative comforts of Washington. He countered with a plan of his own. He would first drive the enemy from the peninsula between Lakes Erie, Ontario and the Niagara River. Having cleared that territory and, assuming that Harrison and Perry had failed in their mission, he would next proceed westward and reduce Fort Malden. With the peninsula and Upper Canada subjugated, it would be time enough to move on Montreal and deliver the *coup de grâce*. Armstrong began to question whether he had been wise in his choice of a commander. He put his foot down upon so extravagant and chimerical a proposal as a march on Malden and eliminated it from the field of operations, but stuck to the campaign against Montreal. Yet after almost two weeks of conferences, when Wilkinson was ready to depart for Sackett's Harbor where he was to make his headquarters, no definite plan of action had been determined upon by the new leader and his chief in the War Department. (See Map III, p. 156)

With an astonishing lack of tact, and simultaneous with Wilkinson's transfer, Armstrong shifted General Wade Hampton, of South Carolina, from the southern to the northern front to command the American troops on Lake Champlain. Hampton was a proud and wealthy planter who had seen service under Marion in the southern area during the Revolution. He knew Wilkinson, distrusted and detested him. Hampton was under the impression that his army of 4,000 men at Burlington, Vermont, was an independent command. But no sooner had Wilkinson reached Albany, New York, than he tried Hampton out by issuing an order to him. Hampton protested directly to Secretary Armstrong, refusing to take orders from Wilkinson and offering his resignation. Armstrong, however, prevailed upon him to remain at his post and hastened north to be on the scene and help keep the peace between his two subordinates who seemed more interested in waging war against each other than against the British. Whatever the understanding may have been between Armstrong and Hampton, Wilkinson was determined to assert his authority. He reached his post at Sackett's Harbor on August 20 and four days later dispatched a letter to Armstrong in which he cautioned him against meddling. "I trust," he wrote, "you will not interfere with my arrangements, or give orders within the district of my command, but to myself, because it would impair my authority and distract the public service. Two heads on the same shoulders make a monster." The campaign could not have got off to a worse start.

Wilkinson's command consisted nominally of from 12,000 to 14,000 men. Of these, 5,000 were at Sackett's Harbor, 5,000 at Fort George on the Niagara; and 4,000, if they could be called Wilkinson's, were with Hampton at Burlington. Sickness had been very prevalent on the Lakes during the summer so that of the force mentioned it was estimated that the effective strength was not more than 9,000. Wilkinson himself was soon added to the sick list and his reports began to take on the aspect of a hospital chart. "I dictate this under much depression of head and stomach," he wrote Armstrong on September 11. Five days later he was little improved. "I have escaped my palet, and with a giddy head and trembling hand will endeavor to scrawl you a few lines."

The season was already growing late, yet valuable days were wasted in lengthy discussions of plans between the Secretary of War and his obstinate lieutenant. Opposing the American forces, the British had in the field an army of 8,000 men spread out all the way from the Niagara Peninsula to Montreal, with Kingston as its center. It was finally agreed to abandon the attack on Kingston, Commodore Chauncey blockading the naval forces in that harbor, while Wilkinson should enter the St. Lawrence and set out toward Montreal. At the same time Hampton was ordered to set his army in motion from Burlington and form a junction with Wilkinson on the St. Lawrence at the mouth of the Chateaugay River for the final assault upon Montreal.

Troops were drawn from Fort George to swell the ranks at Sackett's Harbor and Colonel Winfield Scott, who had been on the Niagara during the summer facing Vincent, was told that if Vincent left that front he might take more troops from Fort George and realize his ambition of having a part in the campaign against Montreal. While the final preparations were being made September sped by and it was not until October 12 that Wilkinson was ready to order a rendezvous at Grenadier Island where the waters of Lake Ontario enter the St. Lawrence. Five more days passed before the little army set out in scows, bateaux and sailboats accompanied by an inadequate number of pilots who knew the treacherous currents in that neighborhood.

The day of departure could hardly have been worse. As the expedition put out into the lake a gale set in, attended by snow and sleet. In the ensuing darkness 15 of the large boats were lost, many others were damaged, and the whole force was thrown into confusion. It was three days before the remnants of the expedition were collected together on the island, still in a disorganized and damaged condition. Wilkinson wrote courageously to his superior that, in spite of this initial disaster, he would proceed to carry out his mission. The Commander needed all the courage he possessed, for the storms continued, battering the boats and creating intense suffering among the men. Finally the temperature dropped and the rain was followed by a snowfall of 10 inches. The fury of the elements added to all the other difficulties so that the reorganizing and re-equipping of the expedition consumed two more weeks.

At last, on November 5, the army again embarked and entered the St. Lawrence River. Commodore Chauncey's operations on Lake Ontario throughout the summer had proved quite ineffectual. He and Yeo, who commanded the British naval forces on the lake, had played hide and seek with each other and occasionally exchanged shots, but without bringing about a decisive action. Now that Chauncey's task was blockading Kingston he allowed the British gunboats to slip through and these immediately proceeded to harass Wilkinson from the rear. At the same time British troops from Kingston pursued the expedition by the road which followed the river along the Canadian shore and caused it further annoyance, taking pot shots at the boats whenever occasion offered.

Unable to put up with this persistent pressure on his rear Wilkinson detached Colonel Alexander Macomb with 1,200 picked men and ordered him to clear the Canadian shore. Hearing that the British were being reinforced he sent General Jacob Brown with more men to support Macomb and, after that, General John P. Boyd with still more men to assist Macomb and Brown. November 10 found the expedition at the head of Longue Saute, a rapids eight miles long. Once the boats were in them there would be no way of getting out. To make matters worse news came that the British had seized a blockhouse at the foot of the rapids and were preparing to contest the passage of the Americans. Wilkinson dispatched General Brown down the river road to dislodge the British. Meanwhile the enemy in the rear were making things unpleasantly hot for him and, to cap the climax, the pilots refused to enter the rapids and run the risk of being caught in them during the night. There was nothing for Wilkinson to do but to moor his boats, take shelter for the night and await favorable news from Brown. The spot selected lay below an island known as Chrysler's and opposite a farm of the same name.

The night passed without incident and, early in the morning, the reliable Brown sent back the encouraging news that he had dislodged the British at the foot of the rapids. Wilkinson gave the order for the flotilla to move. But it was too late; the British in his rear were already upon him. In this critical moment Wilkinson again fell ill. A note headed "From My Bed" was dispatched to Brown advising him of the situation and in it Wilkinson wailed, "It is now that I feel the heavy hand of disease—enfeebled and confined to my bed while the safety of the army intrusted to my command, the honor of our arms and the greatest interest of our country are at hazard."

Wilkinson roused himself enough to direct General Boyd to turn and outflank the enemy. Indeed, the situation had become unendurable and there was no chance of relief until the Americans stood and fought. Boyd took up a position with his left on the St. Lawrence, his right protected by a swamp and heavy woods. Opposite him on the Chrysler farm was the British line, protected by a heavy rail fence and ravines near the riverbank. In the St. Lawrence the American gunboats took up position to fend off any possible attack from the gunboats of the British. On the American right General Swartout was in command, on the left General Leonard Covington, mounted upon a snow-white charger. The day was cold and raw with flurries of snow and sleet, and the ground over which the battle was to be fought was a sea of slush.

Yet the Americans proceeded gallantly to the attack. Swartout opened the engagement by charging upon the enemy's advance guard and driving it back upon the main line. The fighting then became general. As the Americans moved forward they were met by a hail of shrapnel and bullets but kept stoutly on. In spite of the ravines, the fence and the mud, the cold that numbed their fingers so that they could with difficulty load their muskets, and the enemy fire that tore holes in their ranks, they succeeded in dislodging the British and driving them back a whole mile.

But their temporary advantage had been gained at considerable cost. Covington on his white charger, gallantly leading his men, proved too good a target. He fell, mortally wounded. And, when the Americans needed it most, their ammunition gave out. There was nothing to do but retire over the ground they had just gained; and the British, seeing them withdraw, set upon them with everything they had in the way of shot and shell. When the Americans who were in the reserve observed their comrades retreating they fell into a panic and soon the whole army was running helter-skelter from the field. Fortunately, at this moment a reinforcement of 600 men dispatched by Wilkinson reached the scene, and its arrival halted the rout. The battle of Chrysler's Field ended with both armies facing each other, but neither daring to go forward. The American losses were heavy. They included 102 men killed and 137 missing as compared with a British loss of only 22 killed, 150 wounded and 15 missing. One account gives the forces engaged as from 1,600 to 1,700 Americans against 800 British; another declares they were about even, including the Indian allies of the latter. The most serious loss of the Americans was General Covington, who died of his wounds shortly after the battle.

In any event, it was not an engagement of which the Americans could feel proud, indicating as it did poor organization and incompetent leadership. Wilkinson in his report to Armstrong enlarged upon his physical handicaps. "The disease," he wrote, "with which I was assailed on the 2nd of September, on my journey to Ft. George, having with a few short intervals of convalescence, preyed on me ever since; and at the moment of this action, I was confined to my bed, and emaciated almost to a skeleton, unable to sit on my horse, or to move ten paces without assistance."

The demonstration of Chrysler's Field augured ill for success against Montreal. But then Wilkinson counted upon meeting Hampton down the river with fresh men and much-needed provisions. The following day the expedition proceeded unmolested through the rapids, joining General Brown and his detachment, which was waiting at the bottom. And there Wilkinson received the disappointing news that Hampton would not meet him. Wilkinson could not appeal to the Secretary of War to enforce the order, for the third member of this strange triumvirate had departed for home, leaving the other two members to settle their differences as best they could.

Hampton, too, had been having his difficulties. He set out from Burlington for the Canadian border but ran into a drought which threatened to cut off the supply of water for men and horses, and he was forced to change his route. He then found himself facing a British army. He attempted a flanking movement, but the troops assigned to the task lost themselves in a swamp and, when they came into conflict with a small detachment of the enemy, fled in dismay. The British were equally surprised and fled as rapidly in the opposite direction.

After this unsatisfactory contact between two small detachments, the main bodies approached each other. The British, under Lieutenant Colonel De Salaberry, numbered 1,000 men; Hampton's force, 3,500. De Salaberry, however, stationed his buglers at a considerable distance from each other and ordered them to sound off. Hampton, hearing the bugles so far apart, assumed that he was facing an army of immense proportions and, rather than sacrifice his command, gave the order to retreat. He did not halt until he reached a place called Chateaugay Four Corner from which he had set out and a considerable distance from the St. Lawrence.

After these experiences Hampton was in no mood to keep his rendezvous with Wilkinson. It was absurd for Wilkinson to talk of Hampton supplying him with rations when Hampton himself was short of supplies. Besides, his personal animosity toward Wilkinson encouraged him to keep as far away from that gentleman as possible. So it was that Hampton's adjutant appeared to report that the meeting was definitely off.

So, too, was the campaign against Montreal. Wilkinson and his generals contented themselves with drawing up a paper condemning Hampton's behavior. Armstrong presumably had not entertained the idea that an attack on Montreal by Wilkinson would be successfully carried out; for, before his departure, he designated a site for winter quarters at French Mills, a few miles up the Salmon River. To this spot the dispirited army now repaired, suffering great hardship on the way and after they reached the camp. Wilkinson turned over the command to General Brown and set off for a place where he was much more at home than on the field of battle—a hospital at Malone, not very far away. Wilkinson's career was drawing to a close. Later in the winter he attempted another expedition in the direction of the Canadian border, but it was brief and as disastrous as his first. After that he went home to face a court-martial where, as usual, his conduct was exonerated. Wade Hampton, too, gave up his command and retired to his broad acres in South Carolina. Of the three bunglers Armstrong alone held on to resume his bungling in an even more conspicuous field.

Throughout December and January Brown and the army remained at French Mills where they constructed rude huts that afforded little comfort. The cold was intense and the men were short of blankets. In the trip down the St. Lawrence most of the medicines and hospital stores had been lost and the nearest source of supply was Albany, a good 250 miles away. Provisions were scarce and of poor quality. And throughout the whole time the Americans were menaced by the enemy who gave them no peace. It was a great relief when at last in February orders were received to move. Through the snow and along the shores of the St. Lawrence Brown led the forlorn army back to Sackett's Harbor, from which it had set out so hopefully five months before. In that time all it had gained was bitter experience and the loss of a leader who never should have attempted to lead.

Meanwhile disaster had struck the American cause on the Niagara front. It will be recalled that Colonel Winfield Scott was told that if Vincent left the Niagara he might take the 800 regulars at Fort George and join the expedition against Montreal. Vincent did leave, and so did Scott, though his men had to march by land and never reached Wilkinson. General McClure took over the command at Fort George but his force was now composed only of militia and volunteers and, as was usual with these soldiers in time of emergency, their enlistments were about to expire.

Vincent's abrupt departure was due to the fact that he had received news of the defeat of Proctor in the battle of the Thames and naturally assumed that Harrison would immediately follow up his victory by marching eastward and joining forces with the Americans on the Niagara, at Sackett's Harbor and on Lake Champlain. He therefore hastened by forced marches to Burlington Heights, at the western end of Lake Ontario, to intercept him. There he learned to his relief that, instead of advancing, Harrison had retired to Detroit. There being no further threat in that direction, Vincent retraced his steps to the Niagara to resume his harassment of the Americans.

Vincent's action placed McClure in a predicament, as the force under the latter was reduced and of poor quality. McClure deter-

mined to abandon Fort George and retire across the river and concentrate his men on the defense of Fort Niagara. In his alarm he
seems to have lost his head for he not only attempted to blow up
Fort George but, for no apparent reason, he set fire to the village of
Newark, destroying all the houses and leaving the inhabitants without shelter in the bitter cold of the Canadian winter. His action was
as strongly condemned by Americans as by Canadians but this did
nothing to palliate the demand for retaliation that arose throughout
Canada.

It was not long in coming. On December 18 the infuriated British
took possession of Fort George and, in the night, crossed the river.
A body of 1,000 men, including Indians, attacked Fort Niagara,
which with criminal negligence had been left unguarded, captured
the fort and deliberately slaughtered the greater part of the garrison.
The raiders now swept up the American side of the river while
another British force crossed at Queenston. The combined forces
gained momentum as they went, bringing terror and destruction to
Lewiston, Manchester, Schlosser and Tuscarora. At Black Rock they
burned the *Ariel, Little Belt, Chippawa* and *Trippe* which had lain
at anchor there since their part in the battle of Lake Erie. The raid
ended with the plunder and destruction of Black Rock and Buffalo
attended by the excesses that were customary when Indians had a
hand in the game. The whole of upper New York was thrown into a
state of terror and militia and volunteers were called out in a hurry
to stem the tide. The British at last concluded that they had done
enough to avenge Newark, retired as they had come, and left the
border towns mourning their dead and the destruction of their property.

During the year 1813 the American operations on land had met
with complete failure, with the exception of the battle of the
Thames. Yet the records of the Adjutant General's office show that
during the year the United States Army reached a total of 149,148
men, of whom 19,036 were regulars and 130,112 were militia. These
figures are exclusive of volunteers and rangers. That would indicate
a tremendous effort and a force far outnumbering any British force
that could have been brought against it. Yet so short were the individual terms of enlistment and so widely distributed were the
troops that never were more than a few thousand brought together

on a battlefield. As an example of the waste of man power, no fewer than 66,376 militiamen from Delaware, Maryland, Virginia, North Carolina and the District of Columbia were employed in observing no more than 2,600 regulars and sailors on British ships marauding in Chesapeake Bay.

As for the colossal failures in Canada, well might the Federalists continue to declare that the Virginia Dynasty and its Southern and Western supporters had never intended Canada to be taken and that the failures were deliberate.

231

CHAPTER TWENTY

Jackson Justifies a Nickname

THOUGH Tecumseh was dead and the Northwest subdued, the seeds of dissension he had sown in a distant country took root and produced distressing and bloody consequences.

In northeast Alabama, where the Coosa and the Tallapoosa rivers join to form the Alabama, lay the center of the Creek country. The Creeks came under the classification of "good Indians." Game in that region was scarce so that the Creeks perforce abandoned the chase for the plow. Besides, Colonel Benjamin Hawkins, the government's Indian agent, was exceptional in that he was honest and had the interests of his charges at heart. (See Map V)

The Creeks might have continued to live in peace and comparative serenity if they had not come under the spell of Tecumseh. Tecumseh's mother was a Creek; so when he went on his southern mission at the time of the battle of Tippecanoe he was able to present himself as a kinsman. After the victory of the British and Indians at Detroit, in which Tecumseh played such a conspicuous role, the chieftain made a second visit to the Creek metropolis at the Hickory Ground, the peninsula above the confluence of the Coosa and the Tallapoosa. Along with him came his brother, the Prophet. Several thousand Creek warriors assembled to greet the distinguished visitors; and, after Colonel Hawkins had tactfully left the meeting, Tecumseh and his retainers danced the war dance while the Prophet moved among his fellow medicine men doing missionary work. The purpose of the visit was to encourage the Creeks to combine forces with their northern brethren and present a united front to their white oppressors.

The older warriors, content to let well enough alone, were cold to the proposal, but Tecumseh's eloquence, his commanding pres-

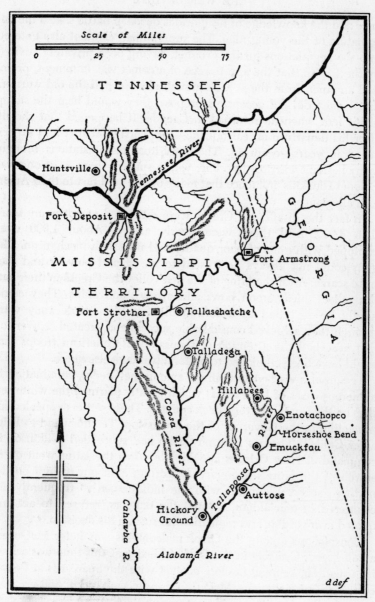

Map V. Creek Campaign

ence and the knowledge of his glorious deeds in battle seized the imagination of the young men. The superhuman element also entered into the negotiations for the Prophet, having been privately advised by the British that the appearance of a comet was imminent, promised an omen from the sky. Tecumseh also warned the old warriors that if they did not accept his proposal they would hear the stamp of his foot when he returned to Canada. It happened that shortly after his departure an earthquake—the worst Alabama had experienced in years—occurred. These spiritual manifestations brought many hesitant warriors into line; yet, in spite of them, so strong was Colonel Hawkins' influence that many others held fast to their American allegiance.

In fact the disaffected Creeks were estimated at not many more than 4,000. And these were poorly armed. About 1,000 were equipped with guns of poor quality and uncertain mechanism. The guns could not always be trusted to go off and powder and shot were scarce. After the firing of the first volley the Creeks in their battles relied chiefly upon bows and arrows, and clubs. They could hardly be regarded as a formidable foe. Yet before they were through they achieved considerable success and created a diversion that absorbed the attention of thousands of American troops that might have been employed to better advantage elsewhere.

Tecumseh's visit created unrest among the Creeks, culminating in numerous cases of lawlessness which greatly alarmed the white settlers on the frontier of the Creek country. These settlers appealed for protection to the Governor of the Mississippi Territory and to Brigadier General Thomas Flournoy, who had succeeded Wilkinson in command at New Orleans and Mobile when the latter went off in search of the laurels Secretary Armstrong held out to him on the northern scene. Flournoy, with the indifference so frequently encountered in officialdom, scouted the dangers, refused to act and quoted army orders and regulations to sustain his decision.

Conspicuous among the Creek malcontents was Peter McQueen, a half-breed. Cruising in the Gulf of Mexico at this time was a British squadron, keeping in close contact with the Spaniards at Pensacola. To Pensacola went McQueen, heading a band of 350 warriors in quest of ammunition; and to each man the Spanish Governor gave balls and powder. Not more than enough for a hunting expedition, explained the Governor. The white settlers got wind of McQueen's expedition, and, by now fully alarmed, determined to take matters into their own hands. They dispatched Colonel James Caller and a force of 180 mounted men to intercept the Indian party on its return. The two forces met at a spot called Burnt Cork Creek and the Indians had the advantage in a brief skirmish in which Caller lost two men killed and 18 wounded.

Encouraged by this initial triumph, McQueen returned to Pensacola for more supplies and ammunition. Meanwhile General Flournoy had aroused himself sufficiently from his lethargy to order General Ferdinand L. Claiborne, a brother of the Governor of the Orleans Territory, into Mobile county where the white population was hastily constructing forts and gathering refugees from the countryside into them. Claiborne was all for going straight into the heart of the Creek country but was overruled by Flournoy. He then proposed calling out the militia. Flournoy replied that he lacked the necessary authority. So Claiborne had to be content to distribute his regulars among the forts, while the situation grew successively worse.

One of the largest of the forts was Mims, on the Alabama River a short distance north of the Florida border, where over 500 persons— wealthy half-breeds, whites and Negroes—had taken refuge behind a stockade. To Fort Mims Claiborne sent Major Daniel Beasley with 175 volunteers and 16 regulars. Beasley entered upon his duties with greater zeal than good sense. He weakened his force by sending detachments of troopers to other forts and made reports to Claiborne in which he assured the general that Mims was perfectly secure.

On a sultry summer day, August 29, 1813, two Negro slaves who had wandered outside the stockade rushed in ashen with terror to report that they had seen several dozen Indian braves in war paint within a short distance of the fort. Beasley sent out a reconnoitering expedition to investigate the story and, when it returned and reported having seen nothing, Beasley charged the Negroes with lying and ordered them lashed. The master of one of them objected. Beasley replied that he could either obey the order or leave the fort. The master yielded and the whipping was set for the following day.

August 30 dawned clear and oppressively hot. The morning passed uneventfully. The women were busy with preparations for dinner, as there were many mouths to feed. The young people amused themselves with dancing, children played innocently inside the stockade while the old people dozed or gossiped in the shade of the cabins. The only discordant note in the establishment was the sight of the Negro slaves bound to a post and waiting for their beating. But that was scarcely noticed, for the punishment of a slave was not unusual. Sentries walked their posts methodically, but without especial diligence. In spite of all the rumors, nothing really alarming had happened and perhaps the dangers had been exaggerated.

While this carefree scene was being enacted in the fort, in the tall grass that waved not more than 400 yards away lay no fewer than 1,000 Creek warriors, armed and in war paint, waiting the signal to spring upon their unsuspecting victims. McQueen had now yielded his command to another half-breed, one William Weathersford, in whose veins mingled Indian, French, Spanish and Scottish blood. Weathersford might easily have passed as a white, as one of his brothers did, but he preferred the Indian life. A man of proud bearing, a superb horseman and distinguished for his courage, he compared favorably with the great Tecumseh himself.

Noon arrived and the cooks had completed their task. A drum beat to summon the hungry garrison to dinner. That, too, was the chosen signal for the Creek warriors to leap to their feet and, with savage yells, to charge the fort. Major Beasley was among the first to hear the war whoops and take in the situation. He ran at top speed to close the gate to the stockade before the Indians reached it. But he was too late. Sand had drifted against it and while Beasley struggled to release it the Indians fell upon him and clubbed him to death.

With Major Beasley dead, command of the fort fell to Captain Dixon Bailey, a half-breed, who proved equal to the occasion by stemming the confusion inside the fort and rallying the garrison to withstand the attack. The Indians swept into the first enclosure, cut two companies of soldiers to pieces and slaughtered the poor slaves where they stood strapped to the whipping post and but for whose unjust punishment the fort might have been saved. Before they could penetrate the second enclosure Bailey had organized his forces, which put up a stout resistance, the women of the garrison fighting side by side with the men.

For three hours the battle raged, the Indians letting loose a storm of arrows and endeavoring to find a vulnerable spot in the ranks of the defenders, the men of the fort holding them back with well-directed shots which took a heavy toll among the Indians. Bailey moved from place to place, encouraging his people, exhorting them to hold out and reminding them of the Indian practice of abandoning an attack after encountering stout resistance. Gradually the fierceness of the assault diminished and the Indians retired out of range. It looked as though Bailey had judged them correctly. But he failed to take their leader into account. Weathersford's Scotch blood seemed to come to the surface and he refused to admit defeat. Instead he rallied the warriors and persuaded them to renew the attack.

The resistance of the whites centered around the Mims house which provided shelter for sharpshooters whose accuracy of fire was creating much havoc among the Indians. Weathersford now ordered his warriors to tip their arrows with fire and direct them at the houses. Soon every house inside the stockade was aflame and the people who had taken refuge in them, afraid to leave and expose themselves to the Indians, were roasted alive.

Captain Bailey himself was severely wounded. When this disaster became known all resistance gave way. The Indians rushed the second enclosure and, brandishing their tomahawks and mad with the lust for blood, set to work upon the massacre of every white they could find. Men, women and children were indiscriminately slaughtered and soon the fort presented a spectacle of indescribable horror, the dead and dying strewn about everywhere in all stages of mutilation. Even Weathersford was shocked by the scene of brutality that lay before him. He pleaded with his warriors to end the unnecessary carnage but his appeals went unanswered. He was quite unable to control the force which he himself had unleashed. And so the work of murder went on. When, at last, the hot summer sun sank below the horizon not a white person remained alive. The Negroes were spared to be made the slaves of the victors. Of the 553 persons who, in the morning, had imagined that their presence inside the stockade and under the protection of the military made them safe from Indian attack, 400 now lay silent in death.

One Negro woman in the heat of the battle escaped from the fort, found a canoe and paddled alone down the Alabama River to Fort Stoddard where she broke the news of the disaster to General Claiborne. Word of what had occurred at Fort Mims spread swiftly from mouth to mouth through Alabama and Mississippi, east to Georgia and north to Tennessee. And wherever it was heard a cry of vengeance went up. The Creek country lay equidistant from Mobile and the borders of Georgia and Tennessee. Extermination of Weathersford's band called for a march of 150 miles through a roadless wilderness from whichever direction an expedition might set out. From all three directions plans got under way. General Thomas Pinckney, of South Carolina, who commanded the Sixth Military District, comprising the Carolinas and Georgia, called out the militia and an expedition was organized under Georgia's General John Floyd. From New Orleans Flournoy sent instructions to Claiborne to do whatever he deemed necessary. But to Tennessee was to fall the most conspicuous part in the reprisals, thanks to the initiative and driving power of her most distinguished citizen.

From the outset of the war Andrew Jackson, planter, turfman and general of militia, had been impatient for active duty. Unfortunately, his tact was inferior to his military ardor. In Richmond, Virginia, during the trial of Aaron Burr, he delivered a speech on the street soundly berating Jefferson's administration. He called Secretary of War Dearborn "an old granny." When Jefferson chose Madison as his successor, Jackson ignored Madison's claim to the presidency and came out openly for Monroe. And, until he discovered the true nature of the man with whom he was dealing, he had been a friend of Aaron Burr and had unwittingly entertained him at his home. In consequence of these numerous indiscretions Jackson's stock was not as high in Washington as it was in Tennessee. When he volunteered for service on the Canadian border his offer was politely ignored.

A crisis in the South in the autumn of 1812, however, afforded Jackson an opportunity. Britain and Spain were threatening Mobile and New Orleans, where Wilkinson was then in command, and the administration in Washington determined to settle the problem once and for all by marching into Florida and taking possession. The government thereupon asked Governor Blount of Tennessee for 1,500 militia to reinforce Wilkinson. Though he was aware of the strained relations between the administration and Jackson, Blount took the bull by the horns and commissioned Jackson to lead the expedition.

On December 10, 1812, Jackson assembled 2,000 men at Nashville in the bitterest winter weather that town had ever seen. On January 7 he embarked his infantry in flatboats lying in the Cumberland River and dispatched 670 cavalrymen under Colonel John Coffee by land direct to Natchez on the Mississippi. Jackson and the infantry put out down the stream and made the arduous journey of over 1,000 miles by way of the Cumberland, Ohio and Mississippi rivers to Natchez in 39 days, joining Coffee and the cavalry on February 15. There he received a message from Wilkinson to stay where he was. The commander at New Orleans was far too shrewd a man to ignore the danger that lay in receiving to his bosom an ambitious military leader, 46 years of age.

Meanwhile the situation altered in Washington. A stubborn Senate refused point-blank to support the administration in its designs on Florida and, consequently, all military plans had to be canceled. It devolved upon General Armstrong, but two days in office as Secretary of War and unfamiliar with the department's details, to communicate with Jackson, thank him for his services and direct him to disband his army.

Upon receiving this unexpected order Jackson assumed that the old animosity of the administration against him had been revived. How, he argued, could his men get back to their homes hundreds of miles away after they had been disbanded, without food or means of transportation? He interpreted the order as nothing less than a shrewd scheme to get rid of him and, through necessity, to force his militia into the regular service. On the matter of shifting militia into the regular army Jackson was peculiarly sensitive. He was not the kind of man to accept defeat calmly. Without waiting for explanations of the order, he dispatched blistering letters to Washington and New Orleans telling his superiors in no uncertain terms just what he thought of them. Furthermore he made it known that he would arrest any Federal recruiting officer who dared set foot in his camp. He then addressed himself relentlessly to the task of collecting supplies and equipment to be used by his troops on the long march by the land route back to Tennessee, giving his personal notes for the purchases made, since he was acting without authority from the government. Traveling at the rate of 18 miles a day the army of West Tennessee reached Nashville on May 18, where Jackson dismissed it, confident that he had thwarted the administration in its clever scheme. It was not until then that he received a letter from Armstrong explaining the true reason for the cancellation of the original orders and also explaining that when he directed the disbanding of the army he had no idea that it was so far away from home. Where Armstrong was to blame was that after this episode he did not have the intuition to recognize that here was a military leader of astonishing resources and initiative—something that was just then very much in demand as Wilkinson was making his tediously prolonged journey from the land of the cypress to that of the laurel.

Jackson's move to Natchez and return was not, however, altogether barren of results. It gave the General valuable experience in handling a large body of men on the march. And it was through his untiring efforts on the trying journey back to Nashville that he earned from his men the nickname of "Old Hickory," which was to stick with him all the rest of his days and stand as a perpetual memorial after his death.

Events moved swiftly in Tennessee in those frontier times. Tennesseans were a proud people and their blood was hot. A chance word, a mistaken meaning and the friend of yesterday was the enemy of today. Jackson's friend and lieutenant on the trip to Natchez was Colonel Thomas H. Benton. Yet a few weeks after their return to Nashville they were in an altercation; Jackson attacked Benton with a horsewhip and Benton retaliated by plugging Jackson with lead, several bullets entering the General's shoulder. So Jackson was in bed recovering from his wounds when news arrived of the massacre at Mims.

The Tennessee Legislature acted promptly and authorized Governor Blount to call out 3,500 volunteers in addition to the 1,500 militiamen already in service. Too weak to mount a horse, Jackson dispatched Colonel Coffee with 500 dragoons to Huntsville, Alabama, below the Tennessee border, and ordered his militia division to assemble at Fayetteville just above the line. He joined them there on October 7. At the same time General John Cocke, with a division of 2,500 men recruited in East Tennessee, arrived at Knoxville.

It was one thing to mobilize an army, but quite another to feed it. The army contractors were inefficient, the Tennessee River by which Jackson had hoped to obtain supplies on barges from East Tennessee was too dry to serve for the transportation. From the very outset hunger became as dangerous an enemy as the hostile Creeks. For his 2,500 men and 1,300 horses Jackson figured that he needed each week 1,000 bushels of grain, 20 tons of meat, 1,000 gallons of whiskey and many other miscellaneous provisions that would have been hard to obtain in the city of Nashville, much less in so remote a place as Fayetteville. But Jackson was not to be discouraged from carrying out his plans by the shortage of provisions. He determined to live off the land and sent Colonel Coffee to forage, hoping that his supplies would eventually overtake him.

Hearing that the Creeks were planning to attack a small body of loyal Indians at a place called Ten Islands, some 50 miles away on the Coosa River, Jackson determined to go to the rescue. He set his men to work building a road through the mountain wilderness and established a post of supplies which he called Fort Deposit. On October 24 he set out from Fort Deposit with only two days' supply of bread and six days' supply of meat. Coffee went ahead of him, burned two Indian villages and brought in 300 bushels of corn. On the 29th Jackson arrived in the vicinity of Ten Islands and learned that the Creeks had assembled near by in a settlement named Tallassahatche. On November 3 he and his men reached the outskirts of the town and prepared for the attack.

Jackson's tactics were simple. They consisted of disposing his force in a semicircle, then sending a small body ahead to serve as bait for the Indians. As soon as the Indians attacked, the advance guard was directed to retire on the main body. Then, when the Indians were well within the semicircle, the two ends were to come together and the Indians would find themselves surrounded and ready for unhurried and systematic slaughter. That was, of course, provided no part of Jackson's line, upon seeing the Indians, turned tail and ran. At Tallassahatche the plan worked to perfection. The Indians took the bait, rushed pell-mell into the trap and the ends closed on them while the sides held firm. The bag on that occasion was 186 Indian braves killed outright at the cost of five Americans killed and 41 wounded. After this easy victory Jackson retired tri-

241

umphantly to Ten Islands where he built a fort which he named Fort Strother.

Four days after the fight on Tallassahatche information reached Jackson that 160 friendly Indians were being besieged by 1,000 Creeks at Talladega, 30 miles distant. The General also learned that the vanguard of General Cocke's army was approaching Fort Strother. In spite of his experiences with Wilkinson he did not realize that other military commanders were somewhat loath to come into close contact with his dynamic personality. Assuming that Cocke would soon be at Strother, Jackson left his sick and wounded without protection and plunged headlong toward Talladega with a force of 1,200 infantry and 800 horsemen. He had arrived within a few miles of his destination when his column was overtaken by a mounted messenger who informed him that Cocke had withdrawn his vanguard and that, therefore, Strother could not count upon him to defend it. In spite of this alarming news Jackson decided to carry out his attack on Talladega, praying that nothing would happen to his sick and wounded at Strother.

On November 9 Jackson attacked, employing the same method that had proved so successful at Tallassahatche. Unfortunately, on this occasion some of the militia lost courage when the Indians rushed against them 1,000 strong, and so the circle was broken and many of the Indians escaped. But in spite of this flaw the Americans did not do so badly. This time 290 Indians were slaughtered. Jackson's own losses were higher than at Tallassahatche, the fight costing him 15 dead and 85 wounded.

As soon as the battle was over Jackson hastened back to Strother and, to his intense relief, discovered that the fort had been unmolested during his absence. Hunger, and not the Indians, was now his most formidable adversary. The Tennessee River was still low and no supplies were coming through from East Tennessee. Nor could he expect assistance from Cocke who built his own fort 70 miles away and named it Armstrong. Following the slaughter at Tallassahatche the Hillabee Indians, who lived along the Tallapoosa River, sent envoys to Jackson to sue for peace, and Jackson accepted their offer. Cocke was unaware of these negotiations, separated as he was by many miles from Jackson, and almost simultaneously with the peace settlement he decided to attack the Hillabee towns. The Hillabees were, of course, quite unprepared for an attack so shortly after concluding a peace. Cocke advanced upon them from Fort Armstrong, burned three of their towns and slew 60 warriors before the error was discovered. The Hillabees naturally blamed Jackson for what they considered a breach of good faith and, when Jackson heard what Cocke had done, he was as furious as the Hillabees. Furthermore, he suspected Cocke of withholding provisions from him. But on this occasion he managed to keep his temper in control and avoided an open breach with Cocke by inviting him to come with his division to Strother. Cocke accepted the invitation and arrived on December 12.

It will be recalled that Jackson first assembled his army at Nashville on December 10 of the previous year. The men, who had enlisted for a year, held that their time was now up, and just then the comforts of home held out inducements far more compelling than the loneliness and hardships of Strother. Jackson, on the other hand, argued that the time during which they had been demobilized in the summer did not count as part of their enlistment. Jackson's arguments failed to impress his homesick troops; they showed as much determination as Jackson and plans for mutiny were whispered throughout the camp.

The militia were the first to break the deadlock. They packed their knapsacks and turned their faces northward. Jackson discovered the plot in time and as the militia set out they found the volunteers blocking the road. The volunteers next made the same attempt but again Jackson thwarted their plans, employing the militia against them just as he had used the volunteers against the militia.

The solution, however, proved to be temporary, for within a few days militia and volunteers combined and prepared to walk off in a body. But even a whole army in revolt could not overawe the redoubtable Commander. Jackson's wounded shoulder was still so weak that he could not raise a gun to it. Alone and disabled though he was, he dismounted from his horse on the road by which the troops had to pass. Then he rested a gun on the horse's back, placed a finger on the trigger and dared the soldiers to approach him. For a moment the men hesitated, overawed by the fire in the General's eye and the determination in his lined face and jutting chin. There could be no question that Old Hickory was in dead earnest.

There was no telling what might have happened had not Colonel Coffee and a troop of loyal cavalry arrived on this strange scene where commander and men glared at each other across an intervening space of a few yards. Coffee's appearance was sufficient to turn the tide. Silent and glum the men returned to their billets.

Having won a moral victory Jackson at last decided to let those go who wished to leave and the majority seized the opportunity. The army was virtually disbanded. From Governor Blount, Jackson received an urgent appeal to return home himself, but Jackson refused. His expedition had failed thus far to crush the Creeks and he no longer had an army, yet Jackson was determined not to leave Strother. Instead, he urged the Governor to recruit a new army and send it to him, and he dispatched Cocke to Tennessee to speed the word. Such determination was all too rare among the commanding generals.

Meanwhile the American forces to the east and south had not been idle. Brigadier General John Floyd with 950 Georgia militia invaded the Creek country from the east and, on November 29, attacked the village of Auttose, 20 miles above the Hickory Ground, where the Creek warriors a short time before had listened to the exhortations of Tecumseh. Artillery and a bayonet charge combined were too much for the nerves of the Creek warriors. Floyd slaughtered 200 of them with the loss of only 11 killed and 54 wounded in his own force. But, like Jackson, he was handicapped by lack of provisions and had to retire instead of following up his victory. He halted at Fort Mitchell on the Chattahooche River.

General Claiborne, to the south, received orders from Flournoy to march to the heart of the Creek country, drive the Indians to the frontiers and "kill, burn and destroy all their negroes, horses, cattle and other property that cannot conveniently be brought to a depot." Claiborne set out and on December 3 reached Econochaca, Weathersford's own town. At the cost of one man killed and six wounded he accounted for a modest 30 Indians, and burned the town. He almost captured the half-breed chief himself. In the course of the fight Weathersford found himself surrounded by Claiborne's men as he sat on his horse on a high cliff above the river. Rather than suffer the humiliation of surrender, as the Americans approached Weathersford dug his heels into the ribs of his mount and horse and rider together plunged into the stream. Both came to the surface uninjured and made good their escape. Then the familiar bogey of short-term enlistments appeared to blast Claiborne's hopes as it had done Jackson's. Within a month only 60 men remained on duty with him in the fort to which he had retired and which bore his own name.

When the books were balanced at the close of the year 1813 the Creeks were on the credit, the United States on the debit side. More than 7,000 troops had been poured into the Indian country and in the course of the several expeditions 800 Creek warriors had been slaughtered. Yet, after six months' effort, the seat of the trouble had not yet been reached and the principal malefactors remained at large. It could not be said that Fort Mims had been avenged or even that guarantees had been created against a similar occurrence.

On the American side, however, there was one potent factor. The tall, iron-gray soldier with the piercing eye and the determined chin was still at Fort Strother. Jackson's indomitable will had not been broken. The obstacles that had stood in his way had merely served to strengthen his resolution. Slowly but surely he was convincing the administration in Washington, as he had already convinced his soldiers on the march back from Natchez, as to what sort of a man he was.

Shortly after New Year's there arrived at Strother 900 Tennesseans enlisted for 60 days' service. Jackson was determined to make those 60 days count. On January 15, hardly before the new men had had time to settle down to camp routine, he set out with them on a raid in the direction of the Tallapoosa River. Accompanying the expedition were 200 friendly Cherokees and Creeks and Colonel Coffee with 40 volunteer horsemen, all that remained of his command after the choice had been given the men of staying at Strother or going home. The expedition gained contact with the Indians near Emucfau and at Enotochopco Creek, and results were achieved as was customary where the American forces could get within striking distance. Some 189 Creeks were killed with a loss to Jackson's force of 20 killed and 75 wounded. After this minor success Jackson withdrew to Strother. It had served to keep his hand in and also to distract the Indians from a similar raid being made by General Floyd from the east. Floyd's column struck on the Calebee River. As soon as the Americans attacked the Indians retired, leaving 37 dead behind them, but in their retreat they took a somewhat costly toll of 17 Americans killed and 132 wounded. The losses served to dampen Floyd's enthusiasm and, besides, his men were on short enlistments which were about to expire; so he, too, withdrew his force.

Unimportant as these various expeditions had been in bringing about a decision they taught Jackson that he could not lead a large body of men into the wilderness of central Alabama and count upon their living off the land. Arrangements had to be made for carrying provisions and maintaining supplies. He also learned that 60-day militia and volunteers were not dependable for a sustained campaign. By February 6, thanks largely to the efforts of Governor Blount at home, Jackson had under his command a force of 5,000 men, including some friendly Choctaws. Most important of all was the arrival of 600 regulars of the 39th U. S. Infantry. Jackson used them to brace his command and also to help him in instilling discipline among the recruits.

Some of the Tennessee volunteers were not altogether satisfied with conditions as they found them at Strother and openly expressed their opinions. Jackson perceived that here were the seeds of the insubordination that had given him so much trouble a few months before and he had no intention of allowing them to germinate. When word came to him that General Cocke, who had returned to Strother, had addressed the malcontents in a manner that might be interpreted as sympathetic toward their complaints, Jackson, indifferent to Cocke's high rank, relieved that officer of his sword and ordered him placed under arrest. A private willfully disobeyed an order. Jackson called a court-martial and, when the charges were proved, had the boy executed. It was harsh action and caused a stir in Tennessee. But, at Fort Strother, it put an abrupt end to all rumors of mutiny. With this housekeeping attended to, Jackson could proceed with the war.

Word now reached Fort Strother that a force of 900 Creek warriors with 300 women and children had taken refuge on a peninsula made by a sharp bend in the Tallapoosa River known as Tohopeka, or the Horseshoe, and that they had fortified the position and were awaiting attack. The Horseshoe was protected on three sides by the river itself. In its front, and extending all the way across the peninsula, the Indians had erected a rampart of stout logs.

Jackson accepted the challenge and prepared to move against the Horseshoe. To insure adequate food supplies for his men he arranged for boats to pass down the Coosa River and he also set his men to work cutting a military road through the woods. At one point on this road he erected a fort. As soon as he was assured that his line of communications was intact he marched his men to within a few miles of the Horseshoe.

It was now March 27. Along the line of communications Jackson distributed troops to protect it so that his effective force for the actual assault on the Horseshoe was reduced to about 2,000 men. This was more than twice the size of the Creek garrison; but, on the other hand, the Indians were protected by fortifications. Having given the last instructions to his officers and inspected his men to see that they were adequately equipped with arms and ammunition, Jackson was ready to strike.

Early on the morning of the 27th Colonel Coffee, his cavalry and some friendly Cherokees were ordered to cross the river above the Horseshoe and make their way to the rear of the Indian stronghold. Jackson waited until he received a message from Coffee announcing that this movement had been successfully accomplished. With Coffee in the rear of the fort and separated from it only by the river, Jackson ordered the main body to advance until it was within 80 yards of the ramparts. On a near-by hill, and commanding the fort, he placed two cannons, weapons the Indians most dreaded.

At 10 A.M. the engagement commenced with artillery fire. Jackson hoped to blast a breach in the defenses, but the shells from the cannons had little effect on the heavy logs which reinforced the ramparts. However, while Jackson was engaging the Indians in front, the Cherokees with Coffee swam the river and made off with the canoes of the Creeks which lay in the river behind the fort. Two hundred of Coffee's men embarked in the captured canoes, recrossed the river, set fire to the fort and attacked it from the rear. The defenders thus found themselves caught between two groups of assailants and were forced to weaken their front line in order to meet the threat in their rear.

The battle had now raged for two hours and the Indians were desperately holding on to their position. At noon Jackson determined to decide the issue by storming the ramparts. For this bold task he selected the 39th Infantry to lead the van, supported by a brigade from East Tennessee. When the order was given the regulars, their bayonets flashing in the sun, rushed forward with a shout, to be met by a storm of bullets and arrows fired by the Indians concealed behind the breastworks. Men fell mortally wounded, but still the regulars pushed on. Major L. P. Montgomery, at the head of his men, was the first to reach the breastworks. He leaped onto them and shouted to his men to follow. As he did so a bullet pierced his brain and he fell to the ground dead. Thus, at the most critical moment of the battle, the 39th lost its leader, but a young ensign was on the spot to take over the command. He was a Virginian and his name, later to become famous, was Sam Houston. Houston himself had been wounded by a barbed arrow but, unmindful of his injury, he ordered his men to give the Indians the bayonet.

The Creeks with their tomahawks and clubs were no match for the cold steel of the Americans wielded at close quarters. Some stood their ground bravely and were cut down, but the majority broke and fled. Some tried to swim the river and while they were in midstream became targets for the sharpshooters on the banks. Others sought shelter under a bluff and refused to obey Jackson's command to come out and surrender. Ensign Houston was ordered to dislodge them but before he could carry out the command he received another wound which put him out of the battle. Then the torch was applied and the Indians were smoked out of their hiding place.

The battle now degenerated into a slaughter. Throughout the rest of the afternoon the Americans occupied themselves rounding up and killing Indians and among them some of the squaws and children. Jackson expressed regret over the slaying of the noncombatants which, he said, was accidental. From the standpoint of the Indians the Horseshoe presented a tragic spectacle. On all sides lay the corpses of Indians. Nine hundred warriors had faced Jackson from behind the ramparts in the morning. As the sun went down in the evening the bodies of 550 were counted on the peninsula alone, not including those who had attempted unsuccessfully to escape by the river. Of the original 900 only 200 remained alive. Compared to the victory achieved the American losses were slight. The cost to Jackson was only 32 killed and 99 wounded; the friendly Cherokees lost 18 killed and 36 wounded.

At last Jackson had made good his purpose. Fort Mims had been thoroughly avenged.

Equally important was the fact that the Horseshoe was the decisive battle in the war with the Creeks. Some of the Indian ringleaders remained at large and sought protection from the Spanish and British at Pensacola, but the Creek nation had been crushed. Weathersford did not wait to be hunted down but voluntarily went to Jackson, who withdrew to the Hickory Ground after the battle, and surrendered, asking Jackson to do with him whatever he pleased. Jackson, who admired Weathersford's courage, magnanimously forgave him. Weathersford walked out of the General's tent a free man, and also out of history. He gave no trouble again.

A deputation of Creeks, representing principally those who had remained loyal to the United States, appeared before Jackson to arrange terms of peace. The General had in his possession drastic articles of capitulation which had been prepared for the hostile Indians. But what hostile Indians survived had fled. Since the loyal Indians were the only ones with whom Jackson could deal he applied the capitulations to them, a proceeding that only impressed them all the more with the strange ways of white men. The Creeks could do nothing but accept the terms which hemmed them in on all sides by the whites.

The Creeks had at last been conquered, but the victory was hardly to the credit of the United States. For six months no more than 3,500 Creek warriors, incompletely equipped with guns and ammunition and dependent chiefly upon their bows and arrows, had defied no fewer than 15,000 American regulars, volunteers, and militia. It had cost the United States Government thousands of dollars for food, pay and equipment, not to mention the thousands of dollars that were to be paid out to the survivors and their widows after them over more than a hundred years.

The victory, if it can be called one, really belonged to the British. For at the cost of a small quantity of powder and shot dealt out to the Indians at Pensacola by their Spanish allies they had succeeded in distracting the attention of 15,000 troops that could have been put to more effective use elsewhere.

CHAPTER TWENTY-ONE

Glory, But Nothing More

WHEN the Canadian campaign of 1813 closed with the failure of Wilkinson's expedition to Montreal the forces on the northern frontier remained inactive throughout the rest of the winter and early spring, save for Wilkinson's brief and desultory attack at La Colle. Upon Wilkinson's departure for home the Army of the North was again in search of a commander.

If Canada was to be conquered something had to be done and done quickly. In Europe, from the American standpoint, matters had gone from bad to worse. On March 31, 1814, the Allies entered Paris and the fall of the French Empire became a matter of days. This was of vital consequence to the American cause, for the government in Washington had been informed that, with the collapse of the Empire, fourteen more British regiments of Wellington's veterans would be released for service in America and that plans already had been made to have them in Halifax by August at the latest. If the Americans could not achieve a victory over the limited forces already in Canada there was little hope of achieving it after the arrival of these reinforcements.

It devolved upon Secretary Armstrong to select a new leader. William Henry Harrison, who showed considerable promise, was no longer in the running. Ignored by Armstrong after his victory at the Thames he had resigned his commission and quit the Army in disgust. Jackson was still occupied with his Creek campaign. But even if he had been free it is doubtful if Armstrong would have risked adding to Jackson's prestige by moving him to the Canadian theater of the war.

Armstrong's choice for the post was the Quaker, General Jacob Brown. Under the circumstances, assuming the disqualification of

Harrison and Jackson, the Secretary of War could not have made a better selection. Prior to 1812 Brown's military experience had been limited to the militia. However, he had displayed rare courage and initiative in his defense of Sackett's Harbor and his conduct during Wilkinson's expedition had been uniformly good; in fact, one of the few bright spots in that disastrous campaign. What Brown lacked in the arts of strategy and tactics was fully made up for by his zeal, and he enjoyed the confidence of his fellow officers and his men, which is more than could be said of Wilkinson.

The selection of a commander accomplished, the next thing was to devise a plan of action. Armstrong first proposed the now-familiar scheme of attacking Kingston in conjunction with Commodore Chauncey's squadron at Sackett's Harbor, preceding it with a feint on the line of the Niagara River. But Armstrong's wording of the order was so ambiguous that Brown assumed the main attack was to be made along the Niagara and lost considerable time marching his men back and forth before an understanding was reached. Eventually, however, Armstrong's first plan was scrapped; it was decided to ignore Kingston for the time being and concentrate on Niagara. (See Map II, p. 110)

Brown's available force consisted of some 3,500 men. Its nucleus was two brigades of regulars, one under Brigadier General Winfield Scott, the other under Brigadier General Eleazar Ripley. Scott's brigade was encamped at Buffalo and consisted of 65 officers and 1,312 men recruited from Massachusetts, Vermont, Pennsylvania and Connecticut. Ripley's brigade, 36 officers and 992 men from Massachusetts and New York, was stationed at Black Rock, a few miles from Buffalo. Also under Brown was Brigadier General Peter B. Porter with a force of 600 militia volunteers from Pennsylvania and a detachment of friendly Seneca Indians. Artillery to the number of 15 officers and 330 men completed the army.

The British at this time held Fort Niagara on the American shore at the mouth of the Niagara River, Fort George on the Canadian shore directly opposite, and Fort Erie on the Canadian shore overlooking Lake Erie, Black Rock and Buffalo. The British army confronting the Americans, and distributed among the three forts and in the towns of Queenston and Chippawa, was composed of 2,300 officers and men, including a detachment of Indians, all under the immediate command of Brigadier General Riall, an Irish officer of questionable ability who was said to have bought his way to his distinguished rank. However, at Burlington Heights and York were reinforcements capable of increasing Riall's force to 4,000.

According to the final plan Brown was first to cross the Niagara at its source, capture Fort Erie, sweep down the left bank of the river through Chippawa and Queenston and capture Fort George, recross the river and recapture Fort Niagara. At the mouth of the Niagara he was to be met by Chauncey's squadron from Sackett's Harbor and, protected by the fleet, march on Burlington Heights, thereby driving the British out of the whole of the peninsula between Lakes Erie and Ontario. But a British attack on Oswego, New York, destroyed American supplies and weakened Chauncey's position at the harbor where he was virtually bottled up.

It was an ambitious proposal. The United States had at last got together an army with more than a semblance of discipline and order. This time there was to be no hesitation about serving on foreign soil, no quitting the field because the term of enlistment had expired. Scott, in particular, had not wasted the winter months in idleness but instead had devoted them to the serious purpose of whipping his brigade into shape. Report had it that he drilled his men regularly from eight to ten hours a day, so that they had become an efficient, hard-hitting force.

There was, however, one serious drawback. Defenders of Ripley say that he was a gallant soldier but admit that he was cautious, a characteristic that was possessed by neither Brown nor Scott. This cautiousness kept him out of tune with his superior and his fellow brigadier. He was not long in displaying the fact that he was not in accord with the expedition and questioned the likelihood of its success. Certainly his reticence did not make success more likely.

Brown selected July 3 for the attack on Fort Erie and gave orders for the army to embark before dawn in boats provided for the crossing. Scott's brigade was to set out from Buffalo and attack the fort above, Ripley's brigade simultaneously was to cross from Black Rock and attack below. But the order did not suit Ripley. He doubted that the fort could be taken and said so. Furthermore he supported his objections by tendering his resignation. Brown, perhaps unwisely, refused to accept it and told Ripley to go ahead and execute the order.

Pursuant to his instructions Scott crossed the river in the early morning darkness and when dawn broke his brigade was on Canadian soil drawn up in line of battle ready for the assault. Ripley, on the other hand, had not left the American shore. Nevertheless Brown attacked without the aid of Ripley who a few hours later made the crossing. As matters turned out Ripley's dilatory behavior made no difference in the outcome, for Fort Erie proved to be poorly fortified and weakly garrisoned. After the exchange of a few shots the British officer in command raised a white flag and the defending force of less than 200 men walked out and were sent as prisoners back to Buffalo. The skirmish cost the Americans four men killed and one wounded; the British lost one man killed.

Meanwhile Brigadier General Riall, receiving word of the attack, hurried forward reinforcements composed of 1,500 regulars and 600 Indians and militia. These had reached Chippawa, a few miles distant, when they learned that Fort Erie had already been captured and there Riall halted to await eventualities. On the following day, the anniversary of Independence, Brown ordered Scott's brigade and Captain Nathan Towson's battery to advance in the direction of Chippawa. Scott drove in the British pickets and marched to Street's Creek, about a mile from Chippawa, where he encamped for the night. He was joined at midnight by Ripley's brigade and Major Hindman with the rest of the artillery. Brown's army numbered in all 3,500 men exclusive of the Indians.

The American and British forces were now not much more than a mile apart. Between them lay a plain about a mile wide, flanked on the east by the Niagara River and on the west by a dense wood. South of this plain and emptying into the Niagara was Street's Creek which served as a protection to the American army, and north of it was the Chippawa River behind which was the British camp. A road skirted the bank of the Niagara and two narrow bridges carried the road over Street's Creek and the Chippawa River.

The rapidity with which the contending forces approached each other was due more to accident than design. Aware of their nu-

253

merical superiority over the British the Americans did not dream
that Riall would risk an engagement. Riall probably would not have
done so if he had not been misled by one of his subordinates, the
Marquis of Tweedale. It so happened that before the opening of the
campaign Scott's men were in need of new uniforms. The conven-
tional color for regulars was blue but when Scott put in his requisition he was informed by the Quartermaster Department that the
only cloth available was gray. Scott was not the sort of man to hag-
gle over the color of uniforms when his men needed them so he instructed the quartermaster to make them up out of the gray cloth,
and it was these new gray uniforms the brigade was wearing as it
approached Street's Creek. Thus it was that the Marquis of Tweedale, observing the advancing American column through his field
glass, noted the unusual color of the uniforms and concluded that
the troops must be militia. It did occur to him that they were displaying a boldness that was somewhat rare for militia but he attributed this to the probability that they had, as true patriots, been cele-
brating the national holiday and were fortified with Dutch courage.
He therefore reported to Riall that there was nothing but militia on
his front and Riall felt completely assured and did not order a retreat.

At noon on July 5 Scott was reinforced by General Porter with
his Pennsylvanians and Indians. About 4 P.M. he observed British
troops in the woods and, assuming that they were some insignificant
detachment, he ordered Porter to advance and disperse them. Porter
at once set his men to the task and accomplished it so successfully
that he drove the enemy all the way back to Chippawa, never
dreaming that he was running into Riall's main body. It did not take
him long to discover his mistake and, in a few minutes Porter, his
Pennsylvanians and his gallant Seneca warriors were racing back to
the American camp in complete rout with hardly enough breath
left to report that the whole British army was upon them.

Brown, who first received the news, notified Scott. It seems that
the Marquis of Tweedale was about 24 hours off in his calculations
on the celebration of Independence. For some reason that had
been postponed until July 5 when the American troops partook of a
hearty dinner. But, Independence or no Independence, Scott refused to let a holiday interrupt his disciplinary routine. He deter-

mined to make his men sweat out the food and drink they had just consumed and, at the very moment Brown's message reached him, he was leading his brigade across the bridge over the creek and on to the plain for a grand parade and review, as he expressed it, "to keep them in breath." In spite of the information brought back by Porter he remained incredulous and expressed doubt that he would find more than a few hundred British on his front. However, he would drive them off and then proceed with the review.

While these thoughts were passing through Scott's mind Riall's army was already advancing toward him in three columns across the plain. In a few seconds Riall's artillery, planted beside Chippawa bridge, began to play unmercifully upon the American ranks, and then at last Scott realized that he had not a review but a battle on his hands. Undaunted by the unexpected turn of events Scott calmly ordered Major Thomas Jesup and the 25th Regiment to move toward the woods to protect his left flank. On his right flank, near the Niagara River, he posted his artillery to deliver an oblique fire at Riall's advancing column. In the center he placed Major John McNeil and the 11th Regiment and Major Henry Leavenworth with the 9th.

His dispositions were made none too soon, for as the Americans hastened to their positions the British infantry approached within effective range and the battle became general all along the line. Then the full weight of Tweedale's mistake made itself felt. No militia could have executed a difficult maneuver as swiftly as did Scott's regulars after they had been taken by surprise. The long hours of drill throughout the winter upon which Scott had insisted proved their true worth in the test. The American line, instead of breaking as Riall expected it to do, held firm. As the battle raged, gaps began to show in the British ranks. Scott was quick to detect them and equally quick to take advantage of them. He picked out a point where he thought there was a good opportunity to drive a wedge. Then he indicated the spot to McNeil and Leavenworth and ordered them to charge. With a shout the men of the 11th and the 9th moved forward and attacked the enemy with bayonets. And there, within sound of the great falls of the Niagara, on that late summer afternoon, Americans and Britons met in hand-to-hand combat and fought it out.

The issue was not long in doubt. The bright scarlet line wavered under the pressure of cold steel, then broke. And in another instant the Britons, who only a short time before had marched proudly and confidently on the plain, turned about and fled while the men of the 11th and 9th Regiments followed in hot pursuit. The chase did not end until the British pulled up in comparative safety behind the protecting waters of the Chippawa River.

Jesup, on the left flank, was equally successful with his assignment. The British forces against him, seeing the disorder in the center, gave up the struggle and joined in the general rout. Ripley's brigade at last arrived on the field, but too late to take part in the battle. Consequently the American force actually engaged was slightly smaller than the British. For the first time in the war British and American regulars had met on even terms and the Americans held possession of the field. It was a tribute to the American regular but it was even more a tribute to General Winfield Scott.

As the battle drew to a close a thunderstorm broke over the field and both armies were thoroughly drenched by the downpour and their ardor considerably cooled. Reconnoitering parties from the American ranks reported the British position behind the Chippawa too strong to be taken by assault, so Scott called it a day. As the storm passed over and the setting sun broke through the clouds in the west Scott's triumphant army reached its camp by Street's Creek. The rest of the evening was devoted to counting the dead and collecting the wounded. In the engagement the Americans lost 61 killed, 255 wounded and 19 missing; the British, 236 killed, 320 wounded and 46 missing. The plain on which the battle had been fought lay deserted. And, in spite of the American victory, the armies remained in the same positions they had held before the battle commenced.

Next day Brown ordered a bridge constructed over the Chippawa to the left of the British position in order to assault it on the flank. The job was assigned to Ripley but, as usual, he offered objections. Meanwhile Riall got wind of Brown's plan and withdrew out of harm's way, past Queenston and westward up the peninsula in the direction of Burlington Heights. In his train followed Brown's army but it held to the shore road until it came within sight of Fort George. There Brown halted and looked for the sails of Chauncey's fleet which he expected would meet him at the mouth of the Niagara. But no fleet was in view. The General sat down and composed a letter to Chauncey in which he pointed out that with the assistance of the fleet he was prepared to drive the British out of Upper Canada. In language more forceful than was customary in Quaker usage, which prefers affirmation to oath, he concluded, "For God's sake, let me see you."

But Brown was not to see Chauncey, who usually managed to have a good excuse for doing nothing. The Commodore at that moment was ill in bed with a fever; and, even if he had been in good health, he could have been of no help since his fleet was held in Sackett's Harbor by the ships of Sir James Yeo. Chauncey was not long in advising Brown of the situation. In addition, the General received the equally discouraging news that Riall had been reinforced by Lieutenant General Gordon Drummond. Not only was Brown unable to follow up his victory at Chippawa, but his own army was in a critical position where it had halted. There was nothing he could do but retrace his steps. The retreat soon got under way, but not before Colonel Stone of the New York militia had taken it upon himself to burn the village of St. David's, which had no strategic value. Stone was court-martialed and dismissed from the service, but that, as events later proved, was not sufficient to prevent the British from making reprisals.

On July 24 Brown and his army arrived at Chippawa and pitched camp above the Chippawa River. Close behind the retreating Americans followed the British who were soon reported at Queenston. There were rumors, too, that Yeo's fleet was in the Niagara and that a British force had crossed to the American side of the river at Lewiston. This was indeed alarming news, for Brown had a base of supplies at Schlosser, a few miles above Lewiston. Brown knew that a British advance in force on the American side of the river would force his withdrawal from the Canadian side, if he was to maintain his communications. There was one line of action he could take that would discourage the British movement. It required boldness. That was to send Scott forward to threaten Queenston and other points on the Canadian side.

As a matter of fact, the information Brown had received was incorrect. British troops had crossed the river but they were only a small force that was repulsed by a body of American militia before it reached the base at Schlosser. The British main body was still on Canadian soil and advancing rapidly from Queenston. The head of the column had already reached Lundy's Lane, a road which ran due west from the river a short distance below Chippawa.

Pursuant to Brown's order Scott, at 5 p.m. on July 25, with less than 1,200 men including Towson's artillery, crossed the bridge over the Chippawa and prepared to move forward. No sooner had he done so than he discovered the British drawn up in line of battle along Lundy's Lane. Scott did not dare to turn back for he realized what might happen if his brigade were seized by panic while attempting to escape by the narrow bridge in its rear. Besides, retreat was not welcome to Scott's nature. Instead he decided to put on a bold front and lead Riall to believe that he had the whole American army to fight, hoping that aid might come to him in time.

As a result of the battle of Chippawa Brown's army had been reduced to 2,644 effectives. Riall and Drummond, on the other hand, had 2,995 men. Of this force Riall, with 950 men, was already at Lundy's Lane, Drummond was three miles away with 815 men and six miles away was another British force of 1,230. Though Scott's force was slightly superior to Riall's, on the other hand Riall had materially strengthened his position by posting his artillery on a hill in the center of the line.

As Scott faced the enemy his keen eye, always on the lookout for any object of tactical value, fell upon a heavy growth of brush near the river's edge which afforded excellent cover. He directed Major Jesup to use the brush as a screen for his movements, to intercept the British reinforcements which were coming up and turn Riall's left flank while Scott himself attacked the center of the British line. Jesup, who had undertaken the flanking movement in the battle of Chippawa, now essayed the same task at Lundy's Lane. His men crept stealthily through the brush, completely hidden from view. All the while Scott monopolized the enemy's attention with a heavy fire directed at the center.

Before the British suspected what was happening Jesup's men had gained not only their flank but their rear. They even overran the British headquarters and among the prisoners captured was General Riall himself. However, by this time the British reinforcements were reaching the field in such numbers that Jesup could not hold his ground and, to escape capture, he had to retreat.

Brown, back at Chippawa, heard the sound of the guns and realized that Scott had run into the enemy. He ordered Ripley's brigade and Porter's militia to follow him at the double quick to the scene of action. When he arrived he found Scott still holding on but his brigade badly cut up. It was now 9 P.M. The sun had long since set and the field of battle was lit by a July moon, shining faintly through the smoke of the guns. In the semidarkness it was virtually impossible to distinguish friend from foe and confusion reigned in both armies. It was worse among the British where detachments became lost and fired into each other.

Scott's brigade had borne the brunt of the fighting for something like four hours. The men were exhausted and their ammunition was giving out. The General himself had been severely wounded in the shoulder but continued in command. Brown therefore ordered Ripley's brigade to relieve Scott. It soon became clear that the key to the British position was the battery of guns mounted on the hill. Turning to Colonel James Miller, a veteran of Harrison's campaign in the west who was standing beside him, Brown ordered him to take a detachment of his 21st Regiment, all Massachusetts men, and capture the guns.

"I'll try, Sir," was Miller's reply, which was to become a classic and to be drummed into the heads of American schoolboys for many years to come. Taking advantage of every bush and shadow and keeping low to the ground Miller and his men crept up the side of the hill. Without being detected they came so close to the British position that they could hear the talk of the gunners and see them distinctly silhouetted against the sky in the moonlight. There was a brief moment of suspense. Then, at a given signal, the attackers fired a volley at point-blank range which mowed down every man in the gun crews. With a shout the men of the 21st rushed forward and seized the guns, beating back the British infantry that had been stationed behind the crest of the hill to protect them.

Reinforcements now came up, for news of the capture of the guns spread swiftly through the British ranks, but though they suffered heavy casualties Miller and his men beat off every attack and remained in possession of the guns. By many people the capture of the British battery at Lundy's Lane was regarded as the most gallant action on the field throughout the whole war. The hour was now 10:30 P.M. Not only had Scott been forced to leave the field, but General Brown also had suffered a flesh wound from a bullet and a bruise from a fragment of shell. His pain was so intense that he could scarcely sit his horse and he, too, had to withdraw.

Brown's injuries seemed to affect his mental processes for he then issued an astonishing order. Though the enemy was still on the field he directed Ripley to march his brigade back to Chippawa, feed, rest, and reorganize his men and return to the battlefield at dawn to renew the engagement. There were no horses available to draw the captured guns which had to be left on the hill. Ripley obeyed this fantastic order, but it was 1 A.M. before he reached Chippawa. And, very naturally, it was considerably after dawn before the brigade was again on its way to the battlefield. Before it arrived a courier galloped up bringing the distressing news that the British had risen earlier in the day and that they were already in possession of the guns, the hill and the field. All of the previous day's labors had been in vain. As for Major Miller who, with the men of the 21st performed such heroic action, he might just as well not have tried.

The American losses at Lundy's Lane were 171 killed, 572 wounded and 110 missing; the British, 84 killed, 559 wounded, 193 missing and 42 captured. The British claimed the battle as a victory. In view of the fact that they held the field and suffered the smaller losses in killed, the claim is justified in spite of the gallantry displayed in the combat by the Americans. Most serious, however, were the wounds of Generals Brown and Scott and Major Jesup. Worst of all, the fight at Lundy's Lane proved the last for General Scott for many years. His shoulder refused to heal and he left the front to go to Philadelphia where he was treated by the capable Dr. Physic. Before he was again ready to take the field the war had come to an end.

By this time General Brown had lost all confidence in Ripley and sent for General Edmund Pendleton Gaines, who was at Sackett's Harbor, to take over the command. Pending Gaines' arrival Ripley was ordered to fall back to Fort Erie. Ripley was all for returning at once to American soil, but was overruled by his fellow officers.

While Drummond lingered at Lundy's Lane awaiting reinforcements the Americans set to work with a will to strengthen Fort Erie which was badly in need of it. From July 27 to August 2 they labored manfully digging entrenchments and constructing an abatis all the way from the star fort on the right to Snake Hill on the left, where Towson's battery was stationed. Another battery was moved into position to the right of the star fort. The stronghold now had an impressive line of fortifications in its front while its rear was protected by Lake Erie. Adding power to the defenses were two armed schooners on the lake whose guns could be trained on advancing enemy columns.

On July 29 Drummond received reinforcements of 1,100 men and immediately put his army in motion toward Fort Erie. He halted and pitched camp two miles away and raised fortifications of his own. A detachment was sent across the river to attack Black Rock but failed in two attempts and returned to the Canadian side. The British now commenced a methodical siege of Fort Erie. From August 7 to August 14 they maintained a heavy bombardment, but without doing serious damage to the fort or its garrison. General Gaines had by this time arrived and assumed command.

In some manner Gaines obtained the vital information that Drummond had selected the night of August 14 for his assault. While he could not be sure of the truth of the report, nevertheless he took the precaution of keeping his men on guard. It was fortunate for him that he did so. At midnight a strange silence fell over the British line. Two hours later it was broken when the American pickets, who had been thrown out in the front of the fortification, fired their muskets to give the alarm and fell back hurriedly upon the works. The British attackers, bringing scaling ladders with them, followed close behind. They were divided into three columns; one to assault the left of the American position, one the right and one the center. On the left Towson's battery opened up; and, though it had to fire blind, it succeeded in driving back the enemy in that quarter. Five times the British charged against the center where Ripley's men were stationed along the breastworks, and each time the attackers were repulsed.

The defense on the right was less successful. There the British managed to gain a foothold and gradually made their way into the bastion. The Americans met them in a hand-to-hand encounter and, though they held the enemy at bay, they were unable to drive them out. Dawn broke and disclosed the British still in possession. Having gained this advantage the British had more than an even chance of strengthening their hold and enfilading the whole of the American line of fortifications. Indeed at that moment the defense of the fort seemed exceedingly doubtful.

At this tense moment a terrific explosion occurred. The bodies of British and Americans were hurled into the air along with dirt, stones and timbers. By some accident the magazine under the bastion had been touched off. Those of the attackers who survived the explosion imagined that they had walked into a trap deliberately set for them. Fearful that this was only a prelude to something even worse they retired to their entrenched camp, leaving the fort safe in American hands. So, thanks to an accident, the Americans won the day though in the course of the action the two schooners on the lake were captured by the British. Drummond's losses were severe. No less than 221 of his men were killed outright, 174 were wounded and 186 captured. The Americans got off with only 17 men killed, 56 wounded and 11 missing.

Gaines became the hero of the hour. He was promoted to major general, a gold medal was struck in his honor, resolutions were drawn up by numerous patriotic bodies and he received swords from the grateful states of New York, Virginia and Tennessee.

Soon after the attack of the 14th Gaines was wounded and forced to give up his command. Brown again called on Ripley to take over the defense of the fort, an appointment that proved highly unpopular with the garrison. When he learned the state of affairs Brown, in spite of his wounds, assumed command himself. Meanwhile typhoid fever broke out in the British camp and Brown decided to profit by the enemy's misfortune, make a sortie from the fort and attack the fortified camp. He was encouraged in this resolve by the arrival of General Porter with 2,000 fresh troops. Ripley lived up to his reputation by offering objections to the proposal. In the attack on Fort Erie he had shown that he was not lacking in courage when he was on the defensive, but the mere suggestion of an advance threw him into a fit of alarm and foreboding. Ripley's attitude, however, had no effect upon Brown. He proceeded with his plan.

September 17 was the day selected for the operations. Under cover of a thick fog the Americans moved out of their lines in three columns and approached within a short distance of the British position before their presence was discovered. They proceeded to storm the works and in less than forty minutes captured four batteries, two blockhouses and the whole line of entrenchments. But the success was not without cost. Eighty of Brown's men lost their lives and 480 were wounded. Though the British lost 500 men in killed and wounded, and 385 of their number were captured, the Americans could not break their resistance. Having considered the situation carefully Brown decided to call off the attack and return to Fort Erie. The assault, however, had its effect upon Drummond for soon after he retired voluntarily to a less exposed position behind Chippawa.

Preceding the battle of Plattsburg, General George Izard led an army of 4,000 men from the Champlain front to Lewiston and replaced Brown in command on the Niagara. Izard conducted several raids on the peninsula which were fruitless. His only tangible gain was the destruction of 200 bushels of wheat. In fact the American invasion had so far degenerated that Izard was ordered to abandon Canada altogether. On November 5, Fort Erie was blown up, and the same day the last of the American troops embarked and put off for the American shore.

In the course of the summer of 1814 an American army of 3,500 men had taken Fort Erie, swept clean the line of the Niagara and fought two pitched battles. It had boldly withstood an attack on Fort Erie and gallantly assaulted the camp of the attackers. Then, after some three months of marching and countermarching, it had withdrawn to the place from which it had started. It had made history, but it had not gained an inch of new territory. The operations had made the reputations of Jacob Brown and Winfield Scott; they had damaged the reputation of Eleazar Ripley. And this was strange, for Ripley's continued reluctance was due primarily to his belief that the campaign would accomplish nothing. The results stand as irrefutable evidence of the correctness of his belief.

CHAPTER TWENTY-TWO

Washington Burned, the Government in Flight

ON JULY 15, 1813, when Admiral Cockburn was spreading terror in the Chesapeake Bay country, General Philip Stuart, member from Maryland, arose in the House of Representatives and offered the following resolution:

"Whereas the seat of government, from the unprepared and defenseless state of the District of Columbia, is in imminent danger if an attack should be made thereon; and whereas the fleet of the enemy is understood to be within a few hours' sailing of the capital, and whereas the immense value of public property exposed to destruction, the great value of the public records, and other deeply interesting considerations, render it peculiarly important that any invasion of the metropolis should be met with vigor and successfully repelled, whereupon

"Resolved: That in the opinion of the House, a distribution of such arms as are in the possession of the government within the District of Columbia should be immediately made to be placed in the hands of all able-bodied men within the district willing to be embodied to perform military duty, and also in the hands of such members of the House as may be willing to receive them, to act against the enemy in any matter not incompatible with their public duties."

Here was a suggestion to do something. But in mid-July Washington is oppressively hot. At that season of the year people who suggest doing something are unpopular. Not only was General Stuart proposing that the men of the town shoulder guns and knapsacks and execute military maneuvers in the broiling sun, but he was asking his fellow members of the House to set the example. Such energetic action would be almost as bad as being conquered by the

British. Besides, Cockburn was so fully occupied in the Bay country that it seemed unlikely he would go out of his way to attack Washington which, though it was the seat of government and contained many fine buildings, was merely a straggling village of 8,000 inhabitants. At any rate, as the members mopped their brows, that was the more comfortable attitude to take.

After the House had gone into secret session to discuss the resolution a motion was made to lay it on the table. Indicative of the indifference of the House toward the emergency, 64 of the members voted in the affirmative, though the motion was defeated by ten votes. A motion to strike out the preamble was then carried and the resolution, in abbreviated form, was turned over to the Committee on Military Affairs.

The Committee lost no time in bringing in its report. Indeed, the speed with which it did its work suggested that it had been content to ask the opinion of the Secretary of the Navy and the Secretary of War. However the information was obtained, it was most reassuring. "The Committee on Military Affairs," read the report, "to whom was referred a resolution of yesterday, having relation to the present movement of the enemy, report, 'That they have examined into the state of preparation, naval and military, made to receive the enemy, and are satisfied that the preparations are, in every respect, adequate to the emergency, and that no measures are necessary on the part of the House to make it more complete.'"

Having thus met the matter to their satisfaction, the members dismissed it from their minds, hoped for the best and turned their attention to the more pressing problem of how to keep cool.

The inertia of the House was fully justified by subsequent events. In that summer the British fleet sailed up the Potomac but remained a good 70 miles from Washington. Almost a whole year passed before the capital had further cause for alarm. When it came, the House and the whole administration had an admirable, though unfortunate, precedent for doing nothing.

Events had moved rapidly in Europe. After the Russian campaign ended in rout and disaster, Napoleon organized a new army and invaded Germany. In October, 1813, the Battle of Leipsic was fought and lost by the French. Central Europe and Holland rose against Napoleon and the Allies invaded France. On March 31, 1814,

Paris fell and the Emperor departed in exile to Elba. On June 27 a British expedition, composed of veteran troops released from the war in Spain, set sail from the Gironde for Bermuda. It was under the command of Major General Robert Ross, an Irishman who had distinguished himself under Wellington in the Peninsular War. Ross's mission, as outlined to him by the war office, was to create a diversion to relieve the American pressure on Canada. He was not to extend his operations at a distance from the coast nor to hold permanent possession of a conquered district. The point of his attack was to be determined by Vice Admiral Sir Alexander Cochrane, in command of the British base at Halifax.

The Canadians were still smarting over the needless destruction done by the Americans to their own capital of York and to the towns of Newark and St. David's. Sir George Prevost had made known the feelings of his countrymen to Cochrane, and Cochrane accommodated himself to their desires. To the commanders of his ships from St. Croix to St. Mary's he gave orders to "destroy and lay waste such towns and districts upon the coast as you may find assailable." On June 2 he wrote a letter to Ross enjoining him to "assist in inflicting that measure of retaliation which shall deter the enemy from a repetition of similar outrages." To Secretary Monroe he penned another letter threatening fire and destruction unless the United States Government should offer to make reparations for the damage done in Canada. Whether by accident or design—some held that the letter was antedated—Cochrane's message did not reach Monroe until the destruction had been accomplished.

Ross's expedition reached Bermuda on July 24 and, after revictualing, set sail for the Chesapeake where it joined Cochrane's fleet. On August 15 the armada with Cochrane, Cockburn and Ross aboard, dropped anchor at the mouth of the Potomac River. There the three distinguished commanders engaged in a council of war and devised a plan of operations. In the Chesapeake was Commodore Joshua Barney with a strong flotilla of gunboats. Upon learning of the arrival of the British fleet Barney had taken refuge in the Patuxent River, a tributary of the bay, wide and deep enough at its mouth to harbor a modern fleet but narrowing into little more than a creek midway between Washington and Baltimore.

The first objective, as agreed upon at the council, was the destruc-

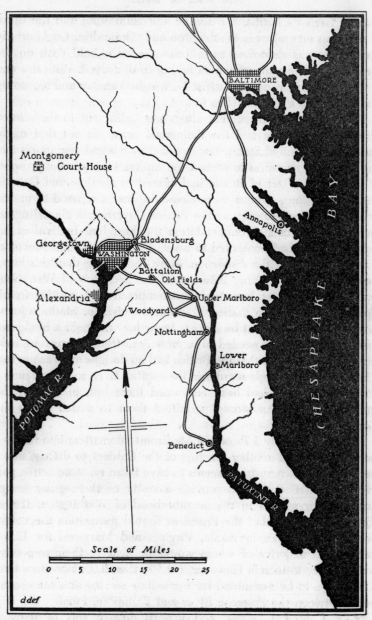

Montgomery Court House

BALTIMORE

CHESAPEAKE BAY

Annapolis

Georgetown
Bladensburg
WASHINGTON
Battalion
Old Fields
Alexandria
Upper Marlboro
Woodyard
Nottingham
Lower Marlboro
POTOMAC R.
Benedict
PATUXENT R.

Scale of Miles

0   5   10   15   20   25

ddef

Map VI. Washington Campaign

tion of Barney's flotilla; the second was Baltimore; and the third, if occasion offered, was Washington and Alexandria. Cockburn, in particular, was described as enthusiastic for a bold dash on the capital once the gunboat flotilla had been destroyed. With this end in view, the squadron, on August 17, weighed anchor and moved up the bay to the Patuxent. (See Map VI)

President Madison was not altogether indifferent to the altered situation in Europe and the dangerous consequences that might ensue in the United States. But two factors worked against his taking energetic measures to protect the capital. One was the prospect of peace. The Czar of Russia had offered to mediate and Gallatin and John Quincy Adams were already abroad prepared to undertake negotiations so soon as the British Government should agree. In answer to their recommendation the President had called his cabinet and it had consented to waive the issue of impressment as a *sine qua non* of the discussion. More compelling than this hope, however, was the stifling influence of the Secretary of War. General Armstrong was brusque, short-tempered and positive in his opinions. He was the soldier, Madison the civilian. Madison knew how to wield a pen but he did not know how to wield a bludgeon, and a bludgeon was needed to impress Armstrong. Armstrong held firmly to the opinion that the British had no designs on Washington. There was not a single regular in the capital. Even so late as June a company of them had been encamped there but, in spite of the gathering storm, Armstrong permitted them to march off to the Canadian front.

However, on July 1 President Madison took matters into his own hands and called another meeting of the Cabinet to discuss measures of defense. Armstrong seems to have taken no more active part in the discussion than to provide a roster of the regular troops available for service in the neighborhood of Washington. It was thereupon agreed that the President should requisition the neighboring states of Pennsylvania, Virginia and Maryland for 12,000 militia, the majority of whom would be held in their respective states, ready to march. However, not less than 2,000 nor more than 3,000 were to be assembled for immediate service at some central point between the Potomac River and Baltimore. Finally, the District of Columbia militia, and various detachments of regulars amounting to about 3,000 in all, were to be put at the disposal of the commanding general. On paper this made a rather impressive little army of 15,000 men.

The question was who was to command them. Armstrong's preference was Major General Moses Porter, an old soldier of the Revolution who had risen from the ranks, and who was now in command of the 5th Military District, with headquarters in Norfolk. In this particular instance the Secretary of War was overruled by the President who, instead, selected Brigadier General William H. Winder, of Maryland. To save the feelings of General Porter the District of Columbia and the neighboring territory were divorced from his command and established as the 10th Military District.

William Winder was an estimable gentleman, springing from the best stock of Maryland. His ancestry and environment were irreproachable. He received a liberal education, moved from Somerset county to Baltimore and became a distinguished ornament of the Maryland bar in competition with such astute legal minds as Luther Martin, William Pinkney and William Wirt. At the outbreak of the war he relinquished his practice and patriotically offered his services to his country. He led Maryland troops to the Canadian border and there engaged in several campaigns. It will be recalled that he had the misfortune to be made prisoner along with General Chandler in the ill-fated pursuit of Vincent after the capture of Fort George.

The close of Winder's career on the border was somewhat inglorious, though he was exonerated from blame. Upon being paroled he returned to Baltimore where he received all the honors customarily bestowed upon a returning hero. Yet, in spite of his distinction, the fact remained that he had never commanded a force larger than a brigade, he was not a soldier by profession and the services he had rendered, though adequate, had not been brilliant. His selection was not based entirely upon his military achievements. There was also a political consideration which weighed heavily with Mr. Madison in making the choice. The state of Maryland had a large Federalist contingent and, when Maryland was suffering under the heel of the invader during the preceding summer, the Madison administration rendered little or no assistance and the state had to depend upon its own resources. Now the shoe was on the other foot. It was Washington that needed the assistance of Maryland and needed it badly. The Federalist governor of the state was Levin Winder, an uncle of the General. So, reasoned Mr. Madison and his advisers, if the nephew of the Governor were given command of the 10th District, Maryland might be expected to enter more heartily into the defense of the capital.

Never was an honor more fraught with impending disaster than that bestowed upon General Winder by President Madison. It was already known that a British expedition had set out for the United States and that its arrival was imminent. To meet the crisis, Winder had been given an army of 15,000 men but as yet it was an army on paper only. His superior, the Secretary of War, had not favored his appointment and did not promise the most complete cooperation. The newly created district was without magazines, provisions for forage, transport tools, general staff or troops. As one observer remarked, Winder "was left to the necessity of being his own commissary, his own secretary, his own vidette and to be himself his own express rider." In short, instead of finding glory, he was about to endure a nightmare lasting no less than six weeks.

Winder was notified of his appointment on July 5 and immediately entered with zeal upon his duties. At once the hopeless inefficiency of the preparations began to assert itself. General Armstrong delayed several days sending out the requisitions to the governors for the militia. When the Governor of Pennsylvania received his he replied that he lacked constitutional powers to raise his quota. At once Winder's paper army was reduced by 4,000 men. The Maryland quota called for 6,000, but Baltimore, Annapolis and Chesapeake Bay were as greatly threatened as Washington and Governor Winder was naturally unwilling to surrender all his troops for the defense of Washington.

The 2,000 or 3,000 militia that were immediately to be concentrated at a point between the Potomac and Baltimore failed to put in an appearance and Winder appealed to the Secretary of War. But General Armstrong, it appeared, had a pet aversion to keeping militia idle in camp before the arrival of the enemy. The Secretary, according to Winder, replied that "the most advantageous mode of using militia was upon the spur of the occasion, and to bring them to fight as soon as called out." This remarkable theory was to have an excellent practical test a few weeks later at Bladensburg.

For 18 days, between July 9 and 27, while awaiting the raising of his army, Winder traveled constantly on horseback through the country he was expected to defend. He was at Baltimore, Annapolis, Marlboro, the Wood Yard, Nottingham, Piscataway, Warburton, and Port Tobacco; several times at the same place and several times at Washington. That area is included in a triangle with sides roughly 30 miles in length, which gives some idea of the distance he must have covered.

Bladensburg, a few miles north of the national capital, Winder had selected as the rendezvous. Yet as late as July 23 he was writing to Armstrong: "It will be necessary that arms, ammunition, accoutrements, tents and camp equipage be deposited there for them [the troops]. I have no knowledge where these articles are in store nearest the point, nor under whose charge they are."

Already weary in mind and body Winder established his headquarters in Washington on August 1. At that late date no line of defense had been selected. Not a breastworks had been raised. Not a single tree was felled across a road to delay the march of the enemy. The total force assembled at Bladensburg amounted to one lone company of Maryland militia.

On August 18 a messenger dashed into Washington to announce the alarming news of the arrival of the British fleet in the Patuxent. Then, at last, the President ordered out all the militia and regulars near Washington and sent fresh requisitions to the near-by governors for militia. Yet even at that late hour the Secretary of War remained unconvinced of the peril that hung over the capital. To General Van Ness, commander of the District of Columbia militia, who expressed grave anxiety over the situation, Armstrong replied, "What the devil will they do here? No, no; Baltimore is the place, Sir; that is of so much more consequence."

To Winder during the next few days Armstrong gave abundant advice. What he failed to provide was the means of carrying it out. While the commanding officer remained in Washington to catch up on his paper work and respond to the hundreds of miscellaneous duties that fell to his lot, James Monroe volunteered to go to the front to see what the enemy was up to. And so, at least for a time, was presented the rare spectacle of the Secretary of State of a nation acting as a vidette, a task which a staff officer might ordinarily have been expected to perform.

On August 19 the British fleet sailed some 20 miles up the Patuxent, as far as the large ships dared go, and anchored off a small settlement known as Benedict. Under the protection of the guns of the men-of-war the disembarkation began. Small boats loaded with soldiers put out for the shore and, as they landed, the men formed into line of battle while pickets were thrown out and all houses were seized. The precautions proved quite unnecessary. Not a single defender was in sight, not a shot was fired to break the serenity of this peaceful countryside on a fine summer day. If the Secretary of State was watching, he was carefully concealed. By 3 P.M. the whole force of 4,500 men was on Maryland soil without having met any opposition. Barney's flotilla of 30 gunboats had fled farther up the river.

At Benedict the invaders spent the night and the morning of the following day. About 4 P.M. of the 20th the troops were formed in column with advance guard, flank patrols and rear guard and marched northward on a road parallel with the river, keeping abreast of a force of barges which were going in search of Barney. Not American troops, but the southern Maryland climate turned out to be the most formidable enemy. It was a hot summer day; the air was humid and the afternoon sun beat down mercilessly upon the heads of the poor Britons, clad in heavy uniforms and every man weighted down with a gun, 60 rounds of ball cartridges; a knapsack containing extra shirts, boots and socks; a blanket; a haversack with provisions for three days, and a canteen filled with water. There were no horses except those of the officers and 100 sailors cursed and sweated as they hauled the expedition's meager artillery—one 6-pounder and two 3-pounders. Men who had been through the worst of the campaign in Spain and imagined that Spain was hot confessed that they had never felt anything equal to southern Maryland on an afternoon in August.

The troops had been cooped up aboard ship for several weeks and were out of condition for marching. The column had advanced only a few miles when the men began to collapse; first singly, then by half dozens, dozens and scores. It looked as though Ross was about to lose two-thirds of his command without the firing of a single shot. After dragging along for seven miles the army, completely exhausted, encamped for the night and waited for the stragglers to catch up. Hardly had the men finished their supper and laid down when a thunderstorm broke over their heads and drenched them.

On the 21st the army was up bright and early and the sun soon dried them out. They had now been in enemy country two days without seeing a single armed man. Camp was broken and the column advanced toward Nottingham. This day's march was less wearing as it led through a thick wood which afforded protection from the sun. For the first time the pickets captured two Americans armed with muskets. On being questioned the prisoners professed to know nothing of the American army, explaining that they were only out to shoot squirrels. They had some difficulty in explaining to their captors why they were hunting squirrels with bayonets on their guns. Light skirmishing began during the day, but when the British reached Nottingham they found the place deserted.

The following day, August 22, the column resumed its march in the direction of Upper Marlboro, the next settlement on the road and only about 20 miles from Washington. Here the army camped. In the middle of the night the troops were awakened by a series of loud explosions off to the east. They came from Barney's flotilla. The Commodore, it seems, had abandoned his boats, taking 400 sailors with him and leaving a skeleton crew with orders to blow them up to prevent their falling into the hands of the British. Thus, by Barney's own act and without an engagement, the expedition achieved its first objective. With the flotilla out of the way it was free to proceed either against Baltimore or Washington. At Upper Marlboro Ross remained during the morning of the 23rd, resting his troops and discussing with the members of his staff what his next move should be.

Though Ross did not know it, as he marched from Nottingham to Upper Marlboro quite an impressive American force was within striking distance of his flank. It was composed of 300 infantry regulars, 120 dragoons, 250 Maryland militia and 1,200 militia and volunteers from the District of Columbia in the aggregate, 1,870 men. It carried with it 12 field pieces. Its ostensible mission was to harass the British without bringing on a general engagement. It had marched out of Washington by the Navy Yard bridge over the eastern branch of the Potomac River and continued 12 miles to a place called the Wood Yard. There, on the evening of the 21st, General Winder caught up with it and took command.

Secretary Monroe's reconnaissance had not been particularly successful and, indeed, Winder had great difficulty in getting any reliable information as to the strength and nature of Ross's army. As a matter of fact, from the reports he received, he was under the impression that the British numbered 10,000, more than double their actual strength. This serves to explain why he let them pass from Nottingham to Upper Marlboro without attacking. Throughout the brief campaign the Americans assumed not only that they were facing veterans but also a much superior force.

The approach to Washington from the east was protected by the eastern branch of the Potomac which also goes under the name of the Anacostia River. From Bladensburg, five miles to the north of the capital, to the point where the branch joins the main stream below the town, the river was not fordable. Two bridges spanned the stream directly east of the town. Thus, if the bridges were destroyed the British would be forced to enter Washington by the Bladensburg road. Even if the attacking forces had been equipped with pontoon bridges the banks of the river were such that the pontoons could have been thrown across only with the greatest difficulty. That was why Winder believed he could make this approach secure and had selected Bladensburg for his rendezvous.

But Winder was not at all sure that Washington was the objective, an uncertainty in which he was encouraged by the Secretary of War. He, personally, felt that Annapolis was the more likely goal, since it had a good harbor and would afford an opportunity for cooperation between the British land force and the fleet and would serve admirably as a jumping-off-place for an attack on Baltimore. On the other hand, he was afraid that Ross might march against Fort Washington, which stood on the east bank of the Potomac south of the capital, take the fort in the rear and cooperate with a British squadron coming up the river for an attack on Alexandria and the capital from the south. In case of an attack on Fort Washington he would himself need the bridges to cross his own force and go to its aid. The uncertainty as to Ross's next move and a desire to meet every eventuality led Winder to divide his army, basing half of it on Bladensburg and the other half on the bridges. It also made him reluctant to burn the bridges.

Upon learning that Ross was at Upper Marlboro, Winder fell back five miles from the Wood Yard to Battalion Old Fields, the junction of three roads leading respectively to Bladensburg, the eastern branch bridges and the Alexandria ferry. Here he spent the night of the 22nd and was joined by the President and the members of his Cabinet. Next morning the diminutive Commander-in-Chief, wearing a hat with a tall cockade in an effort to look as martial as possible, solemnly reviewed the troops as they broke camp and packed up in preparation for whatever the day might bring forth. Winder was considerably cheered by the arrival of Barney and his sailors. Having dragged their guns by hand all the way from the Patuxent they were thoroughly exhausted. The President and most of his Cabinet returned to Washington while the Commanding General went out on another of his scouting expeditions.

Meanwhile a brigade of Baltimore militia, about 2,000 strong, under the command of Brigadier General Tobias Stansbury, was arriving in Bladensburg. It occurred to Winder that this would be a good time to combine his forces so he sent word to Stansbury to move forward from Bladensburg along the road to Upper Marlboro. In the afternoon he himself rode off to confer with Stansbury. Hardly had he left Battalion Old Fields when scouts arrived there to announce that Ross had left Upper Marlboro and was advancing on the American position by the way of the Wood Yard. A messenger caught up with Winder before the general had gone five miles and reported the alarming news. Winder, who had failed to find Stansbury anywhere on the road to Upper Marlboro, at once sent word to him to withdraw to Bladensburg and defend it at all cost, while he returned to his troops at Battalion Old Fields. Actually Stansbury had received a false report that the British were advancing from Upper Marlboro on him and had quickly withdrawn to a position on Lowndes Hill, just east of Bladensburg.

When Winder arrived at Battalion Old Fields the baggage trains had been sent back to Washington and his troops had taken position to meet the enemy, who were now seen advancing not more than a mile away. Fearful of being overwhelmed, Winder gave the order to retreat. Once their backs were turned to the enemy the raw troops felt their courage leaving them. The commissary wagons which should have supplied them with food had been commandeered to remove the official records from the capital, and they had drawn only two rations since leaving Washington. On the night of the 23rd they had been awakened and frightened by a false alarm that the British were coming. They had marched and countermarched to no purpose, and they were losing confidence in their leader. Tired, hungry and dispirited they set off for the capital. With the thought of the British regulars behind them, each step they took was faster than the preceding one. They did not slow up until they reached the eastern branch and were safely over the Navy Yard bridge.

Winder had been in the saddle since daylight and already had worn out two mounts. It was growing dark, but a sense of duty impelled him to go three miles more to report in person to the President, though there could not have been much for him to tell that the President did not already know. The little town of Washington was seething with all sorts of rumors. Winder's horse was by this time played out, so he left it at an inn and, because he did not know where to find a fresh one, proceeded back to camp by foot.

Arrived at the camp Winder was not satisfied that the preparations for blowing up the bridges were adequate. He thought more powder was needed. Instead of leaving these details to a subordinate he set out again in the dark to find Commodore Tingey, commanding the Navy Yard near by, get him out of bed and ask for more explosives. On the way he fell into a ditch, sprained his ankle and wrenched his shoulder. The strain of the past few weeks evidently was telling on him. He had exhausted his body by keeping constantly on the move and exhausted his mind by listening to counsel not only from the high officers of government but from the countless busybodies and cranks who found ready access to his headquarters with their pet theories of what should be done in the nation's hour of peril. Finally, between 2 A.M. and 3 A.M., according to his own account, he lay down to snatch an hour or two of sleep.

Madison was beginning to doubt the wisdom of his choice of a commander. He even suggested to the Secretary of War that he take over, but Armstrong declined to interfere. Heartily enjoying the situation was another old soldier. Major General James Wilkinson was in the capital and relieved of duty, awaiting an inquiry into his futile campaign against Montreal. But he was willing to forget the insults and injuries he had endured from his government and magnanimously offered to take command, defend the capital from the invader or die in the attempt. His services, however, were declined and he lived to set down in his memoirs just what ought to have been done, a much more agreeable task to him than trying to do it.

Daylight of the 24th found the commanding general little refreshed by his nap. It has been said that he was handicapped by interference from those higher up. On this occasion he invited it, sending a messenger to the President appealing to him and the Cabinet for counsel and advice. President and Cabinet were not long in responding cordially. They were soon at his side—the President, the Secretary of State, the Secretary of the Navy, the Attorney General and the Secretary of the Treasury. The Secretary of War was late in showing up. And there the military commander, the President and government argued and debated what Ross might or might not do.

The suspense, however, did not last long. Suddenly a messenger burst in upon the council of war to announce that Ross had broken camp at Old Fields and was already well on his way to Bladensburg. So Bladensburg it was to be, after all.

Immediately the little group broke up. Monroe offered to gallop ahead and look to the disposition of the troops on the field. Winder had his men called to arms and set himself at the head of the column. At last the Secretary of War appeared. President Madison hastily outlined the situation and the measures that were being taken to meet it, and asked if Armstrong had any suggestions. The Secretary replied that he had not, but remarked wryly that it was to be a fight between regulars and militia and that the latter would undoubtedly be beaten.

The President now set out courageously for the scene of the battle, accompanied by the Secretary of War, the Secretary of the Navy, and the Attorney General. The Secretary of the Treasury was indisposed and did not take the field, but presented the President with a pair of dueling pistols which the latter thrust into his holster. These, combined with his cockade, made him appear more martial than ever. Unfortunately, in the heat of the battle or the confusion of the retreat, some miscreant stole the President's pistols. The Secretary of the Navy was feeling none too happy as he had had to submit to a dressing down from Commodore Barney in the best nautical language. The Commodore had been ordered to stay behind with his guns and sailors and defend the Navy Yard. This was not to his liking and he expressed himself so volubly and profanely that the crestfallen Secretary was prevailed upon to change the order and send him on the double to the front.

As Winder, the District Militia and the other miscellaneous units hastened from Washington, things were in considerable confusion at Bladensburg. Stansbury, on learning that Ross was making for the place, called a council of war to discuss what should be done. Though Winder had ordered Stansbury to hold the position at all cost, Stansbury's council took upon itself to overrule the Commander, contending that the attempt would be futile. During the night he and his command moved from their strong position on Lowndes Hill and started off for Washington. Winder heard of the movement and ordered Stansbury to stay where he was. Again Stansbury called a council and again the council overruled the Commander. It was only upon receiving the order a third time that Stansbury decided to obey it and remain at Bladensburg.

The village of Bladensburg, composed of a few scattered houses, stood on the east bank of the Potomac's eastern branch which, at this point high upstream, was little more than a wide ditch, everywhere fordable. The highway from Baltimore to Washington passed over a narrow bridge, turned abruptly to parallel the stream, then ran west for about 60 yards where it forked; one fork going on to Washington, the other making an angle of 45 degrees and leading to Georgetown. In the field in the angle formed by the two roads were stationed a battery of volunteer artillery from Baltimore, six 6-pounders and 160 men under Captains Myers and Magruder, placed inside breastworks that had been constructed for heavy guns. The front of the works had been hastily reduced in height but, even so, the 6-pounders were slightly tilted so that they could not fire at point-blank range. They did, however, cover the bridge with oblique fire. Supporting the battery was Major William Pinkney, who for the time being had exchanged the robes of the hustings for a uniform, and commanded 160 riflemen. On that day he had no need to black beneath the eyes to appear dramatic. The setting was dramatic enough. To the rear and left were two companies of militia; and, forming a line 50 yards behind, in supporting distance and protected by an orchard, were two newly organized militia regiments commanded by Lieutenant Colonels Ragan and Schutz and the well-trained and uniformed 5th Regiment of Lieutenant Colonel Sterett, of Baltimore. The whole force was on a hill that sloped gently toward the river.

As the Washington road leaves Bladensburg it continues to climb, and a mile from the village the hills through which it passes attain considerable height. Here the District militia, including infantry and artillery, the several small units of regulars and Virginia militia, Barney's flotilla men and marines deployed as they came up after their hurried march from Washington to form a second line. Barney planted his guns in the center of the road and on the hill to the right.

The whole of the American force numbered between 6,000 and 7,000 men, about equally divided between Stansbury's Marylanders who were on the scene at the start and the troops that had followed Winder from Washington. But the contour of the land was such that the troops from Washington were concealed from the view of those nearer Bladensburg and, in the excitement preceding the battle, Winder neglected to inform the latter of the arrival of reinforcements. Consequently, though the total American force outnumbered the British force by almost two to one and had an overwhelming superiority in artillery, Stansbury's men imagined that they were a forlorn hope—3,000 militiamen pitted against 10,000 British regulars!

To make matters worse Monroe, for reasons best known to himself and without consulting Stansbury, moved Ragan's and Schutz's regiments and Sterett's 5th back a quarter of a mile, so that they were too far in the rear to support the artillery that had been pushed out front and also lost the cover of the orchard and stood in clear view of the British. When Stansbury discovered what had been done the British advance guard was already coming into view. While these preparations were being made to receive the attack, the President and his Cabinet rode majestically over the field inspecting the disposition of the troops. In fact so absorbed was the President that he was on the point of crossing the Bladensburg bridge and riding right into the British lines when an American outpost fortunately warned him of his danger.

As disturbed as were the President, the Commanding General and the other dignitaries in that moment of peril, their anxiety was no greater than that of one John P. Kennedy, a modest private in the rear rank of one of the companies of Colonel Sterett's 5th Regiment. The 5th was distinguished as a regiment of dandies and the young man was living up to its reputation. Before leaving home he assumed that victory would crown the American arms and that such a victory would undoubtedly be followed by a victory ball, probably in the White House itself. Therefore, to make sure that he would be dressed as befitted a soldier of the 5th, he packed into his knapsack a pair of white duck trousers and a pair of patent-leather dancing slippers. On the night before the battle the regiment was aroused out of its sleep by a report that the British were coming. The young man took off his marching boots and, in the darkness and excitement, could not find them. Then he thought of the slippers, fished them out of his knapsack and put them on, expecting to recover his boots at dawn. But before dawn the regiment shifted its position. So here he was waiting for the engagement to begin and about to become famous as probably the only private ever to fight a battle in dancing pumps!

It was now high noon. As the Americans looked anxiously out toward Bladensburg they saw the British Light Brigade appear, the men magnificent in their scarlet coats, marching six abreast with the cadenced step of regulars. In sorry contrast was the appearance of the American force which had been so hastily brought together. Part of the Baltimore militia was uniformed but, said an observer in the British ranks, the rest looked like a group of country people.

Without hesitating an instant the Light Brigade started to cross the bridge on which the American 6-pounders were trained. At the command of Captain Myers and Magruder the guns thundered, and the shells hurtled across the field. The first shot killed one Briton and wounded two, driving the brigade back in temporary confusion. For a moment Bladensburg seemed free of the enemy as the attackers took cover behind Lowndes Hill and the houses in the village. But in a few minutes they rallied and returned to the attack, wading through the stream above the bridge and heading straight for the center of the American line. One American militia company fired a single volley, then broke and fled to the rear. The rest stood fast.

The British advanced and again the volunteer artillery in the front line poured shot into them and Pinkney's riflemen joined in with a volley. Once more the Light Brigade was driven back, but now it was reinforced and came on a third time. Six times Pinkney's men loaded and fired but their best efforts were not enough to stem the red tide which was momentarily growing larger and nearer. So close were the British now that the volunteer artillerymen could no longer bring their guns to bear. To escape capture they unlimbered and rushed their guns to the rear, spiking the only one that they were forced to leave behind. Pinkney's men also fell back taking station beside the 5th Regiment. Pinkney himself was wounded. Not even his worst enemy could deny his fortitude and courage that day.

The three infantry regiments on the hill were having their own troubles. The British had now laid down a barrage of Congreve rockets. These were a new and terrifying weapon which, the inventor believed, would eventually replace artillery. The rockets had a range of two miles and came over with a crazy roar. To men in trenches or under cover they gave little concern, but to the troops of Sterett, Schutz and Ragan who stood open to view, thanks to Colonel Monroe's dispositions, they proved a very definite menace. The first volleys flew high but those that followed were lower and grazed the heads of the militiamen. What with the rockets and the confusion caused by the retirement of Pinkney's riflemen, Ragan's and Schutz's men next were seized by the surrounding panic and with a few marked exceptions turned and raced for the rear. Sterett's 5th, on the contrary, moved boldly forward to attack, keeping their line like regulars, and firing a volley at the enemy. But its men were getting severe punishment from the British who had now reached the orchard which might have sheltered the Americans and which prevented them from giving punishment in return. Other enemy troops were working their way to its rear. Winder, who had stationed himself well to the front, saw the predicament of the 5th and ordered it to retire. The regiment up to this point had behaved with gallantry; but, once its back was turned to the enemy, its men lost control of themselves and joined in the general rout.

Nothing was now left of the American advance forces and first line and the British proceeded relentlessly against the second line which, up to this time, had taken no part in the battle. As the red-coats came into view on the road Barney's men let them have a salvo from the guns, driving them into the fields on either side. The artillery stationed to the left of Barney joined in but had little effect on the attackers. Believing that the day was lost at Bladensburg, and before more than a few units in the second half of his army had been engaged, Winder ordered a general retreat, hoping to halt and reorganize his straggling army before Washington. Barney's flotilla men, however, continued to hold fast. They were veterans of many a battle at sea and the noise of cannon and the whiz of shot and shell were familiar music to them. The British attempted a flanking attack but the flotilla men beat it off, killed several of the officers who were leading it and pursued the fleeing foe with cries of "Board 'em!" But Barney's brave stand was not for long. Five hundred sailors could not hold off 3,000 British regulars. Soon the sailors were being assailed on the flanks and in the rear. Barney himself was badly wounded and he and most of his men surrendered to the enemy. At this point Ross and Cockburn appeared on the scene and recognized Barney whom they knew by reputation as a gallant sailor. They treated him with unusual courtesy, had his wounds treated by a British surgeon and removed him to a field hospital at Bladensburg.

Back to Washington streamed the District Militia, the Virginia Militia and the odd lots of regulars with Winder at their head. They were not a beaten army, for most of them had not yet had a chance to fight, and there was still some semblance of order. Winder halted them near the capital. He had directed Stansbury to retreat by way of the Washington road and hoped there would be time to reorganize the Marylanders and make a last stand before the town with a combined force. But the British attack had been launched in such manner as to drive Stansbury's men in the direction of the Georgetown road instead of the Washington road. Thus as the two halves of the army retired they moved farther and farther apart. None of Stansbury's men showed up in Washington. Winder now held a hurried consultation with the Secretary of War and the Secretary of State. They agreed that the defense of the town was hopeless under the circumstances and Winder received their permission to evacuate the capital and continue his retreat through Georgetown in the hope of reassembling his army at Montgomery Court House. As the weary and crestfallen men resumed their march to the west, Washington lay open to the enemy.

Throughout these trying days, while the President was so much at the front, the First Lady of the Land maintained an anxious vigil at the White House. On the morning of the 22nd Mr. Madison had set out to join Winder, first asking his beloved Dolly if she had the courage and firmness to remain alone until his return. She assured him that she had no fear except for him and the success of the army. In her charge the President left the cabinet papers and, begging her to take care of herself, he mounted his horse and rode off.

In spite of his official duties the President had time in the course of the day to scrawl two notes in pencil and dispatch them by messenger to his wife. In the last he told her that the enemy was stronger than had been imagined and might reach the capital. He directed her to have the carriage ready to enter at a moment's notice. Dolly set to work packing the cabinet papers into trunks and stowing the trunks in the carriage. Rumors of disloyalty in the town reached her and increased her alarm for the President's personal safety. The guard of 100 men which had been left to protect the White House vanished. She felt very much alone, except for the presence of a loyal servant, French John, who offered to spike a cannon at the gate and lay a train of powder which would blow up the British if they attempted to enter the executive mansion. Dolly declined this well-intentioned, if fantastic, proposal.

There was little sleep in Washington on the night of the 23rd, but nothing serious happened. While she waited for news Dolly was disturbed by terrifying rumors. Anonymous letters were received threatening the President's life by dagger or poison. There were reports of British spies disguised in women's clothing trying to gain access to the White House to seize the cabinet papers. A less courageous woman than Dolly Madison might well have lost her nerve and fled. Dolly's one thought, however, was the President. From sunrise until noon she repeatedly took out her spyglass and searched the horizon in the hope of catching sight of her husband returning with his friends. All she saw were groups of soldiers "wandering in all directions as if there was a lack of arms or of spirit to fight for their own fireside."

Yet, in the midst of fear and confusion, the women of Washington did not forget the strict conventions of society. A dinner had been planned at the White House for the 24th to which the Secretary of the Navy, his wife and daughter had been invited. As Dolly waited expectantly for news of the President a servant handed her a letter. Excitedly she opened it, hoping it might contain some news of him and the fortunes of the battle.

"My dear Madam," it began, "In the present state of alarm and bustle of preparation for the worst that may happen, I imagine it will be more convenient to dispense with the enjoyment of your hospitality today, and, therefore, pray you to admit this as an excuse for Mr. Jones, Lucy and myself. Mr. Jones is deeply engaged in dispatching the marines and attending to other public duties. Lucy and I are packing with the possibility of having to leave; but in the event of necessity we know not where to go nor have we any means yet prepared for the conveyance of our effects. I sincerely hope and trust the necessity may be avoided but there appears rather serious cause of apprehension. Our carriage horse is sick and our coachman absent, or I should have called last evening to see your sister. Yours very truly and affectionately, E. Jones."

The lady of the Secretary of the Navy had observed the customary amenities. Had General Ross seen the letter he would, no doubt, have admitted the hopelessness of conquering a nation of such indomitable women, however scornfully he may have regarded the men.

The afternoon wore on. The distant boom of guns shook the windows of the White House. At three o'clock Dolly, perhaps to quiet her nerves, sat down to pen a note to her sister, Anna Payne Cutts: "Will you believe it, my sister? We have had a battle or skirmish near Bladensburg and here I am still within sound of the cannon! Mr. Madison comes not. May God protect us! Two messengers covered with dust come to bid me fly; but here I mean to wait for him."

Mr. Carroll, a friend, had come to urge her to leave. He did not conceal his ill-humor when she refused. But there was still much to be done. A wagon had somehow been obtained and Dolly superintended the packing of silver plate and other valuables to be consigned to the Bank of Maryland, though she doubted if they would ever reach their destination. Then there was the great portrait of Washington by Gilbert Stuart which hung in the White House. It would be sacrilege to allow it to fall into the hands of the British. Two gentlemen fortunately arrived at this moment to help in the work of rescue. The canvas was obstinate and could not be got from the heavy gold frame. Dolly gave orders to smash the frame and the portrait was soon on its way to safety in Georgetown.

At any moment the British might appear. There was still neither sign of nor word from the President. Finally Dolly was prevailed upon to leave. She entered her carriage, the coachman whipped up the horses and the First Lady and the cabinet papers were off to the hills of Virginia that never seemed more hospitable.

Late in the afternoon the victorious British column arrived on the outskirts of the capital. A party, which for some reason included General Ross's charger, was sent forward to demand the capitulation of the town. But the government offices were deserted; there was no responsible official with whom to deal. When the party reached a point opposite a house owned by Albert Gallatin a single shot rang out and the General's horse dropped dead with a bullet in his side. The house from behind which the shot had come was immediately ordered to be burned while search was begun for the culprit. He was not found, though the act was commonly attributed to one of Barney's men.

If there had been compassion in Ross before, it was stifled by this inhospitable reception. From now on he took a keen and personal interest in the destruction of public property. Under the orders of Ross and Cockburn the firebrand was applied generously, and shortly the Capitol, the Arsenal, the Treasury, the War Office and the White House were in flames. To save it from capture Commodore Tingey himself ordered the firing of the Navy Yards and the ships that rode at anchor there, including a new ship of the line. This section of the town was soon a roaring furnace. Before long the great bridge over the Potomac between the capital and the Virginia shore was added to the conflagration. The British, fearing reinforcements from Virginia, fired it at the Washington end; the Virginians, to halt the British, fired it at the Virginia end.

Earlier in the evening the President had reached Washington.

Taking a boat at the foot of the White House grounds he had crossed the Potomac; and now, accompanied by the Attorney General, the Secretary of the Navy, Mr. Charles Carroll of Bellevue and Mr. Tench Ringgold, he was again on horseback traveling a rough Virginia road. Behind him his capital and his hopes were going up in flames. Fugitives from Washington who recognized him muttered insults or cursed the President to his face. Political enemies were to accuse him of personal cowardice, laugh at his discomfiture. Rhymesters were to sing satiric songs commemorating "the Bladensburg Races" and putting insulting words into the mouth of his beloved Dolly:

> "Sister Cutts and Cutts and I
> And Cutts's children three,
> Shall in the coach, and you shall ride
> On horseback after we."

The punishment was greater than Mr. Madison's crime deserved. It had been a long, hard day; the longest and hardest in his career. From dawn until long past midnight he had been almost continually in the saddle. How a man over 60 years of age could survive such physical punishment was a marvel. Under Mr. Madison's quiet, unobtrusive exterior there was tough fiber. In the middle of the night the presidential party arrived at a wayside inn that was little more than a hovel. But to the President it appeared as magnificent as the finest of palaces. For inside it was Dolly, still courageous and with her faith in him undiminished. Just then, more than anything else in the world, the President needed her.

Throughout the 25th, the British remained in Washington and made themselves thoroughly at home. The gayest spirit among the visitors was Cockburn, who had proposed the raid and was delighted with its success. In a jestful mood and casting dignity to the winds he rode through the town on a brood mare while a black foal trotted at its mother's side. The *National Intelligencer,* official organ of the administration, had bitterly denounced Cockburn as a marauder and the Admiral now seized the opportunity for revenge and ordered the establishment burned. He was restrained by residents living near by who pleaded that their homes would be endangered, and compromised by having the offices of the publication sacked and the type dumped into the street. "See that all the C's are destroyed," he admonished his men, "so that the editors can no longer vilify my name."

Other marauders singled out the Tripoli Monument in the Navy Yard and, in high good humor, amputated the thumb and index finger of the "Genius of America" who pointed to the inscription, robbed "History" of her pen and removed the palm from the head of "Fame."

The work of vandalism received a sudden and unexpected check when one of the invaders tossed a firebrand into a dry well. The well happened to be stored with kegs of powder; there followed an explosion in which 12 soldiers were killed and 30 wounded. This disaster considerably dampened the ardor of the incendiaries.

As evening came on strict orders were issued to all the natives to remain indoors. The injunction was hardly needed, for there broke over the city a thunderstorm almost of tornado proportions. Trees were uprooted and houses were blown down. The British camp was said to have borne the brunt of the wind and rain. Once more the local elements were doing their best to discourage the enemy.

When the rain had ended and a few bold spirits ventured to look out of doors they noticed an unusual quiet in the British camp. Further stealthy investigation revealed that the place was deserted. Under cover of the storm the raiders had slipped out of the town. As a matter of fact Ross realized the weakness of his force and the distance he was from his base. He was fearful that, once the Americans had recovered from their surprise, they would collect a large force to cut him off and destroy him. So, by forced marches, he hurried his men back by the road they had come and did not slacken the pace until they were safe again on the boats.

In the battle of Bladensburg the British loss was more severe than that of the Americans. A British surgeon estimated it at 150 men killed and 300 or 400 wounded, though the official report gave the total as 64 killed and 185 wounded. The Americans, with their backs to the wall and fighting for the possession of their nation's capital, had been considerably less profligate with their blood. Their total loss was 26 killed and 51 wounded.

When news of the treatment meted out to Washington reached the rest of the country indignation ran high; except, of course,

among the extreme Federalists who looked upon it as the just desert
of the administration's folly. But the attitude of the Federalists was
balanced by the attitude of His Majesty's Loyal Opposition in England which soundly berated the government for the conduct of its
armed forces. "A return to barbarism," commented *The British Annual Register.* "It cannot be concealed that the extent of the devastation practiced by the victors brought a heavy censure upon the British character not only in America but on the Continent of Europe."
"Willingly would we throw a veil of oblivion over our transactions
at Washington," chimed in *The London Statesman.* "The Cossacks
spared Paris, but we spared not the capital of America."

England had its political die-hards, too.

CHAPTER TWENTY-THREE

Plattsburg Stands Fast

ON THE evening of July 14, 1814, little more than a month before the raid on Washington, 100 gentlemen sat down to dinner at Butler's Hotel in Hartford, Connecticut. The toastmaster was the Reverend Timothy Dwight, President of Yale College, and among the toasts proposed and drunk were:

> *"The minority in Congress.* Had they appealed to patriots they would have been heard."
>
> *"The Administration*—Prodigal enough, but too proud to return."
>
> *"The Royal Family of France*—Our friends in adversity, we rejoice at their prosperity."
>
> *"The Democratic Party of America*—If not satisfied with their own country, they may seek an asylum in the island of Elba."

The dinner at Hartford was only one of many celebrations of the fall of Napoleon indulged in by Federalists throughout the country who interpreted it as being as great a defeat for Mr. Madison as for the Emperor, as great a victory for themselves as for the Allies. They did not allow their rejoicing to be dimmed by the fact that the fall of the French Empire was releasing veterans of Wellington's army for service in America and that many regiments were already at Halifax and Bermuda or on the high seas. Many good Federalists believed that the Union was on the eve of dissolution and the sooner it was over the better, so that the states could go their several ways.

Indeed, the situation in the United States was dark and growing darker every day. Almost simultaneously with the dinner in Hartford, Brown's courageous little army was engaging the British at Chippawa and American troops were achieving glory that many of their fellow countrymen scorned, yet the conquest of Canada was as remote as ever. A few days later Lieutenant Colonel George Croghan, the young hero of Fort Stephenson, was leading an attack against Mackinac Island in an effort to wrest its control from the British. But Croghan, on this occasion, lacked the fire that distinguished his conduct in the previous year. The attack failed and the expedition returned home with nothing accomplished.

On the other hand the British had taken the initiative and met with startling success. As early as April British seamen and marines boldly raided the Connecticut River and destroyed 22 American vessels to the value of $120,000 which had sought refuge there. In June other landing parties from the blockading fleet fell upon Wareham, Massachusetts, and burned $40,000 worth of shipping, while still others committed depredations around the mouth of the Saco River in Maine.

In July Sir Thomas Hardy commanded a squadron which set out from Halifax, entered Passamaquoddy Bay, seized Fort Sullivan at Eastport, met with faint opposition from the militia and declared the town and neighboring villages the permanent possession of His Majesty King George III. Fresh from this triumph Hardy sailed west and threatened Boston where the citizens, at last aroused, threw up fortifications in great haste. But Sir Thomas passed by and, on August 9, appeared off Stonington, Connecticut, ordered the women and children out of the town, and prepared to destroy it. Displaying a zeal in marked contrast to their rulers, who had refused to lend a hand in the war by honoring the President's call for the Connecticut militia, the good people of Stonington dragged guns to the end of the peninsula, trained them on the British fleet and fired with such good effect that they drove the marauders off. The ships returned next day, but after 48 hours' bombardment, abandoned the attack and retired to Fisher's Island.

Late in August General Sir John Sherbrooke, Governor of Nova Scotia, led 4,000 men in transports accompanied by a fleet upon an expedition whose object was the conquest of Maine from Passamaquoddy to the Penobscot River. Learning that the frigate *John Adams*, 24 guns, had taken refuge in that water, Sherbrooke landed

600 men to effect her capture. Captain James Morris tried to save his ship by using her guns as a battery manned by the crew and supported by local militia. But, upon the appearance of the British, the militia fled and Morris was forced to burn the ship to prevent her falling into enemy hands.

The people of the Maine coast treated their conquest with surprising indifference. Making little or no resistance they resigned themselves to the inevitable, apparently regarding their United States citizenship as not worth a fight. At least two-thirds of them took the oath of allegiance to King George and settled back quietly as his loyal subjects. For a whole hundred miles the coast of Maine became once more a part of the British Empire. After all, why not? The Boston banks were lending money to the British and the thrifty farmers of New York and Vermont were continuing to supply the British army with beef. General George Izard, who had succeeded Wilkinson in command on the northern front, lamented to the Secretary of War that cattle driven across the border beat paths "like herds of buffalo." And on top of all this the nation's capital itself had been sacked.

In the projected invasion of Canada the right wing of the United States Army based itself on Lake Champlain as the natural gateway to Montreal. But now the tables were turned and the lake served equally well as a gateway into the United States, especially adapted to severing New England from the rest of the country. Burgoyne had attempted it in the Revolution and there was every reason to believe that the same strategy would be pursued again. To meet the threat Izard, in the spring of the year, stood in the way with an army stationed at Plattsburg, supported by Captain Thomas Macdonough with a flotilla at Vergennes, Vermont, at the head of the lake. Izard was ably assisted by a capable staff of officers including Alexander Macomb and Thomas A. Smith as brigade commanders and Major James A. Totten as Chief Engineer. Izard himself was an engineer and the combination proved to be of supreme importance.

Hardly had spring broken when, on May 9, word reached Izard that a British flotilla under Captain Pring, of the Royal Navy, was passing up the Sorel River toward Lake Champlain. The naval force consisted of the brig *Linnet*, five armed sloops and 13 row-galleys. Izard summond Macdonough to his aid and Pring was driven off.

291

Macdonough then sailed back to Plattsburg Bay where he anchored his fleet.

During May both armies awaited reinforcements and in June Izard moved a large part of his army to the lower end of the lake, within a few miles of the Canadian border. Late in the month a small body of American riflemen crossed into Canada, but they were quickly driven off and their leader killed. Soon after, news reached Izard that Sir George Prevost was planning an invasion by way of Lake Champlain and that he would use some 15,000 regulars, Wellington's veterans, who even then were pouring into Montreal from Halifax. This host was far larger than the army Izard had at his command to oppose them. The situation was critical. Izard and Totten, skilled engineers, set to work converting Plattsburg into a citadel of redoubts, trenches and strong points to offset the inequality in men.

Far off in Washington General Armstrong was busy with his pins and maps and his own peculiar theories of strategy. Unlike the leaders in the field he could see the problem as a whole, or thought he could. Just at the moment General Brown was having all he could do to handle the British on his front on the Niagara. Armstrong, after due consideration, arrived at the conclusion that Brown needed support. So absorbed was he in the grand strategy that he overlooked the storm that was brewing on Lake Champlain and the anxiety with which Izard was awaiting the British attack. Imagine, then, Izard's surprise when word came to him from the Secretary of War to take the major part of his force, march to Sackett's Harbor, create a diversion in the direction of Kingston and cooperate with Brown's army on the Niagara!

Izard protested vigorously against the order. He pointed out that the Army of the North was already outnumbered, that Prevost was on the point of swooping down upon him. He predicted that if he were to move with part of his force to a new front, the remainder would have to retire to Plattsburg and that, within a few hours, the British would be in possession of every post at the mouth of the lake. He might just as well have saved his breath. The Secretary of War had spoken and the Secretary of War declined to change his mind.

Like the good soldier he was Izard prepared to obey the order and take 4,000 men with him. To General Macomb fell the unhappy task of assuming command of what seemed a forlorn hope. Izard's departure left him with a force reduced to 3,400 of whom he reported only 1,500 as effectives. His ordnance was in bad shape and the fortifications at Plattsburg were unfinished. Macomb's first move was to recall all detachments from the mouth of the lake and concentrate his whole army at Plattsburg. His next was to appeal to Governor Martin Chittenden of Vermont for the help of his militia. Governor Chittenden was a conscientious man who had brought himself to the belief that he had no right under the constitution and laws of his state to order the militia outside the state borders, even if the might of the British Empire was passing his doors. However, if the Vermont militia cared to go as volunteers he would not forbid it. From the militia officers Macomb received the reassuring news that the Vermonters, 2,500 strong, would be there. To reinforce Macomb came also 800 militia from the New York counties of Clinton and Essex under the command of General Benjamin Mooers, a veteran of the Revolution. Yet what were all these compared to the 15,000 veterans of the Peninsular War now posted all the way from Montreal to Lake Champlain and only awaiting the order to move on Plattsburg and crush the handful of defenders?

Plattsburg stands on high ground overlooking Lake Champlain, at the mouth of the Saranac River. The Americans elected to establish their defenses in the lower end of the town on a peninsula almost square in shape lying between the river and the lake. The river protected their front, the lake the rear and one flank. On the open side Izard and Totten employed their engineering skill in the construction of three formidable redoubts. A ravine cutting through the center of this fortified area from the river almost to the lake contributed another natural obstruction to an attack. This well-selected position was further strengthened by two blockhouses and a stone mill, which served as strong points. Two bridges, leading to roads by which the British would come, spanned the Saranac. The lower bridge was near the mouth of the river, the upper bridge about a mile upstream. There was a ford three miles above the lower bridge, but the river for the most part was deep and, in some sections along the Plattsburg bank, cliffs rose to considerable height. Across Plattsburg Bay lay a long peninsula known as Cumberland Head, and guarding the entrance to the bay was a good-sized piece of land known as Crab Island. (See Maps VII & VIII)

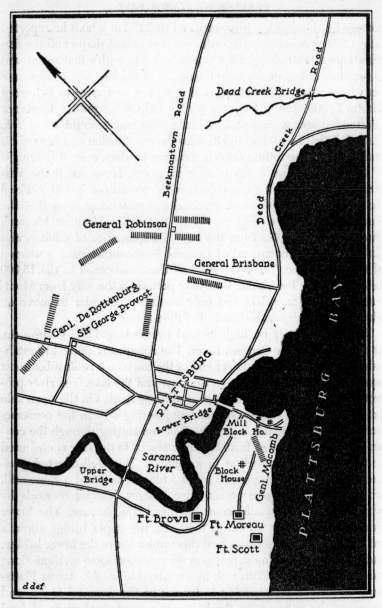

Map VII. Battle of Plattsburg (Land)

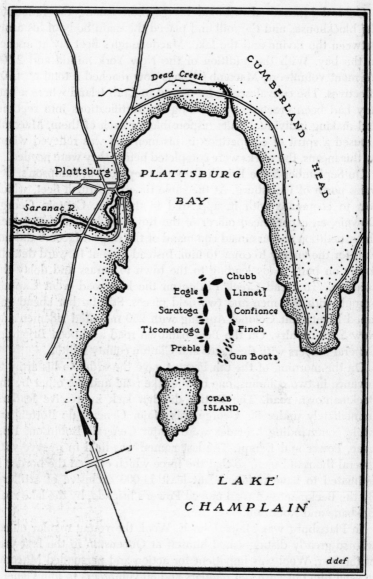

Map VIII. Battle of Plattsburg (Sea)

General Macomb distributed his garrison among the redoubts, the blockhouses and the mill and placed the main body of his army between the ravine and the lake. Macdonough's fleet lay at anchor in the bay. With the addition of the New York militia and 2,500 Vermont volunteers, Macomb's troops now reached a total of 4,700 effectives. The convalescents he moved to Crab Island where a battery had been erected. By dividing the fortifications into sections and making individual units responsible for each of them, Macomb aroused a spirit of competition in his men and was relieved when, by this means, the works were completed before they were needed.

On September 5 the British army was reported at Sampson's, five miles north of Plattsburg. At the same time the British fleet, which was to cooperate with it, appeared in the lake. Captain George Downie, an experienced officer of the Royal Navy, had now joined the expedition and assumed command of the ships. Macomb did not wait for the enemy to come to him. Instead he sent forward detachments on both roads leading to the town to harass and delay the attackers. To Dead Creek Bridge on the lake road went Captain Sproull with 200 men and two field pieces. Still farther ahead galloped Lieutenant Colonel Appling with 250 mounted riflemen and New York cavalry. On the Beekmantown road advanced Brigadier General Mooers with the Essex and Clinton county militia.

On the morning of the 6th Prevost gave the order to his army to advance in two columns, one by the lake road and the other by the Beekmantown road. The British did not lack impressive leaders. Immediately under Sir George was Major General de Rottenberg while commanding brigades were Major Generals Robinson, Brisbane, Power and Kempt. The last named was held in reserve with several thousand men, so that the force which crossed the border is estimated to have numbered at least 11,000 exclusive of artillery. By the Beekmantown road moved Power's brigade, by the lake road Brisbane and Robinson.

In Plattsburg was Major John E. Wool, the young regular officer who so greatly distinguished himself at Queenston in the first year of the war. Wool was impatient for action and persuaded Macomb to send him out with 250 regulars and 30 volunteers to join General Mooers and meet the enemy on the Beekmantown road. Wool and his detachment arrived on one side of Beekmantown as the British arrived on the other. The New York militia, inexperienced in battle and frightened by the first exchange of volleys, broke. Wool placed his regulars across the road where they stood firm and poured a volley straight into the British ranks checking the advance and giving the militia time to reorganize. Wool now fought a brilliant retiring action against the advancing column, moving back slowly to a hill where he made a stand which drove the British spearhead back on the main body with the loss of several officers. He pursued the same tactics until he was within half a mile of Plattsburg Bridge where he was joined by Captain Leonard with two pieces of artillery which went into action and helped further to annoy the British. General Power had to order a bayonet charge to drive the Americans off, but Leonard succeeded in escaping with his guns and crossing the Saranac.

Meanwhile Macomb ordered the withdrawal of Appling and Sproull who had been performing a similar task with the second British column on the lake road. Just as the left column came into sight of the town, Appling and Sproull crossed the bridge and destroyed it behind them, while from the bay Macdonough's guns gave the British a warm welcome. Mooers' New Yorkers crossed by the upper bridge and then destroyed it. All the Americans were now on the far side of the river.

This preliminary action had a salutary effect upon Prevost, a timid man at best, who now was brought to the realization that he had a formidable foe in his front. Looking across the Saranac Sir George saw before him the new fortifications bristling with guns and men, obviously too strong to be taken immediately by storm and with no intention of yielding without a struggle. Prevost therefore halted his men and set them to work erecting artillery emplacements on the heights commanding the town from the far side of the river, while he waited for his heavy guns to come up.

For five days the two armies faced each other, separated only by the waters of the Saranac, and idle save for a casual exchange of shots between the batteries. There was one exception. On the night of the 9th Captain McGlassin, a Scotsman in Macomb's army, with 50 men slipped across the river in front of the town and stealthily made his way to the foot of a hill on which a battery was being erected. The first the British knew of the attack was when they heard the shouts of McGlassin's men as they clambered up the hill. Taken completely by surprise and assuming that the whole of the American army was upon them, the British departed precipitately leaving the guns behind them. The Americans seized the works, spiked the guns and retired across the river without the loss of a single man. The incident proved highly mortifying to Sir George and his distinguished major generals.

Prevost selected September 11 for his grand assault. According to his plan the land forces and the fleet were to attack simultaneously. The appearance of Captain Downie's squadron as it rounded Cumberland Head was to be the signal for the advance of the army on all fronts. Downie's force consisted of his flagship, the *Confiance*, a frigate of 38 guns, the brig *Linnet*, of 16 guns, commanded by Captain Pring, and the sloops *Chub* and *Finch*, each mounting 11 guns. In addition he had 12 gunboats or row-galleys, eight of which mounted two guns, the other four mounting one gun each.

The responsibility for dealing with this enemy rested upon the broad shoulders of Captain Thomas Macdonough, a native of New Castle, Delaware. Macdonough had entered the Navy as a midshipman in 1798, and had taken part in the Tripoli campaign in which he distinguished himself in Decatur's bold entrance into the harbor of Tripoli and in the burning of the *Philadelphia*. At the outbreak of the War of 1812 he was immediately sent to Lake Champlain and there he had remained. So it was that the war was two years old and Macdonough had so far failed to share in the glory that had come to so many of his contemporaries in the naval service. Thirty-one years of age, courageous and alert, the responsibility did not weigh heavily upon him. Rather his mind was occupied by the thought that at last his great opportunity had come.

Macdonough's little fleet was composed of the frigate *Saratoga*, 26 guns, which served as his flagship, the brig *Eagle*, 26 guns, under the command of Captain Robert Henley, the schooner *Ticonderoga*, mounting 17 guns and commanded by Lieutenant Stephen Cassin, and the sloop *Preble*, seven guns, under Lieutenant Charles Budd. He had also 10 gunboats, six mounting two guns each, and the other four a gun apiece. The opposing fleets were manned by about 800 men each. The British had a slightly greater number of guns but the Americans threw a greater weight of metal. On the whole, the forces were fairly evenly matched.

Macdonough, however, enjoyed a decided advantage in position. He had anchored his fleet across the mouth of the bay all the way from Cumberland Head to the shoal water off Crab Island. At the head of the line he placed two gunboats. Then came the *Eagle*, the *Saratoga*, the *Ticonderoga*, and the *Preble* in the order named. In a second line, and filling the gaps between his ships, he placed the remainder of his gunboats which were kept in position with oars. He took the wise precaution of using spring cables which afforded him an opportunity to turn his ships while at anchor and bring their guns to bear. Thus Macdonough stood ready to receive the enemy who had to deploy and form into line before engaging him. (See Map VIII, p. 295)

The morning of the 11th was clear and calm. It was still forenoon when, from the masthead, a lookout gave the warning and the first enemy vessel rounded the Head and hove into sight. This was a sloop which apparently had come merely to see the fun, for she took no part in the battle. Next to appear was the *Finch*, which bore down upon the *Preble*, at the right of the American line. She was quickly followed by the *Chub* and the *Linnet*, which sailed to the left of the American line to engage the *Eagle*; while last to arrive was the *Confiance* followed by the gunboats, which took station off Crab Island, joining the *Finch* for an attack on the *Ticonderoga* and the *Preble*. When the enemy came into view Macdonough, a devout man, called his officers and crew together and offered up a short prayer for victory before sending the men to their stations. The *Eagle* had the honor of opening the engagement, Captain Henley firing a broadside with his four long 18-pounders at long range. As the *Linnet* passed to engage the *Eagle* she fired on the *Saratoga*, but the shot did little damage except to a coop in which the less devout members of the *Saratoga's* company had housed a champion game cock. The cock was released unharmed and flew to a gun slide where it crowed defiantly. This brought cheers from the sailors and provoked an unanswerable question as to how much they were inspired that day by their commander's prayer and how much by the champion of the cockpit.

The *Confiance* was now within range and Macdonough with his own hand sighted a long 24-pounder which sent a shot crashing across the water. It passed through the hawsehole of Downie's flagship, killed several men on her deck and smashed her wheel. Downie tried to close with the *Saratoga*, but the wind was against him and he was forced to anchor at a distance of 300 yards. He did not answer the *Saratoga's* fire until his ship was in position. Then from the larboard battery of the *Confiance* thundered a broadside from 24-pounders, double-shotted and fired at point-blank range. The guns were well aimed and found their mark. The *Saratoga* shivered from stem to stern under the impact, her sails and rigging were ripped and torn and her decks were red with the blood of 40 of her complement who were killed or wounded in this first salvo.

Undismayed by the disaster Macdonough rallied and reorganized his men and kept them at the business of serving the guns. Fifteen minutes later a shell from the *Saratoga* landed squarely on one of the *Confiance's* guns and sent it hurtling crazily across the deck where Captain Downie was standing. The full weight of the carriage was thrown against the British commander and he was killed instantly. His loss at the crucial moment of the battle had a disastrous effect upon the British morale.

A like fate threatened Macdonough. Three times in the course of the action he was knocked unconscious and three times he revived and returned to duty after his men had supposed him dead. The battle now raged all along the line. A well-directed broadside from the *Eagle* crippled the *Chub* which slipped her moorings and drifted helplessly. A shot from the *Saratoga* finished her and she struck her colors. An hour later, at the far end of the British line, the *Finch* received such punishment from the *Ticonderoga* that she was driven from her position and went aground on the shoals off Crab Island. There the convalescents, who were not too ill to man the battery on the island, turned its guns on the *Finch* with such effect that she, too, struck.

The British gunboats now entered actively into the engagement and pounded the *Preble* so hard that she had to cut her cables and withdraw inshore. The *Preble* out of action, the gunboats next gave their undivided attention to the *Ticonderoga* and attempted to get close enough to board her. But Lieutenant Cassin was equal to the occasion. Indifferent to the hail of shot and shell around him he urged on his gunners and the *Ticonderoga* gave back as good as she received and the attack of the gunboats was repulsed.

At the other end of the line the *Eagle* now was in distress. In the heat of the conflict she sprang her cables and was exposed to the combined fire of the *Linnet* and the *Confiance*. Captain Henley, however, skillfully maneuvered his ship until the *Eagle* had dropped back between the *Saratoga* and the *Ticonderoga*, where he brought his larboard broadside to bear and continued the action.

Both the *Saratoga* and the *Confiance* were badly hurt and, in addition, the shift of the *Eagle* exposed the bow of the *Saratoga* to a raking fire from the *Linnet*. In fact Macdonough did not have a single starboard gun that was not disabled. His situation was critical, but here his excellent seamanship came into play. By means of a stream anchor and hawser he managed to wind his ship until her fresh larboard guns bore on the *Confiance*.

The British flagship attempted the same maneuver, but failed and she quickly found herself at the mercy of the *Saratoga*, which poured shot into her. In a few minutes her crew gave up hope and surrendered. The *Saratoga* now turned her attention to the *Linnet*, which fought on alone for 15 minutes before abandoning the struggle. Seeing that disaster had overtaken the ships, the gunboats followed their example and struck. Thus, after a struggle which lasted two hours and 20 minutes, the whole of the British fleet surrendered. Macdonough's ships, though victorious, had suffered almost as severely as the British, and the crews of the enemy gunboats took advantage of the temporary confusion to bend to their oars and row away from the scene of conflict. They were pursued for a short distance but made good their escape.

Macdonough now received the officers of the captured fleet on the deck of the *Saratoga*, complimented them on the fight they had put up and refused to accept their swords. After the events of the last two hours he could afford to be magnanimous. Then he dispatched a message to shore addressed to the Secretary of the Navy, which read:

"Sir,—The Almighty has been pleased to grant us a signal victory on Lake Champlain in the capture of one frigate, one brig, and two sloops of war of the enemy." It was just a simple statement of fact.

Had Macdonough possessed a gift for phraseology commensurate with his ability as a commander he might have become as immortal as Perry. In a later and more detailed report he stated that his losses were 52 killed and 58 wounded, and attributed to the British a loss of 200.

While the two fleets fought it out on the bay, the opposing armies battled on land. When Prevost learned of the arrival of Downie, according to the prearranged plan, he ordered his batteries to open up on the American position. Under the protection of the bombardment three columns advanced to the attack; one toward the site of the lower bridge, one by the upper bridge and the third by way of the upper ford. The first two columns were met by a fusillade from the defenders and, in spite of determined efforts, were unable to cross the river. The third, at the ford, was more successful. Here the attackers gained a foothold on the opposite shore and forced General Mooers and his New Yorkers to give ground. The retreat of the militia might have developed into a rout if the Vermonters had not arrived at this moment and steadied the nerves of their New York brethren. And then as the two forces faced each other, anticipating a renewal of the attack, a horseman dashed up to the American line to announce to General Mooers that the British fleet had surrendered. Inspired by this news the militiamen steadied themselves for the next onslaught. But it did not come. Instead, to their surprise, the British turned and retired from the front, yielding the ground they had recently gained. Prevost, it seems, upon learning of the defeat on the lake, ordered their recall.

The British attempted no further assault and the rest of the afternoon was spent in an exchange of desultory shots between the opposing batteries. There is a story to the effect that on the day of the battle the American secret service prepared a letter which purported to be addressed by Colonel Fassett of Vermont to General Macomb and in which he bade the latter to be of good cheer as Governor Chittenden was marching to St. Albans with 10,000 men, that 5,000 more were on the march from St. Lawrence county and an additional 4,000 from Washington county. This letter was intrusted to an Irishwoman who lived on Cumberland Head and who presented it to Prevost. Whether the letter was responsible, or whether the operations of the day were sufficient in themselves, Prevost became greatly alarmed. In the course of the night he dismounted his guns from the batteries and before dawn the whole of his army was retreating in haste across the border.

And so it came about that the forlorn hope was converted into an overwhelming victory. A British fleet had been captured by an American fleet of its own size while an American army, stiffened by regulars but composed in large part of militia, had successfully resisted a force of veteran British regulars outnumbering it three to one! The threat of invasion by way of Lake Champlain was definitely ended. And Washington, in part at least, had been avenged.

Years later the aged Duke of Wellington was reviewing the exploits of his men when someone in the company recalled the Battle of Plattsburg and commented upon the strange fact that his veterans of the Spanish Peninsula had received so ignominious a defeat at the hands of an inferior number of Americans, for the most part receiving their baptism of fire.

"They did not turn out quite right," admitted the old warrior. Then, holding up his clenched hand, he added with conviction, "They wanted this iron fist to command them!"

CHAPTER TWENTY-FOUR

"The Flag Was Still There"

"THE American navy must be annihilated, his arsenals and dock-yards must be consumed, and the truculent inhabitants of Baltimore must be tamed with the weapons which shook the wooden turrets of Copenhagen."

Thus fulminated the editor of a London newspaper. The American people had been humiliated by the raid on their capital. No less humiliated were the British people in the utter inability of their navy, in spite of the proud boast that "Britannia rules the waves," to protect shipping even in home waters against American privateers and letters of marque. Baltimore was the chief nest of these swift and graceful clippers that lay in wait on the trade routes and struck devastating blows at Britain's commerce; and, consequently, it was upon Baltimore that the British people cried out for vengeance.

Hardly had war been declared before commerce raiders set sail from American ports upon their voyages of destruction and plunder. Privateering was a legalized form of piracy that, in 1812, was recognized by all nations. The vessels themselves were owned by individuals or companies whose stockholders advanced money for the purchase and outfitting of the ships and shared in the division of the spoils. The risks were great and the profits proportionately large. The nature of the investment was a subject of popular debate. Albert Gallatin, always conservative in matters of finance, regarded the industry as being in the nature of a lottery; others contended vehemently that it was a quite legitimate speculation.

To each vessel the President issued "a letter of marque and reprisal" which amounted to a commission to prey upon enemy ships. These vessels were known either as privateers or letters of marque, the only difference being that the privateer was bent solely upon

304

voyages of plunder, while the letter of marque engaged in regular trade, carried a cargo and plundered when occasion offered. The standard privateer was a trim schooner armed with from six to 10 carronades and a single long gun mounted on a swivel in the center. She was manned by about 50 men, not including her officers, and carried a complement of muskets, cutlasses and boarding pikes for use in fighting at close quarters.

However, as privateering was primarily a business enterprise, a privateer's aim was to capture an enemy ship and get off without damage to herself. Fighting was engaged in only as a last resort. Therefore speed was an essential quality, and the graceful Baltimore clippers, packing on a maximum of canvas, could run away from anything on the seas. When a ship was captured a prize crew was put aboard her and she was sailed to the nearest American port. There her cargo was appraised and a duty upon it exacted by the government. When the duty and other charges had been paid, the cargo was sold and the net proceeds divided among the officers, the crew, and the owners of the vessel which had made the capture. Success of a venture depended upon the skill of the captain and crew and the number and value of the ships captured. The promoters were soon complaining of the government imposts and the difficulty of making a profitable voyage.

During the first months of the war privateers were few, since most of the American merchantmen had fled their home ports to escape the embargo and were on their way abroad when the President's proclamation was issued. They had to return to be fitted with guns and altered to meet the requirements of their new duties. Those that first went out did their hunting near home waters, either in the neighborhood of Halifax or of the West Indies. Conspicuous among them was the *Rossie*, of Baltimore, commanded by the redoubtable Commodore Joshua Barney, who was always ready for new adventure on the high seas. On two voyages in 1812 he took 13 prizes and captured or destroyed enemy property to the estimated value of $1,500,000. Even more successful was the *America*, of Salem, which made four cruises, took 41 prizes and, after deduction of expenses and government charges, had $1,100,000 left to divide among her crew and owners.

As the war advanced the number of privateers increased through the refitting of old vessels and the building of new ones. During 1813 New York alone built 26 privateers and letters of marque. And, as the number increased, the privateers ventured farther afield until they penetrated the China Seas, boldly attacking heavily armed East India merchantmen, and even setting up a blockade of the English Channel and the coasts of Great Britain, so that British vessels did not dare to venture out except under convoy.

By 1814 experience had brought improvements in the design of the vessels and in the skill of their captains in handling them. The English lamented that even the Thames was no longer safe. Another famous marauder was the *Governor Tompkins,* of New York, which stood at the mouth of the English Channel for several weeks, challenging every ship that passed, and capturing and burning 14 of them. Meanwhile the *Harpy,* of Baltimore, cruised for three months off the coast of Ireland, in the English Channel and in the Bay of Biscay taking numerous prizes and returning eventually to Boston with rich booty which included $500,000 in British Treasury notes and bills of exchange. The *Prince of Neufchatel,* of New York, boldly entered the Irish Channel and demoralized coastal traffic.

Finally Captain Thomas Boyle, a daring and picturesque skipper commanding the *Chasseur,* of Baltimore, cruised for three months off the British coast, spreading terror among shipping. He had the presumption to send a "Proclamation of Blockade" to Lloyd's with a request that it be posted. In it he declared, with mock seriousness, that his blockade now extended to "all the ports, harbors, bays, creeks, rivers, inlets, outlets, islands and seacoast of the United Kingdom."

Insurance rates skyrocketed and, in the case of vessels trading between England and Ireland, insurance was virtually unobtainable. British merchants, who had been jealous of American trade and keen for the war, now complained bitterly of their lack of protection. How was it, inquired the *Annual Register,* that while Britain had a navy of nearly 1,000 ships "it was not safe for a vessel to sail without convoy from one part of the English and Irish channels to another?" The merchants of Glasgow, Liverpool and Bristol solemnly met in the Scottish port, drew up and addressed a remonstrance to the government in which they declared that "there is reason to believe, in the short space of 24 months, above 800 vessels have been captured by the Power whose maritime strength we have hitherto impolitically held in contempt." Lloyd's published a list showing the names of 825 prizes that had been taken by the Americans.

The British Admiralty could not then deny the charges made against it, but blamed the merchantmen for failing to stick to the convoys. The Navy, stung by the taunts of the American captains and the criticisms at home, lost its temper and, on occasion, violated the international code of laws in its anxiety to run down and punish the privateers. Thus, for example, the *Plantagenet*, a 74-gun ship of the line, tracked the American privateer *General Armstrong* to the neutral port of Fayal in the Azores. The British commander, Captain Robert Lloyd, waited until night, then, in total disregard of Portuguese rights, he sent out 12 boats containing 200 armed men to the side of the privateer. Captain Samuel C. Reid, of the *General Armstrong*, discovered the visitors in the moonlight and shouted to them to keep off. When they failed to obey quickly enough to suit him he ordered his crew of 90 men to fire. The *Plantagenet's* boats withdrew but not before the men in them had suffered severely. Reid meanwhile had grounded his ship under the guns of the Portuguese fort. The boats from the *Plantagenet* soon returned with reinforcements and a sharp exchange of shots followed. Rather than surrender, Reid scuttled his ship. He lost in the engagement only nine men killed and wounded. The *Plantagenet's* loss was 34 killed and 86 wounded, more than that of the *Guerrière* in the battle with the *Constitution*.

Another engagement between a British man-of-war and an American privateer took place off Gay Head, New Jersey, when the frigate *Endymion* came up with the *Prince of Neufchatel*, of New York, put out boats and tried to board her. Again the British came off the worse, losing 28 killed and 37 wounded to the American loss of 31 killed and wounded. The privateers did not look for a fight but they showed that they knew how to take care of themselves when they ran into one. In view of the spectacular activities of the privateers well might the London *Times* lament: "The American cruisers daily enter in among our convoys, seize prizes in sight of those that should afford protection, and if pursued put on their sea wings and laugh at the clumsy British pursuers. To what is this owing? Cannot we build ships? It must be encouraging to Mr. Madison to read the logs of his cruisers. If they fight, they are sure to conquer; if they fly, they are sure to escape."

It is not surprising then that, after the destruction of Barney's flotilla and the easy capture of Washington, the thoughts of the British expeditionary force should have turned toward Baltimore; or that Lord Bathurst who directed operations from the War Office in London, while complimenting Ross on his victory in Washington, should have suggested that he deal more severely with the Baltimoreans after he had conquered them in order to give them a real taste of the bitterness of war. Besides, as General Armstrong had pointed out, Baltimore was a place of consequence. It was in that day the third largest city in the country, with a population of 40,000 and a thriving commercial center. Here was a better opportunity than in Washington to inflict material damage upon the enemy.

Ross and Cockburn, upon rejoining the fleet at Benedict, did not immediately set sail for the city on the Patapsco. There was more urgent business elsewhere. While the battle of Bladensburg was being fought, a British squadron under Commodore Gordon was sailing up the Potomac River. It consisted of two frigates, two rocket ships, two bomb vessels and one schooner. On August 27 the British force appeared off Fort Washington, 12 miles below the capital and guarding its southern approach. In spite of the threatened invasion the fort had been neglected and it was now held by a force of only 80 men under Captain Samuel T. Dyson. General Winder had warned Captain Dyson against capture and his order was followed literally. Upon sighting the British Dyson laid fuse to the magazine, blew up the fort and fled without firing a single shot.

This left Alexandria, Virginia, undefended; and, on the following day, Commodore Gordon moved up the river and anchored off the town where his guns frowned ominously upon the inhabitants. The psychological effect was instantaneous. A deputation of prominent citizens waited on Gordon and asked him what his price would be for sparing the town. The British commodore was not modest in stating his wants. He demanded naval stores and ordnance, shipping, merchandise and refreshment for himself and his men. The Alexandrians had scuttled several ships in the harbor to prevent their capture, and Gordon ordered these raised. There he remained while vessels were loaded with valuable cargoes of flour, cotton and tobacco.

Meanwhile Commodore Rodgers, who had yielded command of the *President* to Decatur, assembled at Philadelphia a force of 450 seamen and 50 marines, armed with four 12-pounders. He was too late to take part in the defense of Washington. However, when the government returned to the capital immediately after the departure of the British and resumed its functions, Rodgers received orders to move posthaste to the Potomac and, if possible, cut off Gordon's retreat. Rodgers at once set out to fulfill his mission. At Baltimore the column was joined by Commodores Perry, Porter and Creighton and when they reached the Potomac they were reinforced by Virginia militia and proceeded to erect batteries at the White House, below Mount Vernon on the Virginia shore, and at Indian Head on the Maryland shore.

When the British squadron appeared on its way down the river the batteries were turned loose and gave Gordon considerable trouble; but, by concentrating his fire first on one and then the other, Gordon succeeded in getting by. Hearing of his predicament the British fleet in the Patuxent made sail for the mouth of the Potomac to go to his assistance. Upon its arrival it learned that he was no longer in need of help. At last the British were free to devote their undivided attention to Baltimore.

Washington had been taken by surprise; but for a year—ever since the British fleet entered Chesapeake Bay—Baltimore had been anticipating the blow that was now about to fall. As early as April of the previous year the City Council voted $26,000 for the improvement of the fortifications and, when Cockburn threatened the town during the same summer, 5,000 militia and 40 pieces of artillery were paraded, a gesture which proved sufficient to frighten him away. The city sprawls over the banks of the Patapsco River some 12 miles from the bay. Within the city itself the river forks, the north branch forming a narrow channel which leads to the inner harbor. At the tip end of the peninsula between the two branches lies Fort McHenry guarding the approach to the inner harbor and also the approach to the city by way of the south or ferry branch. From the city to the Chesapeake the Patapsco is a wide, irregular stream distinguished by numerous bays, inlets and peninsulas. At

Map IX. Battle of Baltimore

the time of the attack Fort McHenry was a thoroughly modern fortress of masonry and earth that had but recently been strengthened by the mounting of 32-pounders. It was garrisoned by regulars and volunteers numbering 1,000 men under the command of a regular army officer, Lieutenant Colonel George Armistead. (See Map IX)

Further to protect the inner harbor, a cable had been stretched across the entrance between the fort and Lazaretto Point, where a battery had been erected, and 24 ships had been sunk in the narrows effectually blocking the channel. To the west and rear of the fort, and guarding the ferry branch, were two other fortifications, Fort Covington and City Battery, both manned by sailors and the latter by a detachment of Barney's flotilla men. These fortifications took reasonably good care of any attack on the south of the city by a fleet sailing up the river.

To meet an attack by land from the east, a fortified line a mile long had been constructed on an elevation known as Loudenslager's or Hampstead Hill. At several points in the line were semicircular batteries and one near the southern extremity bore on the harbor, thus linking the defenses with those at Lazaretto Point and McHenry. The batteries were manned by the sailors under the command of Commodore Rodgers who had hastened back from the Potomac. In the trenches between the batteries were volunteers and militiamen. The construction of the works was accomplished by the townspeople under the direction of a Committee of Vigilance and Safety which divided the city into four sections and called on the sections to labor alternately. The appeal met with universal response, for the fate of Washington was fresh in everybody's mind.

On September 10 General Winder arrived in the city with Maryland troops which had been with him at Bladensburg, now reorganized and somewhat recovered from their unfortunate experiences in that battle. There were present, too, for the first time on the field, Pennsylvania volunteers from the near-by towns of York and Marietta. There was also a brigade of volunteers from Virginia. The defenders numbered in all over 10,000 and in supreme command was General Samuel Smith, 62 years old, a hard-bitten veteran of the Revolution. Though Winder protested being superseded by a militia general, the Baltimoreans would not have him after what had happened at Bladensburg. In short, the city was protected on the east, from which direction the British were expected to come, by a fortified arc bristling with guns and manned by troops among whom there were enough regulars and sailors to act as a steadying influence upon the less experienced volunteers and militia.

Such was the situation when, on Sunday, September 11, anxious lookouts on the housetops, scanning the east through their glasses, made out the British fleet as it came into view at the mouth of the Patapsco. At once the watchers announced the news and the ringing of church bells spread the alarm throughout the town. In short order the place was in turmoil, dispatch riders galloping through the streets, volunteers saying good-bye to their families and hastening off to take their posts in the fortifications, and townspeople with worried looks collecting in little groups to discuss the situation. Many of the more timid fled the city, and the roads leading to the west were filled with refugees toiling under the weight of the few personal possessions they could take with them. All the inns in the surrounding country that night were packed with old men, women and children who, remembering what had happened to Washington, were fearful that a like fate awaited Baltimore. Before the mansions of the wealthy merchants, which lay on the outskirts of the town, family coaches waited at the doors ready at an instant's notice to convey the womenfolk and the jewelry, silver and plate to places of safety.

The fleet itself presented such a spectacle of naval strength as no Baltimorean had ever seen. No less than 50 sails were spread to the wind, from a distance looking like so many great white birds settling on the broad bosom of the Patapsco. Included in the array were ships of the line, frigates, bomb ships and rocket ships; and crowded in among the sailors and marines were some 6,000 soldiers. Commanding the fleet was Admiral Sir Alexander Cochrane, and also aboard were those two old companions in arms, Ross and Cockburn. Two miles off shore, where North Point juts out toward the bay, the vessels lowered their sails and dropped anchor for the night.

The day had been warm; after sunset the air cooled and dew was thick on the grass. It should have been a good night for sleeping, but there was little sleep in Baltimore. Many had left the town, yet the majority remained, and observers say that following the excitement which attended the news of the enemy's arrival and in spite of the danger that hung over the city, there set in a surprising calm. There could, however, be no sleep for there was hardly a household that did not have a son, a father or a husband in the fort or in the entrenchments. In anxious silence they awaited what the following day might bring forth.

Shortly after midnight American horsemen who watched from North Point noticed activity on the ships. At 2 A.M. the first boats were lowered and shortly thereafter their prows became visible as they were rowed to shore. As the boats touched land and delivered their cargoes of armed men, the videttes withdrew; and while some continued to observe, others galloped back the 15 miles to the fortifications to report that the British were landing. From the information that reached him General Smith estimated that the land force must be in the neighborhood of from 7,000 to 8,000 men. He at once ordered Brigadier General John Stricker with his City Brigade to advance to meet them. Stricker's force was composed of 3,185 men and included the 5th, 6th, 27th, 39th and 51st Regiments of Baltimore militia and small detachments of artillery, cavalry and riflemen.

Some five miles from the fortifications the North Point Road crosses a neck of land little more than a mile wide which separates Bear Creek on the south from a branch of Back River on the north. Here, as the troops arrived, Stricker arranged them in line of battle. In the front line he placed the 5th Regiment with its right resting on Bear Creek, and the 27th Regiment with its left reaching out toward a swamp at the edge of Back River. The two regiments were separated by the North Point Road and on this he stationed the Union Artillery, a volunteer force, with six 4-pounders to sweep the road. Three hundred yards to the rear he posted the 51st Regiment and the 39th Regiment, the former on the right supporting the 5th and the latter on the left supporting the 27th. A half mile farther to the rear he held the 6th Regiment in reserve.

Having completed these dispositions Stricker sent forward riflemen to feel out the enemy. The advance guard had not gone far when someone spread the rumor that the British were landing at Bear Creek or Back River; and, without waiting to confirm it, the riflemen, fearful of being taken in the rear, came scurrying back as fast as their legs could take them without seeing the enemy or firing a shot. After this somewhat discouraging prelude to the day's events Stricker placed the riflemen on the line beside the men of the 5th.

Meanwhile the British force, consisting of soldiers, sailors and marines, and accompanied by six field pieces and two howitzers, had formed into column and set out on the 15-mile march to the city. At the head rode Ross and Cockburn. The day was warm and about noon, when the column had covered half the distance, a halt was ordered at Gorsuch's farm, to give the troops rest and a breathing space in preparation for the more strenuous work that lay ahead of them.

News that the enemy was at Gorsuch's was quickly brought back to Stricker who detached 150 men of the 5th, 70 of Aisquith's riflemen, a field piece and some cavalry, placed Major Richard K. Heath in command and ordered them to move on to the farm and break up the siesta. When this advance guard gained contact with the enemy a sharp skirmish ensued. While leading his men, Major Heath's horse was shot from under him and several Americans were killed.

But a greater misfortune befell the British. When Ross heard the firing he quickly mounted and galloped to a knoll the better to observe the field and determine the size and nature of the force that was being brought against him. As he sat his horse in this exposed position he did not know that concealed in a hollow near by were two Baltimore youths, Daniel Wells and Henry McComas, members of Aisquith's rifle corps. Recognizing the general the youths took careful aim and fired. Ross fell to the ground mortally wounded. Infuriated by the loss of their commander the British swept forward and drove off the attackers. In this engagement both Wells and McComas were killed, but they had made the enemy pay dearly. Ross was lifted from the ground by his aides and hurried to the rear; he died in the arms of one of them before he reached the boats.

Their mission accomplished, Heath's men now fell back upon Stricker's brigade, closely pursued by the British. When Ross fell his place was taken by Colonel Arthur Brooke who, according to British estimates, was an inferior officer. By ten minutes to three in the afternoon the main bodies were facing each other across the narrow strip of land between Middle River and Bear Creek. Adopting the same tactics that had served them so well at Bladensburg the British opened the engagement by firing a barrage of Congreve rockets in an attempt to shake the American morale. The American artillery planted in the center of the road responded, the British guns came into action and soon the battle was being hotly fought all along the line. From a vantage point behind the front line General Stricker and his aides endeavored to penetrate the pall of smoke that soon fell over the battle ground. To his relief he found that the men of the 27th and of the 5th had withstood the first assault and remained firmly planted in line.

Having failed to shake the center, the British now directed their attention to the left flank. As we have noted, the line of the 27th Regiment extended toward, but did not reach, the swampland along the shore of Middle River. Here was an opening by which the flank could be turned. To close it Stricker ordered the 39th Regiment, which had been stationed 300 yards to the rear of the 27th, to move up and extend the front line to the swamp. This the 39th accomplished.

Further to strengthen his left Stricker then directed Colonel Amey to move the 51st, which was stationed to the rear of the 5th, across the front and place it at right angles to the 39th, thereby forming two sides of a hollow square. But there were two disadvantages to this maneuver. The order entailed their passing across a field of fire and, when they reached their new position, facing away from the enemy. The 51st, it must be remembered, was composed of green troops who were receiving their baptism of fire.

Execution of the order was attended by some confusion, involving marching and countermarching, which was seen by the British. Taking advantage of it they trained their guns on the area through which the 51st had to pass. The shriek of the rockets overhead, the bursting of shells and the whizz of bullets proved more than the taut nerves of the men of the 51st could stand. They hesitated, then broke. Ignoring the appeals of their officers they fled the field, every man for himself, in a wild rush to get out of range of shot and shell.

When the 51st broke the panic was communicated to a company of the 39th whose men threw down their arms and followed the 51st in flight. This exposed the American left flank and, to save the

rest of his force, Stricker ordered a general retreat. He did not have
to give the order twice. In a twinkling the whole of his force was
marching at the double to the rear, and it did not halt until it had
reached the fortifications on Loudenslager's Hill, while the British
were left in possession of the field. The whole engagement lasted
just 55 minutes, but it had been hotly fought. The Americans lost
35 killed, 115 wounded and missing. The British loss was estimated
at twice the number. In contrast to Bladensburg the invaders did
not attempt to follow up their success, but bivouacked on the field.
Had they continued their pursuit they might have profited by the
confusion among the American forces. They missed the driving
power of Ross. Brooke preferred caution and so lost whatever opportunity he might have had. On the other hand the situation was
not altogether the same as that at Bladensburg. Stricker's men had
been driven from the field but they had not been demoralized.
And they had accomplished their mission which was to fight a
delaying action. There still stood between the British and the city
a fortified line such as had not stood between them and Washington. Under the circumstances Brooke's caution may have been
justified. As darkness descended there ensued a few hours of quiet
among the forces on both sides.

It had been the British plan to attack simultaneously by land and
by sea. The land force was now within striking distance of the fortifications; so, pursuant to the plan, the fleet now entered into the
engagement. At dawn on Tuesday, the 13th, five bomb vessels approached to within two miles of Fort McHenry and opened a heavy
fire. On the previous day soundings of the river had been taken and
the waters near the fort were found to be so shallow that the frigates
did not dare to approach closer than two miles and a half and, consequently, did not take part in the action.

Major Armistead ordered his artillerists to reply, and the big guns
thundered at each other across the water. Armistead soon perceived
that the shots from the fort were falling short and reluctantly gave
the command to cease firing. There was nothing for the Americans
to do but take refuge in the entrenchments and, without replying,
accept the punishment of the bomb ships. From early morning until
the afternoon this one-sided engagement continued. It was enough
to try the nerves of the most hardened veterans. Very soon the Amer-

icans discovered that though the British bombs were terrifying, actually they were doing little damage. There was one critical moment when a bomb landed squarely on top of the magazine but, fortunately, it failed to explode and so the Americans were spared a disaster.

Finally, at 2 P.M., an enemy shell scored a direct hit on one of the fort's 24-pounders, killing one of the gun crew and wounding several others. The incident caused some confusion which did not escape the enemy observers and they seized the opportunity to move one of the bomb ships closer for a last assault. No doubt they assumed from the fort's silence during the morning either that the gunners had fled or that the batteries had been put out of action. In this, however, they were mistaken. Armistead now had the opportunity for which he had been waiting throughout the day. A bomb ship was within range. It was a welcome development for the Americans who at last had a chance to return the compliments the British had been paying them for what seemed an eternity. At Armistead's command the gunners leaped to their stations, trained their guns on the enemy and let them have it. The bomb ship lost no time in retreating to safety, well out of range. From a distance the British returned to the methodical business of pouring fire on the fort. And so the bombardment continued throughout the afternoon and on into the evening while "the rocket's red glare" added a dramatic touch to the scene and served to illuminate the target.

It was now clear to the British high command that little progress was being made by the frontal attack. If the fort was to be taken it would have to be taken in the rear. The American left flank offered little promise. The approach by way of the north branch of the river was blocked by the sunken vessels in the channel and protected also by the battery on Lazaretto Point facing the fort. On that side, too, was Commodore Rodgers' semicircular battery on the hill that might be expected to enter into the engagement. There was no question that the ferry branch offered better prospect of success and upon the ferry branch the British high command decided.

The night was dark, affording an excellent opportunity for a surprise attack. Shortly after midnight 1,200 men, equipped with scaling ladders, embarked in barges and put out silently, passed the fort undetected and glided up the ferry branch. But here they faced the problem of finding a suitable landing place. The darkness which up to this point had protected them now proved a serious handicap. There was no other way except to send up rockets to illuminate the scene of operations.

The decision proved fatal, for immediately the attackers revealed themselves and right before them was the City Battery. In an instant Barney's men were at their guns pouring a murderous fire into the barges while Fort Covington, farther inshore, joined the City Battery in the defense. Even the guns on Lazaretto Point, and some of those in McHenry, uncertain where the attack was being aimed, added their voices to the chorus. The barges were unprepared for this hot reception. One of them was sunk by the fire and members of its crew drowned in the black waters of the Patapsco, while others struggled to safety. In a few minutes the attack was repulsed and the barges were driven back without reaching the shore.

Once more the British returned to the attack on McHenry and kept it up until after dawn of the 14th. For 25 hours the garrison of the fort had been subjected to a gruelling rain of missiles. General Armistead estimated that in the course of the day and night the British fired from 1,500 to 1,800 shells and bombs. Of this number, 400 had found their mark in the fort. Yet, strange to relate, in the course of the bombardment, only four men were killed and 24 slightly wounded. At 7 A.M. the attackers ceased firing while they considered what next should be done.

In keeping with other anomalies that gave the War of 1812 its peculiar character was the fact that the words of our national anthem were composed by a patriot who, at the time of the battle, was a visitor with the enemy fleet. During their Washington campaign the British seized as prisoner a Dr. Beanes, a prominent physician of Upper Marlboro and a friend of Mr. Francis Scott Key, who then resided in Georgetown. Appeals for Dr. Beanes' release were ignored by Cockburn, who appears never to have lost an opportunity to make himself objectionable. As a last resort Dr. Beanes' friends determined to try Mr. Key's acknowledged charm of manner upon Sir Alexander Cochrane. To this end President Madison was petitioned and consented to send Mr. Key to Cochrane aboard a cartel ship under a flag of truce to plead for the good doctor's release. The ship selected for the purpose was a packet that ordinarily plied between Baltimore and Norfolk. Mr. Key set out in the vessel and came up with the British fleet as it reached the mouth of the Patapsco. The messenger proved equal to the estimation of his friends. Sir Alexander consented to the release of Dr. Beanes; but, as the attack on Baltimore was about to take place, he refused to let either Dr. Beanes or Mr. Key go for fear of their carrying valuable information back to the Americans.

So it was that Francis Scott Key witnessed the preparations for the assault and the bombardment itself from the enemy's position. As a patriot his agony of mind may be imagined while he observed the operations, and wondered what would be the result of the prolonged fire. The flag which waved above the ramparts was the only evidence upon which he could rely. If the flag disappeared, he might know that the stronghold had fallen. Throughout the bombardment of the 13th it continued to fly defiantly, but as night came on its "broad stripes and bright stars" faded out of sight in the enveloping gloom; and, as the battle continued on until midnight, Key's hopes faded almost as completely, to be raised at intervals when

> the rockets' red glare, the bombs bursting in air,
> Gave proof through the night that our flag was still there.

And so, at last, when "the dawn's early light" revealed the flag in all its might and glory still flying "o'er the land of the free and the home of the brave," Mr. Key drew a sigh of relief and also a letter from his pocket and on the back of it began to compose his immortal lines. Upon his return to Baltimore Key brushed up his poem and submitted it to his uncle, Judge Nicholson, who had commanded a battery in the fort. The Judge was enthusiastic, gave the work his imprimatur and the verses were rushed to a printer. Set to the tune of a drinking song, it was sung by an actor before a limited number of patriots in a restaurant adjoining the Holliday Street Theater and was so heartily applauded that its rendition became the feature of the performances on succeeding nights in the theater itself. From there it spread throughout the country, establishing itself as the song hit of the day, laying the groundwork for its eventual immortality. Though critics have decried the meter and hinted that as a poet Key was no better than he should be; though prudists have lamented the ribald origin of the music and patriots by the hundreds of thousands have faltered over words which defy the memory and high notes which their voices cannot attain, nevertheless the anthem has stood up gallantly against the bombs and rockets that have been hurled against it; and, like the flag it honors, "is still there."

While the British fleet was launching its attack upon McHenry, Colonel Brooke and his victorious column, it will be recalled, was left bivouacked upon the field of battle. On the morning of the 13th he broke camp, formed his men for an attack and made a feint to the north of the fortifications as though intending to turn the flank. But here he met a strong force under General Winder and was driven back. He then moved to within a mile of the fortifications and made a careful study of their strength in men and guns. Having checked the information gained, he arrived at the conclusion that the American position could not be taken by storm. On the 14th he conferred with Admiral Cochrane who had arrived at the same conclusion with reference to the chances of the fleet against McHenry. And so it came about that further efforts to capture Baltimore were abandoned.

Rain set in during the afternoon and, under cover of darkness, Colonel Brooke proceeded unmolested on his march back to North Point to re-embark on the fleet which had dropped down the Patapsco to meet him. But not before some of his officers had discovered the home of Colonel Sterett, of the 5th Regiment, which lay outside the fortifications. They made free with the Colonel's wines, plundered the bureau drawers in search of valuables, ordered the servants about and, after enjoying a sumptuous meal, left an impudent note on the sideboard informing the owner that "Captains Brown, Wilcox and McNamara, of the Fifty-Third Regiment, Royal Marines, have received everything they could desire at his house, notwithstanding it was received at the hands of the butler, and in the absence of the colonel."

"Awful was the period from Sunday till Wednesday evening," wrote Margaret McHenry, wife of the ex-Secretary of War for whom the fort was named and whose son John was with the 5th Regiment in the battle, to a cousin in the country. "John was taken with a chill, obliged to go to bed, poor fellow. He had undergone a great deal in body and mind of late—he had just recovered from a fever, and had not recovered his strength when he went out with the troops, to meet the enemy; great fatigue and laying on the ground all night in a heavy rain has laid him up again, but Blessed be God, that he is still living.

"Oh, that we may be truly thankful for our present relief;—but we are by no means certain that they will not return; from all we can hear we have every reason to fear it, if they see any prospect of success—the thought is overwhelming. Oh God, in thine infinite mercy preserve us from this dreaded event—poor Sophia has an intermittent, her dear child is also unwell . . .

"Mr. McHenry desires me to tell you that a fullblood Marino ewe would sell here for a hundred dollars and a ram from 50 to 70; the salt herrings and other articles remaining at Mr. McMahon's proper to be sold you will request him to dispose of . . . Sophia's and Charlotte's cloaths please to send as soon as possible . . .

"Mr. McHenry has got over the effects of the mercury, & notwithstanding his late agitations is rather better than a month ago." *

After the glorious defense of their city the Baltimoreans were once more back at their homely pursuits.

---

* Reprinted by permission of Juliana Keyser Clark.

CHAPTER TWENTY-FIVE

The Die-hards Play Their Hand

"UNCONSTITUTIONAL and treasonable . . . wholly abnormal and wicked." Such was John Quincy Adams' declared opinion of the Hartford Convention. But then John Quincy Adams was a renegade from the Federalist Party and could not escape the suspicion of speaking with strong political bias.

The Hartford Convention was the very natural outcome of the injuries, both real and imaginary, that New England Federalists had suffered at the hands of the Republican majority. More than a decade had passed since the Federalists enjoyed the spoils of a national election; and as new states in the South and West, strongly Republican, were added to the Union, the hope of a Federalist revival grew dimmer and dimmer. Ambitious men like Quincy and Pickering sat in the halls of Congress and saw their opinions ignored while national policies were dictated by the homespun statesmen from the South and West led by the Virginia dynasty.

The New England Federalists opposed the war with all their might, but war was declared. They refused to take an active part in it, declined to lend money to support it, turned their faces against applauding its few heroes; but still the war went on. The last straw was Madison's embargo of December, 1813. Though Jefferson's had done more good to New England than to any other part of the country, the very name embargo was hated in that quarter. And now the poor, hard-pressed little President brought the skeleton out again and rattled it in a desperate effort to put a stop to New England's trading with the enemy.

The embargo was a new challenge to battle, as though one were needed. The New England Federalists promptly accepted it. From 40 town meetings in Massachusetts went out memorials breathing hatred of the administration and a determination to submit no longer to oppression, praying the General Court to take action. Conspicuous among the protests was a circular letter sent out by a group of Federalists in the township of Northampton asking for "some amendments to the Constitution, which shall secure to the Northern States their due weight and influence in our national councils." Even more inflammatory was a memorial from Newbury, in Essex county, Timothy Pickering's stronghold, which declared outright: "We call our State Legislature to protect us in the enjoyment of those privileges to assert which our fathers died, and to defend which we profess ourselves ready to resist unto blood." Northampton and ten other town meetings proposed a convention of the New England States to initiate the reform.

When the General Court met in January repercussions were immediately heard. Senator Blake, of Worcester, rising from his seat, declared frankly that if the Constitution permitted embargoes, then he personally preferred the British constitution, "monarchy and all." With fire in his eye Samuel Fessenden boldly proclaimed that "it is time to take our rights into our own hands." These threats against the national government by the extremists alarmed such moderate Federalists as Harrison Gray Otis, Quincy and James Lloyd. They were not prepared to join forces in open rebellion. They set to work with a will to silence the more violent members and keep the sessions under control and met with such success that incendiary resolutions were defeated and the proposed northern convention was postponed until the people could vote on the proposal.

So unpopular was the embargo that even the Republican candidate for governor, Samuel Dexter, did not dare defend it in the spring election. But his silence was not sufficient to remove the taint that New England attached to all Republicans and the Federalist Caleb Strong was swept into office by a plurality of over 10,000. The Federalist victory in the General Court was equally convincing; 360 members were elected as against only 156 Republicans and all the Federalists were instructed for the convention of the Northern States. At last, realizing the futility of the embargo, but too late to influence the election, Madison brought about its repeal; and with this grievance out of the way and the pressure reduced, the idea of a convention was temporarily put aside.

The summer, however, brought with it new alarms. The battles of Chippawa, Lundy's Lane and Fort Erie were indecisive, the invasion of Canada was definitely halted; and, on the other hand, the British were diverting the war with a will to American soil. Indeed, the battle of Bladensburg, the raid on Washington and the flight of the government gave every indication that the Union was on the point of disruption. On the border Sir George Prevost with his army of British veterans was about to launch an attack by way of Champlain and the coast of Maine was already occupied by the enemy.

Boston itself was threatened with invasion and little or no preparation was made for its defense. The Federalist leaders of the city rather welcomed the arrival of the British, whom they had favored throughout the war. Some of them asserted openly that Boston ought to capitulate and that the British could be counted upon to respect private property. The fate of Alexandria, Virginia, however, revealed that the British were not as particular about private property as the Boston Federalists imagined. The flour, tobacco and other goods belonging to individuals had been seized. When the Bostonians heard of that the instinct of ownership triumphed over the instinct of party politics. At last even the most violent of the Federalists forgot their prejudices, took off their coats and set to work on the city's fortifications. Proud and haughty members of the Suffolk Bar and students from Harvard rubbed shoulders with the masses as the earthworks went up. But the threat did not materialize. The British fleet left Boston in peace and, as the fear of invasion receded, Boston's sense of grievance rose.

The chief bone of contention was the state militia. Upon the threat of invasion Governor Strong called upon the National Government for funds to support the troops. The Secretary of War replied that the support would be forthcoming if the Massachusetts militia were placed under the command of regular officers. This Governor Strong refused to do, fearing that once under Federal control the militia would be marched out of the state and into Canada. The Secretary of War made the same offer to the Governors of Connecticut, Rhode Island and Vermont; but, like Governor Strong, all of them refused. Such being the case the Secretary of War declined to provide the funds. In the eyes of the Secretary of War his decision was logical enough, but not to the New England States who saw their revenues turned over to the National Government for the maintenance of the troops from other states while, in addition, they were called upon to support their own. To make matters worse even the Boston bankers, when approached, refused to advance the necessary funds.

To meet the emergency Governor Strong summoned the General Court to a special session which convened on October 5. The proposal for a convention was revived and a resolution passed calling for the appointment of 12 delegates from Massachusetts "to meet and confer with Delegates from the other States of New England, or any of them, upon the subjects of their public grievances and concerns, and upon the best means of preserving our resources and the defense against the enemy, and to devise and suggest for adoption by those respective states, such measures as they may deem expedient; and also to take measures, if they shall think proper, for procuring a convention of Delegates from all the United States, in order to revise the Constitution thereof, and more effectually to secure the support and attachment of all the people, by placing all upon a basis of fair representation."

To the other New England States went the invitation of Massachusetts. Connecticut and Rhode Island promptly accepted it and chose their delegates. They had just been aroused by two more irritating proposals of the National Congress; one calling for conscription to fill the meager ranks of the regular army, the other permitting youths of 18 to volunteer without the consent of their parents. Just another wicked scheme on the part of the Southerners and Westerners to drag the New Englanders into the war and, worse than that, to destroy the very foundation of the American home by encouraging boys to defy the authority of their parents.

But the enthusiasm for a convention halted abruptly. The New Hampshire Legislature was not in session and the governor questioned his authority to send delegates. Governor Chittenden of Vermont was a loyal Federalist, but his spirit had been chastened by the narrow escape at Plattsburg. He had come to the conclusion that, with the British within a few hours' march of his state, this was no time to satisfy party grudges or to engage in domestic squabbles. He declined the invitation for Vermont. But two townships in New Hampshire and one in Vermont took it upon themselves to send delegates. Thus, at the very outset, the Hartford Convention was handicapped. Only three out of the five New England States were fully represented, and in the three states that were represented sentiment in favor of the convention was far from being unanimous.

On December 15 the 26 delegates assembled in the old State House in Hartford, elected George Cabot president and Theodore Dwight secretary; and for three weeks the eyes of the country were on the Connecticut capital. The convention enjoyed all the publicity the press could give it. The Boston *Sentinel* sounded the Federalist keynote when it presented an address to the delegates in which it declared: "At your hands, therefore, we demand deliverance. New England is unanimous. And we announce our irrevocable decree that the tyrannical oppression of those who at present usurp the power of the Constitution is beyond endurance. And we will resist." Other Federalist newspapers displayed an equally chauvinistic spirit. Some of them warned the President to get himself a swifter horse than he used at Bladensburg if he intended to bend the New England States to his will.

The Republican press was quite as noisy in exaggerating the treasonable aspect of the assembly. Its editors asserted that the true object of the convention was to set up a New England confederacy. Some of them published addresses begging it not to start a civil war. The *National Intelligencer,* organ of the administration, recalled that the people, not the states, adopted the Constitution and possessed the sovereign power. The Richmond, Virginia, *Inquirer,* warming to the subject, expressed its unreserved opinion that "nullification or secession was treason and that the respectable gentlemen assembled at Hartford, if they attempted either course, should be treated as traitors." New England threatening secession, the South crying out against it. How embarrassing to both were these declarations of rights to appear some 45 years later!

Stimulated by the press public excitement rose to fever pitch. The war was almost forgotten in the interest over what was taking place at Hartford. Extreme Federalists, whose necks were not at stake, urged the delegates to go the limit. Pickering's idea was to kick the West out of the Union and return to a union of the thirteen original states with New England again holding the balance of power. Gouverneur Morris, in Philadelphia, was enthusiastic over what the convention would achieve. To Pickering, sitting in the Senate in Washington, he wrote, "I care nothing about your actings and doings. Your decree of conscription and your levy of contributions are alike indifferent to one whose eyes are fixed on a Star in the East, which he believes to be the day spring of freedom and glory. The traitors and madmen assembled at Hartford will, I believe, if not too tame and timid, be hailed hereafter as the patriots and sages of their day and generation. May the blessing of God be upon them, to inspire their counsels and prosper their resolutions!"

John Randolph of Roanoke was so concerned over the imminent prospect of civil war that he addressed an open letter to James Lloyd, a moderate Federalist, begging him to intercede before it was too late. Lloyd was quite as alarmed as Randolph. He advised that the Virginians persuade Madison to abdicate and place Rufus King in the Presidency as the best means of saving the Union. The administration itself feared the worst. There were not 500 Federal troops in the whole of New England to suppress a rebellion. The Secretary of War, Mr. Monroe, sent orders to Colonel Thomas S. Jesup, commander of the military district of Connecticut, to keep a sharp lookout on the doings of the convention and to make reports directly to him.

When John Adams, then in his 81st year, heard of Cabot's election, the old fellow exclaimed, "Thank God, thank God! George Cabot's close-buttoned ambition has broke out at last. He wants to be President of New England, Sir!"

But there John Adams was wrong. Cabot's close-buttoned ambition had not "broke out." It was as close-buttoned as ever. It was as close-buttoned as when, a year before, he had retorted to the indefatigable Pickering, "Why can't you and I let the world ruin itself in its own way?" Cabot, most unwillingly, had allowed himself to be drafted for a job which had little appeal. His attitude was made apparent in his reply to a young friend who asked him what he hoped to accomplish at Hartford, "We are going to keep you young hot-heads from getting into mischief." Sixty-two years of age and inclined to accept philosophically the trials and tribulations of life, Cabot was hardly the man to lead a successful rebellion.

As for the rest of the delegates, to a man they were typical of the ruling aristocracy of New England. Harrison Gray Otis, who took a leading part in the discussions, was a polished gentleman of 49 and generally acclaimed as the handsomest man of his day. Witty and easy of manner he moved among the delegates like a gracious host. There were Nathan Dane, a prominent citizen of Beverly; Judge Joseph Lyman of Northampton, kindly, dignified, religious; Timothy Bigelow, a leader of the Suffolk Bar, who had been six times speaker of the Massachusetts House. Two delegates were to be more distinguished in history as sires than for their part in the Hartford proceedings. They were Stephen Longfellow, father of the poet, and William Prescott, father of the historian. Others of the Massachusetts delegation were George Bliss, a prominent lawyer; Joshua Thomas and Hodigah Baylies, judges of probate; Daniel Waldo, a wealthy merchant, and Samuel Sumner Wild, a lawyer and politician.

Equally distinguished were the delegates from Connecticut and Rhode Island. Among the former were white-haired Chauncy Goodrich, veteran legislator and lieutenant governor; James Hillhouse, a giant in stature and with the looks and walk of an Indian, who had fought in the Revolution; Zephamiah Swift, Chief Justice, Governor John Treadwell, Judges Nathaniel Smith and Calvin Goddard, and Roger Minott Sherman, a lawyer and scholar. From Rhode Island came Colonel Samuel Ward, blue-blooded son of the founder of Brown University and himself a wealthy merchant; Daniel Lyman, Chief Justice and the President of the Society of the Cincinnati; Benjamin Hazard, Lyman's son-in-law, and Edward Manton, a merchant and state senator, who shrank into insignificance in such brilliant company. Benjamin West and Mills Olcott, New Hampshire lawyers, and William Hall, a prominent merchant of Vermont, completed the group. Of them all, Bigelow, a member of the Essex Junto and a disciple of Pickering, and Bliss were the only two who could be classed as extremists. Of the 26 delegates, 22 were college graduates and nine were jurists. Their average age was 52.

These were men of maturity and responsibility, capable no doubt of solemn deliberation and protest; but not the sort to erect barricades, defy authority and risk their property and their necks in an abortive revolt. Observers closest to the scene quickly recognized the convention for what it was. Colonel Jesup lost no time in assuring Secretary Monroe that the people of Connecticut were not prepared for rebellion and that the actions of the convention were no cause for public alarm. John Lowell, a pamphleteer and firebrand, who acted as a mouthpiece for Pickering and who was doing his best to egg on the delegates to extreme measures, soon reported in disgust to his master, "They are not calculated for bold measures." Of Otis in particular, who was looked upon as the leader and archconspirator, he wrote, "Mr. Otis is naturally timid, and frequently wavering—today bold, tomorrow like a hare trembling at every breeze." In short, Lowell declared, he did not know "a single bold and ardent man" among the Massachusetts and Connecticut delegations.

The Hartford Convention might have ceased then and there to be news, and doubtless would quickly have been forgotten, had it not, almost by accident, hit upon the one possible means of redeeming itself. The ruling aristocracy of New England was not accustomed to taking the public into its confidence. It deemed it sufficient to apprise the people of its decisions after its deliberations had been completed. And so, rather as a matter of course, on the afternoon of its first session it adopted a rule to the effect that "The most inviolable secrecy shall be observed by each member of this convention, including the Secretary."

The effect of the resolution was overwhelming. If inviolable secrecy was to be observed, then it was as plain as a pikestaff that there must be goings on that could not bear the light of day. The most vivid imaginations were now free to conjure up and enlarge upon what was taking place behind those closed doors. Nullification, secession, conspiracy, treason and rebellion, insidious plotting, nefarious schemes—any and all of them were now considered not only possible, but probable. Honest men walked in the light of day, conspirators sought the shadows. What good did it do for the delegates later to protest that in the discussions and decisions there was nothing said or done that could not bear the fullest scrutiny? What if Otis declared upon his word of honor that the convention

329

was designed solely to soothe the popular excitement, provide for defense against the British and save the Union? If that was true, then why the secrecy? What if the members, feeling themselves unjustly accused, by common consent allowed the journal of the convention to be published, in the hope of silencing the scandal and the rumors? Ah, but there may have been things both said and done that were too incriminating to be set down in black and white. Thanks to the secrecy resolution, the convention was either high-minded and constructive as Otis claimed, or it was "hideous and wicked" as John Quincy Adams charged. A choice could be made according to a man's political prejudices.

The mature judgment of historians, far removed from the excitement and turmoil of the times, is that in spite of the mystery with which its actions were surrounded the Hartford Convention had nothing to conceal. It sat from December 14, 1814, to January 5, 1815, and on the day after adjournment its report was published in a special edition of the Hartford *Courant,* and soon was in circulation throughout the country. This report consisted of some 23 closely typed pages and its authorship was attributed to Otis. It began with a summary of the iniquities of the administrations of Jefferson and Madison and of New England's grievances. It declared that there prevailed to no inconsiderable extent a sentiment "that the time for a change [of government] is at hand," that the evils were due to intrinsic and incurable defects in the Constitution, and offered to present some general considerations in the hope of reconciling all to a course of moderation and firmness.

As to a dissolution of the Union, if that were destined then it should "if possible be the work of peaceable times and deliberate consent." Having mentioned possible dissolution to please extremists of the Pickering type, the report then endeavored to reassure the moderates by stating that "the severance of the Union by one or more States, against the will of the rest, and especially in time of war, can be justified only by absolute necessity."

Under the heading of "Dangers and Grievances" the report next dealt with the matter of the proposed conscription bill and the enlistment of minors without the consent of their parents. And here it reached its most extreme position, for it advised the states, assuming the passage of the bills, to devise such measures as would effectually protect their citizens from the operation of the laws. That was pure and unadulterated encouragement to nullification.

For the solution of the militia problem the report suggested that the states be permitted by Congress to assume their own defense, withholding from the national taxes such portion as might be needed for that purpose.

The report finally proposed seven amendments to the Constitution. These were (1) that slave representation be abolished, (2) that a new State could be admitted to the Union only by a concurrence of two-thirds of the members of both houses of Congress, (3) that embargoes be limited to sixty days, (4) that non-intercourse acts should require a two-thirds vote, (5) that no naturalized citizen be eligible to an elective or appointive office under the national government, (6) that a declaration of war should require a two-thirds vote of both houses of Congress, and (7) that no president should serve more than one term, and that the same State should not provide a President twice in succession.

In other words, the Constitution was to be amended to suit the specific needs of New England with little consideration for the rest of the country. It was an ultimatum to which the rest of the states were hardly likely to consent unless they were in a desperate situation. But the situation was desperate. The war was still in progress and a British army was knocking at the gates of New Orleans with every prospect of getting in. For the satisfaction of these extravagant demands everything depended upon an American defeat in the South and a continuation of the war.

Yet even these proposals were not sufficiently drastic to satisfy the stalwarts of the Essex Junto, the shock troops of the extreme Federalists. Lowell was disappointed because the convention had not declared for New England's neutrality for the rest of the war. Federalist editors complained because it had not assumed that the Union was already dissolved, and that the amendments had been "requested." In the opinion of the editors they should have been demanded. Others noted the omission of a call for a constitutional convention. Gouverneur Morris, who had called the delegates the "Wise Men of the East," now retracted his words, and ridiculed their deliberations in an open letter. The Republicans, on the other hand, were relieved that the report was no worse. "Certain it is, that the proceedings are tempered with more moderation than was to have been expected," admitted the *National Intelligencer.* If, said the editor, the convention was called to effect separation from the Union, at least the delegates appeared to be going about it in a peaceable way.

Yet in spite of all that had happened in New England, President Madison was still willing to try appeasement. In fact his situation was then so precarious that there were no means of using force. The militia question was the immediate bone of contention. Madison would see what he could do with that. So, on January 27, the President signed an act of Congress that authorized him to accept into the Federal service and pay "any corps of troops, which may have been, or may be raised, organized and officered under the authority of any of the States." These troops, though in the Federal service, were to be employed only in the states in which they were raised or in adjoining states and not elsewhere except with the consent of the executive of the state raising them. The act was no less than a flat surrender by the administration to the Hartford Convention on the most vital grievance of the moment. Well might Otis exclaim that "the egg that was laid in the darkness of the Hartford Convention was hatched by daylight under the wing and incubation of the National Eagle."

But these New England Federalists were meticulous. While the act agreed that the United States Government would foot the bill it did not agree that the states could deduct the expenses from the Federal revenues. The United States Treasury was known to be on the verge of bankruptcy. What guarantee, then, was there that the bill would eventually be met? None. The New Englanders were not satisfied with that. The surrender must be complete. On January 31 Governor Strong appointed three commissioners—Otis, Thomas H. Perkins and William Sullivan—to go to Washington, beard the President in his den and make the "request" for this concession. The gentlemen immediately were dubbed "the three Ambassadors."

A few days later the ambassadors set out on their long journey to the national capital. Otis seems to have had some misgivings about his mission for, in a letter to his wife, he remarked that between New York and Philadelphia the party was followed by a flock of crows and that, whenever the crows came to ground, three of them stood apart from the rest. "These are ill omen'd birds," he wrote, "and in days when augury was in fashion would have been considered as sad precursors of the three ambassadors. What the Blackbirds at Washington will say or do with us remains to be seen."

And evil omens the three black crows proved to be; for, on February 12, soon after the travelers had passed through Philadelphia, they received news of the American victory at New Orleans. This was good fortune that was likely to stiffen the Washington blackbirds. Nevertheless the ambassadors continued on their way and arrived in Georgetown, which boasted a considerably more genteel atmosphere than that of Washington with its official rabble. Georgetown was far more congenial to the delicate sensibilities of the Federalist gentlemen. And there President Madison, emboldened by the victory in New Orleans, allowed them to cool their heels before receiving them. Mr. Monroe, the Secretary of State, they had to confess, treated them with courtesy and civility.

But the worst was yet to come. For, on February 14, Washington received news of the treaty signed at Ghent. At last the war was at an end! And with the end of the war came an abrupt end to the mission of the three ambassadors. Payment of militia in the national service ceased to be an issue. So it came about that the three haughty ambassadors who had gone to deliver terms of surrender to the President of the United States were left dangling in air and looking exceedingly foolish. So, too, did the rest of the Federalists who had taken part in the Hartford Convention.

The Republican press and Republican wits did little to relieve their adversaries of their embarrassment. The joke was much too good for the country to miss. In cartoons, verse and editorials the Federalists came in for lampooning and satire that set the nation laughing. The best epitaph of the Hartford Convention appeared in Henry Wheaton's New York *National Advocate:*

"Missing.

"Three well looking, responsible men, who appeared to be travelling towards Washington, disappeared suddenly from Gadsby's Hotel, in Baltimore, on Monday evening last, and have not since been heard of. They were observed to be very melancholy on hearing the news of peace, and one of them was heard to say, with a great sigh, 'Poor Caleb Strong.' They took with them their saddle-bags, so that no apprehension is entertained of their having an intention to make away with themselves. Whoever will give any information to the Hartford Convention of the fate of these unfortunate and tristful gentlemen by letter (post paid) will confer a favor upon humanity.

"The newspapers, particularly the Federal newspapers, are requested to publish this advertisement in a conspicuous place, and send their bills to the Hartford Convention.

"P.S. One of the gentlemen was called Titus Oates, or some such name."

CHAPTER TWENTY-SIX

The Final Chapter at Sea

AT LAST the overwhelming superiority of the British Navy began to tell, and by the end of the year 1814 the effective strength of the American frigates was considerably reduced. The *Chesapeake* was at the bottom of the sea, the *Essex* had fought her last fight. The *United States* and the *Macedonian* were blockaded in the Thames at New London, the *Constellation* at Norfolk. The *Constitution* was in Boston harbor. The *President* alone was on the high seas and she was making for home. She managed to slip through British men-of-war guarding the entrance to New York harbor and there she remained blockaded for the rest of the year, while Commodore Rodgers was transferred to the command of the *Guerrière*, then being completed.

But if the American Navy was badly wounded its fighting spirit had been in no way diminished. It was still capable of striking a few hard blows however ineffectual they may have been in changing the inevitable decision. The *Adams*, rating 18 guns, ran the blockade of Chesapeake Bay in January and cruised until summer, taking nine prizes in the course of six months. In August she took refuge in the Penobscot and then, as we have seen, she was burned to escape capture by the invaders.

Since the beginning of the war three new sloops had been commissioned, and two of them gave good accounts of themselves. The three were the *Frolic*, *Peacock* and *Wasp*. The *Frolic* was ill-fated; she had not been out of port two months before she was captured. More fortunate was the *Peacock*, under the skillful hand of Master Commandant Lewis Warrington. She sailed from New York in March, 1814, and on April 29 sighted a large convoy on the way from Bermuda to Havana under the protection of the British brig

Epervier, of 18 guns. Though weaker in guns and men than the *Peacock,* the *Epervier* stood up to her task of protecting the convoy.

Her decision was courageous but fatal. In less than an hour the guns of the *Peacock* had hulled her in nearly 50 places, cut her rigging and sails into shreds, shot away her main boom and shattered her foremast, while her decks were slippery with the blood of 23 of her crew killed or wounded. The *Peacock* lost not a single man and only two were wounded. Warrington returned with his prize to Savannah.

In June the *Peacock* again set sail and crossed the Atlantic to join the privateers that were harassing British commerce in the narrow seas. There, during July and August, she burned or sank 12 prizes, made cartel ships of two, and returned triumphantly home to New York where she arrived at the end of October.

Equally distinguished was the career of the *Wasp,* Commander Johnston Blakeley. She sailed from Portsmouth, New Hampshire, on May 1, and made for the English Channel where she burned or sank five merchantmen. On June 28 the *Wasp* came up with the British brig *Reindeer,* commanded by Captain Manners. The fight was short and sharp. In 19 minutes the heavier weight of metal of the *Wasp* made a wreck of the *Reindeer* and the British commander was killed along with 32 of his men, not to mention 34 wounded. The *Wasp,* too, suffered badly. She had six round shot in her hull, her foremast was shot through, and her rigging and spars were mangled. Eleven of her crew were killed and 11 wounded. She was obliged to put into Lorient for repairs.

Refitted and her crew reorganized, the *Wasp* left Lorient on August 27 and five days later fell in with the British sloop *Avon.* Both ships cleared for action and engaged. Blakeley handled his ship brilliantly throughout a two-hour fight. When the *Avon* struck her colors she had in her hold two feet of water, which inundated her magazine, five of her guns had been dismounted, her tiller, foreyard, main boom and rigging were shot away and 40 of her crew were killed or wounded. The *Wasp's* loss was only two men. In the course of her brief career as a Channel blockader she took 14 prizes in all, while eluding three frigates and 14 sloops which the Admiralty detailed to the vain task of guarding British shipping.

Turning from these rich hunting fields after her fight with the

Avon, the *Wasp* clapped on sail and sped for Madeira. On September 21 she captured the brig *Atlanta* and on October 9 spoke a Swedish vessel. And that was the last that was ever seen of the stout little sloop and her gallant commander and crew. Her fate remains to this day one of the mysteries of the sea.

The *Constitution*, which had been under repair, once more ventured out to show that an American frigate could still sail the seas. Captain Charles Stewart had replaced Commodore Bainbridge as her commander. She left Boston on January 1 and for 17 days did not encounter a single vessel. At last, in February, cruising off Dutch Guiana, she captured a British schooner and a letter of marque and, returning home, was herself almost taken by two British frigates off Cape Ann. She succeeded in making Marblehead, and eventually Boston, after a not particularly successful voyage. During November, 1814, not a single ship of the United States Navy remained on the ocean.

This situation, however, did not continue long. In December Captain Stewart again hoisted sail, ran past the blockaders and made the Bay of Biscay his goal. There he cruised until February 20, when he ran up with the British frigate *Cyane*, of 36 guns, and the British sloop *Levant*, of 18 guns, and captured both of them, after which he put in with his prizes at Santiago in the Cape Verde Islands. To Santiago he was followed by the British frigates *Leander*, of 50 guns, *Newcastle*, 50 guns, and *Acasta*, 40 guns. Stewart thought little of the protection afforded by Portuguese neutrality and did not wait to test it. Instead he decided to make a run, ordering the *Cyane* and *Levant* to do the same. The *Constitution* and the *Cyane* escaped and returned to the United States to learn that peace had been declared. The *Levant* was recaptured by the British.

In November, 1814, the Navy Department decided to send Commodore Decatur to sea in command of a squadron. With this end in view the *President*, Captain Warrington's *Peacock*, Captain Biddle's *Hornet* and the supply ship *Tom Bowline* were assembled in New York and careful preparations were made for a prolonged voyage. The ships were to slip past the British blockade separately and meet at sea. Decatur designated the lonely island of Tristan da Cunha in the South Atlantic as the rendezvous.

On January 14 the *President* dropped down to Sandy Hook, leaving the rest of the squadron off Staten Island. Hardly had she hoisted her sails before misfortune overtook her. She grounded on a sand bar, but succeeded in getting off with the tide. Hugging the shore of Long Island, she successfully eluded the blockaders during the night and put out to sea. Decatur was congratulating himself on his luck when, as day dawned, he discovered that he was in the immediate vicinity of four British men-of-war. These turned out to be the *Endymion*, 40 guns; the *Pomone*, 38 guns; the *Tenedos*, 38 guns; and the *Majestic*, and they saw him as soon as he saw them. The *President* spread all her canvas and dashed away with the British in hot pursuit, like a fox pursued by a pack of hounds. But in spite of all Decatur could do the *Endymion* began to gain on him. Throughout the morning and early afternoon the race continued while the decks of the *President* were cleared for action and her crew stood at their stations. As a last resort Decatur lightened the ship, but still the space between the *President* and the *Endymion* continued to narrow.

A 3 P.M. the *Endymion* opened at long range with her bow guns. The *President* replied, but her shots fell short. Decatur was disappointed with the behavior of his guns which he attributed to inferior powder. By 5 P.M. the *Endymion* was on top of her prey and pouring a fire into her which did great damage while Decatur could not bring the *President's* guns to bear on her adversary. All hope of escape was now gone. In spite of the odds against him Decatur had no other recourse except to stand up and fight. Still the *President's* guns refused to act as Decatur thought they should and the Commodore determined upon the bold plan of running the *Endymion* down and boarding her. Captain Hope, of the *Endymion*, however, preferred to fight it out with the guns and skillfully maneuvered his ship so as to keep out of harm's way. The ships were now only a quarter of a mile apart and, for two and a half hours, poured broadsides into each other. The battle was hard fought and both of the contenders were badly damaged, but gradually the *President's* superiority in metal began to tell. The *Endymion*, her sails in shreds, gave evidence of exhaustion and fell astern.

The *Endymion*, however, had successfully performed her mission in overtaking and holding the *President*, for by this time the *Pomone*, the *Tenedos*, the *Majestic* and also the *Dispatch*, which had joined in the chase, arrived on the scene and entered the battle. Decatur had had as much as he could do to contend with the *Endymion;* he was in no condition to take on four more adversaries. So, with a heavy heart, he ordered the *President's* colors to be struck. Thus ended the career of the newest and finest of the American frigates, while one of the United States Navy's most distinguished captains and his ship and crew were conducted to Bermuda by their triumphant conquerors.

Ignorant of the fate that had overtaken their leader, the *Peacock, Hornet* and *Tom Bowline* set out on January 22 and eluded the blockade. The *Peacock* and the *Tom Bowline* were the first to reach Tristan da Cunha, arriving off the island by the middle of March, but were driven away by a storm. On March 23 the *Hornet* sailed into the harbor. Captain Biddle was about to anchor when he sighted a strange vessel and set out to investigate her. When the *Hornet* was within musket-shot range of the stranger the latter raised the British colors and opened fire. The newcomer was the 18-gun brig *Penguin,* under the command of Captain Dickenson. Biddle at once accepted the challenge and for 15 minutes the guns of the two ships thundered at each other. They were as evenly matched in size, crews and weight of metal as two ships could be. Dickenson proceeded to run down the *Hornet* in order to board her and settle the dispute on deck in a hand-to-hand fight. The ships crashed and the *Penguin's* first officer shouted to her boarders to follow him over the side of the *Hornet,* but the men held back. Meanwhile Biddle was urging on his gun crews and raking the decks of the *Penguin* with broadside after broadside. Above the din of the battle a British officer's voice was heard shouting that the *Penguin* had surrendered.

Biddle ordered his guns to cease firing; and as the gunners obeyed the command, two British marines drew a bead on the American commander and fired. Biddle dropped to the deck with a bullet through his neck. With a shout of anger the Americans fell upon the marines and killed both of them. It was with difficulty that peace was restored. Biddle's wound proved slight. The *Penguin* was so severely damaged that she could not be taken as a prize and Biddle scuttled her. In the fight the *Hornet* lost only one man killed and 10 wounded. The battle, modest as it was, had an especial significance;

for it was the last to the present day to be fought between men-of-war of Great Britain and the United States.

The sun had not set when the *Peacock* and the *Tom Bowline* arrived on the scene to join the victorious *Hornet*. Biddle now converted the *Tom Bowline* into a cartel ship and sent her off with his prisoners to Rio de Janeiro. The *Hornet* and the *Peacock* continued to cruise about Tristan da Cunha waiting for the *President,* though meanwhile news reached them that she had probably been captured. The two sloops then set off to try their luck in the East Indies. On April 27 they came up with the British ship of the line *Cornwallis,* rating 74 guns, and at once separated and started to run from so formidable an adversary. The *Hornet* was slower than the *Peacock* and the *Cornwallis* singled her out for special attention. For a time it looked as though the end of the *Hornet* had come as the *Cornwallis* was overtaking her. Biddle's only hope lay in lightening his ship. Overboard went shot, anchors, cables and all the heavy gear that served to hold her back. When these proved to be not enough, spars and boats followed and then all the guns except one which Biddle saved for emergency. The plan worked. Gradually the *Hornet* drew away and at last threw off her pursuer. Thus bared of all her fighting gear the *Hornet* set out on her long journey back home. She arrived safely at last in New York harbor on June 9 without an anchor left aboard her to drop.

The *Peacock* continued on alone, looking for further adventure. She eventually came up with the British cruiser *Nautilus,* with whom she exchanged a broadside before the *Nautilus* struck. From her Captain Warrington learned that the war was over and also the period of grace allowed by the treaty for ships at sea. So the *Nautilus* was given her freedom. To Captain Biddle went the honor of fighting the last battle; to his colleague, Captain Warrington, of the *Peacock,* the honor of firing the last shot.

While these final chapters were being written at sea the war was coming to an end as well on land. The British had made a thrust from Canada. They had harried the Eastern seaboard and raided the capital. It was now time to try the South.

Before the British War Office learned of the death of General Ross in Baltimore it had ordered him, upon the completion of that campaign, to sail for Jamaica, await reinforcements and prepare for an expedition against the troubled territory of Louisiana. The British counted upon the disaffected French and Spaniards to further their cause. The main objects were the capture of New Orleans and the closing of the mouth of the Mississippi to commerce. The direction of the attack and the steps to be taken if it proved successful were left to Ross and Admiral Sir Alexander Cochrane, who was to share in this amphibious operation. The death of Ross, when it was reported in England, did not greatly alter the plans.

The situation of the Federal Government, following the humiliation to the capital was bad enough in all conscience. In New England, the people were willing for peace at any price. When, in October, 1814, the British conditions were made known in this country, and included the cession of part of Maine and the abandonment of New England's fishing rights, Governor Strong, of Massachusetts, considered the terms reasonable and the Federalist leaders saw in them no cause for prolonging the war. They blamed the American negotiators for rejecting the offer.

But in other parts of the country the disgrace of the raid on Washington brought about a solidarity that President Madison hitherto had been unable to achieve. Particularly in the West was there a cry for revenge, and the West had a leader capable of making revenge possible. General Andrew Jackson had a personal score of many years' standing to settle with the British; for, as a youth in the days of the Revolution, he had felt the edge of a British officer's sword across his face and the bite of it was still there. It so happened that he was now present for duty at the most threatened spot. When General William Henry Harrison, in a pique, resigned his commission after the battle of the Thames, a major-generalcy in the regular army was left vacant and to it Andrew Jackson, fresh from his victory against the Creeks, was appointed. He was now Commander of the Seventh Military District, with headquarters at Mobile.

The West had always laid covetous eyes on the Floridas and this may well have colored Jackson's estimate of the problem which confronted him. He arrived at Mobile on August 15, 1814, and, because of the demoralization at Washington just at that moment, he was left largely to his own resources. Jackson had informers everywhere and soon received news that the Spanish authorities in Pensacola were closely allied with the British and Indians. He also was convinced in his own mind that any attack on New Orleans must be made by way of Mobile, a conviction he held up to the last minute and which, as we shall see, nearly led to disaster.

The information he had received was shortly verified by the arrival at Pensacola of several British men-of-war, under the command of Captain William H. Percy, from which were landed a few hundred marines under Lieutenant Colonel Edward Nicholls, a somewhat bombastic Irishman. They were hospitably received by the Spanish governor, Don Matteo Gonzalez Manrique, and the British flag was flown from Fort St. Michael, on the outskirts of the town, and from Fort Barrancas, six miles below it. Agents were sent among the Creeks and Seminoles inviting them to join the British in the war against the Americans, while Nicholls issued a proclamation to the people of Louisiana urging them to cast off the American yoke. He talked so loudly of an invasion by way of Mobile that Jackson could not have been better deceived as to their true purpose had the British deliberately employed Nicholls to throw Jackson off the scent. Nicholls' force was totally inadequate for so ambitious an undertaking but the rumor was spread and actually believed that the Russian Czar was lending 50,000 men to the British for the conquest of Louisiana.

In their zeal to gather recruits the British were not squeamish about whom they asked. Their only requirement was that a man should know how to fight. If he had a grievance against the United States, so much the better. In Barataria Bay, west of the Mississippi delta and some 60 miles below the city of New Orleans, was the headquarters of a picturesque band of outlaws under the leadership of a shrewd Frenchman named Jean Laffite. Laffite, according to his own way of putting it, was an honest man who was the victim of what he called "vices of the law." These "vices," for example, forbade American citizens to attack the vessel of a country with which the United States was not at war. Laffite and his gangsters preyed upon Spanish commerce, seizing and robbing every Spanish ship that ventured too near his stronghold.

The "vices of the law" also forbade the entry of goods into the United States upon which a duty had not been paid. Laffite smuggled his captured goods in small boats through the lonely bayous which led to New Orleans and there disposed of them to merchants who were only too glad to get them. New Orleans was a gay, cosmopolitan city where life was free and polite custom forbade the asking of embarrassing questions. In New Orleans Laffite was favorably known and enjoyed the friendship of men in high places. A merchant of his importance naturally needed the service of legal counsel and Laffite engaged Edward Livingston, former mayor of New York, who had been involved in a financial scandal, lost his fortune and gone to New Orleans to start life over again. Livingston was a man of distinguished bearing and he and his charming wife were leaders of the American colony in the city.

Governor William C. Claiborne, however, had sworn to uphold the "vicious laws" of which Jean Laffite complained. In spite of the popular sentiment in favor of Laffite the Governor determined to perform the unpopular task of breaking up the Laffite gang. He offered a reward of $500 for the capture of its leader, but the clever pirate, with a touch of Gallic humor, promptly countered and set all New Orleans laughing by offering a reward of $30,000 for the capture of the Governor. Claiborne, however, was not discouraged. Under his direction a combined military and naval expedition was organized to set out for Barataria Bay and beard the pirates in their den. Before it started Pierre Laffite, a brother of the leader, who lived in New Orleans, was clapped into jail.

Such was the situation when British agents arrived at Barataria Bay bearing a letter from Colonel Nicholls giving a glowing account of the prospects offered if Laffite would join the British and a more pointed one from Captain Percy warning him of the jeopardy he would be in if he didn't. Spanish ships did not always surrender without putting up a fight and the Baratarians were therefore quite accustomed to the smoke of battle and knew how to handle a cannon and other weapons. They could be most useful to the British cause.

Laffite asked for time to think the matter over. But even as he entertained his visitors his alert mind realized that an opportunity had come to him, like manna from heaven. He was now possessed of valuable information about the enemy and, if he delivered that information to New Orleans, the United States authorities ought to see him in a different light. Where all had seemed hopeless before, here at the ninth hour was a promising means of extricating himself from the toils that were tightening about him. Laffite immediately reported the offer to his lawyer, Livingston, and through Livingston begged of Governor Claiborne forgiveness for himself and his men. He promised that, if pardoned, they would faithfully serve the Americans. Claiborne, nevertheless, carried out his raid on Barataria; but, at the same time, Pierre Laffite mysteriously escaped from prison. Thus the dignity of the law was upheld and the Baratarians also scored a point. Everybody in New Orleans was pleased.

Soon after Jackson learned of Nicholls' activities at Pensacola he appealed to Governor Blount of Tennessee for troops for an expedition against the town. But it would be a month or more before the levy could be raised. Meanwhile his immediate concern was Fort Bowyer, 30 miles south of Mobile on a point of land guarding the entrance to Mobile Bay. The fort was poorly constructed and mounted only 20 guns. Major William Lawrence, of the United States Army, was dispatched there with 120 regulars under orders to hold it at all cost. These precautions were taken none too soon for, on September 12, Nicholls landed in rear of the fort with a small band of marines and Indians; while late in the evening the British men-of-war *Hermes, Sophia, Carron* and *Anaconda,* commanded by Captain Percy, sailed up and anchored offshore.

The following day Nicholls posted a howitzer within 700 yards of the fort and tossed over a few shells, to which Lawrence's guns responded. This desultory exchange of shots continued for two days. Then, on the evening of the 15th, the ships approached close to the fort and delivered their broadsides while Nicholls attacked from the land. The British had anticipated an easy victory but they failed to take into account Lawrence's courage and the marksmanship of his gunners. The little garrison in the fort responded vigorously to the attack, keeping Nicholls' force at a respectful distance while at the same time they directed fire with great effect upon the men-of-war which lay nearest them.

In short order the *Hermes* and the *Sophia* found themselves in serious trouble and the *Hermes* was so badly damaged that Percy had to abandon and set fire to her. The joint attack ended in a bloody repulse in which the British lost 162 killed and 72 wounded. Though the American gunners were fully exposed to the broadsides of the men-of-war Lawrence got off with only four men killed and four wounded. The defeated force retired to Pensacola while Lawrence's fine little victory greatly damaged British prestige among the Indians.

A few days after the events at Fort Bowyer Jackson received from the people of New Orleans a memorial in which they begged him to come to their help. This he was not yet ready to do. But he had been smarting under Nicholls' boasts and now was his opportunity for revenge. To Nicholls' proclamation he issued a counter proclamation to the people of Louisiana urging their continued loyalty to the United States. By way of sealing the argument he reminded them of the British offer to the Baratarians and asked how they could trust anyone who had sunk so low as to attempt an alliance with these "hellish banditti." Thus publicly he expressed his opinion of Laffite and his gang.

The British, in spite of their defeat, were welcomed back to Pensacola by Governor Manrique and once more occupied Forts St. Michael and Barrancas. The circumstance strengthened Jackson's belief that Pensacola and its complaisant governor must be brought to book. The government in Washington had recovered from its paralysis and once more began to function. Monroe, who replaced Armstrong as Secretary of War, learned of the British plans against New Orleans, since they were discussed openly in the British press, and hastened to warn Jackson. On October 21 he wrote actually forbidding Jackson to attack Pensacola, stating emphatically that the President did not wish to become embroiled in a war with Spain.

Whether or not Jackson received the order, he nevertheless went ahead with his project. On October 25 his trusted lieutenant, General Coffee, arrived at Mobile with the newly raised Tennessee brigade, bringing Jackson's force there to 4,000. Jackson now judged that he was sufficiently strong to move. On November 3 he set out for his objective and on the evening of November 6 arrived within two miles of Pensacola and encamped for the night. The army he took with him, numbering about 3,000, was composed of two regiments of regulars, Tennessee volunteers and militiamen and a detachment of Choctaw Indians. An officer was dispatched under a flag of truce to demand the surrender of the forts and was fired upon by the Spaniards. After reporting the incident to Jackson the officer set out a second time and succeeded in reaching Manrique who, however, refused Jackson's demand that the forts be turned over to the Americans until the Spanish Government should be strong enough to defend its neutrality.

Next day Jackson's army was up and stirring while it was still dark. Taking to the shore on the east side of the town to avoid fire from the guns of Fort St. Michael, the attackers advanced in three columns, making a desperate effort to drag cannon with them through the sand. The Spaniards were ready to meet them. They had planted two guns in the center of the main street, while houses and gardens were thick with armed men. Not waiting for his own cannon to come up, Jackson ordered the regulars to charge the Spanish battery. They went forward with a shout to be greeted by a burst of grape and solid balls from the battery and a hail of bullets from the defenders in all parts of the town.

Nothing daunted by this warm reception the Americans made a final dash that overwhelmed the battery. In the lull which followed, and as the smoke lifted, a flag of truce appeared. Under it was Don Matteo Manrique asking to be led to General Jackson. His Spanish pride was humbled as he offered to kiss the General's hands and begged him to spare the town. Old Hickory was indifferent to having his hands kissed. At the moment he was more intent upon taking possession of the forts and to this the thoroughly cowed Manrique promptly consented.

Fort St. Michael had already been evacuated by the British, but Barrancas still remained in their hands. Jackson spent the day resting his men and planned to move on Barrancas next morning, seize it and turn its guns on the British fleet which lay offshore. But in the middle of the night the British blew up the fort, and the garrison embarked on the ships which then sailed away. Fearful that the British meant to attack Mobile during his absence, Jackson set his army in motion toward Fort Montgomery to face them should they succeed in passing Fort Bowyer.

Jackson has been severely criticized for this descent on Pensacola. Its capture did, of course, injure the prestige of the British in that quarter. On the other hand it gave the Federalists in Washington the opportunity to raise a clamor over what they called an unwarranted attack on a friendly power. More to the point, it was a waste of valuable time in view of the fact that Jackson was completely deceived as to the actual direction of the invasion.

Jackson reached Mobile on November 11. He found there, not the British, but another urgent appeal from the people of New Orleans to hasten to the defense of their city. New Orleans knew that it was a rich prize. It was fully conscious of the peril in which it stood, but its power of defending itself was virtually paralyzed by petty jealousy, political intrigue and strife. Conscientious and well-meaning though he was, Governor Claiborne lacked the force to weld together the cosmopolitan elements which composed the town's population. Americans, Spaniards and Creoles were divided into factions; the Legislature wrangled with the Governor and its members wrangled among themselves. As a result, nothing was being done by the constituted authorities to put the place in a state of adequate preparedness against the threatened attack. As events proved, the genius was there if it were properly directed. New Orleans needed an iron hand and that hand was at Mobile.

Despairing of getting the Legislature to act, Livingston, the ex-mayor of New York, took it upon himself to call a mass meeting of the citizens. He addressed them with all the eloquence at his command and the result was the organization of a committee of safety with Livingston as its chairman. The next step was the letter to Jackson. Having achieved his ambition in striking at Pensacola Jackson was now ready to go to New Orleans. But he continued to believe that Mobile would be attacked first. He therefore split his army, leaving several thousand men at Mobile under General James Winchester, while he proceeded with the remainder to New Orleans.

The General was at the time in wretched health, suffering from dysentery and exhausted from his strenuous campaigns, between which he had enjoyed practically no rest. His digestion was so poor that he could eat little more than boiled rice, and his tall slender frame and his sunken cheeks gave him a ghostlike appearance. He was so weak that he could not stand, or even sit, for any length of time and many of his orders were issued as he lay on a couch. But his eyes were still full of their accustomed fire and his state of emaciation gave to his chin an even more determined firmness.

Upon his arrival in New Orleans he found plenty of work to do. Livingston had not exaggerated the condition of stagnation. The only military consisted of a battalion of uniformed volunteers and a handful of militia. Arms were scarce and there was neither money

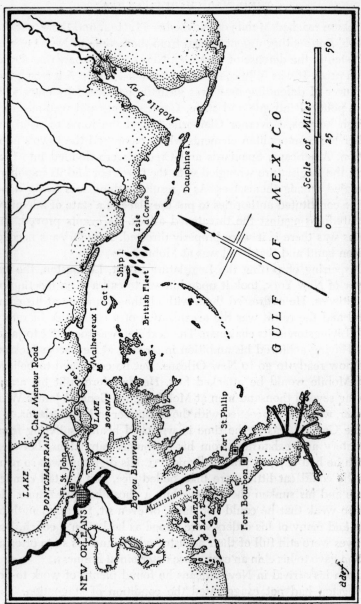

Map X. New Orleans Campaign

nor credit with which to increase the supply. The government had shipped arms from Pittsburgh but they were still on their way down the Mississippi, having been shipped by slow boat by the contractor to save money! Furthermore there was present a defeatist group, composed chiefly of wealthy merchants whose warehouses were stocked with valuable goods and who preferred surrender to the possible loss of their possessions in a siege.

Jackson got swiftly through with the formalities of his arrival, made a speech which was translated by Livingston and created a favorable impression, then declared martial law and set out upon the arduous task of converting the gayest city in the New World into an armed camp. The Governor was immediately directed to call out all the militia, orders were issued to fell trees and raise other obstructions in all the bayous leading toward the city deep enough to float barges. The old fortifications were strengthened and new ones built. Jackson himself pored over maps and in person made long trips outside the city to inspect the operations and study the terrain in order to familiarize himself with the country in which he would probably have to fight. (See Map X)

The city of New Orleans lies on the left bank of the Mississippi River some 100 miles from its mouth. To the north and east is Lake Pontchartrain and still farther east, Lake Borgne. The lakes are joined by a narrow strait known as Les Rigolets and between them is a flat and rather wide peninsula extending from the city to the strait. Through the center of this peninsula, known as the plain of Gentilly, ran the Chef Menteur Road. This would be the most obvious route for an invasion based upon a fleet coming in from the Gulf.

However, there were several other lines of attack. Were the British to take possession of the lakes they could enter Pontchartrain and from there use the Bayou St. John which was sufficiently wide and deep to carry an invading force straight to the center of the city. The entrance to the bayou was protected by Fort St. John, which Jackson garrisoned. A fort also stood at the entrance to Les Rigolets.

South of the city the river winds its way to the delta. For many miles below New Orleans the banks were lined by successive sugar plantations on a strip of narrow dry ground flanked by cypress swamps and marshes. In numerous places the swamps were cut by bayous sufficiently large to float an expedition. The British might come straight up the river or they might use one of these bayous.

To the west of the river was a series of bayous and lakes leading all the way from Barataria Bay to the city. This was the route favored by the Baratarians in bringing their contraband to New Orleans. Jackson's problem of defense was greatly magnified by the choices, of which there were at least five, presented to the enemy and the great danger involved in dividing his limited forces in an effort to guard all approaches.

To protect the direct river route Jackson manned Fort St. Philip, some 20 miles from its mouth. At a broad bend in the river 12 miles from New Orleans, known as English Turn, he erected a battery. Since he had given the orders he assumed that all the bayous had been blocked. On Lake Borgne was a flotilla of five gunboats under Lieutenant Thomas Ap Catesby Jones to lie in wait for the enemy and report his arrival. Having taken these precautions Jackson believed that for the time being he was secure against surprise.

Long before this the British expedition had begun to rendezvous at Negril Bay, in Jamaica. The troops which had taken part in the invasion of Washington and the attack on Baltimore were joined by others fresh from Wellington's campaign in Spain and one Scottish regiment which came all the way from the Cape of Good Hope. The expeditionary force was augmented by several regiments of native Jamaicans. The land troops in all numbered from 7,000 to 8,000, and sailors brought the total to the neighborhood of 10,000. No less than 50 ships, including men-of-war and transports, were assembled to carry this impressive host to the scene of combat. On the way from England to take command of the expedition in place of the now-deceased General Ross was Major General Sir Edward Pakenham attended by Major General John Keane, both officers of the first rank.

Everything being in readiness the armada set sail on November 26. Officers and men were in excellent spirits for they had heard much of New Orleans and anticipated enjoyment of the spoils after what they hoped would be an easy victory. The ships made good time and less than two weeks later, on December 9, they arrived off the Gulf Coast and dropped anchor between Ship and Cat Islands, at the entrance to Lake Borgne. Within 24 hours Lieutenant Jones had sighted the expedition and reported its presence to his superior, Master Commandant Daniel Patterson, in command of all the naval forces in the neighboring waters. Admiral Cochrane also caught sight of Jones and forthwith ordered an attack by his light sailing ships. Jones maneuvered skillfully to lure the ships into the treacherous shallows of the lake where many of them grounded.

This attack failing, Cochrane ordered out 60 barges, each with a carronade in the bow and manned by 1,200 men in all. This was too much for Lieutenant Jones to handle and he prepared to retire under the guns of the battery overlooking Les Rigolets. But at this crucial moment a calm set in rendering flight impossible. So, forming his flotilla in line near Malheureux Island, he cleared his decks for action and stood ready to receive the attack.

The Americans held their fire until the British had come within close range, then met them with a barrage of ball and grape. The damage to the enemy was severe; but, regardless of their losses and counting upon their numerical superiority, they continued forward. The battle raged fiercely for an hour before the gunboats were surrounded, boarded and captured. Jones lost in the engagement all his boats and six men killed and 35 wounded, he himself being among the latter. But he had made the British pay dearly for their success, their loss running to 300 killed and wounded.

However, Jackson had lost his eyes in Lake Borgne as well as the lake itself. The British quickly followed up their success by seizing Pea Island, a desolate spot in the lake at the mouth of Pearl River, part swamp inhabited by alligators but with enough firm land to serve as an advance post for the attack on New Orleans. For the next few days the British set themselves to the laborious task of rowing men and matériel across the 30 miles that lay between the fleet and the island.

As soon as news of the capture of the gunboats reached New Orleans the town was thrown into a fever of excitement and alarm. Jackson at once recognized the plain of Gentilly and the Chef Menteur Road as being his most vulnerable spot and dispatched Major La Coste with a battalion of free men of color and detachments of dragoons and artillery to guard them. General Coffee with half of his mounted riflemen was at Baton Rouge. The other half, unfortunately, had been left in the Mobile area. Jackson ordered him to march posthaste to New Orleans.

General William Carroll with more Tennesseans had set out weeks before and was somewhere on the Mississippi on the way to New Orleans. So, too, was General John Thomas and the Kentucky militia. Jackson had heard nothing from them and had no idea where they were. Nevertheless he dispatched couriers to intercept them if possible and urge them forward with all speed. The time devoted to the attack on Pensacola now began to make itself felt. The enemy, formidable in numbers and equipment, was within striking distance of New Orleans. But as yet Jackson's army was scarcely in being. So firm had he been in the belief that invasion would come by way of Mobile that, at the crucial moment, he was painfully unprepared to meet it.

CHAPTER TWENTY-SEVEN

Old Hickory Avenges His Scar

ON DECEMBER 18 the General held a grand review of the battalion of uniformed companies, the pride of New Orleans, under the command of Major Jean Plauché, and D'Aquin's free men of color led by white officers. The free men of color had fought in Haiti and then fled the island and found refuge in Louisiana. Their organization was Jackson's own idea and it had not been without opposition from persons disturbed over the arming of former slaves.

It was Sunday and the historic Place d'Armes was thronged with people who had turned out to view the spectacle and hear an address from Livingston. The war spirit was now running high in the city. Military bands stirred the emotions of the populace and appealed both to the Americans and the French by playing "Yankee Doodle," "The Marseillaise" and the "Chant du Depart," while the belles of the town displayed their charms on balconies and at windows and waved encouragement to the military with their lace handkerchiefs. A general holiday was declared and people of all classes, regardless of race and color, joined forces in strengthening the fortifications.

The review over, Jackson ordered Major Plauché and his men to the Bayou St. John to watch the northern approach to the city. At the fort itself he stationed a detachment of regulars. At Fort St. Charles, across the Mississippi, he posted the 44th U.S. Infantry and a detachment of regular artillery, 800 men in all. The 7th U.S. Infantry he kept with him in the city. On December 20 Coffee's vanguard, 800 in number, responding to the urgent summons of his chief, arrived from Baton Rouge and encamped several miles to the north of the town. But best of all was the arrival of Major General William Carroll with his 2,000 Tennessee militiamen who at last had completed their long and arduous trip down the Mississippi. What is more, they were equipped, well disciplined and ready for action.

A problem of immediate importance was the disposition of Laffite and his fellow Baratarians. They were experienced fighters, of which Jackson could not have too many, and they had volunteered their services. But the General proved a stumbling block. Having publicly declared them to be "hellish banditti" and condemned the British for trafficking with them, how was he now to do an about-face and accept them into his army? Livingston pleaded with him; so did Governor Claiborne and the local judge. The General brushed their arguments aside. Then, as a last resort, Jean Laffite presented himself in person before Jackson. The conference was held behind closed doors and what went on was never disclosed. But Laffite must have exerted his utmost charms for, when he departed, he carried with him Jackson's permission to muster himself and his men into the service. Most of the Baratarians were sent to the Bayou St. John.

On the barren waste of Pea Island Admiral Cochrane and General Keane received visits from numerous influential Spaniards from New Orleans. The Spaniards were more than willing to give aid and comfort to the enemy. They pictured Jackson as a tyrant, the city poorly defended and the people ripe for revolution. Of even greater importance was their disclosure of the existence, at the northwest end of Lake Borgne, of a bayou which extended almost to the Mississippi, nine miles south of the city, and which was navigable for small boats a good part of the way. This was the Bayou Bienvenu. Cochrane and Keane were sufficiently impressed to send two officers to investigate. The latter were well received at a Spanish fishing village at the mouth of the bayou, and, disguised as fishermen, were conducted all the way to the river.

What is more, they made the astonishing discovery that this vital approach to New Orleans was totally unobstructed and undefended, in spite of Jackson's orders. To the Bayou Bienvenu, therefore, the British leaders decided to direct their expedition.

December 22 broke cold and rainy over Lake Borgne. Undaunted by the weather the vanguard of the British host, 1,800 men, put out in open boats on the first lap of their great endeavor. From

Pea Island to Bayou Bienvenu was a matter of some 30 miles. In command was Lieutenant Colonel William Thornton, the same officer who had played so distinguished a part in the battle of Bladensburg. Through the day the sailors stood to the oars while the soldiers crouched in the boats without protection, the rain beating down upon them and soaking them to the skin. As evening came on the temperature fell below freezing and the wet uniforms of the men stiffened on them. Throughout the night the expedition continued across the lake and in the early morning arrived at the fishermen's village and landed safely. At this spot the British were within 15 miles of New Orleans and up to this time, in spite of all of Jackson's studied precautions, not a person in the city knew of their presence.

However, since the reconnaissance of a few days before, a handful of pickets had been placed at the entrance to the bayou. They were part of the command of Colonel Pierre De La Ronde, next-door neighbor of Major General Jacques Villeré, of the Louisiana militia, whose sugar plantation lay between the Bayou Bienvenu and the river. Most of the pickets were immediately overpowered and captured.

This accident was not without benefit to the American cause. For among the pickets was one Joseph Rodolphe Ducros, a young man of nimble wit and a gift for lying convincingly. Upon being questioned he informed the British that the American force holding New Orleans was composed of excellent troops, thoroughly equipped and trained and, at a conservative estimate, numbering from 10,000 to 15,000 men. Cochrane and Keane, though not convinced, were impressed. The report was sufficient to make them cautious, and that caution was to prove costly.

The expedition now proceeded up the bayou, guarding against surprise, and eventually emerged from the swampland onto the solid ground of the Villeré plantation. The British surrounded the dwelling and, to their delight, discovered that they had bagged Major Gabriel Villeré, the general's son. But while they were congratulating themselves on their good fortune they momentarily relaxed their vigilance. In an instant Major Villeré had leaped a fence and was fleeing to the house of Colonel De La Ronde. Together the two men crossed the Mississippi, obtained horses and galloped all the way to New Orleans to give the alarm. Splashed with mud they

355

burst into Jackson's headquarters and told their story. It verified the news that had been brought to him a few minutes before by one of the pickets who had escaped from the fishermen's village.

Jackson rose from his couch to receive them and listened intently to what they had to say. It was the news for which he had been waiting, for now he had an idea of the direction from which the attack would be launched. The day was already well spent for it was two hours after noon. Jackson's army was spread over a wide area. Considerable time might reasonably be expected to elapse before he could bring it together. Even after that several hours would be needed for the march to the Villeré plantation; an attack could hardly be staged before nightfall. A cautious general would, no doubt, have considered the factors, compared them with the advantage of setting out early next morning when there would have been more time to prepare and make sure that all was in order. Besides, how did he know that this was not a feint? What if the real assault were to be launched from the most obvious direction, the plain of Gentilly and the Chef Menteur Road, or even from a branch of the Bayou Bienvenu that stretched northward toward the city?

But Andrew Jackson was not a cautious general. As soon as he knew where the enemy was, instinct told him to come to grips. He stood for an instant in thought. Then, turning calmly to the officers present, he said, "Gentlemen, the British are below; we must fight them tonight!"

The General fell heir to another piece of good fortune. It so happened that on this very morning Major A. Lacarrière Latour, his chief of engineers, was on reconnaissance in the neighborhood of the Bayou Bienvenu. Latour was an experienced soldier and knew the importance of accurate information. When he heard of the arrival of the British he approached within rifle shot of them, made an estimate and judged that the force amounted to from 1,600 to 1,800 men. He hit the number almost exactly. That was at 1:30 P.M. and within half an hour the information was in Jackson's hands. Thus the General knew the size of the opposition and what force he would need to defeat it.

A cannon was fired to give the alarm, marching orders were issued and by 4 P.M. Jackson, with a force of over 2,000 men, was advancing down the river road on the way to the Villeré plantation.

This force was composed of the advance guard of Coffee's mounted riflemen, Hind's Mississippi dragoons who galloped on ahead of the column, Beale's New Orleans riflemen, Plauché's uniformed battalion, D'Aquin's free men of color, the regulars of the 7th and 44th U.S. Infantries and two 6-inch guns manned by regular artillerists and guarded by a detachment of marines. Carroll's Tennesseans were left behind to guard against a surprise attack closer to the city.

On the river at New Orleans were two armed schooners, the *Carolina* and the *Louisiana,* both under the command of Master Commandant Patterson. The *Carolina* was fully manned and ready for action; the *Louisiana* was still without a full crew. Jackson gave orders to Patterson to dispatch the *Carolina* down the river to cooperate with the land troops.

At the Villeré plantation the British troops had encamped during the afternoon on the riverbank near the levee, taking their last rest before advancing on the city. Thornton counseled immediate action but he was overruled by Keane. Reinforcements were expected during the night and, after Ducros' story, Keane was taking no chances. It never entered the heads of the British that they might themselves be attacked. Since, as one of their officers argued, the Americans had never dared to attack before, there seemed no great probability of their doing so on the present occasion. This man had fought at Bladensburg and Baltimore. He had yet to make the acquaintance of Andrew Jackson. Dark had descended when, around 7 P.M., the *Carolina* quietly anchored off the Villeré plantation. She was so near the British camp that some of the soldiers on the levee hailed her. They eyed her with curiosity but not with fear, never dreaming what her true purpose was. At the same time the American column was moving forward silently on the road that paralleled the river. Arrived within a few miles of the British camp Jackson himself continued to follow the river road. With him were the two guns, the 7th and the 44th, Plauché's and D'Aquin's men. Here Coffee's brigade turned off to the cane fields on the left. With it went Beale's riflemen and Hind's dragoons. The purpose of Coffee's force was to make an encircling movement, cut the British line of communications with the Bayou Bienvenu, and take the enemy in the flank while Jackson attacked them in the front. Coffee was fortunate in having as guides Colonel De La Ronde and Major Villeré who knew every foot of the

357

country. His men moved close to the cypress swamp, which was separated from the river by the flat lands of the sugar plantations.

According to Jackson's orders the action was to be opened by the *Carolina*. The crew were now at their guns which they had trained on the British camp. Promptly at 7:30 P.M., the appointed hour, the *Carolina* let go her first broadside. In a flash the quiet scene was transformed into one of confusion and death as the shells ripped into the groups of men sitting around the fires and left scores of them torn and bleeding on the ground.

Nothing could testify better to the quality and discipline of those British veterans of Wellington's army than their behavior on this occasion. In spite of the entirely unexpected attack they recovered at once from their first surprise, put out their fires and within a few minutes were replying with rockets and musketry. As yet they had no cannon with them. But rockets and small arms did no damage to the *Carolina* which continued to pour in a devastating fire. The critical position of the British was alleviated by the fact that an old levee which paralleled the new one gave them a place where the fire from the schooner could not reach them. This space served as a rallying point as the battle proceeded.

No sooner had the British recovered from the first shock than shots on their northern picket line announced a threat from another quarter. With presence of mind born of long experience in battle Colonel Thornton, though working in the semidarkness, gathered together detachments from two regiments and rushed to the support of the pickets. In fact his counterattack was so successful that he almost overran the American guns. General Jackson saw the danger and dashed forward on his horse to encourage the artillerists with his presence and urge them to save the guns at all cost. Thus inspired by the commander the men stood their ground, drove the British off and the guns were saved. The 44th Infantry joined with the 7th and Plauché's and D'Aquin's commands to drive Thornton back to his original position.

While these events were taking place on the American right and center, General Coffee arrived on the De La Ronde plantation, which adjoined Villeré's on the north, and there dismounted his riflemen. A part of his force made their way on foot almost to the center of the British camp. Here again Thornton came to the rescue and directed a counterattack against Coffee. In the dark friend and foe were virtually indistinguishable; little groups formed and met in hand-to-hand combat. A detachment of Beale's riflemen lost their way and were captured by the British. To add to the difficulty of night fighting a fog came up and further obscured the field. Concluding that nothing further could be accomplished under such trying conditions Jackson called off his men. The hour was 9:30 o'clock and by now the expected British reinforcements were arriving from the Bayou Bienvenu. Jackson no longer knew with how large a force he had to contend.

The battle of the evening of December 23 was inconclusive, yet the result was highly favorable to the American cause. Jackson, through his intuitive genius, had accomplished the rare feat of turning a surprise into a countersurprise. Within a few hours the British had expected to be in New Orleans. Instead they had been roughly handled, losing 277 men in killed, wounded and missing. The American losses were a trifle less, totaling 217. Jackson left the enemy not a little bewildered and disheartened. The men also were critical of General Keane whom they held responsible for the predicament in which they found themselves.

While the regulars and the dragoons remained on the field facing the enemy, Jackson fell back with the rest of his force about three miles to the Rodriguez Canal. This was a dry ditch some four feet deep and 20 feet wide, entering the river at a right angle and extending eastward to the cypress swamp. The line had been selected by the engineers because it was the narrowest piece of dry land between the river and the swamp. It gave Jackson a line of about three-fifths of a mile to defend. Here the men were set to work at once digging a trench 30 feet back from the canal and raising a parapet about three feet in height. Thus the little army spent the whole of Christmas Eve. (See Map XI)

The day in the British camp was cheerless enough, for the weather was cold and blustery with occasional rain. However, the spirits of the expedition were considerably raised by the arrival of a new commander. Rumor spread in the American camp that it was the great Wellington himself. Actually he was the Iron Duke's brother-in-law, General Pakenham. Sir Edward was the beau ideal of a soldier whose rise to high rank was due not alone to family influence

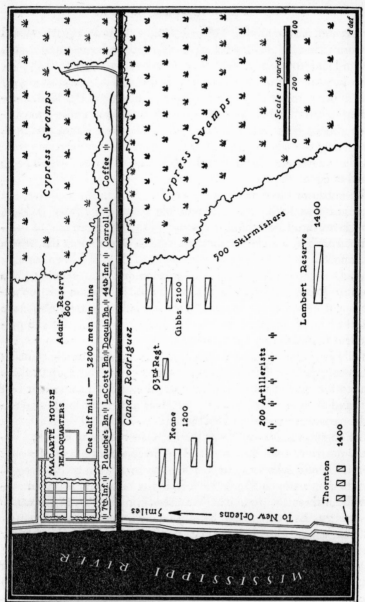

Map XI. New Orleans, January 8

Cypress Swamps

Cypress Swamps

Scale in yards
0   200   400

500 Skirmishers

Lambert Reserve   1400

Adair's Reserve
800

One half mile — 3200 men in line

Coffee
Carroll
44th Inf.
Daquin Bn.
LaCoste Bn.
Plauche's Bn.
7th Inf.

MACARTÉ HOUSE
HEADQUARTERS

Canal Rodriguez

93rd Regt.

Gibbs 2100

Keane 1200

200 Artillerists

To New Orleans   5 miles

Thornton   1400

MISSISSIPPI RIVER

d def

but also to native ability. He had fought through the Peninsular War and, because of his exploits in that adventure, won the sobriquet of "Hero of Salamanca." He was 37 years of age, 10 years junior to Jackson. If reports are to be credited, on this present expedition he was subjected to the salty jibes of Admiral Cochrane who compared unfavorably the fighting qualities of the soldiery to those of his sailors. This may have warped Pakenham's judgment in the critical days ahead and induced him to take heavy risks.

After the punishment the British had taken from the *Carolina* on the evening of the 23rd Pakenham wisely decided not to attempt an advance until that annoying vessel had been got out of the way. That meant waiting for guns which had to be brought the 30 miles from Pea Island and then dragged laboriously through the mire on the last few miles that lay between the bayou and the Villeré plantation.

Jackson employed the interim to examine and strengthen his defenses. He posted two 6-pounders near the levee on the right flank to cover the river road. Across the Mississippi he ordered Brigadier General David Morgan, of the Louisiana militia, to withdraw from the English Turn and take station on a line with the Rodriguez Canal. Major Latour cut the levee in several places in the hope of inundating the strip of flat open land that lay between the two forces on the east side of the river, but the Mississippi was too low and the scheme failed. Buildings were blown up so that the artillery might have a clean sweep of the field.

The General made his headquarters in the château of a M. Macarté and from a window on its third floor, with the aid of a telescope, he could follow the activities in the British camp. As the guns arrived the enemy set to work erecting a heavy battery near the river to oppose the *Carolina*. Detachments of Louisiana militia arrived on the field, increasing the American forces to 4,000, and pieces of artillery were distributed along the line. With the arrival of another division Pakenham's army numbered about 5,000.

On the morning of the 27th the British battery was completed and its guns were leveled at the *Carolina*. The broadside of the schooner was no match for the battery. Hot shot was hurled into her and in a few minutes she caught fire and had to be abandoned by her crew. They got off just before the fire reached the magazine and the ship blew up. The *Louisiana* had by this time been manned and prepared for action and had joined the *Carolina*. Having disposed of the latter the British next turned their guns on the *Louisiana*. But, before any damage had been done, her crew manned the boats and, battling the current, towed her out of harm's way. The *Louisiana* now took station in the river just to the right of Jackson's line and was placed so that she could throw an oblique fire from the river across the plain.

Pakenham now prepared for his next move. On the evening of the 27th he advanced his whole force forward to within a few hundred yards of the American line to be ready for an assault on the morrow. His plan of battle was to divide his army into two columns and send them forward simultaneously. The column on the left, under General Keane, was to stick close to the levee and the river road and attack the American right; the other, under Major General Sir Samuel Gibbs, was to attack the American left over by the cypress swamp. Arrived at their jumping-off-place the British settled down for the night. But Jackson gave them little peace, sending out raiders who kept them so constantly on the alert that they had little chance to sleep. This, apparently, was contrary to European custom where opposing armies by mutual consent allowed each other a good night's rest. The British regarded this breach of good manners on the part of the Americans as little short of barbaric.

As the morning of the 28th dawned a fog enveloped the plain. It rose like a curtain at a play, disclosing the two solid columns of scarlet and, between them, General Pakenham and his staff. At this critical moment Jackson observed a rabble advancing at the double from the direction of the river road. He soon recognized them as Laffite's Baratarians who had trotted almost all the way from the Bayou St. John to be in on the fight. Jackson rewarded their zeal by giving them a 24-pounder to serve which had just been placed in the line. Sailors from the *Carolina* also arrived on the scene and these experienced gunners were assigned to a howitzer.

General Gibbs ordered a gallant young colonel, Rennie by name, to move with a detachment through the edge of the cypress swamp and endeavor to flank the American left. As Rennie obeyed the fight was on. Simultaneously Keane's column advanced and made good headway toward the American line in spite of fire from the guns and small arms that greeted them. The British anticipated this first stand. They had seen it at Bladensburg and in the skirmish on the North Point Road outside of Baltimore. But they assumed that the resistance of raw American troops could not be expected long to endure against the steady pressure of Wellington's veterans.

Here, however, there was a difference. The British again used rockets to strike terror into the Americans. But rockets were nothing like so fearful when they were observed from behind a parapet. Further, the American gunners knew their business. This was by no means a baptism of fire for the Baratarians or the sailors of the *Carolina* or others who manned the pieces in the line. Nevertheless Keane's men were making good headway. They were approaching the canal and the Americans lay only 30 yards behind it.

From the deck of the *Louisiana* Master Commandant Patterson bided his time. Then came the chance for which he had been waiting. As the scarlet column nearest the river came within range of his guns he opened on them. So quickly did the schooner's crew work that, in the course of a few minutes, they sent over more than 800 shots. And those shots were well aimed, ripping holes in the closed ranks that presented so admirable a target. A single shot was said to have killed or wounded more than a dozen men.

Caught between a frontal fire from the trenches and the oblique fire from the *Louisiana* Keane's column broke. It was more than human flesh and blood could stand. Veterans though they were they had experienced nothing like this in the battles of Spain. It soon became apparent even to General Keane that he could expect no more of his men. He ordered them to take cover, but there was little cover to be had except the canals which cut across the plain. To these the troops retired, standing in mud and water up to their waists.

On the American left the British met with greater success, where they faced Carroll's Tennesseans. Colonel Rennie made a spirited attack with his advance guard; Carroll countered by sending out a force to get around Rennie's flank and rear but it was discovered and hurled back. Rennie was now free to proceed with his flanking movement, and with every prospect of success. General Gibbs, however, had witnessed the disaster which overtook Keane and at the very moment of Rennie's triumph saw fit to recall him. Rennie obeyed, though indignant at being denied the opportunity of a victory. Given a few more minutes he was confident he could have achieved his objective. Parkenham now ordered a general retirement. In the morning's fight he lost 150 men killed and wounded; the Americans got off with nine killed and eight wounded. The British were bitter over the outcome, for Wellington's men were not accustomed to being bested. There was a feeling in the ranks that Pakenham had let them down.

Jackson was not a man to rest on his laurels. He had seen the danger to his left flank and set to work to strengthen it. The line was carried well into the swamp itself. Logs were chained together to form rafts and on these for the next few days the hardy Tennesseans ate, slept and fought. Further to strengthen the position a battery of two 12-pounders was erected near the swamp and placed in charge of General Garrigue Flauzac, a veteran artillery officer who had served under Napoleon. Also near this flank he mounted a 6-pounder and an 18-pounder, bringing the number of batteries in his line to eight.

Similar precautions were taken across the river on the extreme right of the American defenses. The *Louisiana*, after her decisive action of the 28th, saw no further service. Her heavy guns were removed and used to establish a battery to deliver an oblique fire across the plain as she had done. The Americans now had in their line 15 guns in all which could be considered effective.

Throughout the last four nights of the dying year the Tennesseans amused themselves at the expense of the British by what they described as "going hunting." They slipped out of the line in the darkness and stalked their human game with rifle, knife and tomahawk. Soon the British did not dare place a sentinel alone within several hundred yards of the Tennesseans' front. In fact, to protect themselves, they constructed a redoubt and mounted it with heavy guns which they put to work shelling the American left.

History speaks of the battle of New Orleans. Actually there were four separate and distinct battles covering a period of two weeks. We have seen how Jackson on the 23rd scotched the immediate march on New Orleans and how, on the 28th, the guns of the *Louisiana* turned the tide and sent the British back whence they had come. Pakenham salved his conscience by calling that not "a battle" but a "reconnaissance in force." But by now he had learned enough to know that, with the armament he had at his disposal, he could not take the American line. Another possibility occurred to him. If he used heavy cannon to blast holes in the American line he and his men could walk right through. That line, after all, was no more than mud raised to a height of three feet, capable of warding off small-arms fire but not a concentrated bombardment. There was a purpose in the four-day respite. Heavy siege guns were on the way from Pea Island.

Jackson planned to celebrate the New Year with a grand review and visitors came from the city to attend it. As day dawned a fog again covered the plain, but it promised to burn off before the time set for the festivities. However, there was no parade that day. The British had seen to it. During the night of the 31st Pakenham moved his whole army forward to be in readiness for an assault, and the Americans heard the sounds of work coming from the British lines. When the fog cleared there, within 600 yards of the American ramparts, stood three half-moon batteries armed with heavy siege guns. These batteries were at the right, left and center of the American position ready to blast it into bits.

The British attack opened with an artillery barrage supplemented by rockets. For ten minutes the British guns concentrated their fire on Jackson's headquarters and, in that brief interval, more than 100 shots landed on or near the Macarté château. The General and his staff wasted little time in getting out of the house while the troops which were being assembled for the review rushed back to the comparative safety of the fortifications. After the first surprise the American guns replied in kind, and with an accuracy that astonished the British. Master Commandant Patterson from across the river engaged in a duel with the British batteries on the levee while the Baratarians, the sailors from the *Carolina*, General Flauzac and the other artillerymen gave as good as they received, and even better. Rank played little part in Jackson's choice of battery commanders, who ranged from a general to a corporal. What counted with him was that they knew how to handle their pieces. Pakenham tried an attack on the American left, but it had been greatly strengthened since his attack on the 28th by the extension of the line into the swamp and the addition of the batteries. Coffee's men withstood the onslaught and began a counterattack which drove the British back.

The artillery duel continued and, under the grueling American fire, the British batteries were severely punished. The British used hogsheads of sugar to protect their guns, assuming that sugar would prove as effective as sand. But they were mistaken. The American fire smashed them to pieces, many of the guns were dismounted and others so badly thrown out of alignment that the gunners could scarcely fire them. The American guns also did not escape damage. Cotton bales had been used to shield them and these proved to be no more effective than the sugar hogsheads similarly employed by the British. Several of the American guns were dismounted and a caisson was blown up.

From 8 A.M. until after noon this battle of the opposing artillery went on. Then, at 1:30 P.M., the British fire ceased. It was a shocking thing for them to admit that British artillery had been outshot by the Americans. More remarkable still, according to a careful estimate, the Americans had only 15 guns to 24 of the British and the American guns threw a smaller weight of metal. British military critics shook their heads and reflected that this was one of the worst setbacks their artillery had ever encountered. There was nothing for Pakenham to do but call off the attack. His men found what shelter they could during the afternoon and, when night came on, retreated to their camp behind the lines. Some of their heavy guns were hauled to safety, but several could not be moved and fell into the hands of the Americans.

Three times so far the British had tried and three times they had failed. While their spirits ebbed the Americans grew in enthusiasm and confidence. Welcome also was the announcement of the belated arrival of Major General John Thomas with 2,000 Kentuckians. But the news was not as good as it sounded for the Kentuckians had assumed that arms and equipment would be waiting for them at New Orleans, and there were none. The legislature appropriated money and the people of the city raised a fund for blankets, clothing and bedding. A few hundred small arms, which New Orleans had stored against a possible uprising of the slaves, were commandeered. Nevertheless only a fraction of the Kentucky force found arms and most of it was used as a reserve to bolster the weak spot on the American left where Carroll's Tennesseans joined those of Coffee.

Pakenham, however, had one more trump card to play. His prospects were improved by the arrival of a fresh division under Major General John Lambert. Including Cochrane's sailors and various staff detachments and specialists the British army now numbered close to 10,000 men. Having found the American left flank secure Pakenham's thoughts turned to the right flank across the river. His plan of operations was simple. Sending a force across the Mississippi he would seize Patterson's battery and turn the guns on the American line. Simultaneously his main body would attack the Americans on the Rodriguez Canal from the front.

This plan, it so happened, took advantage of an inexcusable weakness in the American defenses. A commander, perhaps, cannot be expected to look out for every eventuality, but Jackson's indifference to his flank across the river is hard to excuse. He gave the responsibility to General Morgan, who was not an exceptional leader and had at his disposition only some 500 Louisiana militia, by no means the best troops.

To lead the force that was to operate across the river Pakenham selected Colonel Thornton, assigning him 1,200 men for the task. Boats for the crossing were to be brought up from the Bayou Bienvenu and, to facilitate this, the army was set to work digging a canal which would connect the upper arm of the bayou with the river. This was an ambitious undertaking which would require several days. On the east side of the river two columns were to attack the American front, led by General Gibbs and General Keane respectively on the right and left. Since the main effort was to be on the right, Gibbs's force was to consist of 2,100 men while that of Keane was to be 1,200 strong. Added to this force were 200 artillerists and 500 skirmishers. Held in reserve in the rear and ready to move either to right or left as circumstances required was General Lambert with 1,400 men. In view of the strength Jackson's line had already shown it was evident to Pakenham that a frontal attack in broad daylight offered little prospect for success. Consequently the plan called for it to begin before dawn. (See Map XI, p. 360)

An evil genius seemed to pursue the British from the beginning. The canal was completed by January 7 and the assault was ordered for the early morning of the 8th. But when Thornton was ready to move he found that the boats provided were sufficient only for 700 men. To make matters worse the walls of the newly built channel caved in and the boats stuck in the mud. It was only with the greatest effort and the loss of valuable time that they were released and dragged to the river. Then Thornton did not make sufficient allowance for the swift current of the Mississippi so that he landed on the west shore several miles below the point intended.

Jackson knew the attack was coming. From his lookout on the third floor of the Macarté mansion, searching the horizon with his telescope, he had observed the activity in the enemy camp. After darkness on the evening of the 7th he heard the noise of construction gangs as before the previous attacks. An aide came from Patterson on the west side of the river warning Jackson of the weakness of the situation there and begging for reinforcements. But the General was still confident the main attack would be delivered against his front and was reluctant to weaken his force. His only contribution to Morgan was 400 Kentuckians, some of whom were unarmed and who could be sent across the river only by marching all the way back to New Orleans. Less than 200 eventually reached Morgan.

Jackson was asleep when the messenger from Patterson arrived. Now wide awake he announced to his staff that they had rested long enough and, putting on his greatcoat, he went out into the dark to make a final inspection of his lines. Never before had so strange an assortment of men fought under the Stars and Stripes. The Macarté château stood not far from the levee. Beginning at the right of the line, Jackson came first upon the 7th Infantry, regulars all, and with them Beale's New Orleans riflemen. A bastion had been extended in front of the line at this point and it was occupied by the riflemen.

Next in line were Plauché's companies of the smartly uniformed battalion which had taken part in the operations of December 23. Then came La Coste's colored corps, D'Aquin's free men of color, and after them the 44th Infantry, regulars but like the 7th composed mostly of raw recruits. At the far end of the line, in strange contrast to the rest, were Carroll's and Coffee's Tennesseans and a few Kentuckians, the main body of the latter being kept in reserve

368

where Carroll's and Coffee's commands met. Here were rugged frontiersmen in hunting shirts, fur caps and pantaloons, their faces unshaven, their hair unbrushed, uncut and matted, each holding tight to his precious rifle. Their belts were stuffed with tomahawks and wicked-looking hunting knives. Because of illness General Thomas, of Kentucky, had to yield his place to General John Adair. At equal intervals along the line were eight batteries capable of adding greatly to Jackson's fire power, covering every portion of the plain and ready to repeat the performance of January 1. The total force in the line was about 3,200 men, which was as many as could be squeezed into it.

Jackson took nothing for granted. He ordered his engineers to prepare two other lines in his rear to which he might fall back in case of disaster. One was a mile and a half behind the Rodriguez Canal, the other on the outskirts of the city. The people of New Orleans were disturbed, taking this as evidence that Jackson expected to be whipped. They would have been more nearly correct had they guessed that Jackson's plan was to fight where he was and, if beaten there, to fall back on the second line; and, if need be, on the third. He even contemplated fighting inside the city itself. His was not the attitude of a man who expected to be whipped, at least so long as there was anything with which to fight.

Pakenham, on his side of the field, was equally active. Throughout the evening men had been at work preparing emplacements for the artillery and at midnight the General ordered the divisions of Keane and Gibbs to advance and take station within a quarter of a mile of the American line. He also ordered the construction of fascines and scaling ladders to be used by the vanguard in crossing the canal and climbing the breastworks. Pakenham and his staff took station in the center.

The attack was to begin as soon as the fire of Thornton's expedition across the river was heard. All was now in readiness and Pakenham waited anxiously for the signal. But precious moments passed by and no signal came from Thornton. Delayed by the shortage of boats, the late start and the river's current, he was still far from his objective. Dawn was beginning to break and there was the usual fog. Very soon it would lift and reveal the British position. The flaw in Pakenham's strategy was that, for its success, it depended upon simultaneous action by two widely separated forces. It was a flaw that, many times in the history of warfare, has led to disaster.

Soon the critical moment arrived. As the sun rose the fog floated away and there on the plain, in full sight of the Americans, stood the two compact columns. It was too good a target to ignore. In all his campaigns with Napoleon Garrigue Flauzac had not seen a better one. The guns of Battery 7 boomed, and grape and round shot zoomed through the air and ripped a hole in the British ranks which quickly closed, according to the rules, leaving another perfect target.

What was Pakenham to do? He could not let his men stand there and be mowed down while he waited for Thornton. And he could not retire. That was not in the books of Wellington's veterans. What would his brother-in-law say were he to hear that British regulars had incontinently retired in the face of a few thousand American backwoodsmen? That was not in the tradition of the British Army. For a man of Pakenham's training and background there was no choice.

The prearranged signal for the attack was the firing of two rockets, one at each end of the line. The Americans saw them and knew what they meant. Slowly the scarlet ranks moved forward. Again the evil genius that was dogging Pakenham appeared. The advance regiment, whose job it was to carry the fascines and scaling ladders, had forgotten them. But there was no stopping now. Men were sent back for the fascines and ladders while the rest moved ahead. The Americans took advantage of the brief delay to pour in more shot and shell from their batteries, tearing more holes. The infantrymen behind the ramparts withheld their fire. They remembered Jackson's order to wait until the British were within effective range, then to take aim just above the breastplate.

Gibbs's column obliqued toward the cypress swamp to avoid the fire of the batteries in their immediate front. Keane's men, led in person by the brave young Colonel Rennie, were making good progress by the levee and had reached the bastion that stood out in front of the American line. A fast charge and they were in possession of it, driving Beale's riflemen out. But the riflemen and the regulars of the 7th Infantry counterattacked and regained the bastion. In the hand-to-hand fighting Rennie was killed and Keane's attack slackened.

On the British right Gibbs was in even worse plight. His attack was aimed to sever the American line between Carroll and Coffee. Only a few hundred yards now separated the two forces and word came to Pakenham that the fascines and ladders were on the way. The General rode forward to urge on his men for the last assault that would take them across the canal and over the breastworks. An American sharpshooter fired. His aim was a trifle low; the bullet caught Sir Edward in the left hand. Another rifleman shot Pakenham's horse from under him. The General borrowed a Creole pony from an aide and remained on the field.

The British now were within effective small-arms range. It was the moment for which the Tennesseans had waited. It is said that the riflemen were organized in groups of three, one man firing while another stood ready and a third was loading. However that may be, the British who survived reported that they had never before faced such rapid fire or one so deadly.

This was actually true. For as primitive as the Tennesseans might appear, and as remote as was their home from the centers of inventive genius, they possessed the most destructive small-arms weapon the world then knew. This was the Kentucky rifle and its history is interesting. In the eighteenth century the infantryman was customarily armed with the musket, a smooth-bore weapon of questionable accuracy. Fire power was obtained by using it in the mass and at close range. In Germany, however, greater accuracy was achieved by rifling the barrel and this improved arm was carried by the Jäger, or sharpshooter.

The rifle was brought to this country by the Germans who settled in Pennsylvania, and Lancaster became the center of its manufacture. From there it followed the march of migration into Kentucky and Tennessee. Frontiersmen depended upon it for their food and improved it by lengthening the barrel and adding other refinements. Authorities on small arms state that at a range of 150 yards it was as accurate as the modern rifle. Marksmen who were accustomed to picking off a squirrel in the top of a tree found nothing difficult in drawing a bead a few inches above a shining breastplate. On that winter morning below New Orleans the British regulars were walking into the most devastating fire then imaginable, and the slaughter was frightful.

With their customary gallantry the British officers set a good example to their men by taking the forward and most exposed positions. Many of them were killed. The men could no longer keep their line and broke up into little groups. Some of them fell back in confusion behind a portion of the swamp that bulged into the field and afforded cover. There the officers who survived restored some order and prepared for a fresh assault. With the fascines and ladders in front, at the word of command, they rushed forward in a last desperate attempt to break the American line. Only a handful got across the canal and scaled the slippery breastworks. One officer made it and fell dead in the American line.

General Keane, at the other side of the field, witnessed the confusion in Gibbs's column and, without waiting for orders, detached the 93rd Regiment, 900 Scottish Highlanders in kilts and tartans, fresh from a tour of duty at the Cape of Good Hope. They set out to reinforce Gibbs. Halfway across the plain they were caught in an oblique fire from Patterson's guns across the river as well as that of the batteries in front of them. Of the 900 men only 130 survived the devastating fire; of the 25 officers who led them only nine escaped untouched.

In rallying his men Gibbs had been killed. Keane soon was severely wounded and had to leave the field. Shortly after he had been first hit Pakenham received a second wound which put him out of action. He was being led from the field when a shell burst near him, driving a fragment into his thigh which severed an artery. Before he could be moved to the rear he was dead from loss of blood. Thus in a few minutes the British lost all three of their major generals who had taken part in the engagement.

Pakenham's last words before he died were to order Lambert to throw in the reserves who, up to this point, had not been engaged. But, displaying a discretion in marked contrast to the foolhardy boldness of his colleagues, Lambert refrained from obeying the command. He realized that the situation was now beyond retrieving.

Across the river Thornton had a different story to tell. Once he

got under way he drove Morgan's forces before him and, as Pakenham had planned, overran and captured Patterson's battery, though
the American commander had time to spike the guns. No opposition
worth mentioning now lay between Thornton and New Orleans. His
accomplishment, however, was without profit. For, in view of the
disaster which had overtaken the main body, Lambert ordered
Thornton to break off the action and retire by the way he had come.
Though Jackson later rebuked Morgan's command for its flight
and lack of discipline, the latter had exacted a toll from Thornton's
men as they retreated. General Adair came to the defense of his
Kentuckians and the charge was made that Jackson's complaint actually was designed by him to cover up his lack of judgment in
leaving his right so weak.

Throughout the battle the Americans had been cheered by a military band. Now that the fight was over the musicians struck up
"Hail Columbia" while the victorious general and his staff passed
along the whole length of the line, receiving the cheers and applause
of the troops. Not until the smoke had cleared away was the carnage
on the field revealed and the overwhelming nature of the American
victory realized. The plain was covered with the British dead and
wounded, and from among those lying on the field the living now
rose up and ran forward to surrender. The courage and tenacity of
the British had cost them no less than 2,600 men of whom 700
were killed, 1,400 wounded and 500 captured. And this stunning
defeat the Americans accomplished with the loss of only eight men
killed and 13 wounded! Of the several thousand men in the American line only a fraction had been engaged. The British paid a fearful price to maintain their reputation for bulldog determination.
The body of Sir Edward Pakenham took its sad departure for home
preserved in a cask of spirits.

New Orleans without a doubt was the decisive battle of the war.
Or at least it would have been save for one important circumstance.
For, true to the last to the war's anomalous nature, the battle was
fought and won just two weeks after the treaty of peace had been
signed at Ghent!

CHAPTER TWENTY-EIGHT

Ghent, City of Peace

IN MAY, 1813, three travelers set sail from the United States for Europe. One was a man of outstanding appearance: tall, handsome and reserved. One was short, bald-headed and large of feature; not particularly impressive at first glance. A casual observer might have remarked that he possessed a pleasant and intelligent face with more than a suggestion of kindliness and good humor. The last of the trio was a pink-cheeked youth with a somewhat cherubic countenance, still in his teens. Before very long he was to pose as Eros for an allegorical picture by the celebrated French artist, David.

A closer scrutiny of the party might have disclosed that the less distinguished of the two older men was actually the leader, for the other showed him a noticeable deference. Such was, in truth, the case. The handsome man was Senator James A. Bayard, of Delaware. The less distinguished in appearance was Albert Gallatin. The war had not yet passed its first birthday but, nevertheless, the two gentlemen were going abroad to discuss a possible peace, having but a few weeks before been appointed commissioners by President Madison. Gallatin was taking his son along with him to show him something of the Old World. Besides, it would be an education for the boy to be present while such important negotiations were in progress. James had decided to make the most of the opportunity by setting down his impressions in a diary. It was a fortunate decision for posterity, since the diary was actually written and provides a record of interesting details such as no official state papers could ever have included.

Gallatin's spirits must have been more buoyant than usual for even though the mission with which he was entrusted was uncertain, he had left worse troubles behind him. At last he was free of puzzling how to raise money for the war, and faced the more congenial task of finding means to stop the war. His genius for finance and the jealousy of the less distinguished members of his political party had consigned him to the Treasury when his real ambition was to be Secretary of State. Now, at last, his longing for diplomacy was to be gratified. He did not know that, in a last gesture of pettiness, his enemies in the Senate had refused to ratify his appointment.

The third member of the mission was John Quincy Adams, United States Minister to Russia, and it was for St. Petersburg that Gallatin and Bayard were headed. St. Petersburg was a remote spot for the settlement of differences between Great Britain and the United States. The explanation was that the United States commissioners were assembling there in answer to an invitation from the Czar.

Coincident with the declaration of war by the United States Napoleon was launching his memorable campaign against Russia. As the imperial legions swept northward Czar Alexander I found himself in a desperate situation. His only ally was Great Britain and it was hardly to his advantage to have the attention of this ally distracted by a war elsewhere. But there were other equally compelling reasons for Russian intervention. The American war was interfering with quite a lucrative trade between Russia and the United States. Furthermore, the British policy of blockade, of which the United States complained, was equally irksome to Russia. In fact, Alexander's Chancellor, Romanzoff, was anti-British, and saw in the negotiations the opportunity to settle old accounts with England. Finally, and perhaps not the least important of the motives, there was Alexander's own conception of himself as the most enlightened prince of his day. Harassed as he then was by Napoleon, his vanity could not be entirely suppressed. He did not shrink from appearing in the popular role of peacemaker.

So it was that Romanzoff sounded out John Quincy Adams who did not discourage the proposal. Invitations were dispatched to London and Washington offering Russian mediation. The formal offer reached the American capital in March and found the President in a decidedly low state of mind. The invasion of Canada had failed; the expenses of the war were mounting and the Treasury was bare; the patriotic rush to join the colors had been disappointing and

375

the ranks of the regular army could not be filled. The New England Federalists were more than ever opposed to the war. By the time the invitation arrived Napoleon had received his first setback; his army which had swept everything before it and entered Moscow had had to retreat and had been well-nigh annihilated. Should Napoleon fall, Great Britain would be free to throw her whole weight against the United States. Under the circumstances the Czar's invitation appeared to the President as the last ray of hope, dim though it was. Madison accepted with alacrity, not even waiting to learn how the invitation would be received by Great Britain.

Castlereagh, the British Foreign Minister, being well schooled in diplomacy, was immediately suspicious of the kind offices of the Czar. He therefore declined the invitation with almost as much alacrity as Madison had accepted it, on the ground that the war could not be settled by mediation since it was concerned with the domestic matter of impressment. On the other hand he did not feel that Great Britain could afford to take the position of declining an offer of peace. So, in spite of its apparent failure, the Russian invitation had the effect of forcing Castlereagh's hand and leading him to invite the United States to negotiate directly.

Of this the travelers knew nothing when at last they reached St. Petersburg on July 21. They were, however, conscious of a somewhat cold reception. John Quincy Adams was not of great help in making them feel at home. Even the meeting with compatriots in so remote a spot as St. Petersburg failed to break down his chilly reserve. "Mr. Adams is very civil but has a disagreeable manner," wrote young James Gallatin. A few days later he added, "Our position is a very embarrassing one. We plainly see we are not wanted."

There ensued a long period of uncertainty and inactivity that taxed even such patient men as Albert Gallatin and Senator Bayard. Unwanted though they were they stayed on at the Russian capital through the summer and autumn because they did not know what else to do. Romanzoff, who had first proposed mediation, now appeared to have lost favor with the Czar, while Count Nesslerode had become the favorite. Having got them to St. Petersburg the Czar treated the Americans with complete indifference. "Such weary waiting and all seems so hopeless," commented James.

Much more weary waiting would have to be endured before the negotiations got under way. At last, in November, Castlereagh's offer of direct negotiation reached Washington. The war was going no better for the Americans. The summer had witnessed the raids in Chesapeake Bay which more than outweighed the victory of Perry on Lake Erie and of Harrison at the battle of the Thames. The President was as anxious as ever for peace, so he accepted Castlereagh's offer and strengthened the American mission by adding to it Henry Clay and Jonathan Russell, former Chargé d'Affaires in England. The Senate at long last was prevailed upon to ratify the appointment of Gallatin, but not until they had done the same to the other negotiators, so that Gallatin's name was at the bottom of the list and not at the top, as it deserved to be.

In January, 1814, Gallatin and Bayard said good-bye to St. Petersburg, happy enough to be going. Through the good offices of his friend, Alexander Baring, the London banker, Gallatin obtained permission for himself and Bayard to enter England in the hope of speeding the negotiations. Castlereagh had proposed London as the scene of the conference, but Adams and Clay immediately objected. They were afraid, they said, of being snubbed and treated as colonists. The old Flemish city of Ghent was finally decided upon.

Gallatin's visit to London produced no results so far as hastening the negotiations was concerned. Castlereagh would discuss peace, but he was determined to take his own time. In the meanwhile, Paris fell and Napoleon went into exile at Elba. Government, press and public were too taken up with the victories to pay attention to the American emissaries.

In July Gallatin left London and joined the other American commissioners at Ghent. There they awaited the arrival of the British representatives and whiled away the time disputing among themselves. There could hardly have been a less congenial group. John Quincy Adams was the nominal head of the mission, but not one of the other members liked him. It was Gallatin who eventually assumed the leadership. Adams was particularly irritated by Clay who, though ten years Adams' junior, did not hesitate to take issue with him on every point. In his diary for July 15 James Gallatin made the entry, "Nothing to do. Mr. Adams in a very bad temper. Mr. Clay annoys him. Father pours oil on the troubled waters."

Adams did not like the habits of his colleagues, which were the very negation of his own ascetic life. The others did not appear to realize the solemnity of the occasion. "I dined again at the table d'hote, at one," he wrote. "The other gentlemen dined together at four. They sit after dinner and drink bad wine and smoke cigars, which neither suits my habits nor my health, and absorbs time which I cannot spare. I find it impossible, even with the most rigorous economy of time, to do half the writing that I ought."

If Adams disapproved of Clay's ideas he disapproved even more of that young statesman's morals. A man who, like Adams, made it a practice of rising at 5 A.M. and getting at once to work could have little respect for one who gambled the night away. "Just before rising," he reports, "I heard Mr. Clay's company retiring from his chamber. I had left them . . . at cards. They parted as I was about to rise." Gallatin was the peacemaker and so, too, was Bayard whose restraint throughout the whole of the negotiations won praise even from Adams. Bayard was a Federalist and had been selected primarily to give the mission the appearance of national unity. But he was not a die-hard and, in spite of his politics, got on perfectly with his colleagues. In fact the ease with which he did it aroused suspicions of his loyalty among the extremists of his own party. Jonathan Russell, the fifth member of the mission, was a New Englander but, in spite of his nativity, liked Clay much better than he liked Adams.

Not until the 8th of August, 1814, did the British commissioners reach Ghent. Castlereagh could not have selected a less distinguished or less competent group. Lord Gambier, who headed the mission, had had no experience whatever in diplomacy. His own countrymen were his severest critics. The London *Morning Chronicle* could see no reason for selecting a man who, the newspaper said, "was a post-captain in 1794, and happened to fight the *Defence* decently in Lord Howe's actions; who slumbered for some time as a junior Lord of the Admiralty; who sang psalms, said prayers, and assisted in the burning of Copenhagen, for which he was made a lord."

Henry Goulburn, second on the list, was a young and officious undersecretary of state to Lord Bathurst, whose idea of diplomacy was showing his temper and sticking firmly to his opinions. Third and last was William Adams, a Doctor of Civil Law, who was supposed to supply technical knowledge to the mission. He took a subordinate part in the discussions.

It did not take Gallatin long to get the correct measure of his opponents. On the day of their arrival James Gallatin confided to his diary, "Father is not impressed with the British delegates—men who have not made any mark and have no influence or weight, but are puppets of Castlereagh and Liverpool. Father feels he is quite capable of dealing with them." As a matter of fact Castlereagh was saving his best talent for the approaching Congress of Vienna. In comparison with that meeting of all the European powers to settle the affairs of the Continent the negotiations at Ghent were of little importance. Gallatin, unfortunately, could not speak with equal confidence upon the handling of his colleagues of the American mission. "Clay," wrote James, "uses strong language to Adams and Adams returns the compliment. Father looks calmly on with a twinkle in his eye. Today there was a severe storm and Father said, 'Gentlemen, gentlemen, we must remain united or we fail.'"

Now that the commissioners were prepared to face each other the immediate problem was to find questions they could discuss, for each group appeared with positive and conflicting instructions. With from 15,000 to 20,000 trained soldiers already landing in America or on their way the British felt that they were in a position to dictate a peace. The London *Times* expressed the popular attitude bluntly. "Our demands may be couched in a single word—Submission!" The London *Courier*, official organ of the ministry, talked of depriving New England of her fishing rights in British waters, the return of Louisiana to Spain, and American concession of the right of impressment. These were mild in comparison with Canadian demands, made in the official *Gazette*, which included cession to Canada of northern New York and the south bank of the St. Lawrence, a guarantee of the Indian Territory from Sandusky, Ohio, to Kaskaskia in southern Illinois, withdrawal of American military posts in the Northwest, the cession of a part of Maine, and control of the Lakes, in addition to the claims previously made by the London *Courier*.

Quite the contrary were Secretary Monroe's hopes. He was for asking for the transfer to the United States of Upper Canada, or even the whole of it, on the ground that "Experience has shown that Great Britain cannot participate in the dominion and navigation of the Lakes without incurring the danger of an early renewal of the war."

The first conference was held on August 8 at the Hotel des Pays-Bas. After the preliminary formalities had been disposed of, Goulburn, acting as spokesman for his colleagues, informed the American commissioners that the British commissioners were authorized to discuss impressment and allegiance; the Indians and their boundary, which their government considered to be a *sine qua non;* the Canadian boundary, and the privilege of landing and drying fish within British jurisdiction.

The commissioners then retired to allow the Americans time to study the British agenda. The two groups met again on the following day. Adams, speaking for his commission, stated that it had no authority to admit the Indian or the fisheries questions into the discussions. He presented as the American topic the matter of blockades and indemnities. The British commissioners, notwithstanding, reverted to the subject of the Indians and revealed a plan to set up an Indian territory as a buffer between American and British possessions. The Americans refused to consider the proposal and the British commissioners withdrew to communicate with their government and obtain further instructions.

No other meeting was held until August 19. Goulburn then read the instructions he had received from Castlereagh. These were a second demand for the establishment of an Indian territory, a rectification of the Canadian boundary to include Fort Niagara and Sackett's Harbor and a promise from the Americans to erect no fortifications on the Lakes. Gallatin politely called attention to the fact that the territory to be handed over to the Indians included parts of Ohio, Indiana, Illinois and Michigan. He inquired what was to become of the 100,000 Americans already living in the territory. "They will have to shift for themselves," replied Goulburn. The young man then added, by way of encouragement, that he had once known an Indian who was quite a decent fellow.

Such a ridiculous answer to a vital question convinced the American commissioners that, whatever might be Castlereagh's purpose in sending a man like Goulburn to the council table, he evidently had no serious intention of making a peace. That is, all the commissioners were convinced except Clay. The Kentuckian's instinct as a player of the game of "brag," an early form of poker, told him that the British were bluffing. And if they were bluffing, the way to beat them was to put up a bigger bluff.

The Americans retired to formulate a reply. It devolved upon Adams as the chairman to write it. When he read the draft to his colleagues all their animosity toward him was released. They ripped his work to pieces. If Adams rejoiced in heavy labor he now got his fill of it. From early afternoon until almost midnight the commissioners were engaged, as Adams said, "in sifting, erasing, patching and amending until we were all awearied, though none of us was yet satisfied with amendment." Impatient as they were with each other, separated though they might be by personal animosities, there was one point upon which they were unanimous, and that was to utter a defiant "No" to what they regarded as impossible demands. Little did they know that at the very moment they were drawing up a document which all of them, except the ebullient Clay, believed would be their last act as commissioners, the capitol in Washington was in flames and the President of the United States was a fugitive! It was perhaps as well for the future of the country that news then traveled so slowly.

The reply that was presented next day to the British commissioners gave no indication whatever of the discord that had attended its drafting. In conclusion it said of the terms offered, "They are, above all, dishonorable to the United States in demanding from them to abandon territory and a portion of their citizens; to admit a foreign interference in their domestic concerns, and to cease to exercise their natural rights on their own shores and in their own waters. A treaty concluded on such terms would be but an armistice."

Having delivered their reply the American commissioners packed their belongings and gave every evidence of preparing to leave Ghent. Senator Bayard singled Goulburn out and warned him that the exacting terms insisted upon by the British would wreck the Federalist party in the United States and destroy the last vestige of sympathy for his country. Already Madison, who had received the British terms, had had the wisdom to make them public and the country rang with protests against their harshness. "Don't Give Up

The Soil" became the war cry and even some of the Federalist newspapers expressed indignation over the demands. Goulburn, the budding diplomat, reported to his superiors that Bayard's argument "has not made the least impression upon me or my colleagues." It may not have impressed Goulburn, Gambier and Dr. Adams, but it made a profound impression upon Castlereagh, Liverpool and Bathurst. If the negotiations were permitted to end on this note Great Britain would be in the position of refusing a peace in order to engage in a war of conquest. The Americans must be kept at Ghent by whatever means possible. Gambier, Goulburn and Dr. Adams were rebuked by their superiors for their clumsy handling of the negotiations.

Castlereagh had now departed for Vienna and he left the conduct of affairs at Ghent to Lord Bathurst. The President of the Board of Trade lost no time in drawing up new instructions, though in order to keep the negotiations going he had to admit that the Indian territory was not a *sine qua non*, though it had first been described as such. He authorized his commissioners to abandon the demand for the Indian territory and control of the Lakes and merely to require that the Indians be included in the truce. This was a definite victory for the Americans, though Bathurst excused his retreat on the ground that he was merely marking time until the conquest of the United States should be more complete and the original demands could be revived.

Bathurst's policy was to keep the negotiations going by writing notes, confident that the Americans would reply to them. The news of the raid on Washington had reached Europe and increased the confidence of the British as much as it depressed the hopes of the American commissioners. Prevost was poised for his invasion of New York and his victory, which seemed assured, would place the British in a position to obtain anything they demanded.

While the British had surrendered in the matter of the Indians the United States had made a surrender that was of even greater importance in clearing the way toward an agreement. Their surrender concerned impressment. From the very outset the United States had insisted that Great Britain relinquish this right. Had she done so the war would have ended a few weeks after it commenced. But on this point Great Britain remained as firm as ever. In instructing the commissioners Monroe made impressment a *sine qua non* for, he said, quite logically, if this were abandoned "the United States have appealed to arms in vain." However, after the collapse of Napoleon's empire there was no longer a crying need for sailors for the British Navy, and, consequently, while holding to the right the British had abandoned the practice. The result was, of course, to place impressment on a different footing. After considering the issue in the light of the altered circumstances, Madison's cabinet yielded the principle and instructions were sent to the commissioners at Ghent that they might withdraw this demand.

Elimination of the Indians and impressment now reduced the negotiations to a question of territory. Stimulated by the victory at Bladensburg, Bathurst instructed the British commission to negotiate on the principle of *uti possidetis;* that is to say, each country was to keep the territory it then had in its possession. This would have given Great Britain Mackinac Island, Fort Niagara with the territory surrounding it, and all of Maine north of the Aroostook River; while to the Americans would have gone Fort Erie and Fort Malden, at Amherstburg.

Here John Quincy Adams' value to the commission came into full play. In view of Massachusetts' recalcitrance the other members might have felt that loss of her territory was no more than she deserved. But, unpopular though he might be at home, Adams' jealous guardianship of the interests of his native state never flagged. His attitude stiffened the rest of the commission. Close, too, on the heels of the news of Bladensburg, came news of the British retirement from in front of Baltimore, Macdonough's brilliant victory on Lake Champlain, Prevost's retreat from Plattsburg and the repulse of the attack on Fort Erie. This fortunate turn of affairs encouraged the American commissioners to reject the principle of *uti possidetis* and hold out for settlement on the basis of *status quo ante bellum,* or a return to the territorial division that existed prior to the war.

Once more the obstinacy of both sides appeared to obstruct the peace as effectively as the Indians and impressment had done. The war, incidentally, was beginning to be embarrassing to Castlereagh at Vienna. The Czar was making a bid for leadership in that assembly, and the reverses to British arms in America were affecting British prestige at the council table. The war, too, was becoming unpopular in England. The public was complaining of the taxes they were called upon to pay to support it; the price seemed too much to exact for a mere rectification of the Canadian frontier. Merchants were impatient to do business with their old customers in the United States, and the American privateers that still haunted the trade routes were a constant thorn in the flesh.

However, the British had one more trump card to play. The great Wellington, momentarily without a war to fight, was cooling his heels as British Ambassador in Paris. Now if he could be persuaded to go to America and take charge, the United States would surely succumb in short order to British arms. There would follow a dictated peace based upon the cherished principle of *uti possidetis,* and what the British would possess when the Iron Duke was through with the Americans could be left to the imagination.

A messenger was dispatched forthwith to Paris to put the proposition up to the Duke, while the British ministry and the British commissioners awaited his reply with keen anticipation. Surely the Duke would not refuse this opportunity to add new luster to his name. The Duke did not keep them waiting long. Liverpool's invitation was dated November 4. Wellington's reply was dated November 9.

"I have already told you and Lord Bathurst that I feel no objection to going to America," he began. This sounded encouraging indeed, but what followed made melancholy reading for Liverpool. The Duke's letter continued: ". . . though I don't promise to myself much success there." This was hardly the spirit in which to set out upon a campaign of conquest. "That which appears to me to be wanting in America is not a general, or a general officer and troops, but a naval superiority on the Lakes."

In spite of feeling "no objection," nothing could be clearer than the Duke's unwillingness to undertake the mission. From that subject Wellington turned to a discussion of the proceedings at Ghent:

"In regard to your negotiation, I confess that I think you have no right, from the state of the war, to demand any concession of territory from America. . . . You have not been able to carry it into the enemy's territory, notwithstanding your military success and now undoubted military superiority, and have not even cleared your own territory on the point of attack. You cannot on any principle of equality in negotiation claim a cession of territory excepting in exchange for other advantages which you have in your power . . .

"Then if this reasoning be true, why stipulate for the *uti possidetis*? You can get no territory; indeed the state of your military operations, however creditable, does not entitle you to demand any."

The Duke's letter fell like a thunderbolt on British pretensions. Appeal had been made by the ministry to the highest authority on military matters in King George IV's realm and the highest authority had rendered his decision against his own people and in favor of the Americans!

There should have been clear sailing after that. The British accepted the principle of the *status quo,* but they made one exception. They insisted that the United States relinquish her fishing rights in Canadian waters or exchange them for an equivalent. These rights were peculiarly precious in the eyes of John Quincy Adams, not only because Massachusetts chiefly made use of them, but because his own father had wrung them from Great Britain in the Treaty of 1783. The equivalent which the British proposed was their right to navigate the Mississippi. Such an arrangement was quite agreeable to John Quincy Adams, who knew little and cared less about that quarter of the globe. Not so, however, to Henry Clay, the champion of the people of the West.

Just when it appeared that peace between Great Britain and the United States might become a reality, war to the death was declared between the two ill-mated members of the American mission. Adams belittled Clay's objection to the Mississippi concession. "The navigation principle," replied the Kentuckian scornfully, "is much too important to concede for the mere liberty of drying fish on a desert." Clay protested further that, if need be, he was ready to fight the war three years more to protect the Mississippi.

Gallatin found his hands full trying to appease the combatants. But there was a limit to what even he could stand. "Father can no longer support Mr. Adams," wrote James, "he has tried his patience too far." It was the British commission which eventually solved the problem by suggesting that the questions of the fisheries and the Mississippi be reserved for future discussion.

At last, on Christmas Eve, 1814, the treaty was ready for the formal signing. From August through December the negotiators had struggled; yet after five months of labor not a single disputed point found settlement in the finished document. Some of these disputed points were left for future commissions to tackle. Impressment, that bitterest bone of contention, was not mentioned. The treaty was, in substance, a mere agreement to let matters stand as they had stood before the war.

Fruitless though the treaty appeared to be, its signing was the cause of universal rejoicing. A few discordant notes in the British press did not conceal the general satisfaction of all classes in England that peace was once more restored. In the United States Madison breathed a sigh of relief while the public applauded the work of the American negotiators.

The ancient town of Ghent did itself proud in honor of the historic occasion. Prominent citizens who had followed the proceedings with sympathy and interest congratulated the American commissioners and made them all honorary members of the local society of arts and sciences. The bells of the town were rung, and a solemn and impressive service was held in the cathedral. The signing itself took place in the refectory of the monastery.

Next day being Christmas, the British commissioners graciously invited the Americans to dine with them on roast beef and plum pudding imported from England especially for the occasion. Healths were drunk to each other and toasts were proposed to "The King" and "The President" while a band played first "God Save the King" and then "Yankee Doodle." It was a scene to be remembered," wrote James Gallatin. "I never saw Father so cheerful; he was in high spirits and his witty conversation was much appreciated." Even John Quincy Adams for once forswore his custom of dining alone and risked his health and habits in an atmosphere of wine and cigars.

To that angular, quixotic son of New England went the honor, a few days later, of responding to a toast in which he expressed a pious wish that time has gratified—a toast that serves as a most fitting epilogue to the War of 1812.

"Ghent, the city of Peace; may the gates of the temple of Janus, here closed, not be opened again for a century!"

Conclusion

THE WAR OF 1812 was full of absurdities. It was absurd that the orders in council, one of the two main issues in dispute, should have been withdrawn before war was declared. It was absurd that the principle of impressment, the other main issue, should have found no mention in the peace. Great Britain did not formally abandon it until some 50 years later.

It was absurd that the President of the United States should have been driven from his capitol by a handful of British soldiers and absurd that a handful of American privateers should have terrorized commerce in the narrow seas about the British Isles.

The American boast that the conquest of Canada was "a mere matter of marching" was absurd in the light of the futile efforts at invasion. Equally absurd was Sir George Prevost's repulse at Plattsburg in his attempted invasion of the United States. It was absurd that the greatest battle of the war should have been fought and won by the Americans, thereby saving the country, when the country had been saved two weeks before by the signing of the treaty at Ghent.

So insignificant was the war in comparison with the mighty effort required to defeat Napoleon that it is virtually unknown to the average Englishman today. Save for a few glorious episodes that have been woven into our national tradition the War of 1812 is scarcely better known to the average American.

The average American depends chiefly upon school histories for his knowledge of the past, and school histories quite naturally hesitate to stress discreditable and humiliating incidents. Besides, the War of 1812 was quickly overshadowed by the great events of the American Civil War and the heroic figures of Lincoln and the military leaders of both the North and the South. In contrast those of 1812 seem small indeed. Because the American Civil War produced

387

such leaders, was more bitterly fought, caused much more bloodshed and lasted longer, it is understandable that it should long have taken precedence over the War of 1812 in the popular imagination.)

The events of the past quarter of a century have, however, placed the War of 1812 in a new light which calls for a new evaluation. The Civil War and the issues involved, important as they were at the time, are not likely ever to reappear. So far as we can see they represent a closed chapter.

On the other hand the War of 1812 now stands revealed as the initial stage in a logical sequence of historical events in which World War I and World War II have been the succeeding stages. Each is astonishingly like the others in the international situations leading up to them and in the popular reactions.

Three times in the course of the nation's history the whole of Europe has been plunged into war. Each time we have fervently believed that Europe's misfortunes were none of our business and that we should have no part in them. Each time we have displayed a blind faith in neutrality and neglected to take the necessary precautions to put the nation in a proper state of defense. Three times we have seen our hopes crushed and ourselves drawn into the conflict.

But there was one striking difference between the first stage and the two which followed. In the cases of World War I and World War II our allies held off the enemy until we had time to prepare. We fought those wars thousands of miles from our homeland. In the case of the War of 1812 we had time to prepare but we made no use of it. As a result the war was waged at our firesides and we knew the terror and distress of invasion.

"Detroit Falls." "Chicago Garrison Massacred." "New York Blockaded." "Enemy Fleet in Chesapeake Bay." "New England Invaded." "Maine Subjugated." "Boston Threatened." "U. S. Army Driven From Field and Demoralized." "Washington Captured." "Capitol and White House in Flames. President and Congress in Flight." "Baltimore Attacked by Land and Sea." "British Army Before New Orleans."

These are not figments of a fevered imagination. They are the unexaggerated statements of actual events. Detroit and Chicago, of course, were not then the great cities they are today. But Boston, New York, Washington, Baltimore and New Orleans were important places. The flight of the President and the Congress of the United States would be a national calamity at any time. These things did happen here. And, since they happened, it is possible they could happen again. From the disasters of 1812 there are valuable lessons to be learned.

In the first place, there is a popular assumption that we want nothing. Yet we have always wanted something. In 1812 we wanted foreign trade. In consequence Jefferson's embargo to keep us out of the theater of combat was as ineffective as Franklin D. Roosevelt's Neutrality Act prior to our entry into World War II. At long last we seem to be learning that the affairs of the world are our affairs, whether we want it that way or not. Wendell Willkie is credited with bringing the conception of "One World" into being in our own time. Few of us realize that, as regards Europe, we were "One World" a century and a half ago.

We hope that we can avoid war because neither we nor our potential enemy wants war. The War of 1812 reveals the tenuousness of that hope. Neither Great Britain nor the United States wanted war then. Neither had anything to gain by it and both everything to lose. Yet we went to war. The circumstances can hardly be put down to exceptional incompetence on the part of our civil leaders. Canning has gone down in history as one of Britain's most able foreign ministers. Jefferson and Madison are numbered among our nation's Founding Fathers and, as such, popularly endowed with superhuman qualities. The inevitable conclusion is that in spite of a mutual desire not to go to war and statesmen presumably well equipped to carry out the popular mandate, nevertheless we cannot be sure of not going to war.

This brings us logically to the question of preparedness. How far that should go is a matter to be left to the experts on national defense and measured according to our resources and the estimated needs to meet a given situation. But the War of 1812 teaches us that we should not neglect national defense to the point where a potential enemy will assume that we are so ill-prepared we will not go to war under any circumstances. The enemy made that mistake in 1812 just as it did in 1917 and in 1941. The War of 1812 teaches us that pious pronouncements are impressive overseas only so far as there is visible physical strength to support them. Had Jefferson displayed less repugnance to building a navy and maintaining the nucleus of an army Great Britain might well have listened more sympathetically to our protests.

The War of 1812 reminds us, too, of a national characteristic which is that every man, regardless of his training, looks upon himself as a military strategist. When the enemy is in view, like Madison at Bladensburg, we leave the field to the military commander. But, until the enemy appears, we scorn the military commander's advice and belittle his requests for men and the tools of war. Then, in an emergency, we expect him to perform miracles. Jefferson's assumption that gunboats were superior to frigates and ships of the line is reflected in the present belief of many amateur military strategists that the next war can be settled by pressing a button.

Closely associated with this attitude is the bitter criticism of the "brass hats" that follows every war and the popular demand to make our armed forces more democratic. Nowhere is there a better illustration of the ineffectiveness of a democratic army than in the War of 1812. The Ohio militiamen who rode their officer on a rail were, no doubt, merely asserting their democratic rights. The same men, however, did not distinguish themselves a short time later under the severe test of combat. On the other hand the brigades of Winfield Scott and Eleazer Ripley were whipped into shape in anything but a democratic fashion. Then at Chippawa and Lundy's Lane they proved as good as the best that the British could throw against them.

The War of 1812, however, teaches us also that the "brass hats" themselves are by no means always above criticism. Our defeats on land were, in most instances, directly traceable to incompetence in the high command. After the Revolution we allowed our officer corps to deteriorate along with the rank and file. Against a background of blunderers Andrew Jackson stands out alone as a natural military genius. Such fortunate accidents of discovery, however, should not be left until the enemy is at our gates. On the other hand our victories at sea are primarily attributable to the excellence of our naval commanders who maintained the highest standards between wars. We have learned the necessity, in time of peace, of training professional military leaders to serve as a nucleus for the expansion of the armed forces in time of war. Since 1812 the practice has paid off well. It is a lesson that should not be forgotten.

On the whole the War of 1812 teaches us that there are no short cuts to national security. Where we indulged in wishful thinking and dodged individual sacrifice, we lost. We won only where we put our whole soul into the effort. That, it may be reasonably assumed, is as true today as it was then.

It would be remiss to close this story without saying a few laudatory words for the war which, in spite of its many absurdities, it justly deserves. It was a comparatively inexpensive war for the United States. Basing the cost upon the increase in the national debt the bill came to $80,500,000. To this should be added the $46,-217,150.57 paid out as pensions to veterans of the war and their dependents up to December 31, 1940. Who today would not relish a war on land and sea that cost no more than $127,000,000! The killed and wounded did not number much more than 5,000, a third as many as the Union army lost at the battle of Fredericksburg alone.

On the whole it was a war conducted on humane principles. The burning of York, the Canadian capital, and the burning, in retaliation, of the Capitol at Washington were the exceptions rather than the rule. The destruction of Newark by the Americans was uncalled for and caused unnecessary suffering on the part of the civilian population of Canada. But it was heartily condemned by the American Government. The excesses at Hampton, Virginia, were inexcusable, though General Beckwith did the best he could by placing the blame on Frenchmen and dismissing them from the service. Cockburn's raids in the Chesapeake and farther south did considerable damage, but even he made an effort to respect private property, and the British Government paid indemnities to the owners of slaves who were carried away.

The peace stipulated a return to the *status quo* which made it apparent to everybody that nobody had won the war. Consequently there was no desire on the part of either contestant to renew the war to gain something of which it had been deprived. The fact that disputed questions were left to be settled by commissions led to the discovery that commissions could do the job quite as well as a resort to arms.

If many of the acts of our military were inglorious, on the other

391

hand there were acts which testified to the fact that Americans, properly trained and equipped and competently led, could give a good account of themselves. The British gained a new respect for them and thereafter the United States was treated as an independent nation and not as a colony.

More important than all else is the fact that for over a century the frontier between Canada and the United States has remained unfortified and the Lakes have been used jointly with no fear of aggression on either side. And though Great Britain and the United States have had their disagreements, and more than once have come close to a renewal of the conflict, the peace concluded at Ghent has prevailed to this day.

True to Adams' pious wish, so far as the United States and Great Britain are concerned, the gates of the temple of Janus remained closed for a century. As matters stand Adams appears to have been guilty of the New Englander's habit of understatement when he did not wish for two.

Bibliography

ADAMS, HENRY. *History of the United States During the Administrations of Thomas Jefferson and James Madison.* New York, 1889 and 1930.

American State Papers. Military Affairs.

BABCOCK, KENDRICK CHARLES. *The Rise of American Nationalism (1811-19).* New York, 1906.

BAILEY, THOMAS A. *A Diplomatic History of the American People.* New York, 1940.

BARNES, JAMES. *Naval Actions of the War of 1812.* New York, 1896.

BARROWS, EDWARD M. *Matthew Calbraith Perry.* Indianapolis, 1935.

BEARD, CHARLES AND MARY. *The Rise of American Civilization.* New York, 1930.

BRUCE, WILLIAM CABELL. *John Randolph of Roanoke.* New York, 1922.

CLARK, JAMES FREEMAN. *History of the Campaign of 1812 and Surrender of the Post of Detroit.* New York, 1858.

CLEAVES, FREEMAN. *William Henry Harrison and His Times.* New York, 1929.

Dictionary of American Biography. New York, 1929.

DUTTON, CHARLES J. *Oliver Hazard Perry.* New York, 1935.

DWIGHT, THEODORE. *History of The Hartford Convention.* New York, 1833.

ESSARY, J. FRED. *Maryland in National Politics.* Baltimore, 1915.

FULFORD, ROGER. *George The Fourth.* New York, 1935.

GALLATIN, JAMES. *Diary.* New York, 1916.

GAY, S. R. *James Madison.* New York, 1884.

GLEIG, GEORGE ROBERT. *A Narrative of The British Campaigns*

Against Washington, Baltimore and New Orleans. London, 1821.

HOCKETT, HOMER C. *Political and Social History of The United States (1492-1828)*. New York, 1925.

INGRAHAM, PRENTISS. *Land of Legendary Lore*. Easton, Maryland, 1898.

JAMES, MARQUIS. *Andrew Jackson, The Border Captain*. Indianapolis, 1933.

JAMES, WILLIAM. *Military Occurrences of the Late War Between Great Britain and the United States*. London, 1818.

JOHNSON, GERALD W. *America's Silver Age*. New York, 1939.

JOHNSON, GERALD W. *Andrew Jackson*. New York, 1927.

JOHNSON, GERALD W. *Randolph of Roanoke*. New York, 1929.

LA TOUR, MAJOR A. LACARRIÈRE. *Historical Memoir of the War of 1812 in The West*. Philadelphia, 1816.

LOSSING, BENSON J. *Pictorial Field Book of the War of 1812*. New York, 1868.

MADISON, DOLLY. *Memoirs and Letters*. New York, 1857.

MAHAN, ALFRED THAYER. *Sea Power in Relation to the War of 1812*. Boston, 1905.

MARINE, WILLIAM MATTHEW. *The British Invasion of Maryland*. Baltimore, 1913.

MARRIOTT, J. A. R. *George Canning and His Times*. London, 1907.

MORGAN, GEORGE. *Life of James Monroe*. Boston, 1921.

MORISON, SAMUEL ELIOT. *Harrison Gray Otis*. New York, 1913.

MORRIS, WILLIAM O'CONNOR. *Napoleon*. New York, 1893.

Niles' Register. Baltimore.

OWENS, HAMILTON. *Baltimore on the Chesapeake*. New York, 1941.

PRATT, JULIUS W. *Expansionists of 1812*. New York, 1925.

Report of the Trial of Brig-Gen. William Hull. New York, 1814.

ROBERTSON, C. GRANT. *England Under the Hanoverians*. London, 1911.

ROOSEVELT, THEODORE. *The Naval War of 1812*. New York, 1882.

SCOTT, WINFIELD. *Memoirs*. New York, 1864.

SWANSON, NEIL H. *The Perilous Fight*. New York, 1945.

UPTON, EMORY. *Military Policy of the United States*. Washington, 1917.

VAN RENNSELAER, SOLOMON. *Notices of the War of 1812*. New York, 1836.

WILKINSON, JAMES. *Memoirs of My Own Times*. Philadelphia, 1816.

WILLIAMS, JOHN S. *History of the Invasion and Capture of Washington*. New York, 1857.

ZIMMERMAN, J. T. *Impressment of American Seamen*. New York, 1925.

INDEX

INDEX

Acasta, 337

Adair, John, General, 369, 373

Adams, 112, 192, 335

Adams, Henry, 11, 12

Adams, John, 41, 327

Adams, John Quincy, 21, 46, 268, 322, 330, 375-378, 383-386, 392

Adams, William, 379, 382

Aeolus, 127

African, 127

Aisquith's rifle corps, 314

Alabama, 232, 234, 246

Alexander I (Russia), 33, 375-376, 383

Alexandria, 89, 179, 268, 274, 308, 324

Allen, John, Colonel, 143

Allen, William Henry, Lieut., 190-191

America, 305

Amey, Colonel, 315

Amherstburg, 101, 141, 148, 215-216, 383

Amott (Representative from New York), 89

Anaconda, 344

Annapolis, 179, 270, 271, 274

Appling, Lieut. Col., 296, 297

Argus, 126, 183, 190-191, 198

Ariel, 206, 207, 208, 209, 214, 230

Armistead, George, Lieut. Col., 311, 316-318

Armstrong, John, General, 32, 44, 51, 146, 155, 157, 200, 220, 222, 223, 224, 227, 229, 234, 239, 240, 250-251, 268-271, 277, 292, 308, 345

Arnold, Benedict, 154

Arthur, Stanley M., 65

Asia, 76

Astor, John Jacob, 101

Atlanta, 337

Atlantic, 193

Auckland, Lord, 26, 27-28, 32

Auerstädt, battle of, 28

Austria, 57

Auttose, 244

Avon, 336-337

Bailey, Dixon, Captain, 236-237

Bainbridge, William, Captain, 133, 135-136; (Com.) 183, 192, 337

Baltimore, 12, 74, 89, 120, 168, 173, 179, 181, 266, 269, 270, 271, 275, 278, 304-321, 350, 357, 363, 383, 388-389

Baltimore *Evening Post*, 56

Baltimore *Weekly Register, see Niles' Register*

Baltimore *Whig*, 21, 92

Baratarians, 343-344, 345, 354, 362, 363

Barbary pirates, 15

Barclay, Robert H., Captain, 203-211, 214, 217

Baring, Alexander, 87, 377

Barlow, Joel, 93, 190

Barney, Joshua, Commodore, 266, 268, 272-273, 278, 279, 282, 285, 305, 308, 311, 318

Barrie, Captain, 181-182

Barron, James, Commodore, 34, 35, 45

Barrows, Edward M., 12

Bassano, Duke of, 93

Bathurst, Lord, 308, 378, 382-384

Battalion Old Fields, 275, 277

Bayard, James, Senator, 374-378, 381-382

Baylies, Hodigah, 328

Bayonne Decree, 44, 50, 51

Bayou Bienvenu, 354-359, 367

Beale, 357, 359, 368, 370

Beanes, Dr., 318-319

Beasley, Daniel, Major, 235, 236

Beaver Dams, 162, 164

Beckwith, Sir Sidney, General, 176, 177-179, 391

Belgium, 57

399

Belvidera, 126-127, 129, 172
Benton, Thomas H., Colonel, 240
Beresford, J. B., Captain, 172
Berkeley, George, Admiral, 33, 38
Berlin Decree, 29, 32, 38, 50, 51, 75
Bibb, William, 65
Biddle, Captain, 337, 339-340
Bigelow, Thomas, 328
Bingham, A. B., Captain, 53-55
Black Rock, 120, 158, 163, 203, 230, 251, 252, 261
Black Swamp, 99, 140
Bladensburg, 12, 271, 274-282, 284, 286, 287, 308, 311, 312, 315, 316, 324, 326, 355, 357, 363, 383, 390
Blake, Senator, 323
Blakeley, Johnston, Commander, 336
Blanchard's Fork, 99
Bliss, George, 328
Blockade of France by Great Britain, 25-26, 38-39
Blockade of Great Britain by Napoleon, 29
Blount, Governor, 238-239, 240, 244, 245, 246, 344
Blyth, Samuel, Captain, 191-192
Boerstler, Charles G., Lieut. Col., 164-165
Bonaparte, Joseph, 44
Bonne Citoyenne, 183
Boston, 77, 78-79, 86, 89, 90, 132, 155, 168, 169-170, 185, 186, 290, 291, 324, 325, 388
Boston, 192
Boston *Gazette,* 45, 73-74
Boston *Patriot,* 21, 92
Boston *Sentinel,* 326
Boxer, 191-192
Boyd, John P., Colonel, 61; (Gen.), 225-226
Boyle, Thomas, Captain, 306
Brandt, John, 117
Brisbane, General, 296
British Annual Register, 288, 306
Brock, Isaac, General, 102-103, 105, 106, 111, 114, 115-116
Broke, Philip, Captain, 127, 128, 130, 185-189
"Broken voyage," 18, 28
Brooke, Arthur, Colonel, 314, 316, 320

Brown, Jacob, General, 166-167, 225, 227, 228-229, 250-263, 289, 292
Brownstown, 103
Brush, Henry, Captain, 102-106
Bryant, William Cullen, 42, 94-95
Budd, Charles, Lieut., 298
Buffalo, 111, 157, 230, 251, 252, 253
Burlington (Vermont), 223, 224, 227
Burlington Heights, 163, 164, 229, 252, 256
Burnt Cork Creek, 235
Burr, Aaron, 70, 221, 222, 238
Burrows, William, Lieut., 191-192
Byron, Richard, Captain, 126-127

Cabot, George, 326, 327-328
Cadwalader, John, General, 47
Caledonia, 112, 203, 206, 207, 208, 209
Calhoun, John C., 65, 70, 71, 89, 93
Caller, James, Colonel, 235
Campbell, Hugh G., Captain, 83, 84-85
Canada, 28, 64, 67, 68-69, 71, 75, 91, 96-106, 108-123, 141, 153, 157-167, 168-170, 205, 213-220, 222-231, 234, 250-263, 266, 269, 290, 291, 292, 324, 340, 375, 379, 380, 384, 385, 387, 391, 392
Canning, George, 31-38, 44-45, 47-48, 87
Cape Henry, 171, 172
Carden, John S., Captain, 135
Carolina, 357, 358, 361, 362-363, 364
Carroll, Charles, 286
Carroll, William, General, 352, 353, 357, 363, 367, 368-369, 371
Carron, 344
Cass, Colonel, 105, 106; (Gen.), 213
Cassin, Stephen, Lieut., 298, 300-301
Castlereagh, 88, 92, 95, 376-382, 383
Champagny, de, 38, 50, 51
Chandler, John, General, 163-164, 269
Channing, William Ellery, 94
Chasseur, 306
Chasseurs Britanniques, 177-178, 179, 391
Chauncey, Isaac, Commodore, 125, 157, 158, 160, 161, 167, 197, 200,

201, 203, 205, 206, 212, 224-225, 251, 252, 256-257

Chauncey, Woolcott, Lieut., 167

Cheeves, Langdon, 65, 74-75

Cherokee Indians, 245, 247, 248

Cherub, 194-196

Chesapeake, 33-38, 42, 45, 49, 52, 54, 77, 185-189, 190, 203, 335

Chesapeake Bay, 170-182, 231, 264-270, 309, 377, 391

Chew, Samuel, 75-76

Chicago, 107, 388; *see also* Fort Dearborn

Chippawa, (251-260, 263, 289, 324, 390; *see also* Fort Chippawa

Chippawa, 206, 210, 211, 230

Chittenden, Martin, Governor, 293, 302, 325

Choctaw Indians, 61, 246, 345

Chrysler's Field, 225-227

Chrystie, John, Colonel, 114, 116

Chub, 298-300

Civil War, 387-388

Claiborne, Ferdinand L., General, 235, 238, 244, 245

Claiborne, William, Governor, 82, 343, 347, 353

Clark, William, 16

Clay, Green, General, 147-148, 149, 150, 219

Clay, Henry, 12, 64, 65, 70-71, 75, 91, 107, 123, 139, 377-381, 385

Clinton, George, 89

Clipper ships, 305

Cochrane, Sir Alexander, Admiral, 266, 312, 318, 319, 320, 341, 351, 354-355, 361, 367

Cockburn, Sir George, Admiral, 170-174, 177-179, 182, 264-268, 282, 285, 286, 308, 309, 312, 316, 318, 391

Cocke, John, General, 240-243, 244, 246

Coffee, John, Colonel, 239, 240-247; (Gen.), 345, 351, 353, 359, 364, 368-369, 371

Coleman (editor of New York *Evening Post*), 92

Columbia River, 16

Congress of Vienna, 379, 382, 383

Confiance, 298-301

Congress, 126, 192

Congreve rockets, 171, 281, 315

Connecticut, 324, 325, 328, 329

Connecticut River, 290

Constellation, 171, 335

Constitution, 128-133, 135-136, 183, 192, 205, 307, 335, 337

Continental System (Napoleon), 42, 44

Conway, 221

Copenhagen, 378

Cornwallis, 340

Cotton, 40, 43, 44, 58, 69

Covington, Leonard, General, 226-227

Crab Island, 293, 296-301

Craig, James, Sir, 77, 80

Craney Island, 176-177, 179

Crawford, William H., 190

Creek Indians, 12, 232-249, 250, 341, 342

Creighton, Lieut., 53; (Com.), 309

Crillon, de, Edouard, Count, 78-81

Croghan, George, Major, 150-153; (Lieut. Col.), 290

Crutchfield, Stapleton, Major, 177-178

Cumberland Head, 293, 298-301

Cutts, Anna Payne, 284, 286

Cuyahoga, 99-101

Cyane, 337

Dacres, James R., Captain, 52, 127, 130-132

Dane, Nathan, 328

Danish fleet, 33, 49

D'Aguin, 353, 357, 358, 368

Dawson, Edith, Mrs., 181

Dayton, 98-99

Dearborn, Henry, General, 90, 96, 104, 106, 108, 123, 138, 154-167, 202, 221, 222, 238

Decatur, Stephen, 91, 126, 135, 183, 298, 309, 337-339

Decrès, 32, 38

Defence, 378

De La Ronde, Pierre, Colonel, 355, 357

Delaware, 231

Delaware Bay, 171, 192

Democratic party (former Republican party), 289
De Salaberry, Colonel, 228
Detroit, 96, 100-103, 105, 107, 109, 111, 118, 120, 122, 123, 138, 140, 141, 142, 143, 146, 153, 200, 214, 215, 216, 219, 220, 229, 232, 388
Detroit, 112, 203, 205-211
Dexter, Samuel, 323
Dickenson, Captain, 339
Dispatch, 338
District of Columbia, 231, 264
Dobbins, Daniel, 202
D'Onis, 84, 86
"Don't give up the ship," 188, 207
Dorothea, 197
Downie, George, Captain, 296, 298, 300, 302
Dragon, 181
Drummond, Gordon, General, 257-258, 261-263
Duane (editor of Philadelphia *Aurora*), 92
Ducros, Joseph Rodolphe, 355, 357
Dudley, William, Colonel, 148
Du Ponts, 172
Dwight, Theodore, 326
Dwight, Timothy, Rev., 289
Dyson, Samuel T., Captain, 308

Eagle, 298-301
East Indies, 28
Econochaca, 244
Elizabethtown (Canada), 157-158
Elkswatawa ("the Prophet"), 59, 60-63
Elliott, Jesse D., Lieut., 112, 203, 205, 207-210, 212
Embargo, 23, 88, 89, 305, 322, 323, 331, 389; Embargo Act, 40, 41-46, 47, 50, 73, 82
Endymion, 307, 338-339
Enterprise, 191-192
Epervier, 336
Erskine, David Montague, 47-49, 50, 54
Essex, 18, 22, 26, 28, 124, 192-196, 335
Essex Jr., 193-196

Essex Junto, the, 41, 328, 331
Eustis, William, 90, 91, 100, 101, 104, 109, 139, 140, 142, 155, 200
Evans, Samuel, Captain, 185, 187
Expansionists of 1812, 12

Fassett, Colonel, 302
Federalist party (later Republican party), 18-19, 21, 35, 41-46, 48, 49, 50, 54, 55, 64, 65, 69, 71, 72, 73, 74, 75, 76, 77, 79, 80, 81, 86, 89, 90, 92, 109, 111, 123, 132, 155, 164, 186, 189, 231, 269, 270, 288, 289, 322-334, 341, 346, 376, 378, 382
Fenwick, Lieut. Col., 114
Fernandina, 82-83, 85
Fessenden, Samuel, 323
Field Book, 11
Finch, 298-300
Finnis, Captain, 202, 203
Fisk, James, 75
Fitzgibbon, James, Lieut., 165
Flauzac, Garrigue, General, 364, 370
Floridas, 12, 17, 24, 64, 67, 81-86, 87, 238, 239, 341-346
Flournoy, Thomas, General, 234, 235, 238, 244
Floyd, John, General, 238, 244, 245-246
Folch (Spanish governor), 82
Foreign trade, 17-18, 23, 26-29, 38-40, 41, 47, 57, 58, 65, 66, 70-71, 73, 199, 384
Forsyth, Benjamin, Major, 157-158
Fort Armstrong, 242-243
Fort Barrancas, 342, 345-346
Fort Bowyer, 344, 345, 346
Fort Chippawa, 117, 158, 162, 206; *see also* Chippawa
Fort Covington, 311, 318
Fort Dearborn, 107-108
Fort Defiance, 141, 142-143, 147
Fort Erie, 112, 120, 158, 162, 163, 202-203, 251-253, 261-263, 324, 383
Fort George, 113, 115, 116, 117, 158, 161, 162, 164, 202, 220, 223, 224, 227, 229, 230, 251-252, 256, 269
Fort Harrison, 61

Fort Malden, 100, 101-103, 143-145, 147, 149, 153, 203, 206, 207, 214-216, 222, 223, 383
Fort McHenry, 309-311, 316, 318, 320
Fort Meigs, 146, 147, 149, 150
Fort Mims, 235-238, 240, 245, 249
Fort Mitchell, 244
Fort Montgomery, 346
Fort Niagara, 111, 113, 114, 158, 161, 163, 230, 251-252, 380, 383
Fort St. Charles, 353
Fort St. Jean, 349
Fort St. Michael, 342, 345-346
Fort St. Philip, 350
Fort Stephenson, 150, 151, 153, 217, 290
Fort Stoddard, 238
Fort Strother, 242, 243, 244, 245, 246
Fort Sullivan, 290
Fort Washington, 274, 308
Foster, Augustus John, 52, 54, 56, 83, 84, 86, 87, 104
Fox, Charles James, 23, 24-27, 29, 47
Frame-breaking riots in England, 88
France, 15, 18, 19, 21, 22, 24, 25-26, 28-29, 38-40, 41, 44, 47, 50, 56, 57, 65-66, 67, 70, 75, 81, 92, 138, 168, 265, 289, 377
Fredericksburg (Civil War), 391
Frederickstown (Maryland), 174
"Free men of color," 353, 357, 368
"Free Trade and Sailors' Rights," 15-23, 124-125, 128, 168, 187, 195
French John, 283
French Mills, 228-229
French Revolution, 41
Frenchtown (Canada), 143-145
Frenchtown (Maryland), 173
Frolic, 133-134, 335
Fulton, Robert, 196-198

Gaines, Edmund Pendleton, General, 260-262
Gallatin, Albert, 16, 46, 47, 72-73, 74, 80, 87, 101, 268, 285, 304, 374-386
Gallatin, James, 374, 376, 377, 379, 385, 386
Gambier, Lord, 378, 382
General Armstrong, 307

General Pike, 167
George III, 24, 25, 48, 83-84, 87, 290, 291
George IV, 25, 385
Georgetown, 174, 278
Georgia, 238, 244
Gerry, Elbridge, 89
Gershorn, 76
Ghent, treaty of, 333, 373, 377-386, 387, 392
Gibbs, Sir Samuel, General, 362, 363, 367, 369-372
Gibson, Jacob, 179-180
Giles, William B., 71, 72
Goddard, Calvin, Judge, 328
Goodrich, Chauncy, 328
Gordon, Captain, 34
Gordon, Commodore, 308, 309
Gorsuch farm, 314
Goulburn, Henry, 378, 380-382
Governor Tompkins, 306
Great Lakes, 91, 102, 200-212, 379-380, 382, 384, 392; *see also* Lake Erie; Lake Ontario
Grenadier Island, 224
Grenville, Lord, 23, 25
Griffin, Thomas, 178
Grundy, Felix, 65, 67, 68
Guerrière, 52, 53, 127, 130-132, 307, 335

Haiti, 353
Halifax, 53, 127, 169, 189, 266, 289, 290, 292
Hamilton, Alexander, 42, 72
Hamilton, Paul, 84, 101
Hampton, 177-179, 391
Hampton Roads, 171, 174-179
Hampton, Wade, General, 223-224, 227-228
Hardy, Captain, 198
Hardy, Thomas, Sir, 290
Harpy, 306
Harrison, Benjamin, Governor, 139
Harrison, William Henry, 58-63, 139-153, 200, 203, 205, 206, 211, 213-218, 220, 229, 250, 251, 259, 341, 377
Hartford Convention, 12, 322-334
Hartford *Courant*, 330

Havre de Grace, 173, 174
Hawkins, Benjamin, Colonel, 232, 234
Hazard, Benjamin, 328
Heald, Nathan, Captain, 107-108
Heath, Richard K., Major, 314
Henley, Robert, Captain, 298, 299, 301
Henry, John, 77-81, 86, 87
Henry letters, 12, 78-81, 86, 87
Hermes, 344
Hickory Ground, 232, 244, 249
Hillabee Indians, 242-243
Hillhouse, James, 328
Hillyer, Captain, 194-195
Hind, 357
History of the Administrations of Thomas Jefferson and James Madison, 11
Holland, 57
Holland, Lord, 26, 27-28, 32
Hope, Captain, 338
Hopkins, Samuel, General, 107
Hornet, 92, 183-185, 192, 337, 339-340
Horseshoe, The, 246-247, 249
Houston, Sam, 248
Howick, Lord, 27
Hull, Isaac, Captain, 91, 128-133, 135
Hull, William, General, 90, 96-107, 109, 111, 112, 119, 128, 129, 139, 140, 142, 152, 153, 155, 200, 216, 221
Humphries, Captain, 34-35
Hunter, 206, 207, 209, 210
Illinois, 139, 379

Impressment of American seamen, 19-23, 26-30, 36-39, 42, 52, 57-58, 65-66, 67, 77, 92, 379, 380, 382-383, 386
Indiana Territory, 58-63, 138, 380
Indians, 58-63, 67, 91, 92, 98, 102, 103-106, 107-108, 117-119, 139, 140-153, 158, 159, 162, 164-165, 201, 207, 213, 214-219, 230, 232-249, 250, 251, 254, 257, 341, 342, 345, 380, 382, 383
Irvine (editor of Baltimore *Whig*), 92
Izard, George, General, 263, 291-293

Jackson, Andrew, 12, 220, 222, 238-249, 250, 251, 341-352, 353-373, 390
Jackson, Francis James, 49-50
James, Marquis, 12
Java, 136
Jay, John, treaty negotiated by, 19, 28
Jefferson, Thomas, 15-30, 35-40, 41-46, 48, 64, 74, 92, 123, 126, 154, 197, 238, 322, 330, 389, 390
Jena, battle of, 28
Jesup, Thomas, Major, 255-256, 258-260; (Col.), 327, 329
John Adams, 192, 290
Johnson, Gerald W., 12
Johnson, James, 217
Johnson, R. M., Colonel, 65, 213, 214, 215-218
Jones, E., Mrs. (wife of Sec. of Navy), 284
Jones, Jacob, Captain, 133-134, 135
Jones, John Paul, 133
Jones, Thomas, Lieut., 350-351

Kaskaskia (Ill.), 379
Keane, John, General, 350, 354-355, 357, 359, 362-363, 367, 369-372
Kempt, General, 296
Kennedy, John P., 280
Kenton, 99
Kentucky, 91, 107, 123, 139, 140, 141, 142, 153, 213, 215, 217-220, 352, 366, 368, 369, 371
Key, Francis Scott, 318-320
King, Rufus, 46, 327
Kingston (Canada), 157, 158, 166, 167, 222-224, 225, 251, 292

La Colle, 250
La Coste, Major, 351, 368
Lady of the Lake, 161
Lady Prevost, 206, 207, 210
Laffite, Jean, 342-344, 345, 354, 362
Laffite, Pierre, 343-344
Lake Champlain, 96, 104, 123, 223, 229, 263, 324; battle of, 291-303, 383
Lake Erie, 98, 100, 141-142, 146, 153, 158, 200-212, 213-220, 222, 230, 252, 261-262, 377

Lake Ontario, 109, 125, 157, 158, 163, 203, 206, 219, 222, 224, 225, 229, 252
Lambert, Henry, Captain, 136
Lambert, John, General, 367, 372-373
Lambert's Point, 176
Lancaster rifle, 371
Latour, A. Lacarrière, Major, 356, 361
Laval, Jacint, Major, 85
Lawrence, 203, 204-211, 212
Lawrence, James, 91, 183-189
Lawrence, William, Major, 344-345
Lazaretto Point, 311, 317, 318
Leander, 337
Leavenworth, Henry, Major, 255
Leipsic, battle of, 265
Leonard, Captain, 296
Leopard, 33-36, 185
Letters of marque and reprisal, 304-307, 337
Levant, 337
Lewis, Meriwether, 16
Lewis, Morgan, General, 163
Lewis, William, Colonel, 143-144
Lewiston, 109, 111, 112, 113, 114, 230, 257, 263
Lincoln, 387
Linnet, 291, 298-301
Little Belt, 12, 53, 56, 58, 206, 207, 211, 230
Lively, Robert, 178
Liverpool, Lord, 379, 382, 384
Livingston, Edward, 343-344, 347-349, 353, 354
Lloyd, James, 89, 323, 327
Lloyd, Robert, Captain, 307
London *Courier*, 54-55, 379
London *Gazette*, 55, 379
London *Morning Chronicle*, 378
London Statesman, 288
London *Times*, 307-308, 379
Longfellow, Stephen, 328
Lopez, Justo, 85
Lossing, Benson, J., 11
Loudenslager's Hill, 311, 316
Louisiana, 341-352, 353-373, 379
Louisiana, 357, 362-363, 364
Louisiana Purchase, 15, 16, 41, 81, 82
Louisville, 58
Lowell, John, 329

Lowndes Hill, 275, 278, 280
Lowndes, William, 65
Ludlow, Augustus, Lieut., 187, 188-189
Lundy's Lane, 258-261, 324, 390
Lyman, Daniel, 328
Lyman, Joseph, 328
Lynnhaven Bay, 33, 172-173, 174

Macarté château, 361, 365, 368
Macdonough, Thomas, Captain, 291-292, 296-302, 383
Macedonian, 135, 192, 335
Mackinac Island, 102, 103, 219, 290, 383
Macomb, Alexander, Colonel, 225, 291, 292-297, 302
"Macon's No. 2," 50
Madison, 161
Madison, Dolly, 283-286
Madison, James, 19, 20, 21, 29, 44, 46, 47-50, 54, 64, 65-66, 71, 75, 79, 80, 81, 82, 83, 87, 88, 89, 92, 93, 94, 96, 98, 104, 123, 141, 155, 169, 170, 185, 190, 197, 202, 220, 222, 238, 268-286, 289, 304, 308, 318, 322, 323, 327, 330, 332, 333, 341, 376, 381, 386, 388, 389, 390
Magruder, Captain, 278, 280
Maine, 154, 290-291, 324, 341, 379, 383, 388
Majestic, 338
Manchester, 230
Manners, Captain, 336
Manrique, Governor, 342, 345-346
Manton, Edward, 328
Maples, J. F., Captain, 191
Maps, 97, 110, 156, 175, 233, 267, 294, 295, 310, 348, 360
Marion, 90
Marlboro, 271, 273, 274, 275, 318
Marlborough, 172
Marquesas, 193-194
Martin, Luther, 269
Maryland, 19, 23, 66, 231, 264, 268-273
Massachusetts, 189-190, 251, 259, 322, 325, 328, 383, 385
Masséna, 57
Mathews, General, 82-86

Maumee River, 99, 141, 142, 146, 147, 150, 151
McArthur, Colonel, 105, 106
McArthur, Duncan, General, 213
McClure, General, 220, 229-230
McComas, Henry, 314
McDonnell, Lieut. Col., 116
McGlassin, Captain, 297-298
McHenry, John, 320-321
McHenry, Margaret, 12, 320-321
McHenry, Sec. of War, 320-321
McKee, Colonel, 82
McNeil, John, Major, 255
McQueen, Peter, 234-235, 236
Mediterranean, 32
Meigs, Jonathan Return, Governor, 98, 99, 146, 149
Melampus, 33
Merry, Anthony, 24, 26
Messenger, 181
Michigan, 96, 98, 380
Middle Sister Island, 214
Milan Decree, 51, 75
Miller, General, 111
Miller, James, Colonel, 99, 104, 259-260
Mississippi, 238
Mississippi River, 353-373, 385
Mobile, 82, 234, 235, 238, 341-342, 344, 346-347, 352
Monroe, James, 18-19, 22, 24-30, 32, 36-37, 54, 76, 79, 80, 81, 84, 86, 88, 142, 146, 238, 266, 271, 274, 277, 279, 281, 327, 329, 333, 345, 379, 383
Montagu, 183
Montgomery, L. P., Major, 248
Montreal, 96, 104, 220, 222, 223-224, 227, 228, 229, 250, 277, 291, 292, 293
Mooers, Benjamin, General, 293, 296-297, 302
Moravian Town, 216, 219
Morgan, General, 361, 367, 368, 373
Morison, Samuel Eliot, 12
Morris, Lieut., 130
Morris, Gouverneur, 327, 331
Morris, James, Captain, 291
Moscow, 138, 170, 376
Myers, Captain, 278, 280

Napier, Charles, Sir, 185
Napoleon, 21, 25, 28-29, 32, 33, 38-39, 42, 44, 50-51, 55, 56, 57, 66, 69, 70, 75-76, 78, 81, 82, 93, 138, 157, 170, 265, 289, 364, 370, 375, 376, 377, 383
Natchez, 239, 240, 245
National Advocate, 333-334
National Intelligencer, 286, 326, 332
Nautilus, 83, 127, 340
Negroes, 235-236, 237, 353, 357, 368
Nelson, 28, 204
Nesslerode, Count, 376
New Brunswick (Canada), 28
New England, 16-17, 20-21, 41-43, 45-46, 54, 73, 74, 77, 94, 123, 138, 155, 168, 169, 186, 189-190, 291, 322-334, 341, 376, 378, 379, 388
New Hampshire, 325, 326, 328
New Orleans, 12, 221, 222, 234, 238, 239, 331, 333, 341-352, 388, 389; battle of, 353-373
New York, 192
New York City, 89, 132, 135, 168, 388, 389
New York *Evening Post,* 43, 74, 92
New York *Morning Post,* 92
New York state, 41, 46, 74, 119-120, 121, 262, 291, 302, 379, 382
Newark (Canada), 230, 266, 391
Newcastle, 337
Newport, 200, 211
Niagara, 96, 102, 104, 105, 108, 109, 122, 162, 165-166, 167, 203, 219, 222, 223, 224, 229, 251, 253, 255, 257, 263, 292; *see also* Fort Niagara
Niagara, 203, 204-211
Nicholls, Edward, Lieut. Col., 342, 343, 344, 345
Nicholson, Judge, 319
Niles, Hezekiah, 54, 56-57, 74, 89, 106
Niles' Register, 54, 56, 64, 74, 89, 106
Nocton, 192
Non-Importation Act, 23, 25, 50, 65, 66, 70-71, 73, 82
Non-Intercourse Act, 47, 50-51, 331
Norfolk, 171, 176-177
North Carolina, 231

Northwest Company, 102
Northwest Territory, 108, 139-153, 219, 232, 379
Nottingham (Maryland), 271, 273, 274
Nova Scotia, 28

Ogdensburg, 109, 157-158
Ohio, 98, 99, 101, 106, 139, 141, 142, 153, 379, 380, 390
Olcott, Mills, 328
"One World," 389
Oneida, 161
O'Neil, John, 173-174
Oswego, 252
Otis, Harrison Gray, 323, 328, 329, 330, 332

Pakenham, General, 350, 359-365, 369-372
Patapsco River, 309-312
Patterson, Daniel, Comdt., 351, 357, 363, 367, 368, 372-373
Patuxent River, 268, 271, 272, 309
Peacock, 184-185, 186, 187, 335-336, 337, 339-340
Peake, William, Captain, 184
Pearce, Cromwell, Colonel, 159
Pearson, Lieut., 181
Pelican, 191
Penguin, 339
Peninsular War (Spain), 49, 89, 168, 303, 361
Pennsylvania, 93, 120, 122, 141, 146, 212, 251, 254, 268, 270
Pensacola, 234, 235, 249, 341-342, 344-346, 347, 352
Perceval, Spencer, 49, 51, 54, 58, 87, 93, 95
Percy, William H., Captain, 342, 343, 344
Perilous Fight, The, 12
Perkins, Simon, General, 142
Perkins, Thomas H., 332
Perry, Alexander, 201, 209, 211
Perry, Matthew Calbraith, 12, 52-53
Perry, Oliver Hazard, 91, 161-162, 200-212, 213-214, 216-217, 309, 377
Philadelphia, 74, 89, 132, 173

Philadelphia, 298
Philadelphia *Aurora*, 21, 92, 198
Phoebe, 194-196
Pickering, Timothy, 21, 35, 41, 45-46, 322, 323, 327, 328, 329, 330
Pike, Zebulon, General, 158, 159
Pinckney, Charles Coatsworth, 46
Pinckney, Thomas, 90, 238
Pinkney, William, 18-19, 22, 23, 26-29, 32, 38, 44, 46, 49, 51, 94, 269, 278, 282
Pinkney, William, Mrs., 174
Piscataway, 271
Pitt, William, 23, 25, 41, 197
Plantagenet, 307
Plattsburg, 157, 291-303, 325, 383, 387
Plauché, Jean, Major, 353, 357, 358, 368
Poictiers, 134, 172
Point Petre, 83, 84-85
Polly, 18, 28
Pomone, 338
Porcupine, 206, 207, 208
Port Clinton, 205, 213
Port Tobacco, 271
Porter, David, Captain, 124-125; (Com.), 192-196
Porter, Moses, General, 269
Porter, Peter B., 65, 67, 72, 91, 120, 121, 122, 251, 253, 259, 262, 309
Portland, Lord, 32, 49
Portugal, 56, 57, 168
Power, General, 296, 297
Pratt, Julius W., 12
Preble, 298-300
Preble, Commodore, 15, 200
Prescott, William, 328
President, 12, 52-55, 56, 58, 126-127, 128, 192, 309, 335, 337-339, 340
Presqu' Isle, 202, 203, 204, 207
Preston, James P., Colonel, 163
Prevost, George, Sir, 157, 166-167, 169, 266, 292, 296-298, 302, 324, 382, 383, 387
Prince of Neufchatel, 306
Pring, Captain, 291, 298
Privateers, 88, 199, 304-307, 387
Proctor, Henry, Colonel, 102, 103, 141, 144-153; (Gen.), 206, 207, 214-216, 218-219, 229

"Prophet, the" (Elkswatawa), 59, 60-63, 147, 232, 234
Prussia, 28, 57
Put-in-Bay, 205, 214

Queen Charlotte, 102, 206, 207, 209, 210-211
Queenston, 112-119, 120, 251-252, 256-258, 296
Quincy, Josiah, 71, 89, 93, 94, 189, 322, 323

Ragan, Lieut. Col., 279, 281
Raisin River, 102, 218, 219
Rambouillet Decree, 50, 51
Ramillies, 198
Randolph, John, 12, 23, 64, 65, 67-70, 71, 91, 93, 138, 170, 221, 327
Ratford, 35
Reid, Samuel C., Captain, 307
Reindeer, 336
Rennie, Colonel, 362-364, 370-371
Republican party (later Democratic party), 18, 21, 22, 35, 42-46, 55, 64, 68, 69, 70, 72, 73, 74, 75, 89, 90, 92, 111, 132, 154, 155, 164, 322, 323, 326, 331
Revolutionary War, 41, 82, 96, 107, 140, 142, 154, 173, 213, 221, 223, 291, 311, 328, 341, 390
Rhode Island, 324, 325, 328
Riall, General, 252-258
Richmond *Inquirer*, 326
Ringgold, Tench, 286
Riots in England, frame-breaking, 88
Ripley, Eleazar, General, 251-263, 390
Robinson, General, 296
Rodgers, John, Commodore, 52-55, 56, 91, 126-127, 174, 197, 309, 317
Rodgers, John, Mrs., 174
Romanzoff, 375, 376
Roosevelt, Franklin D., 389
Rose, George H., 45-46
Rose's Bluff, 85
Ross, Robert, General, 266, 273-278, 282, 285, 287, 308, 312, 314, 316, 340-341, 350
Rossie, 305
Rottenberg, de, General, 296
"Rule of 1756," 18

Russell, Jonathan, 87, 88, 377, 378
Russia, 28, 33, 57, 81, 138, 157, 170, 265, 268, 375-376

Sackett's Harbor, 109, 157, 158, 160, 161, 166, 200, 201, 203, 205, 220, 223, 224, 229, 251, 252, 257, 260, 292, 380
St. Augustine, 85
St. Clair, Lieut. Commander, 126
St. David's, 117, 257, 266
St. Lawrence River, 220, 222, 224-229, 379
St. Martial, 78, 79, 81
St. Mary's, 83, 84, 85
St. Michael's (Maryland), 179-180
St. Petersburg, 375-377
St. Vincent, Earl of, 197, 198
Salt tax, 73
Sandusky, 141, 142, 143, 149, 150, 379
Sandwich, 215, 216
Saratoga, 298-301
Sawyer, Admiral, 54, 127
Scandinavia, 57
Schlosser, 230, 257-258
Schutz, Lieut. Co., 279, 281
Scorpion, 206, 207, 208, 209
Scott, Charles, 139
Scott, William, Sir, 18
Scott, Winfield, 112, 116, 117-118, 161-163, 167, 224, 229, 251, 252-259, 263, 390
Scottish Highlanders, 350, 372
Secession, New England proposes, 41, 45, 326, 330
Seminole Indians, 342
Seneca Indians, 251, 254
Seneca Town, 150, 151, 203, 205
Serurier, 76, 78, 79, 81
Shannon, 127, 128-129, 185-189, 190
Sharp's Island, 179
Sheaffe, R. H., General, 111, 117-118, 158-160
Shelby, Isaac, Governor, 139, 142, 213, 215, 218
Sherbrooke, Sir John, General, 290
Sherman, Roger Minott, 328
Short, Lieut. Col., 152
Sidmouth, 88
Sims, Lieut., 113, 114

Smith, Captain, 126
Smith, Nathaniel, Judge, 328
Smith, Robert, 47, 50, 54
Smith, T. A., Captain, 83; (Col.), 85; (Gen.), 291
Smith, Samuel, General, 311, 313
Smyth, Alexander, General, 111, 112, 119-122
Somers, 206, 207, 208, 210
Sophia, 344
Southampton, 124
Spain, 17, 24, 26, 28, 44, 49, 56, 57, 68, 82, 83, 84, 89, 90, 168, 169, 221, 234, 238, 249, 266, 303, 345, 350, 363, 379
Spitfire, 52
Sproull, Captain, 296, 297
Stansbury, Tobias, General, 275, 278, 279, 282
"Star-Spangled Banner," 319-320
Staunton, 99
Stephen, James, 87
Sterett, Lieut. Col., 279, 280, 281, 320
Stewart, Charles, Captain, 337
Stone, Colonel, 257
Stonington, 290
Stony Creek, 163-164
Street's Creek, 253, 254, 256
Stricker, John, General, 313-316
Strong, Caleb, 89, 323, 324, 325, 332, 334, 341
Stuart, Philip, General, 264
Sullivan, William, 332
Sumter, 90
Swanson, Neil, 12
Swartout, General, 226
Swift, Zephamiah, 328

Talladega, 242
Tallassahatche, 241-242
Tallyrand, 64
Tannehill, General, 120
Taylor, Robert B., General, 176, 178
Tecumseh, 59, 60-63, 103, 105, 107, 147, 149-150, 151-152, 214-219, 232, 234, 236
Ten Islands, 241-242
Tenedos, 185, 338
Tennessee, 238, 240, 244, 245, 246,

248, 262, 352, 353, 357, 363, 364, 365, 371
Terre Haute, 61
Thames, 75
Thames, battle of the, 215, 216, 219, 229, 230, 250, 341, 377
Thames River (Conn.), 335
Thomas, John, General, 352, 366, 369
Thomas, Joshua, 328
Thornton, William, Colonel, 355, 357, 358, 367-370, 372-373
Ticonderoga, 298-301
Tigress, 206, 207, 208
Tingey, Commodore, 276, 285
Tippecanoe, 59, 60, 61-63, 67, 68, 107, 139, 219, 232
Tobacco, 43
Tom Bowline, 337, 339-340
Tompkins, Governor, 111
Toronto, 157; *see also* York
Torpedoes, 196-198
Totten, Lieut., 116, 118
Totten, James A., Lieut., 116, 118; (Maj.), 291-293
Towson, Nathan, Captain, 253, 258, 261
Trafalgar, 25, 28-29, 204
Treadwell, John, Governor, 328
Treaty of 1783, 385
Treaty of 1794, 27
Treaty of 1806 (U.S. and Great Britain), 29
Treaty of Ghent, 333, 373, 377-386, 387, 392
Treaty of Tilsit, 33
Tripoli, War with, 16, 91, 126, 183, 200, 298
Trippe, 206, 207, 208, 230
Tristan da Cunha, 337, 339-340
Tucker, Captain, 194
Tupper, Edward W., General, 142
Tuscarora, 230
Tweedale, Marquis of, 254, 255

United States, 126, 135, 192, 335
Urbana, 99

Valparaiso, 192, 194-195
Van Horne, Thomas, Major, 103
Van Ness, General, 271

Van Rensselaer, Solomon, Colonel, 109, 113, 114-115, 116

Van Rensselaer, Stephen, General, 108, 109-119

Van Rensselaer, William, 109

Vermont, 251, 291, 293, 296, 302, 324, 325-326, 328

Vickers, Clement, Captain, 181

Vienna, Congress of, 379, 382, 383

Villeré, Gabriel, Major, 355, 357

Villeré, Jacques, General, 355

Villeré plantation, 355, 356-358, 361

Vincennes, 58, 60, 61, 107

Vincent, John, General, 161-164, 224, 229

Virginia, 141, 146, 171, 177, 231, 262, 268

"Virginia Dynasty, The," 19, 46, 231, 322

Vrooman's Point, 117, 118

Wadsworth, William, General, 111, 116, 118

Waldo, Daniel, 328

"War Hawks" the, 65, 66, 67, 70, 75, 87, 89, 93, 138

Warburton (Maryland), 271

Ward, Samuel, Colonel, 328

Wareham (Mass.), 290

Warren, Admiral, 167, 176-177, 178

Warrington, Lewis, Comdt., 335-336, 337

Warsaw, Grand Duchy of, 57

Washington (D.C.), 179, 264-288, 303, 308, 309, 311, 324, 341, 350, 381, 382, 388, 389, 391; burning of, 285, 381, 388

Washington, George, 41, 154, 221; Stuart portrait of, 285

Wasp, 83, 133-134, 183, 335, 336-337

Wayne, Anthony, 139

"We have met the enemy and they are ours," 211

Weathersford, William, 236-237, 238, 244-245, 249

Wellesley, Richard, Lord, 49, 54, 58, 92

Wellington, 56, 57, 89, 176, 250, 266, 292, 303, 350, 358, 359, 363, 370, 384-385

Wells, Daniel, 314

West, Benjamin, 328

West, expansion of the, 16, 17, 58-63

West Indies, 20, 28

Westwood, Mrs., 178

Wheaton, Henry, 333

Whingates, Thomas, Captain, 133

Whitbread, 87

Wild, Samuel Sumner, 328

Wilkinson, James, General, 68, 90, 220, 221-228, 234, 238, 239, 240, 250, 251, 277, 291

Williams, David R., 65

Willkie, Wendell, 389

Winchester, James, General, 90, 140, 142-143, 144-145, 347

Winder, Levin, Governor, 270

Winder, William H., General, 120, 163-164, 269-271, 274-276, 278-279, 281-283, 308, 311, 320

Wirt, William, 269

Wood Yard, 271, 274, 275

Wool, John E., Captain, 114-116; (Maj.), 296

World War I, 388

World War II, 388, 389

Wright (Republican from Maryland), 73

Yarnell, John J., Lieut., 210

Yazoo scandals, 64

Yeo, James, Sir, 124-125, 156, 164, 166, 203, 206, 225, 257

York (now Toronto), 157, 158-160, 165, 252, 391

York, Sir Joseph, Admiral, 56

Yorktown, 154